ENGLISH LITERARY CRITICISM: THE RENASCENCE

To help posterity to judge rightly of the old, . . . wee must
. . . calmly study the separation of opinions, find the errors have
intervened, awake Antiquity, call former times into question,
but make no parties with the present, nor follow any fierce under-
takers, mingle no matter of doubtful credit with the simplicity
of truth, but gently stirre the mould about the root of the
Question and avoid all digladiations, facility of credit or superstitious simplicity.

—Ben Jonson, *Discoveries*, §§ 116, 123

ENGLISH LITERARY
CRITICISM : THE RENASCENCE

by

J. W. H. ATKINS

M.A., HON. LITT.D., MANCHESTER

FORMERLY FELLOW OF ST. JOHN'S COLLEGE, CAMBRIDGE ;
EMERITUS PROFESSOR OF ENGLISH LANGUAGE AND LITERATURE,
UNIVERSITY COLLEGE OF WALES, ABERYSTWYTH

BARNES & NOBLE, Inc.
New York
METHUEN & CO. Ltd
London

First published in 1947

Reprinted, 1968
by
Barnes & Noble, Inc., New York
and
Methuen & Co. Ltd, London

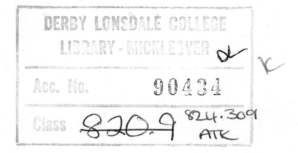
Printed in the United States of America

PREFACE

THIS work is a continuation of studies embodied in earlier volumes—*Literary Criticism in Antiquity* and *English Literary Criticism : the Medieval Phase*—treating of the history of literary criticism. And in continuing a survey of the development of literary criticism in England beyond medieval times an attempt is here made to review the critical achievement at the Renascence by ' stirring the mould about the root of the question ' (as Jonson advised), the aim throughout being to arrive at the ideas of literature then current in England, as revealed in contemporary theorizing and judgments. The period has sometimes been dismissed as lacking great critics ; and the critical works themselves have been described as elementary, second-hand and remote. Viewed, however, in the light of what came before and after, those works will be found to be of considerable interest and possessed of intrinsic, as well as historical, value. Now, without a doubt, a new era was dawning, not only in the problems faced and the manner of their treatment, but also in the glimpses afforded of enduring principles, in the new sense of literary values and in the literary charm that lights up so many of the critical pages. It was now, in fact, that the foundations of modern criticism were being laid ; and, besides, the critical work of the time, so far from being remote or irrelevant, has, on the contrary, a close bearing on contemporary literature.

In the pages that follow, the general course of the movement has first been sketched ; then the main findings and their significance in critical history. And in making the survey what is in some sense a new approach has been adopted. Hitherto attention has been mostly directed to following the fortunes of the new classical teaching, interpreted and modified as it was by 16th-Century Italian critics. The assimilation of classical doctrine, however, was not the only, nor yet the main, concern of English critics ; neither were the 16th-Century Italians, for all their admirable theorizing, the real channels through which Englishmen first became acquainted with classical theory. So that for a clear understanding of what actually took place some regard must be paid to other sources of influence. Hence the efforts here made to indicate the part played by the medieval tradition, with its inheritance of post-classical and patristic doctrine ; the lead given by 15th-Century Italian and other Humanists, by whom the break with medievalism was first effected ; and again, the no less important attempts of independent native writers to work out new artistic and dramatic theories all their own. In this wider perspective the work of

Erasmus and Vives, of Colet, Jewel and Wilson will be found to be not irrelevant ; the later contributions of such writers as Willis and Lyly, Carew, Reynolds and others assume fresh significance ; while clearer conceptions become possible concerning the works of the more familiar critics from Ascham onwards. It may perhaps seem that in tracing this critical development too much attention has been devoted to rhetorical studies, too little to the influence of 16th-Century Italian critics. Yet, at this early stage in the critical history problems of style were necessarily a ' first priority ' with contemporary men of letters, while for reasons suggested later, the direct influence of Scaliger, Castelvetro and the rest would seem to have been comparatively slight.

In making this survey I am grateful for valuable help derived from the labours of earlier workers in the same field, notably from the works of Saintsbury, Gregory Smith, and Spingarn ; though my treatment has been on somewhat different lines. With such scattered material, however, as forms the main body of this Renascence criticism, a further debt is due to those editors and translators who have made accessible a variety of texts ranging from the 15th to the 17th Centuries. For the contribution of 15th-Century Italians and later Humanists I have drawn mainly on W. H. Woodward's *Vittorino da Feltre* and his *Erasmus concerning Education*, with their English versions of relevant Latin texts, as well as on Foster Watson's *Vives on Education*, with its translation of Vives's *De tradendis disciplinis*. Most, though not all, of the remaining texts are included in the well-known volumes of G. Gregory Smith's *Elizabethan Critical Essays* and J. E. Spingarn's *Critical Essays of the 17th Century*, to which (along with the works of Woodward and Watson) references are made throughout the following pages ; while for access to the rare text of Willis's *Disputatio* I am indebted to the courtesy of the British Museum authorities, and to Mr. Scholderer in particular. Mention should also be made of the help derived from M. Castelain's edition of the *Discoveries*, which not only tracks Jonson in his adventures among the ancients, but also makes use of the numbering of passages (first adopted by Gollancz) so necessary for purposes of reference. And finally, a special debt is owed to Professor H. B. Charlton, who, interested in the venture throughout, has been good enough to read the work in typescript and to make some helpful suggestions.

J. W. H. A.

Aberystwyth,
 12th June, 1946

CONTENTS

CHAPTER I

INTRODUCTION

IN the various phases which make up the complicated development of English literary criticism none is of more vital interest than that bound up with the 16th-Century Renascence, the period which marks the break with medieval theories, a renewal of attempts to arrive at clearer conceptions of literature, and a beginning of what is called modern criticism. Not that the break with medievalism was by any means complete. Each period inherits from its predecessors ideas and tendencies of the past ; and this, to a degree that has sometimes been forgotten, is notably true of Renascence times. Along with influences that gave fresh impetus and new direction to critical studies there survived during that period ideas handed down from earlier generations, ideas that were still cherished and tenaciously held. And this fact is one of prime importance in any attempt to understand the actual nature of the critical development at this stage. Moreover, this overlap of old and new traditions persisted until well into the 17th Century, when the formulation of what is known as the neo-classical creed in France diverted attention into new channels, giving rise to new problems, new theories and standards. There was, in short, an unbroken critical development in England from the beginning of the 16th Century to the middle of the 17th, in which Renascence, and to a lesser extent medieval, forces were still active. Hence the scope assigned to the present inquiry, which concerns itself not only with early Tudor and Elizabethan criticism but with the critical activities of the Jacobean and Caroline periods as well.

Of earlier treatments of the criticism of this period there has been no lack ; and valuable light has in consequence been thrown on its progress from various angles. It has, for instance, been viewed as part of a European movement, attempts having been made to indicate sources and the general indebtedness of English critics to 16th-Century Italian scholars mainly, though in a lesser degree to contemporary French critics as well. Or again, it has been considered as a preliminary stage preparing the way for the later formulation of neo-classical doctrine ; and traces of classical theory, modified as yet by ' romantic ' tendencies, have thus been noted, with the main problems described as the inculcation of *decorum*, the treatment of the ' kinds ', prosody, diction and the like. These efforts to explain origins and to read some sort of system into the varied critical activities are undoubtedly of interest, though they tend to simplify unduly what is after all a somewhat complicated development, thus presenting part of the truth for the whole. What is more, they are apt to leave the reader with a sense of detachment, with some relevant facts, it is true, and some amount of abstract theory, but also with a vague and an imperfect notion of the actual performance and its relation to the literary activities of the time. This at least would seem to account for the judgment of certain eminent French critics who, describing the critical achievement of the period as of mediocre value and importance, declared that for the most part it was devoid of originality, dependent mainly on second-hand Italian doctrine, and with practically no bearing on contemporary English literature. In short, ' it remains almost abstract ', they explained,[1] ' by ignoring what was before its eyes '.

Yet nothing is more certain than that, despite some amount of borrowing from various sources, the critical movement at this stage was fundamentally of an independent character, distinct, that is, both in aims and methods, from those of contemporary Italian and French critics, free also from any attempt at a rigid or systematic treatment. For the truth is that so far from ignoring what was before its eyes or being indifferent to contemporary literary work, English criticism at this date, both in its nature and its course, was determined, broadly speaking, by immediate national needs and problems. ' It develops itself ', so wrote a well-known authority,[2] ' if not with entire independence, yet with sufficient conformity to its own needs.' And considered in this light, against the background of contemporary literary conditions, the critical movement at this stage takes on new meaning and significance, as embodying something more than the vain repetition of abstract theories which in practice were for the most part ignored. What criticism there was, in short, is none other than a running commentary on the literary progress ; a commentary, it is true, confused, intermittent, and wholly unregulated, yet one that faithfully reflects the notions of literature then current. It is therefore with the object of arriving at what Englishmen were thinking about literature at this date that the main effort will be made in this inquiry into the contemporary literary criticism, with

[1] E. Legouis and L. Cazamian, *Histoire de la littérature anglaise*, p. 350.
[2] G. Saintsbury, *History of English Criticism*, p. 98.

its various theories, its judgments and appreciations of what was actually accomplished. And with this aim in view no less attention will be paid to conceptions and estimates of historical interest only, than to aesthetic doctrines and judgments of more definite and lasting value. To ignore all that has no bearing on our modern conceptions would be to lose sight of part of the historical picture and of some important features of this phase of criticism.

For a just appreciation of the critical achievement at this stage, however, it is necessary, in the first place, to recall something of those intellectual conditions which went to determine the character and scope of critical activities in England. That the period was one of general enlightenment in which a flood of new ideas came in with the New Learning, accompanied by a revival of men's powers, a fresh vision of things and a new spirit of enterprise and initiative, all this and much else besides were characteristic of the Renascence period; and all alike were calculated to inspire a lively regard for literature, as well as a new critical attitude towards it. At the same time no less significant were the lack of knowledge and the confusion that prevailed in literary practice, as well as the formidable array of problems and difficulties that confronted men's minds in their quest for clear ideas concerning poetry and the like. It was not only that strong prejudices existed against the vernacular in favour of Latin, that the make-up of the vernacular as a literary medium was itself a subject of debate; or again, that rhyming verse was evoking a surprising amount of hostility. Apart from perplexities such as these there existed, for instance, but crude notions of the very nature of poetic and dramatic forms; there had also come down some unfinished controversies relating to the status of both the drama and the romance; while the wealth of new ideas that had now become available was as yet but imperfectly assimilated, owing partly to the native lack of interest in abstract theory, partly also to the failure of Elizabethan scholarship to fulfil the early Tudor promise and to grapple successfully with the difficult Greek text of Aristotle's *Poetics*. Moreover, many of the new doctrines now enunciated were at variance with inherited traditions and native tendencies which still retained much of their earlier vitality; and the situation was further complicated by a violent Puritan hostility to art of all kinds. Most serious of all, however, were the vague and conflicting views current concerning poetry, a confusion due to the multitude of ideas drawn from different quarters. Along with classical theories that now became available, sometimes modified, it is true, by Italian interpretations, there were also post-classical and patristic conceptions which had filtered through from medieval times, Neo-Platonic doctrines relating to the Cabbala and such-like handed on by early Humanists, besides more modern theories based on Italian and French models. All these were presented with the weight of authority, while the native literature continued to develop on lines of its own ; and the confusion was further increased by the limited sympathy of Humanists with poetry as such, and by sundry efforts from abroad to discredit the teaching of the ancients in general and of Aristotle in particular.

Amidst all this confusion the main inspiration of the criticism that ensued has usually been ascribed to the practical recovery of Aristotle's *Poetics* at the end of the 15th Century, and the subsequent exposition of that work by Italian scholars of the century following. It was thus, so it is claimed, that the break with medievalism came and that imaginative literature for the first time was really vindicated. Yet notable as was this new influence in its ultimate effects, another, and an earlier, influence which has hitherto received less notice in this connexion, has also to be taken into account. For it was the 15th-Century Italian Humanists who first broke away from medieval traditions, and by their teaching and inspiration alike made literary discussions possible. By them was inaugurated, for instance, a new approach to literature ; and through their efforts later generations were made acquainted not only with a host of classical texts and theories, but also with a new sense of literary values and a more exalted conception of literature in general. In short, the part they played in the critical development, and this not in England alone, can scarcely be over-rated. Their influence was spread abroad partly by their published writings ; but much also came through by way of the works of later Humanists such as Colet, Erasmus, Vives, Sturm, and Melanchthon. And the essential fact remains that the vital part in the critical development at this stage was played, not by 16th-Century Italian scholars, but rather by Italian Humanists of the preceding century and those later Humanists who handed on their teaching. As Walter Pater later on maintained, ' it is in Italy, in the 15th Century, that the interest of the Renaissance mainly lies '.[1] So that for a proper understanding of the origins of English Renascence criticism some appreciation of the foundations laid by these early Humanists is indispensable.

Most notable of the influences derived by English critics

[1] Pater, *The Renaissance*, p. xiv.

from the activities of these early Italian Humanists was the practice of bringing reasoned judgment to bear for the first time on literature and literary problems. For this, even more than the access afforded to classical literature and theories, was the determining factor in the development of contemporary English criticism. A heightened sense of the power of human reason had been instilled by these early Humanists, and this not only did much to foster critical discussion, it also helped to establish Nature or reason as the recognized instrument of inquiry in all fields of thought throughout the Renascence period. It is true that for this doctrine the Humanists were not alone responsible ; though not without its significance is the fact that the ancient authorities upon whom they drew most freely, namely, Cicero and Quintilian,[1] had long ago adopted as their governing principles the laws of Nature or reason. Already, however, throughout Western Europe the idea was widely and firmly rooted that there existed in man a certain natural faculty which enabled him to arrive at the eternal law of natural fitness, and thus to perceive the light of truth. To this *lex naturalis* or *lumen naturale* scholastic theologians (including Aquinas) had freely subscribed, its source being defined as *summa ratio in Deo existens*, which men were able to perceive by the light of their natural understanding. Among English theologians, moreover, Reginald Pecock (15th Century), for one, had likewise exalted reason's ' doom of kinde ' (or judgment by the law of reason), which he claimed had been written ' in men's souls by the finger of God '. Or again, Italian thinkers in attacking Scholastic dogma had relied at first on the authority of the ancients, but later they had appealed to Nature against ecclesiastical and classical authorities alike.

Of the widespread observance of this doctrine during the Renascence period there is abundant evidence ; for its influence is illustrated by various writers treating of totally different subjects. Thus the Oxford Reformers and Sir Thomas More, for instance, both combined a profound faith in religion with faith in the dictates of natural reason. To Hooker again, in the absence of any fixed or absolute authority, the only guide left was a pure and elevated rationalism, ' the light of the natural understanding, wit and reason ', which, he explained, was the gift of God. Then, too, references to the doctrine are occasionally found in contemporary poetry, as when, for instance, Sir John Davies in *Nosce Teipsum* (1599) declared that ' Nature in man's heart her laws doth pen '. It was, moreover, commonly appealed

---

[1] See Atkins, *Literary Criticism in Antiquity*, ii. pp. 24, 262.

2

to by philosophical writers of the early 17th Century; while
in yet another sphere, that of International Law, both Selden
and Grotius, the most learned men of the age, based their theories
on the same law of Nature or reason.   It is therefore not strange
to find that English critics, seeking for light amidst the literary
confusion of the time, also looked to first principles, and, following the earlier Italians, relied primarily in their treatment of
literary problems on Nature or reason as their main instrument
for arriving at truth.   This is not to say, however, that the New
Learning was without its effects on English critical inquiries and
judgments.   To classical teaching great deference was paid by early
Italian and English theorists alike ; but generally, it should be
noted, with reservations of a rational kind.   Theories of various
kinds were drawn from ancient authorities, and interesting
principles of permanent value were from time to time assimilated.
Nevertheless, the authority of the ancients was in general recognized only in so far as it was capable of being reconciled with the
dictates of Nature or reason ; while where native instincts suggested new theories or methods the necessary departures were
freely advocated by English critics.   And this was due not so
much to a spirit of independence ascribed to the English genius
as to the spirit of rationalism emphasized, though not originated,
by Italian Humanists.   So that, despite constant recourse to
ancient teaching, the fundamental principle which governed
English criticism at this stage was not, as is sometimes assumed,
that of ' following the ancients ', but rather of accepting Nature
or reason as the ultimate guide in theory and practice alike ;
and this fact will be found to explain much in the critical
performance.

For the actual development of English criticism during the
16th and early 17th Centuries we must look to pronouncements
of various forms and kinds, that is, not only to treatises definitely
devoted to literary matters such as the Rhetorics, the *Artes* and
Apologies now appearing for the first time, but also to Prefaces,
Dedications, Letters and the like, and not least, to those sporadic
comments in creative literature itself in which writers casually
explained their ideas of art, thus witnessing to the emergence
of a new critical consciousness at this date.   In general the
movement may be said to have gathered strength under changing
conditions, acquiring greater scope, insight and initiative as time
went on.   First came the critics of the early Tudor period who
under Humanistic influence were interested mainly in the media
of literature, in rhetoric, style, and diction, and who wrote in
scholarly yet unadorned fashion.   In due course they were

followed by the courtly critics of a later date who, concerned primarily with poetry, its nature and art, wrote with lighter touch for cultured circles, explaining what poetry was and its value to the community. Then in the last decade of the 16th Century, in the flowering time of Elizabethan literature, a marked advance was made by men of letters in the range, the methods and the significance of their critical activities. Generally speaking, a more intimate concern with contemporary literature now became apparent and writers from now on more freely expressed their ideas on the literary art. Thus notable attempts for the first time were made at discussing dramatic principles ; judgments and appreciations of considerable value were at times forthcoming ; further recondite theories relating to poetry (and history) were also propounded ; and at a later stage serious efforts were made to recover the teaching of classical antiquity, including some amount of Aristotelian theory. To this movement as a whole contributed most of the outstanding figures in contemporary literary history, notably, Wilson and Ascham, Sidney, Puttenham and Daniel, Nashe, Harvey and Hall, Lyly and Shakespeare, Bacon, Jonson and Milton ; and their writings at their best are full of good things, remarks suggestive and illuminating, and couched in those happy and picturesque phrases, the secret of which belonged to the Elizabethans. The value of this Renascence phase in the critical development has not infrequently been underestimated in the past. The critics themselves, summarily dealt with, have with few exceptions been belittled as a group of writers whose theories were purely academic in kind and with little bearing on the literary practices of the age. The argument has been that the Elizabethan period was above all a creative age, and therefore cannot well have been critical. But this view was based on a superficial scrutiny of what was actually accomplished. The truth is that literary criticism formed an integral element in the intellectual life of the time, and an element closely bound up with the literary development. For a just estimate of its significance and value, therefore, some consideration of the contemporary literary progress and conditions is absolutely essential. And there is also this to be said, that for a full appreciation of the literature of these most stirring times some understanding of the critical background and of current theories is no less desirable.

CHAPTER II

THE BREAK WITH MEDIEVALISM : ITALIAN HUMANISTS

FOR the beginnings of modern literary criticism we must look to Italy of the 14th and 15th Centuries, to that formative period of the Renascence which had drawn its inspiration from the Revival of Learning and the renewed study of the classical literatures of ancient Greece and Rome. At the time in England medieval literary doctrine held full sway, as was evident from the form of much of the contemporary literature, and from the works of Geoffrey of Vinsauᶠ, John of Garland, and still later, Hawes and others. There a body of literary theory had gradually been established, based mainly on post-classical authorities. It was theory which perpetuated many of the errors of the Hellenistic culture of Imperial Rome ; and now, with the recovery of the Greek and Graeco-Roman traditions, a marked change in the conception of literature was effected by Italian scholarship, and that within the course of a single century. This change was mainly the work of enthusiastic Humanists who sought to make use of the vast body of recovered literature in the service of a new education. In the ancient world they had found ample precedent for such an experiment, and in formulating their schemes they were aided by not a few of the ancient writers, notably by Cicero and Quintilian, though other works of classical antiquity bearing on literary matters had also by now become available. Outstanding among these Humanistic contributors to literary theory were Laurentius Valla and Politian ; but valuable assistance came also from others including Vergerius, Vittorino da Feltre, Guarino da Verona, and Leonardo Bruni, besides Aeneas Sylvius, Pico della Mirandola, and Savonarola. And as the outcome of their various activities fresh impetus and a new direction were given to literary studies. A wider vision of literature, new methods of approach, the raising of some vital problems, an increasing concern with literary values and with the relations existing between life and letters, these were some of the results attained. It was, in fact, one of those periods of enlightenment, in which the minds of men, conscious of new powers, become keenly interested in matters intellectual, social and political ; enthusiastic also in applying a newly-acquired critical spirit to all departments of thought. And not least significant were the inquiries into literary questions, which,

8

despite the primary educational motive, despite also the mistakes and excesses inevitable at this date, represented a new phase in critical history and the starting-point of much of the later European criticism.

Already in the 14th Century the task of collecting Latin manuscripts, begun by Petrarch (1304–74), had made considerable progress in Italy ; and, from then on, the salvaging and copying of ancient manuscripts became one of the main preoccupations, thus supplementing the efforts made in Western Europe during the 9th and 10th Centuries to preserve what was left of ancient Latin texts. The search was now carried on with greater zest than ever ; and an air of romance hangs over the relentless quest in monasteries and elsewhere which brought to light a host of works long buried in dusty libraries. Thus Poggio's discovery of a complete Quintilian at St. Gall in 1416 was followed five years later by the finding of complete copies of Cicero's rhetorical works (including *Brutus*, hitherto unknown) in the Cathedral Church at Lodi. The writings also of a long list of other Latin authors—poets, historians, orators, and letter-writers—soon made their appearance, until by the early decades of the 15th Century the main body of Latin classics had been rescued from neglect and oblivion. Even yet more valuable was the work done in connexion with Greek manuscripts which enshrined a literature the very memory of which had faded throughout Western Europe. In the closing years of the 14th Century the Greek scholar, Manuel Chrysoloras, was already at Florence teaching his native language ; and after that time Greek manuscripts poured in freely from the East. In 1418 Guarino (1374–1460) returned to Italy from Greece with considerable treasure, while the Sicilian, Aurispa, some nine years later brought back from Constantinople no less than 238 texts, including many of the great Greek classics. Filelfo in 1427 added some forty more to the list ; and after the fall of Constantinople (1453) several notable Greek refugees, including Theodorus Gaza, Trapezuntius, Argyropulos and Chalcondyles, carried on the work of furthering Greek studies, while also assisting Pope Nicholas V in acquiring for the Vatican Library its famous collection of both Greek and Latin texts. Thus for the first time vast literary treasures of classical antiquity, both Greek and Latin, were rendered accessible to the modern world ; and a new era was opened up for literary studies.

The first effects were seen in the religious care and enthusiasm with which these relics of antiquity were cherished and copied, and were then translated and expounded in the literary academies of Italy at this date. Everywhere men became conscious of a new revelation of literature which set up new standards of literary achievement ; while as records of ancient wisdom, human documents embodying matter of universal import, the newly-discovered texts also appealed strongly to contemporary scholars. Classical texts, it is true, had by no means been wanting to medieval readers ; but now they were more fully represented and were approached in an entirely new spirit and with an enthusiasm of a more enlightened kind. To Italian minds the glories of Augustan literature were none other than part of their ancient patrimony, the fruit of a golden age, in the earlier stages of which Greek literature had also shared ; and for the appreciation of this priceless legacy Italy at this date was peculiarly well fitted. Antiquity, for instance, was now revealed in clearer outline, free to some extent from the mists of post-classical and patristic traditions, free also from medieval ideas of a vague and mysterious past. A more vivid realization of the genuine classical tradition resulted, filling men's minds with a longing to absorb and revive the old civilization, and conducing inevitably to an emulation of the past in all spheres of thought. It was as if new horizons had suddenly been opened in the intellectual world, affording fresh glimpses of the power of letters, the living spirit of which was widely felt. As yet, however, these new finds were to some extent uncritically accepted, the prevailing enthusiasm being extended to all salvaged works alike, to the great masters and to later commentators as well. But purely objective and judicial views were hardly to be expected at this date ; since patriotic fervour, the remoteness of classical times, and the lack of accurate knowledge concerning those times were all factors which made some measure of idealization inevitable. There was thus for a time a lack of discrimination in the matter of values ; and classical standards which had been wanting throughout the Middle Ages were to emerge more clearly in the course of the century.

Nevertheless this revival of interest in ancient literature resulted in something more than mere wonder and passive acceptance by the Italians. By the middle of the 15th Century, with the work of collecting practically complete, a critical attitude towards both life and letters is seen developing at Florence, Naples and other centres of learning, where it was applied to the solution of problems, intellectual as well as literary. In the first place, Greek studies had revealed human nature in the fullness of intellectual and moral freedom ; and a heightened sense of the greatness of man and of the power of human reason therefore

became general. Eloquent testimony of this may be found in
Pico della Mirandola's short treatise, *On the Dignity of Man*,[1] in
which man is described as the crown of creation, a free agent gifted
with reason which distinguished him from brutes and angels
alike, endowed also with the power of growth and development ;
and with this glowing eulogy went a claim for the right of free
inquiry and for an emancipation of the reason in human affairs.

Efforts were consequently made to bring reasoned judgment
to bear on intellectual problems in general. Loftier conceptions,
for instance, were formed of a liberal education, ideas which
differed vitally from those underlying the medieval system of
the seven Liberal Arts. Attacks were also made on scholastic
doctrines and monastic abuses ; the authority of Aristotle and
the Arabic philosophers was questioned ; [2] and in the search for
truth classical learning was applied, and what is more, was sometimes challenged, with a daring that was something entirely new.
Ficino (1422–99), for instance, is seen attempting to reconcile
Platonism and Christianity ; while Pico della Mirandola (1463–94),
imbued with the idea of the unity of all knowledge, sought to
bring into accord pagan, Christian, and Hebrew traditions. At
the same time that writer has also something to say for medieval
schoolmen, as against the one-sided worship of classical authorities. To him the schoolmen were, after all, philosophers,
seekers after truth, and not as the grammarians, triflers with
questions relating to the mother of Andromache or the sons of
Niobe.[3] And a similar independence of mind is shown by L.
Valla (1406–57) when in his dialogue *On Pleasure* (1431) he discusses in rational fashion the problem of conduct. He examines
in some detail Stoic and Epicurean arguments ; but he adopts
as his final criteria, not ancient precepts, but the dictates of Nature
or reason, on the ground that what was ordained by Nature could
not be wrong.[4] And this *interrogatio Naturae*, which amounted
to a challenge of classical authority, is highly significant at this
date. It points to the emergence of a new rational spirit which
was to play a great part in the development of later critical
activities.

But while problems of various kinds were thus being freely
discussed, evidences of the same rational and judicial attitude
were not lacking in connexion with works of literature, which

[1] For the relevant passage see J. Burckhardt, *The Renaissance in
Italy* (tr. Middlemore), p. 354, n.
[2] L. Valla, *On Dialectic*.
[3] *Ep. to E. Barbaro* (1485) : see Burckhardt, *op. cit.* p. 202.
[4] L. Valla, *Opera Omnia* (1465), i. c. 9.

now became subject to criticism from several angles. Already at an early date, when manuscripts were accumulating, the importance of ascertaining what an author had actually written was firmly grasped ; and the foundations of textual criticism were laid by Niccolo de' Niccoli (1363–1437) of Florence, by his collation of manuscripts, his revisions and corrections of texts —a task in which he was followed by L. Valla, Politian, and others. Then, too, it was now that inquiries were first made into the authenticity of ancient works ; and to Valla's well-known denunciation of the ' Donation of Constantine ' [1] is attached a special interest in critical history, apart from its effect in discrediting certain Papal claims to temporal power. In the ' Decree of Gratian ' Valla had noted the passage in which Constantine had presented to the reigning Pope and his successors his own diadem, Rome and all the provinces of Italy. This ' Donation ' Valla now declared to be fictitious, claiming it to have been interpolated at a later date ; and his contention he based on legal, linguistic, political and historical grounds, maintaining further that the style of the passage was inconsistent with the date alleged. Here, then, was the first use made of the historical method of criticism ; and this illuminating example of the method does not stand alone. Elsewhere and for similar historical reasons, the same critic questions the authenticity of the *Celestial Hierarchies* of Dionysius the Areopagite, a work of considerable influence at the time, which was accepted as genuine and translated by Ficino. Then, too, Valla is also the first to suggest, on the strength of internal evidence, that the popular medieval manual, the *Rhetorica ad Herennium*, was unworthy of Cicero and had therefore been wrongly assigned to him. And in this contention he was followed by Raphael Regius, who in 1491 expressly denied Ciceronian authorship, and attributed the work to one Cornificius instead.[2]

Yet more significant, at least for our present purpose, were those further critical activities which concerned themselves with literary values, and which succeeded in throwing fresh light on literature itself, and more particularly on that confused mass of ancient texts which had by now accumulated, ranging from early Greece to the Byzantine Age. For the literary theorizing that resulted we must look mainly to certain educational treatises of 15th-Century Humanists, most of which, after the ancient fashion, were addressed to persons of rank. First came one of

---

[1] *De falso credita et ementita Constantini donatione declamatio* (1439).
[2] Politian is less happy in assigning the *Letters of Phalaris* to Lucian (*Ep.* I. *Pol. opera*, Lyon, 1539, p. 2).

the most widely-read of treatises, the *De ingenuis moribus* [1] (*c.* 1404) of Vergerius, in which the claims of Latin literature to an essential place in a liberal education were cogently set forth. Before the end of the 15th Century at least twenty editions of the work had already appeared; and its popularity remained well into the 16th Century. This was followed by the tractate, *De studiis et literis* (*c.* 1405) of L. Bruni, in which literary questions were discussed from a different angle but with equal enthusiasm and suggestiveness. The value of literature and the art of writing are effectively treated; and some important principles are enunciated in the course of the discussion. Yet more important, however, was L. Valla's *Elegantiae linguae latinae* (*c.* 1435), in which the problem of correct Latinity was subjected to critical analysis, and an art of style established on rational principles. After comparing medieval Latin with that of Cicero and Quintilian, Valla deals with points of grammar and style (Bks. I–V) and then corrects the views of earlier scholars and grammarians, such as Gellius, Donatus, Servius, Priscian and Isidore (Bk. VI). The work was one of the great achievements of the 15th Century in virtue of its methods as well as its teaching; and its influence was considerable. Printed at Venice (1471), it had gone through fifty-nine editions by 1536, and was epitomized by Erasmus in 1484. Of importance, too, was Valla's *Annotations on the New Testament* (*c.* 1444) which submitted the Biblical text to linguistic criticism. His aim was to correct errors in the Vulgate by reference to the original Greek; and the work provided Erasmus with the suggestion for his edition of the Greek Testament.

Less directly influential, but still of great interest, was the treatise, *De liberorum educatione* (1450) of Aeneas Sylvius (afterwards Pius II) in which the principles of the new education were once more set forth. The place of literature as the indispensable foundation is confirmed; the importance of a sound grammatical training is stressed; and attempts are also made at appreciating individual authors. Of similar interest is the treatise *De ordine docendi et studendi* (1459) by Battista Guarino, son of the famous Guarino da Verona, whose educational doctrine is here represented. The work is an attempt at inculcating the value of Greek, as well as Latin, writers; and at the same time suggestions are made concerning the most effective methods of appreciating their writings. It thus afforded a useful introduction to

[1] English versions of this treatise and of those of Bruni, Aeneas Sylvius, and Guarino are supplied in W. H. Woodward's *Vittorino da Feltre*, pp. 93–178, to which references are made in footnotes *infra*.

ancient literature, and supplied guidance that was much needed at the time. For the rest, judgments on literature and literary studies may be found scattered in works of various kinds. Important contributions, for instance, are made by Politian (1454–94) in his *Letters*, his *Miscellanea* and also in *Sylvae*, four Latin poems declaimed as introductions to his academic lectures. From Pico della Mirandola (1463–94), again, came certain theories of poetry which found later echoes in 17th-Century England ; while the agelong hostility to poetry was vigorously voiced by Savonarola (1452–98) in his treatise *De scientiis*.

Such, then, were the indirect contributions to critical literature during this period ; and they owed not a little to the timely recovery at this date of certain works of antiquity which had dealt with literary matters, and which now afforded glimpses of that classical theory which had been inaccessible to the Middle Ages. Inspiration, for instance, was now drawn from Cicero's works on rhetoric ; still more from the newly-discovered complete version of Quintilian's *Institutio*. The latter, the most popular of contemporary finds, was in fact largely responsible for the new attitude towards literature and literary studies ; and after an early exposition of its teaching by Vergerius, the treatise was subsequently reduced to epitome form by F. Patrizi (*c.* 1460–70). Meanwhile other important works had also appeared, though their significance as yet was not fully appreciated. Thus something of Plato's teaching on poetry and rhetoric had been made available by the translation of his *Republic*, begun by Chrysoloras (1402) and completed by Decembrio (1440) ; also by Bruni's Latin versions of *Phaedo, Phaedrus* and *Gorgias* (1423). Later in the century translations of Aristotle's *Rhetoric* came from Filelfo and Trapezuntius ; and, in addition, a Latin version of the *Poetics* (1498) from Georgius Valla—the latter, however, too late to influence 15th-Century thought. Of more immediate influence, on the other hand, was Guarino's version of the pseudo-Plutarchian tractate, *On Education* (1411) ; and there is evidence to suggest that Plutarch's *De audiendis poetis* was also well known at this date. Notable also was Bruni's translation of the *De legendis Gentilium libris* of St. Basil (*c.* 327–79) which appeared in 1405, and was to prove one of the most popular tracts among early Humanists ; while it is also worth noting that Tacitus's *Dialogus*, that *aureolus libellus*, had already been published in Venice in 1470. Altogether a beginning had thus been made—though only a beginning—in restoring the link with classical antiquity which had been severed in the Dark Ages, with disastrous consequences for the centuries that followed.

When we turn to consider what actually was achieved in the way of literary theorizing and judgment at this date, we shall find that such criticism as was forthcoming was largely conditioned by the circumstances under which it appeared. In the first place, the actuating motive of this criticism was throughout educational in kind. It resulted from the efforts of contemporary Humanists to provide a new liberal education, in place of the medieval system bound up with the seven Liberal Arts. The Trivium and Quadrivium had been products of 5th-Century monasticism, though their elements had come down from a yet earlier age. They had presented in an abridged form certain aspects of ancient culture ; but divorced from the texts on which they were based, and consisting as they did of codified and sterilized learning from which the virtue had vanished, they had proved to be seriously lacking in educational value. Now, however, reasoned judgment and psychological insight were brought to bear on the problem. With a deeper sense of the requirements of the human spirit, efforts were made to apply the newly-discovered literature to educational ends ; and definite claims for literature and literary studies were established as essential elements in a liberal education. This preoccupation with educational interests, however, was not without its effects on the criticism involved. With the rational faculty reawakened, and in the absence of a full revelation of ancient classical doctrine, the literary standards adopted were predominantly of a utilitarian and moral kind. Literature was valued not so much for its aesthetic and artistic qualities as for its practical uses, for its influence on character, its ability to train a man for his part in active life, or again, as providing models of expression ; and these tests remained characteristic of Humanistic criticism to the end.

There were other considerations, however, which modified this mainly utilitarian outlook, and which led to a treatment of literature from other standpoints. In the first place, the prevailing enthusiasm for literature now became articulate as never before. A new significance was being attached to literature in general, to literature in and for itself, apart from its educational uses ; and the intimate relations existing between life and letters were accordingly represented in a new and suggestive light. Then, too, the new importance now being attached to literature in the scheme of education also led to some amount of theorizing on literature, its various forms, the art of expression and the like ; and some basic theories were therefore enunciated, thus giving a definite direction to later critical thought. Moreover, in response to the demands of an age bewildered by the vast stores of literature acquired, attempts were also made at distinguishing literary values, at removing that medieval confusion which had failed to discriminate on artistic grounds between Dares and Dictys on the one hand and Homer and Virgil on the other; and in consequence critical judgments were pronounced which established once for all the great classics of antiquity. These, then, were the three main lines along which criticism developed in 15th-Century Italy; firstly, attempts to explain the significance of literature in general, secondly, some amount of theorizing on literature and the literary art, and thirdly, efforts at distinguishing classical values in an aesthetic or historical sense. And it now remains to inquire into the extent to which the understanding and appreciation of literature were furthered by these various activities.

In the first place, no greater service was rendered to literary studies at this date than the recognition given to literature, first, as a study of prime importance, and, what was more, as a precious possession of humanity at large. An acquaintance with ancient literature, as well as literary contributions in the vernacular, had by no means been wanting in the Middle Ages; and statements had been made concerning the value of literature from the time of the early Fathers onwards. Nevertheless, the attitude of scholars had been consistently one of depreciation and even scorn. At Paris first, and later at other Universities, classical studies had been despised as purely ' grammarian ' or elementary, useful only in providing stores of grammatical examples, or else as ancillary to other and more important studies. Pride of place, on the other hand, was given to the professional studies of Law, Medicine, and Theology; and while logic overshadowed all other subjects in the education provided by the seven Liberal Arts, no place was found for the cultivation of literature. And now in 15th-Century Italy a more enlightened scholarship discerned in the art of letters a new and more vital culture than had been afforded by encyclopaedias, epitomes, and the like. Vergerius, for instance, had described it as ' a study adapted to all times and circumstances, to the investigation of fresh knowledge or to the recasting and application of the old '; [1] and with literature thus placed at the centre of things, a readjustment was made in the whole educational scheme. Attention was focused on works of classical antiquity, and literature from now on became the key to the thought and culture of the ancient world.

Of yet greater interest was the value attached to literature

[1] Woodward, *op. cit.* p. 107.

in its bearing on life ; and here appreciation rises above pedagogic levels to higher planes of enthusiastic praise. Thus by Aeneas Sylvius,[1] to begin with, literature is described as a guide to the meaning of life, throwing light on the past, interpreting the present, providing also a sound forecast of the future ; so that ' where letters cease darkness covers the land '. Elsewhere its merits as a source of wisdom are set forth by Vergerius.[2] In literature, he states, are vast stores of knowledge, records of great human achievements and of the wonders of Nature, as well as noble thoughts which by virtue of their expression were destined to be immortal. Then, too, he adds, such knowledge is always and easily accessible. ' At a word ', he explains, ' books speak to you, at a word they are still ; and to all requests their response is ever ready and to the point.' Moreover, ' books ', he continues, ' are indeed a higher—a wider and more tenacious —memory, a storehouse which is the common property of us all '. Nor, again, are the pleasures of literature entirely ignored ; for Guarino [3] recalls Cicero's well-known tribute to imaginative literature, declaring it to be ' the inspiration of youth, the delight of age, the ornament of happy fortunes and the solace of adversity '. In addition, he describes literature as the adornment of leisure, a mental recreation, and a source of harmless emotional delight that ' stirs you, but with no empty hopes and no vain fears '. And finally he adds, ' through books, and books alone, will your converse be with the best and greatest, nay even with the mighty dead themselves '. Thus was voiced some measure of the new feeling for literature ; though as yet there were but few signs of that aesthetic appreciation heralded by Petrarch, who had been the first to recognize the formal excellences of classical literature, its expression of fine thought and delicate emotions, its harmonies of prose and verse, its proprieties of diction and its imaginative effects. Yet certain aspects of literature had now been duly noted, the value of its thought, its intimate bearing on life and something of its manifold delights ; so that altogether a new prestige was being claimed for literature, a prestige which had hitherto been denied it, at least in scholastic circles.

It is therefore not strange to find that efforts were now made to explain in more specific terms the nature of literature and the literary art ; and in the theorizing that resulted will be found the main substance of the Humanistic contribution to literary doctrine. Such theorizing of necessity had obvious limitations,

[1] Woodward, *op. cit.* p. 141.
[2] *ibid.* pp. 105–6. [3] *ibid.* p. 176.

being based on the works of Cicero and Quintilian, together with stray doctrines drawn from Plato, Plutarch, St. Basil, and the Latin Fathers ; while the lines of treatment followed were those of Quintilian's classification of literature, comprising oratory, poetry, history, and philosophy. The determining factor, however, was pedagogic in kind ; and one of the great principles of Renascence studies was the intimate connexion existing between wisdom and eloquence in their relation to life. It had been an ancient commonplace, referred to by Cicero at the beginning of his *De inventione*,[1] that wisdom without eloquence is of little benefit to the state whereas eloquence without wisdom is a great danger ; and this doctrine found fruitful soil among 15th-Century Humanists. Thus Bruni explicitly states that ' these two sides of learning should not be separated ' ;[2] and he condemned as a barren attainment not only proficiency in literary form unaccompanied by a broad acquaintance with facts and truths, but also knowledge, however vast, which lacked grace of expression. Humanistic aims were therefore concentrated, first, on the acquisition of knowledge, and secondly, on the attainment of skill in expression ; and with these as the actuating motives the discussion of literary matters proceeded. Of the several branches of literature mentioned by Quintilian, history and philosophy, in the first place, come in merely for summary treatment ; though not without its interest is the fact that the conception of history as ' philosophy teaching by example ' was already familiar at this date. According to Vergerius, ' History gives us concrete examples of the precepts inculcated by philosophy. The latter shows what men should do, the former what men have said and done in the past '.[3] Of yet greater importance in critical history, however, was the attention given to oratory and the cultivation of prose style, as well as the views expressed concerning poetry. These were in fact the two main themes of Humanistic scholars at this date ; and their theorizing is notable, not only for what it contains, but also for what it omits, namely, those discussions on the drama and other poetic forms which Italian critics of the 16th Century were to supply.

Highly significant, in the first place, was the interest now taken in the study of oratory and prose style ; for there were many factors, other than pedagogic influences, which made such inquiries inevitable. To begin with, oratory at this stage had recovered something of its ancient prestige. It was to the orators of antiquity, for instance, that the Humanists assigned the leading position among classical writers, possibly in their admira-

[1] I. i.   [2] Woodward, *op. cit.* p. 132.   [3] *ibid.* p. 106.

tion for Cicero's orations ; though there was also the fact that it was with the education of the orator that Quintilian had dealt in his *Institutio*, the standard work on education generally. Apart from this it was keenly felt at the time that in medieval Latin the art of expression had been lost, and that the restoration of classical Latinity was thus an urgent necessity ; and besides, the spirit of the age now made for a revival of oratory in Italian public life, as was shown by the great part played by ceremonial eloquence at all functions, whether diplomatic, civic or academic. The results are seen in the attempts now made to revive the study of eloquence, attempts which were productive of what was perhaps the most characteristic of Humanistic theorizing. All such inquiries, it is true, were confined to expression in Latin ; for the vernacular, made up as it was of a number of dialects, was held to be no fit instrument for literary expression. It was to the restoration of Ciceronian and Augustan Latinity as the standard and ideal that the Humanists now addressed themselves ; and their efforts were to prove of the highest significance. They not only directed attention anew to matters of prose style ; they also restated some valuable artistic principles ; and, incidentally, they explain in some measure the course taken by later critical activities.

Of importance, to begin with, was the restoration at this date of the ancient conception of grammar, and its recognition as the essential foundation of an education based on letters ; for by this means fresh impetus was given to the study of both literature and prose style. Throughout the Middle Ages grammar had indeed been studied as one of the seven Liberal Arts. But based as it was on the works of Donatus, Priscian and others, and complicated later by endless glosses and speculations on those particular texts, it had become a mechanical and barren study, deprived of independent status, subordinate to both logic and rhetoric, concerned solely with rules of accidence, syntax and prosody ; and of these limitations the medieval Grammars in current use—the works of John of Garland, the *Graecismus* of Évrard, and the *Doctrinale* of Alexander of Villedieu—all afford abundant evidence. Against this sterile discipline a reaction was now fostered by Italian Humanists ; and grammar, under Quintilian's influence, became a new and more vital study, being regarded as ' the portal to all knowledge ', and the necessary preliminary, not only to correctness of utterance, but also to the acquisition of a sound style and to the interpretation of literature. Moreover, both logic and rhetoric now became in the main ancillary studies, valued chiefly as aids to an effective style ;

though the *Rhetorica* (*c.* 1437) of Trapezuntius, a translation of Aristotle's *Rhetoric*, maintained something of the old tradition and was influential in its own and the succeeding age. The function of grammar, it was generally held, was ' to order expres- sion ', of logic, ' to give it point ', of rhetoric, ' to render it illustrious ' ; [1] and whereas the complexities of rhetoric were now less zealously studied, the syllogistic reasonings and verbal displays of earlier logicians were also sternly discountenanced. ' Logic indeed has no profit ', so writes Aeneas Sylvius,[2] ' except it serve as a direct aid to clear and precise thought and expression.'

Nor was it merely that fresh interest was now aroused in matters of style by this revival of grammar. A new and far-reaching principle relating to literary standards was enunciated by Laurentius Valla, which was to have a vital bearing on literary values generally. Hitherto questions of grammar had been decided on the authority of Donatus, Priscian and others, together with *a priori* reasonings and speculations of later grammarians. And now in revolt against these unstable foundations Valla submits as the one infallible authority the actual practice of the great classics ; and the principle he lays down, *Ego pro lege accipio quidquid magnis auctoribus placuit*,[3] marks a definite stage in the critical development. It is true that his pronouncement relates primarily to matters of accidence, syntax and the like. But it represents, notwithstanding, the earliest Renascence state-ment of the doctrine of classicism, according to which authority in literary matters was vested in the great works of antiquity, as representing the highest artistic ideals then known. More-over, the methods thus advocated for arriving at literary principles were no less significant. They involved a first-hand examination of actual texts, in place of an acceptance of the findings of earlier theorists, often speculative and imperfect. They were, in fact, the methods inherent in Aristotle's critical procedure, rational, analytic and also inductive ; and the way was thus prepared for a sound development of literary theory, which, owing to various causes in the period that followed, was not destined to be realized.

Yet already during this period some consideration was being given to matters of expression in general ; and not a few principles of value were brought to light. The importance of an effective style as an indispensable condition of permanence was in the first place suggested by Vergerius. ' I do not think ', he writes,[4] ' that thoughts without style will secure . . . a sure survival ' ;

----

[1] Woodward, *op. cit.* p. 144.   [2] *ibid.* p. 155.
[3] *Elegantiae Linguae Latinae*, iii. 17.
[4] Woodward, *op. cit.* p. 105.

and the idea in substance was repeated by Bruni [1] and Aeneas Sylvius.[2] Then, in the theorizing that followed, attention was called first to the necessity for the right choice of words; and the essential elements were said to be the accepted vocabulary and the diction of the best writers. Coinages in consequence were thus discouraged; 'to very few, the great creators of a tongue', so wrote Aeneas Sylvius,[3] 'is it given to coin new words with impunity'. Moreover, by the same writer the employment of foreign words was condemned and described as a mere barbarism; while arbitrary changes in word-forms (except for metrical reasons), as well as the use of obsolete words and expressions, were also denounced. Speech, above all, it was added, should be intelligible and without pretension. Thus metaphors which obscured the plain meaning were described as 'no longer ornaments but a weariness'; and not less important was the further injunction he gave, 'to choose the word which will most exactly express the sense you wish to convey'. This, he asserted, was 'the one controlling rule in all composition to be observed'.

Equally suggestive, however, were the remarks made concerning the manner and style of utterance, which in general was required to be in keeping with the subject-matter. Then, too, of interest are the illuminating statements made concerning that 'other harmony of prose', in which the influence of Aristotle's *Rhetoric* or the works of Cicero or Quintilian or both, may be discerned. Guarino, for instance, notes that 'rhythm is not confined to poetical composition'; [4] while Bruni supplies a fuller and more reasoned statement. 'We notice,' he writes,[5] 'in all good prose a certain element of rhythm—though it is not obtrusive—which coincides with, and expresses, the general structure of a passage and gives us a clue to the sense.' 'Different rhythms', he explains,[6] 'arouse different emotions suitable to the matter in hand. To ignore this is to neglect one of the most delicate points of style.' Then, too, attention is called to the importance of obtaining the right order of words in a sentence, or again, to the need for a skilful linking-up of the sentences employed; [7] while not without its significance is the warning issued against affectations of all kinds. These, then, were among the main principles of style laid down at this date; and they are based, so it is claimed, on reason and authoritative usage. The latter, described as 'the final canon to be obeyed in all

---

[1] Woodward, *op. cit.* p. 132.   [2] *ibid.* p. 143.   [3] *ibid.* p. 146.
[4] *ibid.* p. 165.   [5] *ibid.* p. 125.   [6] *ibid.* p. 126.
[7] *ibid.* p. 146.

3

composition ', is further defined as the practice of the best ancient writers, namely, the orators and historians of the Ciceronian and Augustan Ages ; and it is further urged that not only their vocabularies but also their methods of handling their subjects should be studied.[1] It was all a development of the teaching of Valla.

One special stylistic problem of far-reaching significance has, however, yet to be noted. It arose out of the attempt to restore a correct Latinity by applying the accepted doctrine which prescribed an imitation of the orators and historians of the great days at Rome. From the first it was perhaps inevitable that Cicero as a prose stylist should command most attention ; and early in the 15th Century a Ciceronian tradition was established by Barzizza (followed by Vergerius, Vittorino and others), attempts being made by adopting Cicero as their chief model to cultivate a style which should embody his main principles, and yet was adapted to current needs of expression. Imitation was thus interpreted in the most liberal sense, and was not confined exclusively to Cicero. It stood for a revival of classical form and spirit, which yet afforded scope to the national genius and was calculated to produce a style both flexible and spontaneous, with, moreover, the freedom of movement indispensable for a living language. By the middle of the century, however, the tradition had already shown signs of degenerating into a pedantic cult, the views of which were set forth by Bartolomeo Scala, who demanded an exclusive and a meticulous imitation of Cicero, with expression strictly limited to the Ciceronian vocabulary, accidence and syntax. And thus was inaugurated the cult of Ciceronianism, together with the many discussions that followed, regarding the methods by which the ancients were to be most profitably imitated.

Already in 1450 Aeneas Sylvius had issued a warning against ' the forced imitation of an older style ', at the same time recalling the advice of Phavorinus (borrowed from Aulus Gellius) ' to copy the virtues of the great men of old and let their archaisms die with them '.[2] It was by Politian, however, that the challenge was most successfully met, and his treatment of the question bears witness to his fine scholarship and his critical sense alike. In the first place he argues, in a famous letter to Paolo Cortesi,[3] that style after all is a personal thing. One whose style is mere imitation he compares to a parrot repeating what

---

[1] Woodward, *op. cit.* p. 149.   [2] *ibid.* pp. 147–8.
[3] *Politiani Opera*, Gryphius ed. Lyon (1537–9), i. 251 : for translation see C. S. Baldwin, *Renaissance Literary Theory and Practice*, pp. 48–9.

to it are but meaningless sounds ; and he recalls how Quintilian had derided those who claimed kinship with Cicero by concluding a period with *esse videatur*, or again, how Horace had decried writers who were imitators and nothing more. Such writing, he added, was without reality or force ; it lacked the stamp of individuality, was without nerve or life, and failed to arouse emotion in others. He therefore denounces the Ciceronians as ' mere apes of Cicero ' ; and his advice is to discard that ' miserable superstition ' which compelled one to disparage one's own composition and forbade one ever to withdraw one's eyes from Cicero. And if some one should protest that in so doing the writer was not representing Cicero, then the answer should be that he, the writer, was not Cicero, and that he claimed to be expressing himself. (*Non exprimis, inquit aliquis, Ciceronem. Quid tum ? Non enim sum Cicero ; me tamen, ut opinor, exprimo.*)

But Politian in attacking Ciceronianism goes even further than this. He condemns outright the theory of an ideal classical period with fixed and absolute standards, thus exploding the doctrine which held Cicero to be the one and only model ; and this he did in a lecture delivered at Florence on the Silver Age at Rome.[1] He had already noted that the writers of the so-called ideal, that is, the Ciceronian, age had differed considerably in their methods and effects. He now points out that Cicero himself had adopted no one consistent standard, but was influenced in turn by Asiatic, Rhodian and Attic styles, so that he had provided no actual precedent for the doctrine of Ciceronianism. More trenchant still, Politian then makes positive claims for the recognition of the value of those innovations in style introduced by writers who came after Cicero. He discountenances, for instance, the idea that prose-writers after Cicero's day had seriously declined, and suggests that their styles were ' not so much corrupted and debased as changed in kind ', and that they were ' not necessarily inferior because they were different '. In them, on the contrary, he found considerable charm, much liveliness and colour, attractive epigrams and figures, and a host of qualities which made for effectiveness in style. It was therefore in his opinion ' a capital vice to imitate one author and him alone ' ; in imitating the ancients ' many men's excellences were to be considered ', as well as those of Cicero. Moreover, that these writers were to be studied, not with a view to mere copying, but with the development of an

[1] *Politiani Opera*, Gryphius ed. Lyon (1537–9), iii. 108–9 : for translation, see C. S. Baldwin, *op. cit.* p. 47.

individual style in mind, is shown by his further injunction that
' finally, I would have you . . . swim without corks, take sometimes your own advice . . . in a word, risk your whole strength '.[1]
This then was the enlightened conception of imitation submitted
by Politian. It embodied not only the conception of the
relativity of standards, but also the idea that imitation was
only a preliminary to the development of a personal style. And
in adopting this position he was influenced not only by
Quintilian,[2] but in all probability by Tacitus as well who in his
Dialogus [3] had questioned the validity of absolute standards, and
had defended on similar lines the main innovations in post-
Ciceronian prose. Of the importance of this teaching of Politian
at this juncture there can be no doubt. It represented one of
the outstanding pronouncements of the 15th Century; but, as
the sequel showed, the tendency towards a mechanical and
pedantic imitation was by no means checked, and Politian's
counsel was to pass for the most part unheeded in the later
expositions of style and other literary theorizing.

Such then were the Humanistic discussions on oratory and
prose style which took place in 15th-Century Italy; and of
hardly less importance were the views expressed concerning the
nature of poetry, that elusive form of artistic creation which had
hitherto defied all medieval attempts at a satisfactory analysis.
It had previously been treated as a branch of grammar, of rhetoric
and even of logic; and Humanistic doctrine now marked an
appreciable advance on the earlier position. The subject was
now approached with greater respect than formerly as a definite
element of ancient culture. It was frequently discussed, if only
in incidental fashion; and while to some extent, it is true, the
earlier post-classical and patristic doctrines still held their ground,
they were now adopted with occasional modifications that are
not without their interest. Signs of the new attitude are seen,
to begin with, in the stress now laid on the divine origin of poetry,
doubtless under the influence of contemporary Neo-Platonic
studies. Thus ' Poetry ', states Bruni,[4] ' is marked with something of the divine ', such inspiration being suggested by Virgil's
prophecy of the Redeemer's birth, so that, he adds, ' we must
recognize in the poet a certain " possession " as by a power other
and stronger than himself '. A similar claim is likewise made
by Pico della Mirandola when, in a *Discourse on Plato*,[5] he states
that Homer and Tiresias were filled with ' poetic fury ', in

---

[1] *Letter to Cortesi*, see note, p. 23 *supra*.
[2] See Atkins, *Lit. Crit. in Antiquity*, ii. 280.   [3] *ibid*. ii. 188 ff.
[4] Woodward, *op. cit.* p. 130.   [5] fol. 507.

accordance with Platonic teaching ; so that poetry was thus the result of a rapture of the spirit, inspired by a vision of ideal or spiritual beauty, from which proceeded all wisdom, and which opened the poet's eyes to all things both past and future. Of this exalted conception of poetry as an ' inspired thing ' there had been but stray hints in medieval theorizing ; while new also was Politian's contention (in *Nutricia*) that poetry had been given to men as a consolation for the miseries of life. On the other hand, such doctrines, it should be added, were strongly denounced by Savonarola in his *De studiis*.

Then, too, while primary importance was in general attached to the thought contained in poetry, some advance was now being made towards a more adequate understanding of the poetic art and its aesthetic qualities. ' In poetry ', writes Guarino,[1] ' we must fix our thoughts on the underlying truths rather than upon the " imaginations " in which they are expressed ' ; but at the same time he adds that it was ' in purity and grace of style, in worthy deeds worthily presented, in noble thoughts nobly expressed ' that he found nourishment for both mind and spirit. With this consciousness of artistic quality he then declares that ' poetry feeds as nothing else our sense of delight '. But he is also careful to state that emotional effects may sometimes be harmful —a distrust characteristic of a rational age which regarded ' imagination ' as a mental aberration, the view taken by Pico della Mirandola in his *De imaginatione*.[2] No such qualification, however, enters into Bruni's conception of poetry.[3] He notes, for instance, ' its formal charms, the variety and interest of its subject-matter ', and above all, ' its peculiar affinity to our emotions and intelligence '. Its emotional effects he describes as ' a sort of uplifting of the soul ', such as men are wont to experience at sacred moments ; and he unequivocally declares poetry to be ' an ennobling form of pleasure ', which has ' by our very constitution a stronger attraction for us than any other form of expression '. Here, then, for the first time psychological considerations were being brought to bear on literary theorizing ; and Bruni attributes not a little of the poetic effect to the ' peculiar affinity ' of rhythm and metre to the human constitu-tion. The ancients, he pointed out, had held that ' the human soul was ordered in special relations to the principles of harmony and rhythm, and is therefore by no other influence so fitly and so surely moved '. Nor was he alone in associating with harmony and rhythm part of the charm of poetry. It was commonly

[1] Woodward, *op. cit.* p. 175. [2] Translated by Baïf (1557).
[3] Woodward, *op. cit.* pp. 130–1.

held, on the authority of Pythagoras and Socrates, that music
had a soothing and refreshing influence on the mind, and was
thus an aid to ' the inner harmony of the soul '.[1]   Moreover, even
Savonarola allowed that since the soul loved harmony, therefore
poetry made use of harmonic forms; but he also added a
qualification. The Scriptures, which were for him the highest
poetry, were not necessarily in verse-form ; and so verse was
merely an accompaniment of poetry, a welcome feature but not
an essential element.

With regard to the function of poetry, again, new ideas were
now put forward. The Horatian formula of ' delight and
instruction ' had been familiar to the Middle Ages ; and the
ethical function of poetry was generally maintained at this date.
Now, however, stress was also laid on poetry as a civilizing factor
in history.   It was a commonplace of antiquity, applied to poetry,
philosophy, and oratory in turn, that from the first such activities
had been great civilizing agencies, rendering services of a social,
political, and religious kind ; and this idea, handed on by Cicero
and Horace,[2] became one of the main doctrines of Humanistic
critics.   The chief function of poetry was held to be that of
refining and elevating humanity.   Action being the test of all
studies, poetry was valued in that it conduced to righteous and
noble action.   At the same time, however, other and less
serious views were sometimes propounded ; as when Vergerius
suggests that the main concern of poetry and the poetic art was
with ' the leisure side of existence ',[3] and was therefore not
of the first importance—a reminiscence possibly of Plutarch's description of the charms of poetry as ' mere play or amusement '
(παιδιά).

Nor, in addition, must the fresh arguments now brought
forward in defence of poetry be overlooked.   Attacks on poetry,
mainly on the score of immorality, were still being made, in
particular by the Dominicans at Florence ; and replies to
detractors were forthcoming from many of the Humanists.   The
conventional lines of apology handed down from patristic times
were submitted by Aeneas Sylvius.[4] He notes how shallow
minds were wont ' to quote Cicero and Plato, Jerome and
Boethius ' in making their attack, and would then cry out for

[1] Woodward, op. cit. pp. 108, 155, for views of Vergerius and Aeneas
Sylvius.
[2] cf. De oratore, i. 31–3, Ars Poetica, ll. 391–407 : also Isocrates,
Nicocles, 5–9.
[3] Woodward, op. cit. p. 108.
[4] ibid. pp. 149–50 : see also Atkins, English Literary Criticism
Medieval, pp. 17–18.

the banishment of poets. To this he replies that 'Jerome, Augustine and Cyprian all drew illustrations from heathen poets and so sanctioned its use'; that St. Paul likewise 'availed himself of Epimenides or Menander to enforce a doctrine'; and that, besides, there was abundant classical precedent for honouring poets.[1] Now, however, fresh points were also made on poetry's behalf. To the charge that ancient poetry had dealt largely with 'stories of love and sin', Bruni makes reply that such poetry embodied also themes of constancy and devotion, that noble characters in fact predominated in Homer and Virgil, that such unedifying stories as existed were after all mere fiction and had therefore no immoral effect; while the Scriptures, he added, were not without narratives of the kind.[2] Still more significant was Guarino's defence of the 'impieties, cruelties and horrors' found in ancient poetry. Such matters, he claimed,[3] were to be judged, not by moral standards, but by the test of verisimilitude, by 'their congruity to the characters and situations described'; and here Guarino makes a plea for aesthetic judgment where poetry was concerned. 'It is the artist we criticize', he states, 'and not the moralist'; and then proceeds to explain how an artistic representation of things repugnant may yet be pleasing. 'We shrink', he asserts, 'from the sight of a snake or a scorpion, yet a clever drawing of either is a source of pleasure'; and therefore, 'what in real life repels us may in fiction win our admiration by its skilful representation'. This same awareness of other than moral standards is incidentally revealed by Aeneas Sylvius in his confession that when reading 'the loves of Aeneas and Dido' it was to the genius of the poet that he paid his tribute of admiration.[4] And here may be detected the influence of Plutarch,[5] who, following Aristotle [6] in this, had explained that the artistic pleasure arising out of a painful subject was of an intellectual kind and was due to an appreciation of the skill of the artist in presenting it.

But while fresh light was thus being thrown on the nature and function of poetry from various angles, some of the medieval doctrines still held their ground, thus hindering a clearer and fuller apprehension of the truth concerning poetry. For this survival the influence of Dante, Petrarch and Boccaccio may in part be responsible. Dante, for instance, had described poetry as a rhetorical fiction musically arranged; Petrarch and Boccaccio

[1] cf. also Bruni in Woodward, *op. cit.* p. 129.
[2] *ibid.* pp. 132–3.   [3] *ibid.* p. 175.
[4] *ibid.* p. 132.   [5] cf. *De audiendis poetis*, 18 A–C.
[6] cf. *Poetics*, 1448 b. 10 ff.

had conceived of allegory as ' the warp and woof ' of poetry ; and now Mantuan (1448–1516) defines a poem as a literary form bound by the laws of metre, with truth hidden under fables— a conception, it may be added, which prevailed in 15th-Century England. At the same time Savonarola adopted the Scholastic attitude, and regarded poetry as little more than a sort of rational philosophy. Pico, again, with his mystical tendencies, insisted on its esoteric character. He explains, following Jerome and others, that its meaning is disguised so as to hide it from the vulgar ; just as the Books of the Law had been handed to Moses, couched in mysterious terms (dissimulata autem et occultata), with instructions to convey the interpretation to Joshua and his successors alone.[1] And precedents for such enigmatical and figurative writing he found among the earliest Greeks as well as the Hebrews.

Amidst this flux and confusion of thought, however, Humanistic scholars held firmly to some of the traditional ideas, and to none more tenaciously than to the conception of poetry as a form of allegory. In the first place, there is ample evidence of the general acceptance of the allegorical theory, and of the tendency to attach value to the underlying truths of poetry rather than to the fancies in which they were enshrined. Guarino, for one, claims Cicero's authority for stating that the true significance of poetic fiction consists in ' the exhibition of the realities of life under the form of imaginary persons and situations '.[2] Bruni, again, finds in the ancient poets many ' deep speculations on Nature, on the causes and origins of things, as well as many important truths concerning matters of daily life ' ; [3] and this he illustrates by Homer's story of Iris descending upon Agamemnon in his sleep as a warning against the sloth of rulers. Or again, there was Virgil, who was said to surpass all philosophers in displaying the inner secrets of Nature and the soul. From Pico, however, came the most elaborate, if also the most obscure, exposition of the doctrine. In the light of his conception of the esoteric nature of poetry he argues that the arcana of the ancient sages in fabulous attire form the real subject-matter of poetry. Homer, for instance, he claimed to have excelled in magia naturalis, that is, ' in the exact and absolute knowledge of all natural things ', the generation of the elements, the courses of the stars, the secrets of Nature ; and such knowledge is said to underlie the story of the Odyssey.[4] Elsewhere he makes a plea for the art of mystical writing in numbers, on the score that

---

[1] Heptaplus and Apologia, fol. 81. [2] Woodward, op. cit. p. 170.
[3] ibid. p. 129. [4] Apologia, ff. 112, 80.

God disposed all things in weight, measure and also numbers ' ; [1]
so that he who knew numbers was said to know all things. It
was an attempt to extend the accepted allegorical theory by the
inclusion of Neo-Platonic and Cabalistic teaching ; and belated
echoes of the doctrine were to be heard in 17th-Century England.
These then were the conceptions of poetry held by early
Humanists. They were views confused and inadequate still,
despite the new light thrown on some of its essential qualities ;
so that the secrets of its greatness remained yet to be explored.
The truth was that to the Humanistic mind poetry was little
more than a branch of learning ; a means, along with oratory,
history, and philosophy, of recapturing something of the lost
culture of antiquity, rather than a mysterious and independent
art of infinite possibilities.

So far we have been considering Humanistic theories concerned with, first, the cultivation of oratory and prose style, and,
secondly, the nature of poetry ; and it now remains to inquire
into the work done in connexion with the third main object of
Humanistic critical activities, namely, that of attempting some
appreciation of literature in the concrete, by way of discriminating
between the respective values of works recovered from antiquity.
That some sifting had become necessary was generally felt, in
view of the uncertain standards of medieval times, and, not
least, for pedagogic reasons.   ' We must be supremely careful
in our choice of authors ', wrote Bruni,[2] ' lest an inartistic and
debased style infect our own writing and degrade our taste ' ;
and he urges that ' a keen critical sense ' should be brought to
bear on the various texts.   This task had been facilitated by the
elaboration of grammar and the closer study of style ; and
Vittorino had led the way in instilling principles of taste and in
directing attention to the greater classics.   In this he was
followed by Bruni, Aeneas Sylvius, and Guarino, all of whom
supplied brief estimates of ancient writers ; while most compre-
hensive and suggestive of all was the survey afforded by Politian
in his lectures and in *Sylvae*.

Among the considerations which went to determine the
nature of the critical judgments, none was more important than
the fact that they were for the most part estimates borrowed
from Quintilian, whose concern had been primarily with stylistic
qualities and the suitability of the various authors as models for
intending writers.   This had imposed limits on the range of his
appreciation ; and the same limitations are apparent in Humanistic literary judgments.   Then, too, value was frequently assigned

[1] *Apologia*, fol. 115.   [2] Woodward, *op. cit.* p. 124.

by Humanists to literary work for other than aesthetic reasons. Since subject-matter was regarded as the essence of literature, undue value was attached, for instance, to inferior works which threw light on antiquity or conveyed moral lessons under cover of allegory. And in this connexion Aeneas Sylvius (following Plutarch) commends the habits of the bees rather than those of the garland-maker. ' Other creatures ', he writes,[1] ' enjoy the colour or scent of the flower, but bees are wise to extract the honey.' At the same time there were also signs of more en-lightened standards ; as when, for instance, references were made to artistic matters, such as the charm of verse-form, the value of consistency in characterization and the like. Moreover, allegorical interpretation was being challenged by rational minds desiring to find out what an author's words meant to a plain intelligence ; as when Valla approached Moses and the Evangelists as mere historians. Nor, again, without its interest was Bruni's comment with regard to critical judgment, that ' it is unjust to ignore the beauties of a work of art and to call attention only to its blemishes '.[2] Most significant of all, however, was Politian's attempt to supply some amount of historical background for the appreciation of ancient literature. A lack of historical knowledge, for instance, had hitherto prevented Plato from being understood by earlier Humanists. He had been read in the reflected light of Neo-Platonism ; and scholars had yet to learn the need for viewing a writer in his historical setting before attempting to explain him. An effort was now made by Politian to supply this deficiency. In his lectures he attempts a compre-hensive view of the whole ground of classical literature, while in his introductory poerîts, known as *Sylvae*, he treats of Virgil (in *Manto*), Homer (in *Ambra*), Hesiod (in *Rusticus*) and the origins of poetry generally (in *Nutricia*). His appreciations partook too much perhaps of the nature of panegyrics ; but by him, as the first literary historian, the way was at least prepared for an application of the historical sense in forming critical judgments.

    With regard to the value of such judgments as were forth-coming this much in general may be said, that despite all limita-tions they were effective in giving much-needed guidance, and in establishing for the first time something like standards of taste in literary matters. In the survey of ancient literature there were of course gaps. The Greek tradition was imperfectly represented, Greek tragedy, for instance, receiving but slight notice ; though Politian traces the general development from

[1] Woodward, *op. cit.* p. 150.   [2] *ibid.* p. 131.

the mythical bards of Hellas onwards. On the other hand, the main interest was concentrated on Latin writers, on poets, historians, philosophers, and orators ; and Quintilian's classification of poets (epic, lyric, elegiac, comic, tragic, satiric) was also adopted, but without reference to the formal characteristics later on associated with each of the ' kinds '. Nor was the survey limited to writers of classical antiquity. The merits of Jerome and Augustine were duly appreciated ; Lactantius in grace of style was compared to Cicero ; and while Biblical literature including *Ecclesiasticus* was in general commended, the second Book of *Maccabees* was held to approach in dignity of style the finest examples of classical literature.[1]

As for the appreciations of individual writers, they consisted for the most part of brief comments of a stylistic or moral kind. Already Homer and Virgil, Demosthenes and Cicero had been hailed by Vittorino as the supreme masters of expression ; and subsequently most of the ancient writers were summarily characterized. Of the Greeks, Hesiod was admired for his practical reflexions, Pindar for glowing metaphors and epithets, Isocrates for perspicuity, Euripides for weight of sentiment, Demosthenes for energy of utterance ; and while Plutarch was commended as moralist and historian, Herodotus, Xenophon and Arrian were also praised for their historical writings. Among Latin writers, again, Horace was said to rank next to Virgil in charm of theme and style and to possess a ' specially delicate sense of expression ', Ovid was described as luxuriant but wanton, Lucan as impassioned but rhetorical, Juvenal as severe and crude, Persius as obscure, and ' in handling Martial ', wrote Aeneas Sylvius,[2] ' one cannot gather the roses for the thorns '. Of the historians, moreover, Livy was praised for his flowing narrative style, Caesar for elegance and verve, though Sallust also had his admirers. Seneca's tragedies were likewise commended on account of their lofty sentiments, their grave situations and graceful diction ; while Plautus and Terence both received not a little attention. Each was admired for grace of diction ; but Guarino[3] (following Macrobius) placed Plautus along with Cicero at the head of Latin writers, recalling what was then a common saying that ' the Muses, if they spoke in Latin, would choose the Plautine diction '.

From these running comments the limitations of Humanistic judicial criticism may to some extent be gathered. At the same time the indebtedness of poets to their predecessors was already

[1] Vegio, *De educatione liberorum*, p. 252.
[2] Woodward, *op. cit.* p. 151. [3] *ibid.* p. 171.

being discussed, as when Guarino [1] (following Macrobius again) notes in Virgil Homeric reminiscences—incidents, similes, epithets and the like—as well as other borrowings from Theocritus or Hesiod ; he also suggests that Statius's *Thebais* had been modelled on the *Aeneid*. Most significant of all, however, was the judgment being formed of Virgil in comparison with Homer. Ample tribute, in the first place, was paid in general terms to Homer. Thus, by Vittorino, he is described (in terms reminiscent of Quintilian) [2] as *oceano similis*, the source of every stream and river ; and while Guarino acknowledges him to be ' the sovereign master of all ',[3] Politian bears eloquent witness to the universality of his influence.[4] But Quintilian in insisting on Homer's un-rivalled genius, had also asserted that Virgil was, notwithstand-ing, the greater artist ; and this conception became generally emphasized. Vittorino, for instance, held that Virgil had surpassed Homer in *cura et diligentia*,[5] and that he was also supreme in refinement and technique. Aeneas Sylvius called attention to the music of Virgilian language. ' Praise can no further exalt ', he writes,[6] ' nor criticism detract ' ; and he gives special praise to Virgil's varying style, ' now terse, now copious, now severe, now luxuriant '. And again, Politian exalts him in even yet more rapturous strain, placing him above all poets and all wonders of the world.[7] Judgments of this kind were but the prelude to the Virgil-worship of the century following. As yet admiration fell short of absolute idolatry ; but the way was being prepared for a pedantic narrowing of the conception of the poetic art, which kept pace with the growing and con-stricting influence of Ciceronianism.

Such, then, were the main critical activities of 15th-Century Italy, to which contributions were made by most of the early Humanists ; and in critical history their work is of the first importance despite the prevailing pedagogical interests, for it marked a definite break with medieval doctrine and taste, besides providing inspiration and guidance to leaders of 16th-Century thought, such as Reuchlin, Colet, Erasmus, Vives, Melanchthon, 'and Budaeus. But while the movement was thus of a general kind, positive advance came mainly from two seminal minds, whose pioneering work brought to light new methods and ideas of enduring value. Laurentius Valla, in the first place, brought to bear on literary problems a spirit of rationalism, and was thus

[1] Woodward, *op. cit.* pp. 168, 170 ; cf. also Politian, *Ambra*.
[2] *Institutio oratoria*, x. i. 46.   [3] Woodward, *op. cit.* p. 168.
[4] *Ambra*.   [5] cf. Quin. *Inst. orat.*, x. i. 86.
[6] Woodward, *op. cit.* p. 151.   [7] *Manto*.

the founder of critical scholarship and historical criticism. He led the revolt, for instance, against medieval grammarians, placed the practice of composition on a foundation of analysis and inductive reasoning, inaugurated a new phase of Biblical criticism, and in general submitted to cold reason existing authoritative pronouncements in literary and other spheres. Likewise Politian, the greatest scholar of his age, also opened up fresh fields of critical enterprise. He first revealed something of the pageant of classical literature, and commended a wider outlook in enthusiastic and attractive fashion. At the same time he voiced in reasoned form the liberal conception of 'imitation' held by the early Humanists, which had allowed for the development of initiative and personality in style; and in so doing he administered a check to the growing Ciceronianism, which, had it been heeded, would have guided later theorizing on to sounder and more fruitful lines.

Of the actual critical achievement at this stage not the least important features were the new regard for literature engendered by this, the first, impact of classical antiquity on the modern world, and the attempts that were consequently made at systematic theorizing on literature and the literary art. A new critical spirit had in fact emerged, based on rationalism, which submitted to the test of reason or Nature various problems of literature, and which resulted in some amount of original and independent thinking. As yet, it is true, much of the theorizing was borrowed, mostly from Cicero and Quintilian; though post-classical doctrines still survived in the utilitarian and moralistic standards applied to poetry, or again, in the practice of allegorical interpretation which still persisted, though not without challenge. Moreover, the medieval apologetic attitude towards the vernacular was still preserved. It was now even intensified by reason of the enthusiasm for a correct Latinity and a profound belief in the immortality of Latin itself; and, in addition, the earlier objections to poetry still called for adequate answer. On the other hand, contact, though still limited, had been established with classical theory and practice; and not without positive results. A liberal conception had, for instance, been formed of the best method of turning to account the ancient models; and the process of 'imitation' commended aimed at no dead reproduction of the past, but rather at recapturing the ancient spirit by a free adaptation of classical principles in accordance with the national and individual geniuses. Many valuable principles of style at the same time had been brought to light from classical sources; there were also signs of an appreciation of aesthetic values in connexion with both poetry and prose ; and a beginning had been made with the establishment of classical standards and with the sorting and re-ordering of ancient writings in their historical setting. The criticism of this period, in short, is the prelude to the critical activities which followed in Italy, France, and England alike. New and important ideas were later on to be introduced by the discovery of the works of Aristotle and other classical theorists ; but the foundations had been successfully laid in the critical work of these early Italian Humanists.

CHAPTER III

HUMANISM IN ENGLAND: COLET, ERASMUS, AND VIVES

IT was in the opening decades of the 16th Century that a new direction was being given to critical activities in England, when a break, more or less definite, was made with the medieval conceptions of literature and the literary art. Inspired by Italian scholars of the Quattrocento, efforts were now made by Humanists in England to apply the New Learning to educational purposes, with the result that a new approach to literature was inaugurated, involving a heightened conception of the value of literature, the acquisition of some amount of ancient classical theory and the application of sounder methods of literary appreciation. It was, in fact, a phase in the development of literary theorizing in England full of significance and promise; a phase which in spite of obvious limitations marked the entry into a new sphere of thought, and was successful in diverting criticism from the shallows of post-classical and medieval doctrine into the main stream of literary discussion as represented in the works of classical antiquity.

Earlier impulses in this direction had not been wanting in the writings of Englishmen during the earlier period. From John of Salisbury (1110–80), for instance, had come an illuminating appreciation of literature as so many living records of human activities, universal in their bearing—an assertion of the intimate connexion between life and letters. Moreover, in an age of logical studies and of long-harboured prejudices against imaginative art, he had ventured to claim for literature an essential place in a liberal education, had revealed with the help of Quintilian some of the principles which govern good writing, had also introduced to his contemporaries not a few of the literary achievements of classical antiquity, and had thus anticipated by a century or more the Humanist movement in Italy. Then, too, Roger Bacon (c. 1214–92) somewhat later had directed attention anew to the writings of antiquity as the sources of wisdom, at the same time uttering a caveat against the slavish following of the ancients. He had also insisted on the need for a correct reading of what the ancients had written, thus anticipating the textual criticism of the following century; while his inductive method, it might also be noted, was the method later on applied by Valla in the restoration of grammar. In addition, from Richard of

35

Bury (1281–1345) had come an eloquent and enthusiastic tribute to literature in general. But while all three gave evidence of keen Humanistic sympathies, their influence was apparently but slight on later generations. They heralded, but did not inspire, the Italian movement ; and their teaching contributed little or nothing to 16th-Century developments in England.

Nor again can it be said that Humanistic activities in 15th-Century England did much to further an understanding, still less an appreciation, of literature. A newly-enkindled zeal for classical studies there undoubtedly was, fostered by contacts with Italian scholars and Papal officials, as well as by pilgrimages made by Englishmen to Italian centres of learning. Before the middle of the century, moreover, Chrysoloras, Poggio and Aeneas Sylvius had all visited England ; and after that date notable English scholars, including Tiptoft, Earl of Worcester, William Grey, John Free, Robert Flemmyng, and John Gunthorpe had resorted to Guarino's school at Ferrara. In the meantime enthusiasm for book-collecting had also been aroused under the patronage of Humphrey, Duke of Gloucester (1391–1437), Tiptoft, and others ; and not least valuable of the results of the movement were the additions of Latin manuscripts and recently printed books, such as Valla's *Elegantiae*, made to existing libraries at Oxford and elsewhere. Apart from this, classical studies were in the main pursued for utilitarian ends by men who cultivated a correct Latinity for ecclesiastical and diplomatic purposes.[1] The wider intellectual effects of Italian scholarship were thus to some extent missed, the prevailing interests being centred, not on imaginative literature, but on works of theology, philosophy, medicine, and the like. The new studies, in short, were but preparatory work, elementary in kind, and based as yet on Scholastic and medieval learning. And that medieval standards had by no means been discarded was shown by the extravagant and bombastic Latinity displayed by John Whetham-stede (d. 1465).[2] A cultural reaction, it is true, became visible before the end of the century ; and in the work of Sellyng, followed by Colet, Linacre, Grocyn, and others, the change is seen. By them, under the influence of Valla, Guarino, Pico, and Politian, something of the spirit of Italian Humanism was imparted to English scholarship, with results of considerable value for English criticism.

For the change of outlook which marked the opening decades

[1] See R. Weiss, *Humanism in England during the 15th Century*, p. 179.
[2] *ibid*. pp. 28 ff. : also W. F. Schirmer, *Der Englische Frühhumanismus*, pp. 88 ff.

of the 16th Century where literature was concerned we must turn to the work of the three great Humanists, John Colet (c. 1467–1519), Erasmus (1466–1536), and Juan Luis Vives (1492–1540), all of whom, though of different nationalities, were intimately bound up with contemporary English life, and whose influences were definite factors in the intellectual life of the times. In their works, as well as in the works of other contemporaries, a new critical spirit is seen emerging, which was applied, not to literary questions alone, but also to all departments of life and thought, whether intellectual, religious, social or political ; and to this movement many other factors had also contributed. Thus ecclesiastical abuses, earlier superstitions, Scholastic dogmatism, the sterile methods of medieval grammarians and the tyranny of dialectics, all these invited challenge from minds enlightened by the New Learning. Moreover, it was as if the torpor of centuries had suddenly been interrupted by the opening of ancient treasuries, by the invention of printing, or again, by such an event as the discovery of America ; while, not least, a new critical instrument was being forged by the rational spirit which had developed in Italy during the century preceding. This spirit of rationalism, as has already been stated, had not been generated in Italy alone. It was widely spread and deeply rooted in cultured minds elsewhere ; though conditions in 15th-Century Italy had encouraged its free development, and from thence it influenced the Humanistic movement. According to this doctrine the whole world was conceived of as existing under a reign of law, a law, not arbitrary, but an expression of the divine reason ; and, moreover, in man, gifted with reason, there was held to exist an innate sense of right and wrong which was his main instrument for the discovery of truth. It was a doctrine which filled the gap left by the extinction of the supreme medieval authorities of Emperor and Pope : and in the 16th Century it gave direction not only to Humanistic studies, but also to contemporary discussions on all aspects of life and thought.

With this article of faith as a new incentive, traces of a widespread critical spirit are not far to seek in contemporary writings. It may be said to pervade, for instance, almost all the works of Erasmus, and is not wanting even in his religious writings, such as the *Enchiridion Militis Christiani* (1503), where he brings to bear the light of reason on Christian ethics and conduct. Yet more lively and pungent criticism characterizes his *Praise of Folly* (1509) as well as the *Colloquies* (1516), whether he is treating of the foibles of men, of current abuses, or merely topics of

4

daily life. And in the *Praise of Folly*,[1] more particularly, his judgment on Scholasticism is pronounced in the satirical comment beginning: 'and next come our philosophers, much reverenced in their furred gowns and starched beards, looking upon themselves as the only wise and others as shadows '—a passage reminiscent of Boccaccio [2] and suggestive of Sidney's later irony in his *Apology for Poetry*. Critical comment of a more formal kind animates Vives's early work, *In pseudo-dialecticos* (1519), an attack on logicians, or again, his educational treatise, *De corruptis artibus* (1531), in which he discusses the causes of the intellectual decline, and attributes it to the superficiality of Schoolmen, to corrupt texts and the stupefying effects of authority. Elsewhere social and political conditions call forth More's constructive criticism in his *Utopia* (1516) ; while a critical examination of the Vulgate bears fruit in the *Novum Instrumentum* (1516) of Erasmus. Moreover, a further exercise of criticism, both textual and historical, is seen in the doubts cast on the authenticity of writings formerly accepted as genuine. Thus Vives, for instance, declared Dares and Dictys to be ' inventions ' ; [3] both Erasmus [4] and Vives [5] questioned the Ciceronian authorship of the *Rhetorica ad Herennium* ; while Grocyn refused to recognize the *Celestial Hierarchies* as the work of Dionysius the Areopagite.

But it is with the criticism of literature as such that we are here more especially concerned ; and the main contributions of that nature will be found in works of various kinds, in lectures, treatises, satires, and letters, all of which bear in some measure on literary matters. From Colet, to begin with, the central figure in English intellectual life (*c.* 1500) came some significant *Lectures on St. Paul's Epistles*, delivered at Oxford (1497–8), which, together with an interpretation of the first chapter of *Genesis*, contained in a letter to his friend Radulphus, marked a new era in literary interpretation and had considerable influence on Erasmus and other contemporaries. The contribution of Erasmus was more considerable, and apart from his *Praise of Folly*, will be found in his educational works, in *De ratione studii* [6] (1511) dealing with methods of instruction, in *De copia verborum* (1511), a manual treating of ' amplification ' and based on

---

[1] ed. P. S. Allen, p. 112.
[2] cf. *De genealogia deorum*, xiv. v : philosophers represented with downcast eyes, slow paces, unpretentious dress, &c., see p. 126 *infra*.
[3] *De tradendis disciplinis*, v. ii.
[4] *Praise of Folly*, p. 110.   [5] *De trad. disc.* iv. iii.
[6] For an English version see Woodward, *Erasmus concerning Education*, pp. 162 ff., to which references are made in the footnotes *infra*.

Quintilian's *Institutio* (Bk. VIII), and in *De conscribendis epistolis* (1521), a treatise on letter-writing. At an earlier date (1484) he had published an epitome of Valla's *Elegantiae*, and somewhat later, Valla's *Annotations on the New Testament* (1505). Then, in 1516, he produced his *Novum Instrumentum*, consisting of the New Testament in Greek with a Latin translation and a Preface in which he expounded his views on Biblical interpretation ; and this was followed by the dialogue *Ciceronianus* (1528), in which he discussed what was perhaps the most vital question of his day. Hardly less important, however, was the contribution of Vives, who spent some portion of each year between 1522 and 1528 in England under the patronage of Queen Catherine, and who, numbering among his friends Erasmus, Sir Thomas More, and Wolsey, was not without his influence on English thought. In 1523 he had completed *De Institutione feminae Christianae*, and in that same year he wrote for Princess Mary an educational treatise, *De ratione studii*. Later on he published *De ratione dicendi* and his greatest work, *De disciplinis* (1531), consisting of three treatises (*De corruptis artibus*, *De tradendis disciplinis* and *De artibus*) [1] in which he discusses in systematic and historical fashion the main principles underlying a literary education. It is a work comprehensive, cultured, and sensible, full of suggestion on literary as well as pedagogic matters ; and though Vives's works were apparently neglected during the Elizabethan period, owing possibly to political reasons, his merits were later recognized by more than one 17th-Century writer, and notably by Ben Jonson, who drew freely on his teaching in compiling the *Discoveries*.

Such, then, were the main contributions to literary criticism at this date ; and it now remains to inquire into the actual nature of the critical achievement and the extent to which fresh light was thrown on literature and the literary art. Already in Italy, as we have seen, a fresh beginning had been made ; the value of literature generally, and of the literatures of antiquity in particular, had been firmly established, and a fuller understanding of their meaning, an appreciation of their methods, and some discrimination of their artistic values had also been effected. At the same time the preoccupation of Italian Humanists with the classical literatures of antiquity had not passed altogether unchallenged. By the end of the 15th Century

---

[1] See *Vivis Opera omnia*, ed. G. Majansius (1782) : an English version of *De tradendis disciplinis* by Foster Watson is included in his work, *Vives on Education*, pp. 1–304, to which references are made in the footnotes *infra*.

the claims of the vernacular in Italy, and of Italian literature as well, were already asserting themselves ; while a growing scepticism and semi-paganism confirmed the fears of those who held that with a revival of ancient literature paganism would flourish once again. And the influence of these reactions on critical thought in England is seen in the growing concern with the vernacular and with Biblical studies, which represented new factors in the critical movement. It is therefore as a continuation, with certain modifications, of the efforts of Italian Humanists that the critical work in England at this date is best approached ; and its main results will be found, first, in the theorizing on literature that followed, and secondly, in the attempts made at forming literary judgments and appreciations.

When we turn to examine the literary theorizing submitted at this time we shall find that the general lines of treatment are those characteristic of the earlier Humanists. Thus Quintilian's classification of literature—oratory, poetry, history, and philosophy—is still retained, the greatest significance being attached to oratory and poetry ; while, of the latter two ' kinds ', the study of oratory still commands the main attention, though consideration is also given to theorizing on poetry. In the generation that was to follow, the ' courtier ' was to supersede the ' orator ' as the educational ideal ; and poetry was then to be more seriously studied as well as more widely cultivated. As yet, however, Quintilian's influence was still predominant in educational circles ; and oratory, not poetry, remained the chief subject of study. The results were, first, a return to something like the classical conception of rhetoric, in place of the confused and imperfect idea of medieval times ; and, secondly, some treatment of urgent contemporary problems relating to prose expression in general, that is, to matters of style, to the proper methods of ' imitation ', the use of the vernacular and the like.

In connexion with oratory, in the first place, not the least significant of the changes brought about during this period was the reintroduction of the classical conception of rhetoric in place of the confused and vague notion characteristic of the Middle Ages. Throughout the medieval period rhetoric had undergone strange vicissitudes. From being a practical training for life it had become a mechanical technique, based largely on post-classical *Rhetorics*, on the *compendia* of Cassiodorus, Capella, and Isidore, or on elementary school-books such as *De inventione* and *Ad Herennium*. Confined at one time to the treatment of ' civil questions ', it had subsequently been bound up with grammar and logic, had been misapplied to poetic and *dictamen*,

and its technical terms besides had frequently been misinterp
Most serious of all, however, was the influence of the 2nd-Ce
Sophistic which had limited the subject to the study of an
elaborate and ingenious style. This search for a false glamour
obtained by stereotyped ornament had constituted the main
idea of medieval rhetoric ; and in consequence it had ceased to
be either an independent or a useful study.

Now, however, a return was made to the classical tradition
of Aristotle, Cicero, and Quintilian ; and by Vives, to begin
with, some indication was given of the true nature and purpose
of the ancient art of rhetoric. In the first place he reminds his
readers of the essential qualities of ' the arts ' in general.[1] So
far from being arbitrary or mechanical techniques he explains
them as having been arrived at by inductive reasoning, and as
the means of attaining ' sure and pre-determined ' ends, being
based on experience from which reason gathered universal laws,
so that ' what is in the arts was in Nature first '.[2] And in support
of this basic doctrine he quotes Plato's advice to ' let experience
bring forth art and let art rule experience ' ; also Manilius's
dictum that ' experience through various applications has made
art '.[3] Then in connexion with the art of rhetoric in particular
he points out that the power of speech had been the glory of man
as distinguished from the beasts ; and ' eloquence ' he describes
as a mighty instrument of society, a τυραννικόν τι, according
to Euripides, by which men in all ages had acquired power and
authority.[4] It was therefore with the study of eloquence that
the art of rhetoric was concerned ; and rhetoric he describes as
' the most powerful of the arts ', and thus part of practical
wisdom. Its aim, he adds, is not to inculcate a vain use of
words or mere elegance of expression, but rather to instruct men
how to speak (and write) effectively, and (in terms reminiscent
of Cicero) to enable them to ' teach, convince and arouse '. For
this purpose, he states, the study of words in the first place is
essential ; but other matters had also to be considered. It was
necessary, for example, to have regard to the personality of the
speaker, to the nature of the audience and the business in hand ;
and then to consider means suitable to produce a particular effect
in relation to a particular time and place. After this brief
summary he notes that ' confused directions had been drawn up
by our ancestors ' ; and he gives a list of authorities for his
readers. The list is a lengthy one and points to a widening

[1] Watson, op. cit. pp. 20–7.
[2] ibid. p. 20 : cf. Shakespeare's Winter's Tale, IV. iii. 90 ff.
[3] Astronomica, i. 61.   [4] Watson, op. cit. pp. 180 ff.

outlook. It includes, for instance, Aristotle, Cicero, Dionysius Halicarnassus, Demetrius, and Quintilian ; but it comprises also the *Ad Herennium*, as well as the post-classical authorities Aelius Aristides, Hermogenes, Capella, and others.

With rhetoric thus restored to something like its ancient status it is not strange to find that ' eloquence ' at this date commanded considerable attention ; and by Erasmus in his *De copia* and by Vives in his *De ratione dicendi*, as well as elsewhere, valuable comments were made on the cultivation of style. To begin with, Erasmus, following Bruni [1] and other Humanists, insists on the value of both thought and expression as components of literature. ' If the former ', he states, ' is first in importance, the latter is acquired first in order of time . . . for ideas are only intelligible by means of the words which describe them.' [2] Significant of the balance and good sense of these scholars, however, were the warnings that were already being uttered against an undue absorption in matters of expression, that ' first distemper of learning ', later diagnosed by Bacon,[3] ' when men study words and not matter '. Erasmus, for one, had realized that the reaction against medieval Latinity had tended to encourage among Humanists a display of style for its own sake ; and more than once he insists that breadth of culture comes before style.[4] He also condemns an ostentatious display of stylistic effects, stating that ' it is good to speak Attic Greek, but it should not be ostentatiously Attic ' ;[5] and Vives in turn calls to mind the advice of Cicero that the precepts of rhetoric should not be too rigorously followed.[6] Apart from this, some further ideas were set forth in this connexion. Vives, for instance, conceives of style as an expression of personality (*imago est animi parentis sui*),[7] reflecting more faithfully than any mirror the nature of the speaker (or writer) ; and he quotes in support the ancient proverb, *talem esse quemque qualis sit eius oratio.* Serious attempts were thus made to expound some of the main qualities of eloquence ; and it was a development which marked a new phase of critical activities in England.

Among the more detailed principles of style expounded was, first, the need for a proper choice of words ; and Vives here quotes Caesar's dictum (also quoted by Cicero) that *verborum delectus origo est eloquentia.*[8] Moreover, the diction selected should be in keeping with both subject and speaker ; and this

---

[1] See p. 18 *supra*.   [2] Woodward, *op. cit.* p. 162.
[3] *Adv. of Learning*, I. iv. 3.   [4] Erasmus, *Opera*, i. 923 C.E.
[5] *ibid.* iii. 10 D.   [6] Watson, *op. cit.* p. 183.   [7] Vives, *Opera*, i. 103.
[8] *ibid.* i. 85 : cf. Cicero, *Brutus*, lxxvii. 253.

principle of *decorum* runs through the whole discussion of style. Erasmus, for instance, states that ' no form of expression can be pronounced elegant which is not both congruous to the artist and rightly fitted to the subject ' ; [1] while Vives adds that ' nothing is more objectionable than what is unfitting ',[2] or again, ' words behind which there is no meaning are mere bombast '.[3] Erasmus, again, discountenances the interpolation of foreign words with their ' mosaic-like ' effect, as well as obsolete terms ' drawn from some worm-eaten manuscript ' ; [4] and his pronouncement was doubtless not without its effect on later theorists. With correctness and propriety of language thus laid down as prerequisites, it was further recognized that more than this was necessary for effective prose. Erasmus, for instance, notes the need for ' naturalness and sincerity of utterance ',[5] for individuality in expression and the due subordination of style to thought ; [6] while Vives calls attention to that ' other harmony of prose ', declaring that ' prose too has its rhythms, though they are not fixed by definite and constant law as in poetry '.[7] Moreover, a systematic effort at inculcating grace and variety of expression was made by Erasmus in his *De copia*, in which he dealt with ' amplification ', a device for enhancing style, as expounded by Quintilian, but which, applied to poetic in medieval times, had degenerated into a complicated means of rendering expression merely more luxuriant and profuse.[8] Erasmus now describes it as a method of treating more effectively a given topic by means of fables, proverbs, similes, *exempla* and the like. But he also demands a wise discretion in the use of these devices, limiting them to appropriate figures alone and with digressions kept sternly in hand. Such ' amplification ' he commends as a rational device for giving elevation to a theme. It was no *indigesta turba* of illustrations and tedious repetitions as in medieval times ; while brevity consisted ' not in saying as little as possible, but in saying the best that could be said in the shortest way '.

Then, too, Vives in his *De ratione dicendi* has something further to say on matters of style. He emphasizes as fundamental, to begin with, the need for perspicuity, which he describes as the fruit of orderly arrangement (*ordinem sequitur distinctio*) ; [9] he likewise calls attention to those departures from direct expression which add elevation, variety and colour to style, notably

---

[1] Erasmus, *Op*. i. 1026 A.   [2] Watson, *op. cit.* p. 187.
[3] *ibid*. p. 185.   [4] *Praise of Folly*, p. 12.
[5] Erasmus, *Op*. iii. 10 D.   [6] *ibid*. i. 1026 B.
[7] Watson, *op. cit.* p. 40.
[8] See Atkins, *Eng. Lit. Crit. Med.* pp. 101 ff.   [9] Vives, *Opera*, i. 97.

such figures as metaphor (*translatio*), simile, hyperbole and the rest. Like Erasmus he demands that such devices should be used with discretion, that there should be no far-fetched, mixed or unsuitable metaphors, and that similes should not be too long-drawn-out ;[1] while figurative expressions that result in obscurity he describes as mere puerile affectation. Apart from this, Vives, following the ancients, also attempts to distinguish between varieties of style. Thus he remarks on the virtues of brevity in expression, the style which expresses great thoughts in words from which nothing can be taken away without loss and which leaves something to the imagination.[2] He also points out the merits of the periodic style, ' with sentences well fitted together as stones in a wall arranged without mortar ' ; though the period, he adds, must not consist of too many clauses, or clauses too lengthy, else the result will be as ineffective as ' a long and unwieldy spear '.[3] Then, too, he recalls the conventional classification of styles, high, middle and low [4]—the high style with its sonorous diction and swelling periods, the low style flat and colourless, the middle style with its plain words and quiet pleasing movement. And of special interest are his picturesque descriptions reminiscent of Cicero and Tacitus, when he makes use of analogies drawn from human physiology, in describing the rotund, periphrastic style as ' fleshy ', or again, the meagre, bloodless style as ' bony and sinewy '.

The concern with oratory and prose style at this date, however, resulted in something more than the recovery of the ancient conception of rhetoric, or the exposition of some of the classical principles of style. Certain fundamental questions of importance were also being raised ; first, the general attitude to be adopted towards the master-minds of antiquity, and secondly, the proper use to be made of their works, of Cicero's works in particular, in attempts at improving style ; and in the light of later developments, these discussions are of great significance in critical history. With regard to the general question, to begin with, it was commonly held to be necessary to take over what was best in the work of the ancients and to utilize such material as the basis for an advance in literary activities. But while the attitude adopted was thus one of profound respect and admiration, there were already signs that no slavish following was to be advocated. In *De corruptis artibus*, for instance, Vives protested against the

---

[1] Vives, *Opera*, i. pp. 85 ff., 97 ff., 101.
[2] *ibid*. i. p. 96 : concisa [oratio] quae minus exprimit quam intelligentia requirat, sed unus ita loquendi adjuvat sensum et supplet quod deest.
[3] *ibid*. i. 97.   [4] *ibid*. i. pp. 103 ff.

tendency to form an irrational estimate of the ancient classics. They were men, he urged, ' liable to be deceived and to err, . . . neither heroes nor demi-gods ' ; [1] and he condemned as a false and foolish similitude the earlier saying of Bernard of Chartres that, compared with the ancients, the moderns ' were as dwarfs on the shoulders of giants '. The ancients, he added, had excelled in many things, but so might the moderns also, by a judicious use of what had already been discovered ; and, for the rest, the ancients had ' judged it to be of the very essence of the human race that it should progress in the arts '.

Yet more forcibly are these ideas presented by Vives in his illuminating Preface to *De disciplinis*,[2] upon which Ben Jonson was to draw at considerable length. There Vives acknowledges the debt due to the ancients, and states that for Aristotle in particular he has ' admiration and respect unique above all others ', on account of ' his judgment in human arts '. At the same time he suggests that it is far more profitable ' to form a critical judgment of the writings of the great authors than merely to acquiesce in their authority and to receive everything on trust '. Aristotle himself, he points out, had dealt faithfully with the works of his predecessors ; while Seneca had declared that ' those who have been active intellectually before us are not our masters but our leaders '. Hence it could not well be forbidden for later generations to investigate for themselves, and to form their own opinions. Then, striking a more positive note, he boldly asserts that ' truth stands open to all. It is not as yet wholly possessed, since much has been left for later ages to discover '. And upon this fact he enlarges in memorable phrase.

Nature [he states] is not yet so effete and exhausted as to be unable to bring forth in our times results comparable to those of earlier ages. She always remains equal to herself, and not rarely she comes forward more strongly and more powerful than in the past. . . . So we must regard her in this present age as reinforced by the confirmed strength which has developed by degrees through so many centuries.

And, finally, he concludes,

it is therefore clear that if only we apply our minds sufficiently we can judge better over the whole round of life and nature than could Aristotle, Plato, or any of the ancients ; always remembering [he significantly adds] that no knowledge is at the same time discovered and perfected.

It was not in this general statement alone, however, that

[1] Vives, *Opera*, vi. 39.   [2] Watson, *op. cit.* pp. 7–10.

wise counsel was being given regarding the use to be made of the works of the ancients. From both Erasmus and Vives came further advice in their pronouncements on Ciceronianism ; from Erasmus in his dialogue *Ciceronianus* (or *De optime dicendi genere*), in which the ' apes of Cicero ' are satirized in lively fashion, from Vives in his *De tradendis disciplinis*, where the Ciceronian problem is also discussed, and some account given of sound methods of ' imitation '. Of the rise of the pedantic cult of Ciceronianism in 15th-Century Italy something has already been said,[1] as well as of Politian's successful reply to the growing evil ; and now the matter became an outstanding question in scholarly circles. Early in the 16th Century the controversy had been continued in Italy by the Ciceronian, Pietro Bembo, in opposition to the younger Pico della Mirandola, nephew of the more famous Pico, friend of Politian. Then, in 1520, Erasmus, already interested in this much-vexed question, wrote to the Italian purist, Longolius, denouncing the new craze, and afterwards followed this up by writing his *Ciceronianus* (1528). Whereupon the dispute assumed the proportions of a major battle, in which the Ciceronian cause was championed by the scholarly forces of Italy and France, headed suitably enough by the redoubtable Julius Caesar Scaliger (1484–1558), whose scurrilous attack on Erasmus [2] was, however, received with contemptuous silence.

Such then were the conditions which led to the pronouncements of Erasmus and Vives on this particular question, in which both writers adopted the position of Politian in declaring decisively against the Ciceronian doctrine and in condemning the slavish following of a single model. In one of his *Letters* [3] Erasmus, for instance, derides the practice of the new sect in employing only terms and phrases which Cicero had used and in not venturing to speak otherwise than Cicero had spoken. His comment on the practice is brief and to the point. ' If Cicero ', he explains, ' came to life again he himself would laugh at these Ciceronians.' Elsewhere he enlarges on the matter, explaining that ' times are changed, our instincts, needs and ideas are not those of Cicero ' ; [4] thereby suggesting that the ancient material should be treated in accordance with modern needs. Furthermore, he finds in Cicero's style certain defects ; and recalling Quintilian's censure of a blind worship of Cicero, he demands with Politian some expression of individuality in style.

[1] See pp. 22–3 *supra*.
[2] *Pro M. Tullio Cicerone, contra D. Erasmum Roterodamum*, Oratio I (1531).
[3] III. Ep. 28.   [4] Woodward, *op. cit.* p. 53.

His recommendation is therefore that a judicious, but not an exclusive, use should be made of Cicero as a model, and that the spirit, rather than the letter, of his writing should accordingly be studied.

Even yet more definite are the views of Vives who begins by conceding the necessity for some form of 'imitation', since 'Nature fashioned men . . . strangely hostile to art',[1] so that some guidance in artistic matters was therefore needed. The proposal to imitate Cicero alone, however, he promptly rejects, quoting Seneca and Quintilian in support of his position, and recalling Cicero's lapses into 'the luxuriant and Asiatic kind of speaking'.[2] Moreover, while recognizing the excellence of Cicero's art, he points out that Cicero is not the only great stylist, that even he did not embody every quality; and then he significantly reminds his readers of the possibilities of change and development, holding with Tacitus that 'the countenance of eloquence is not always one and the same ; nor is that which is different necessarily worse'.[3] He therefore advises that use should be made of all the great authors of antiquity, and that those should be chosen for 'imitation' which best suited the nature of the intending writer and the immediate purpose in hand ; thus adopting the method of the painter Zeuxis, commended by Cicero, whose portrait of Helen was inspired by the combined excellences of many women of Crotona.[4] Of yet greater value is his conception of the proper method of 'imitation', which he regards as something more than the mere copying of words, inflexions, figures or rhythmic tags ridiculed by Erasmus in *Ciceronianus*. True 'imitation', he maintains, involves a consideration of 'the art and method by which such and such effects were achieved by a given author, in order that similar artifices may accomplish for the imitator his own intention in his own work'.[5] In other words, it is a process in which artistic methods are studied with the view of adapting them for use in work of an original kind ; and here is represented the essence of the classical conception formulated by Horace, Quintilian and others.[6] It was counsel of a sane and judicious kind ; counsel, in short, which had it been followed would have guided later theorizing on to sound and fruitful lines.

While, however, attention at this stage was thus primarily directed to matters of oratory and prose style, the views expressed concerning poetry are by no means without their interest, for

---

[1] Watson, *op. cit.* p. 189.   [2] *ibid.* p. 190.
[3] *ibid.* p. 191 : cf. Tacitus, *Dialoguos de Orat.* c. 18.   [4] *ibid.* p. 194.
[5] *ibid.* p. 195.   [6] See Atkins, *Lit. Crit. in Antiquity*, ii. 79, 279.

they mark some advance on the medieval position, while they also throw light on the conditions which were to call forth the Elizabethan *Apologies*. The views of Erasmus on poetry, in the first place, are incidentally conveyed in his *Praise of Folly* (1509) and in the *Colloquies* (1516). Those works were among the most widely read of 16th-Century writings ; and they undoubtedly did much to perpetuate the Humanistic attitude towards poetry, with its imperfect sympathies, its lack of understanding and imaginative sensibility. It is not without its significance, for instance, that in his *Praise of Folly* Erasmus lets his satire play lightly around some of the conventions of ancient poetry as well as on the poets themselves. Thus in one place he ridicules the idea of Bacchus as the god of poets, because, forsooth, ' wine stirs up wit and makes men eloquent, whereas water-drinkers make poor verse ' ;[1] and elsewhere he derides the whole host of the poets' Olympian gods, ' with which heaven is so thronged that they are not able to crowd one by another '. Apart from this he finds sport in censuring all professors of the art, amongst whom, it is worth noting, he includes players and fiddlers along with poets. He also comments on the arrogance of poets, asserting that ' the more ignorant they are, the more they plume themselves ' ; [2] and in general he regards them as ' vain triflers who aim at tickling the ears with trifles and ridiculous fables, . . . and yet are sure of immortality '.[3]

Nor are his occasional references to poetry in the more serious treatment of men and things in his *Colloquies* much more illuminating. For one thing, he appears to be interested not in the great masterpieces but in the less important developments of poetry, in such forms as the epithalamium, the echo dialogue, the *conflictus* and the Menippean satire ; and of them all he provides illustrations of sorts, the Menippean satire being represented by his *Apotheosis of Capnio* (i.e. Reuchlin), in imitation of the younger Seneca's *Apocolocyntosis*. Then, too, such theory as he presents is suggestive of a limited outlook, and is mainly made up of doctrine characteristically medieval. This fact emerges from the *Conflictus* already mentioned, a dialogue between ' Barbarism ', the representative of an early medieval poetic tradition,[4] and the Muse Thalia, who stands for the later medieval tradition characteristic of Lydgate, Hawes and others ; [5] and here it would seem likely, Thalia is voicing the views of Erasmus himself. Thus Thalia derides that medieval doctrine

[1] i. 133.   [2] i. 88.   [3] i. 106.
[4] See Atkins, *Eng. Lit. Crit. Med.*, ch. v.   [5] *ibid.* pp. 171 ff.

according to which poetry was little more than versified rhetoric, the fruit of a careful study of glosses, vocabularies, arguments and prosody. ' Your poems ', she informs ' Barbarism ', ' are such that if a man understands them he will never be the wiser ; if he does not he will never know the less.' [1] And when ' Barbarism ' confidently refers to John of Garland as his authority, whom he claims to have ' excelled in such elegancy of words and such a majesty of style that few can understand him ', her brief reply is that ' he did not understand himself '. At the same time she also discloses her own poetic theory, which is none other than the late medieval conception of poetic art as allegorical in form and highly decorative in style. Charged with making poetry a matter of ' gilded lies and old wives' tales ', she claims in return the virtue of ' hiding truth in ambiguous words and enigmatical expressions, which, though all may read, yet they may not understand '.[2] Poetry to her, in short, is an esoteric art, based on allegory and rendered ' illustrious ' by elegant diction ; while the labour thus involved is said to make moral truths more pleasing. That such ideas were possibly those of Erasmus himself is suggested by occasional remarks elsewhere in his works, as when, for instance, he stated that ' Homeric and Virgilian poetry was all allegorical (*eam totam esse allegoricam*) ; [3] or again, that ' his greatest praise was for a rhetorical poem ', and that ' the rhetorical art should pervade a poem '.[4] On the other hand it would seem that he had but little enthusiasm or feeling for poetry ; like Bacon he probably felt that ' it was not good to stay too long in the theatre '.

More truly representative of the classical position where poetry was concerned were the views submitted by Vives, which embody Neo-Platonic and Plutarchian ideas set forth by earlier Italians and which carry the discussion into fields remote from medieval technique and allegory. Thus in his exposition of the nature of poetry his main points are that poetry is ' a thing inspired ', is of harmony all compact ; and to these two considerations he attributes its emotional effects, its usefulness and its appeal to human nature. Of the element of inspiration, in the first place, he speaks at some length and in Platonic fashion. ' The poet ', he states,[5] ' is a man who possesses great passion, . . . which raises him above the usual and ordinary state of his nature, and who in this elation conceives lofty, almost heavenly, inspirations. Then the sharpness of his mind contemplates and concentrates itself on great ideas ; it also arranges

[1] *Coll.* i. 273. [2] *ibid.* i. 272. [3] *Enchiridion Militis Christiani*, ch. iv.
[4] Erasmus, *Opera*, iii. 104 D. [5] Watson, *op. cit.*, p. 138.

them and thus causes within his body a harmony derived from the exaltation of his mind.' In this way does Vives analyse the process of poetic creation ; and at the same time he explains, in terms reminiscent of Bruni and others, the essential element of verse. ' Poets ', he asserts,[1] ' write in verse, the characteristic quality of their art being music ; and verse has charm because of this harmony which corresponds with the melody of the human soul.' Then, having stated that poetry has no fixed subjects, that its diction consists of words ' lofty, sublime and brilliant ', and that poetry displays human passions in a wonderful and vivid manner, he has something to say on its emotional effects. Those effects he describes as elevating and invigorating. The minds of readers, being caught by the lofty spirit that breathes in poetry, are said to rise above their own intellects, even above their own natures, thus deriving both strength and refreshment from poetry by reason of its harmonious nature.[2] And here again may be detected echoes of Plato, to whom poetry was first and foremost an influence, rather than a means of instruction. Such theorizing, based on psychological considerations, marked a distinct advance on medieval efforts ; though not without its significance is Vives's further comment, that ' poetry must be relegated to the leisure hours of life and is to be regarded, not as nourishment, but as a spice '.[3] Significant, too, is the fact that Vives's teaching, expounded as it was in 1531, takes no cognizance of the new Aristotelian ideas which had been made accessible by the Latin translation of the Poetics of 1498, ideas which were subsequently to give direction to much of the later theorizing. The truth was that as yet the importance of Aristotle's doctrines was not generally understood, even in Italy. Vives's own surprising opinion was that ' the Poetics contained little good fruit, being occupied entirely with the consideration of old poems and with those niceties in which the Greeks are so tiresome . . . and inept '.[4]

Before leaving the subject, however, Vives endeavours to meet the objections which in his day were being raised against poetry on the score of immorality. As he definitely stated, ' poetry is openly hated by certain people ; there has been a long and varied dispute on the matter '.[5] Throughout the Middle Ages apologies based on patristic authorities had been current, and to some extent they had been utilized by Italian Humanists. Vives, however, now discards the conventional arguments and takes up his own line of defence. Freely recog-

---

[1] Watson, op. cit. pp. 125 ff.   [2] ibid.   [3] ibid. p. 138.
[4] ibid. p. 158.   [5] ibid. p. 121.

nizing the presence of dangerous and unwholesome themes in ancient poetry, he attempts to establish its educational value by suggesting how best ' to gather healthy plants among poisonous weeds '. The task had previously been undertaken by Plutarch in his *De audiendis poetis* ; [1] and Vives now submits Plutarch's arguments to critical examination and then attempts a justification of his own. [2] He points out, to begin with, that Plutarch had suggested as antidotes for the poison the moral maxims of other poets. But such antidotes, argued Vives, were not always available ; and in any case it was wiser to avoid the poison altogether. Plutarch, again, had suggested that poetry was harmless since it was essentially fictitious, and thus represented, not real life, but merely a kind of painting. Vives's rejoinder to this was that if a picture was obscene it necessarily contaminated the mind, and all the more if it was skilfully painted. Nor does he accept Plutarch's further argument that the poets concerned did not actually approve of their own disgraceful subjects. His reply is that some of them did, and he mentions Ovid, Catullus, Martial, and others. Having thus disposed of Plutarch's line of argument he ventures to offer some practical suggestions of his own by means of which the current objections to poetry might possibly be met. His main recommendations are twofold ; either an expurgation of the ancient texts, or else an allegorical interpretation of all obnoxious passages. [3] By such means, he urges, ' poetry will be kept from ignominy and readers from an evil poison '. At the same time he holds that too much should not be looked for in poetry, despite the high esteem accorded to it down through the ages. He recognizes its value in general terms, its antiquity, its charm of expression, its element of instruction ; but then poets, he adds, though men inspired were subject to human frailties and were often deficient in learning and in experience of life. Vives's treatment here is obviously inadequate and unconvincing ; as a rational defence of poetry it ignores essentials. Yet it is not without its interest as illustrating the urgent need for a sounder and more philosophical justification ; and this, in the decades that followed, Aristotle's *Poetics* was to supply to Italian scholars.

Of less importance in the history of literary criticism, though not devoid of interest, were the comments made on history and philosophy, the two remaining branches of literature according to Quintilian's classification. Concerning history, in the first place, Erasmus presents little more than the conventional view

---

[1] See Atkins, *Lit. Crit. in Antiquity*, ii. 310 ff.
[2] Watson, *op. cit.* pp. 126 ff.   [3] *ibid.* p. 128.

of his contemporaries when he describes it as a form of literary activity which had to do with the collecting of accepted facts, marvellous stories and examples of vices and virtues, all of which were said to be useful for the embellishment of style or for providing concrete illustrations of the moral law.[1] Of history as a faithful mirror of the past, or as a record and analysis of human life he has not much to say ; though in one place he remarks that some knowledge of history was necessary as the key to references in other writings.[2] Views of a more rational kind are suggested by Vives, who conceives of history as a branch of literature providing a basis of practical wisdom by means of a review of the experiences of man in past ages, which, so he explains, have a significance for later generations since human nature in its essentials remains ever the same.[3] Apart from this he points out the value of a historical approach to the several arts ; also the need for exactness of truth, for distinguishing between history and myth, between fact and fancy ; and to this end he demands a more exact chronology, the great task to which the younger Scaliger (1546–1609) was subsequently to devote himself. Altogether with Vives a new sense of the nature of history and of its value both intellectual and moral may be said to emerge. ' There is nothing of the ancients ', he writes,[4] ' so worn out by age that it cannot be accommodated to our modes of life. We may employ a different form,' he adds, ' yet its usefulness remains.'

With regard to philosophy, in the conception set forth by Erasmus there are obvious signs of a reaction against medieval traditions, and in particular against the earlier ' preposterous feats of dialectical jugglery '. In his view philosophy treats of little more than the practical wisdom of the Roman world, to the exclusion of dialectic and metaphysics. Logic he regards as no longer a substantive study, but merely an aid to correctness and clarity of expression. ' Natural philosophy ', again, he describes as a futile speculation ; and in his *Praise of Folly* [5] he denounces in withering terms the earlier play with ' Ideas, Universalities, separate Forms, first matters, quiddities ' and the like, as well as the arrogance of those who treated of ' inexplicable things ', as if they were ' Nature's secretaries or had dropped among us from the Council of the gods '. Vives, on the other hand, is more conventional, less revolutionary in his ideas.[6] He commends the study of logic, for instance, as a means of testing

---

[1] Erasmus, *Opera*, i. 389 F.   [2] Woodward, *op. cit.* p. 168.
[3] Watson, *op. cit.* p. 232.   [4] *ibid.* p. 233.
[5] p. 112.   [6] Watson, *op. cit.* pp. 164 ff.

truth; also the pursuit of natural philosophy, provided there was no indulgence in speculation on the unattainable. At the same time, he adds, such inquiries into Nature should be made to serve the useful arts of life, or to raise the mind from the knowledge of the Creation to a knowledge of the Creator.[1] And in general he conceives of philosophy as a useful mental discipline instrumental in acquainting men with causes and first principles, and with generalizations of a universal character based on the particular.

Such then is the main contribution to literary theory made by Humanists in close touch with English thought; and it is not irrelevant to add here that so far all theorizing was based on the literature of the ancients and was largely inspired by the desire to write Latin, the one recognized medium of expression, in accordance with the traditions of classical Latinity. To the Humanists the vernaculars represented no fit instruments for literary expression; though Politian had pleaded for the recognition of Italian in view of the native literature that had previously appeared. In this he was supported, strangely enough, by Bembo, leader of the Ciceronians, who in his dialogue, *Lingua Volgare* (1512), had argued for a standard Italian, based either on the authority of Dante, Petrarch, and Boccaccio, or on Italian as spoken at the court of Rome; and his efforts constituted the first Renascence challenge to the dominant position of Latin. As yet, however, neither Erasmus nor Vives seems to have shared wholly in this more liberal outlook; and Humanistic ideas were summarized somewhat later in the *Apologia* (1537) of Floridus, an intimate friend of Erasmus and a keen anti-Ciceronian as well. In that work it was maintained that the vernaculars lacked fixity, dignity, and universality; that they were unfitted for literary purposes; and that as a product of barbarism they were themselves barbarous by nature. Latin was, in fact, the only medium possible for men of letters; the vernaculars were little more than local, crude, and obscure jargons.[2]

At the same time there were signs that the possibilities of the vernaculars were at least beginning to be realized in scholarly circles. Erasmus, for instance, commends the use of native English for sermons, as being better calculated to stir up emotions and impulses. Or again, there is his eloquent defence of Biblical translation in which he dissents from those who were ' unwilling that the Scriptures should be read by the unlearned translated

---

[1] cf. Bacon, *Adv. of Learning, passim.*
[2] Woodward, *op. cit.* pp. 60–71.

into their own tongue '.[1] ' I long ', he states, ' that the husband-
man should sing portions to himself as he follows the plough,
that the weaver should hum them to the tune of his shuttle, that
the traveller should beguile with their stories the tedium of his
journey.' Nor, again, does Vives fail to see the value of the
vernacular, more especially for educational purposes ; while so
far from regarding the native tongues to be of barbarian origin,
he recognizes in French and Italian honourable descendants of
Latin itself.[2] Apart from this he betrays some concern for the
vernaculars and their literatures, as when, for instance, he urges
the cultivation of their histories in order that earlier writings
should be properly understood, since ' every language ', he
explains,[3] ' in the course of time undergoes multitudinous
changes '.

It now remains to inquire into the Humanistic attempts at
literary judgment and appreciation ; and these critical activities,
like the attempts at theorizing, will be found to be highly suggestive and illuminating; developments which opened up a new
chapter in critical history. To begin with, the fact that systematic efforts were now made to pass judgment on works of literature
is of importance in itself. Throughout the Middle Ages such
judgments as had been pronounced were almost invariably of a
sporadic and occasional kind ; and now that the need for the
formation of literary judgment was for the first time being
recognized as a necessary cultural training, efforts were accordingly made to include literary criticism in the higher educational
system. Thus Erasmus in one place points out the value of
learning the true methods of literary appreciation. ' Once
acquired,' he states,[4] ' this power of insight into the minds of
great writers will lead to the formation of a critical habit of
mind.' Then, too, Vives insists on the importance of clear and
wise judgments of literature, since nothing, he urges, is more
harmful than a confusion of standards. Great writers, he
maintains, should be criticized, adversely if necessary, but always
with knowledge and discretion ; and, deprecating the arrogance
and pedantry of the scholars of his day, he adds, not without
some feeling, that ' if those same keen critics were to offer themselves and their works for judgment they would soon become
more gentle in their charges against others '.[5] The significance
of this change of attitude cannot therefore well be mistaken.
Later influences were undoubtedly to contribute to the revival

---

[1] Preface to *Novum Instrumentum* (1516).
[2] Watson, *op. cit.* p. 94.   [3] *ibid.* p. 103.
[4] Woodward, *op. cit.* p. 177.   [5] Watson, *op. cit.* p. 295.

of critical judgment in the 16th Century; but prior to these came the impetus given by earlier Humanistic studies. Nor are the causes which led to this recognition of the value of judicial criticism without their interest. In the first place they were primarily educational in kind, an outcome of the Humanistic movement. Thus an urgent need was felt for some discrimination in values in connexion with an educational system based on works of literature; and, moreover, there were the examples of Cicero and Quintilian in their educational treatises, from whom had come a considerable body of literary judgments. Apart from this an added impulse was derived from the Biblical studies engendered at this date by the quickening of religion and theology bound up with the Reformation; and the contributions of Colet and Erasmus in this field were of a noteworthy kind. In addition, it was inevitable that comments, however rare, should occasionally be made on medieval and contemporary writings.

Among the results thus achieved not least important was the fresh light now thrown on the classical literatures of ancient Greece and Rome. Erasmus, for instance, asserted that 'the whole of attainable knowledge lies enclosed within the literary monuments of ancient Greece'; [1] and from the accounts supplied by him, and Vives as well, readers were enabled to become acquainted with the ancient classics to an extent not possible before. The whole field of antiquity from Homer onwards was more or less covered in surveys which included orators, poets, historians, and philosophers; some treatment was given to post-classical and patristic writers; while attempts were also made at estimating literary values in general. As yet, however, the judgments supplied were subject to certain limitations. What was aimed at was not so much literary appreciation in the wider sense of the term as a discussion of stylistic qualities, the value of this or that writer as a model of expression, or else as a source of instructive subject-matter. Then, too, both in substance and form, the estimates were largely borrowed, consisting mainly of brief formal comments reminiscent of Quintilian; and these limitations are clearly seen in the accounts given by Erasmus in *De ratione studii*,[2] by Vives in *De tradendis disciplinis* [3] and elsewhere.

As might have been expected, Latin authors are more fully treated than the Greeks; and what is said of the latter is often merely of historical, rather than intrinsic, value. Thus Homer is praised with reservations, Plato is said ' to speak the language

---

[1] Woodward, *op. cit.* p. 164.   [2] *ibid.* pp. 164 ff.
[3] Watson, pp. 131–59.

of Jove ', Euripides is preferred to Sophocles, Aristotle is praised for 'originality of style', Isocrates for 'purity and ease', Demosthenes for vigorous expression, while Plutarch and Lucian are commended for both subject-matter and style. Among the Romans, and apart from Cicero and Virgil, Terence perhaps receives the highest praise. He is said to be unrivalled for pure and terse Latinity, for wit and grace, and for a conversational style which is said to have preserved the ancient speech in living form. Tacitus, on the other hand, is described as difficult, but bold and powerful, Sallust as obscure and rough, Seneca as varied and picturesque, Juvenal as rough and hard, Martial as immodest ; and of post-classical writers Gellius is dismissed as a mere compiler, while Ausonius is described as ' keen and exciting ', Juvencus and Sedulius, again, as ' muddy and disturbed rivers ', whose waters were yet health-giving. Altogether, it must be confessed, the appreciations are but sketchy and superficial, providing little more than a catalogue of ancient literature.

At the same time these accounts of classical writers are not without their more significant items ; and two notable tendencies are revealed, one in the marked preference for Virgil as compared with Homer, the other in the dawning recognition of the evolutionary aspect of literature. In the first place, reference has already been made to the tendency of Italian Humanists to assign the superiority in poetry to Virgil in virtue of his art ; and now Erasmus also regards him as the chief of all poets and for the same reason. By Vives, too, the same judgment is given, only in more detailed form.[1] He points out, first, the excellences of Homer ; his abounding genius, his power of vivid and picturesque narrative, his emotional effects, his reflexions on human life, and finally his undoubted appeal to all ages. But Homer, he adds, had also artistic defects from which Virgil was free ; and referring to Vida's De arte poetica (1527), he includes among Homer's faults verbosity and a love of digression, the use of long descriptions in the midst of action, the employment of mean similes and improbable incidents, as well as the repetition of epithets introduced often as mere metrical tags. It is true that Vives also attempts a sort of defence of Homer by suggesting that such defects were due to the conditions under which he had written, conditions which had compelled him to compose his works, not as complete wholes but as so many separate rhapsodies. Yet the tendency to praise Virgil at the expense of Homer still persisted. Vives recognized that Vida ' was committed as by a

[1] Watson, op. cit. p. 146.

sacred oath to the imitation of Virgil ' ; [1] but as yet no definite stand was made against the growing Virgil-worship.

On the other hand, deserving of notice is also the fact that fresh light was now thrown on these ancient literatures, more especially by Vives, in attempts to view them in their historical perspective. In connexion with Greek literature, for instance, the great age of Pericles was described as the most flourishing period, followed by the century of Plato, Aristotle, and Demosthenes ; while the progress of Latin classical literature was set out in yet more detail, its childhood being said to coincide with the age of Cato, its prime with the age of Cicero, and its old age with that of Trajan. ' For some reason or other,' wrote Vives,[2] ' the works written in the time of Cicero seem more original and natural. . . . After that the language became extravagant and voluptuous along with the ways of the state, and writers seem rather to want to please than to express in words the thoughts of their minds.' At the same time he urges that the works of these later writers, Seneca, Quintilian, Pliny, and Tacitus are not therefore to be neglected. Such comments were calculated to give help and guidance in the evaluation of the ancient literatures. With their suggestions of reasoned order they hinted at the idea of development in literary history.

Timely, however, as were these appreciations of classical literature at this date, even yet more significant were the attempts made to throw light on Biblical literature in which were employed critical methods of a most unexpected kind. Indeed it is not too much to say that with the work of Colet, and subsequently of Erasmus, in this particular field a new epoch in literary appreciation was inaugurated. They were in fact the first to make use of the historical method of interpretation, in advance of their own and many later generations. Colet it was who led the way in his Oxford lectures on the *Epistle to the Romans* and subsequently in his lectures on the *First Epistle to the Corinthians* ; and in a letter to an unknown friend, Radulphus, similar methods of interpretation were also applied to the first chapter of *Genesis*. Then, under the inspiration of Colet, whom he greatly revered, Erasmus in the Preface to his *Novum Instrumentum* (1516) attempted an exposition of the Gospels on similar lines ; and a new and illuminating approach to literature had been opened up. To this surprising development at this early date many influences had contributed. The original impulse, no doubt, was due to a reaction against the arbitrary interpretations of Scholastic divines, for whom the Bible had been largely

[1] Watson, *op. cit.* p. 160.   [2] *ibid.* p. 132.

a collection of detached texts to be used in theological conflict
without reference to their original meaning or context. With
them the ' manifold senses ' had been all-important and everywhere applicable ; the real meaning of the text had been lost
amidst the thousand and one propositions extracted from its
pages. And now arose the desire to arrive at the plain and
original significance, and thus to escape from ' the thickets of
medieval thought '. To this end enlightenment was sought from
the early Fathers and the Christian Humanists of Italy. Jerome
(A.D. 331–420), whose works after twenty years' study had been
edited in 1516 by Erasmus, had long ago warned against the
indiscriminate use of the allegorical method of interpretation.[1]
Chrysostom, again, had urged that in interpreting ' we must
investigate the period, the cause, the motive, the difference of
persons, and all the attendant circumstances, so only can we get at
the truth '.[2]   And while many of the Fathers had been conscious
of the principle of development in the spiritual education of
mankind, Gregory of Nyssa (c. A.D. 343–96) had interpreted
the early narrative of Genesis, not as history, but as doctrine in
the form of a story. In each instance the object had been to
arrive at the actual and original meaning of the text ; and the
results had already been seen in Pico's exposition of Psalm xvi.
in the light of his knowledge of Hebrew and Oriental customs.

Inspired then possibly by Pico and these earlier authorities
Colet attempts an interpretation of St. Paul's Epistles by an
application of the historical method, his main object being to
explain their real meaning by viewing them against their historical
background. Regarding them as letters of the 1st Century A.D.,
written by a religious teacher for contemporary readers under
certain definite conditions, he resorts to Suetonius and others
for light on the society and conditions of the time ; and with this
as the key to the understanding of the works he succeeds in
bringing out their main drift and their bearing on human life.
But he also does more than elucidate their true meaning, though
this in itself was no slight achievement at the time. He also
reveals in part the art underlying the Epistles, as well as certain
aspects of the personality of the writer himself. Thus he points
to the skill with which the arguments are addressed to the reader,
the due regard for persons and seasons, the tact with which blame
is preceded by praise. Or, again, he sees in the vehement statements, the abrupt suspended words, something of St. Paul's fire
and force ; while elsewhere reflexions are caught of his prudence,
his modesty and tolerance. In this way something of the vitality

[1] Ep. liii.   [2] In Mat. Hom. xvii. 6.

of the original writings is recaptured ; it is interpretation merging into appreciation of a psychological kind. Nor is his comment on the first chapter of *Genesis* without its interest ; for here, too, the same historical method is used, but with different results. Centuries had passed since Origen had described the Biblical story of the Creation as a wise and useful poetic figment ; [1] and now Colet sees in that judgment an explanation of things. He conceives of ' Moses ' as writing for a primitive people, and therefore adapting his message to their limited intelligence, by conveying his great truth, the one God as Creator, with the help of allegory, ' after the manner of a popular poet ', as he significantly puts it.

Equally interesting, however, is the work done by Erasmus in the same field, and notably in his illuminating treatment of the Gospel narratives in his Preface to *Novum Instrumentum*. Luther's literal interpretation, in place of the ' manifold senses ' of medieval times, had only succeeded in making the Bible a dead book ; but now Erasmus. gives to it a fresh vitality by applying Colet's historical method. His primary purpose was to explain meanings, first by a reversion to the Greek text, and secondly, by reading in the light of contemporary conditions. To this end he requires in the reader a knowledge of the historical background, the customs of Palestine, its institutions, natural history and the like, as well as a consideration of context, occasion, and speaker. In this way only, he maintains, would men gather the true significance of what was written, and perceive how real and actual was the New Testament story. But his comments go beyond such limits as these. In the first place, he views the Gospels as a whole, and remarks on the vividness with which Christ's character is there revealed, the result being ' a living, breathing picture '. ' If we had actually seen Him ', he writes, ' we should not have had such intimate knowledge as they give of Christ speaking, healing, dying, rising again, as it were in our actual presence.' He then points out the consistency of the narrative, the harmony existing between Christ's doctrine, His nature and His life. ' No lie ', he maintains, ' was ever framed with such skill as in everything to comport with itself ' ; and such verisimilitude, he suggests, is most convincing. Moreover, concerning the teaching itself, he throws out hints of spiritual development. ' Certain Gentile philosophers ', he states, ' by force of Nature discern some matters which agree with the doctrines of Christ ' ; and in heathen philosophy, as well as in the Old Testament, he traces foreshadowings of Christian doctrine.

[1] cf. also Gregory Nazianzus, *Orat.* xxxi. 25.

Here then were brought to light some of the unique qualities of Biblical literature, qualities which for the most part had escaped medieval readers, but which later ages were to appreciate more fully as time went on. The treatment marked a new phase of literary appreciation ; and, as a Christian Humanist, Erasmus makes a plea for the reading of the Biblical text, even by simple minds, in place of the subtleties involved in Scholastic theology.

But while classical and Biblical literature may thus be said to have absorbed almost wholly the attention of Humanists, some casual judgments on medieval activities are also forthcoming, and they too are of interest. Of unmistakable significance historically, for instance, are the strictures passed on medieval romances as the characteristic productions of earlier times ; though of the works of Chaucer and others little or nothing is said. It was by Vives in his *De instructione feminae Christianae* (1523) that the most specific pronouncement was made ; and the work having been translated by Richard Hyrde (c. 1540),[1] the attitude therein adopted, as well as the terms and method of the censure, were destined to have considerable influence on later writers. Thus Vives deplores, to begin with, the great vogue of popular romances still prevalent in his day. 'There is a use nowadays ', he writes, ' worse than among the pagans, that books written in our mother tongue, that be made for idle men and women to read, have none other matter than that of war and love.' And, as examples of the widespread fashion for these ' ungracious books ' he mentions among others, *Amadis*, *Florisand*, *Tristan* and *Celestina* of Spain, *Lancelot du Lac*, *Paris and Vienne*, and *Melusine* of France, *Florice and Blanchefleur* of Flanders, while Hyrde in his translation supplies as English counterparts the stories of *Parthenope*, *Libius and Arthur*, *Guy*, *Bevis*, and others—the very titles of which for modern readers spell the magic that still clings to old-world romance. Then follows the main charge of his indictment.

What delight [he asks] can be in . . . so plain and foolish lies ? One killeth twenty himself alone, another killeth thirty, another, wounded with a hundred wounds and left dead, riseth up again and on the next day made whole and strong, overcometh two giants and then goeth away, loaden with gold and silver and precious stones more than a galley would carry away. What madness is it of folks to have pleasure in these books ! There is no wit in them but a few words of wanton lust.[2]

---

[1] For this English version see Foster Watson, *Vives and the Renascence Education of Women*.   [2] *ibid*. p. 56.

What Vives thus objects to is the unedifying character of the romances, their wanton love-themes and stories of unending warfare, together with the fanciful, far-fetched nature of those stories, conducing to neither morality nor truth. Elsewhere he recalls that even Ovid had warned against the dangers of ancient love-poetry,[1] such as that of Sappho, Anacreon, Propertius, and the like ; whereas Plato, he added, in his zeal for truth, ' had cast out of the commonwealth of wise men . . . even Homer and Hesiod, though they were free from the vices of Ovid's books of love '. Moreover, in this position Vives was supported by Erasmus who also had little use for romances, even in their Latin form ; while he likewise condemned all ' amatory stories and songs '.[2] The romances he had described as so many *fabulae stultae et aniles*,[3] among which he had included the Arthur and Lancelot stories ; and indeed to him the Arthurian cycle was little more than trivial nonsense, neither true to fact nor morally helpful, not even clothed in notable language. In this way was founded a tradition of hostility to the romance, a tradition later on extended, at least by the theorists, to ' romantic ' literature at large. The tests applied were those of morality and factual truth ; and not without its significance is the condemnation of love-poetry at this stage. The position was, obviously due to Humanistic lack of sympathy with the Middle Ages, together with the failure to apply that historical method which had proved so helpful in interpreting Biblical literature. And that Vives's influence in establishing the tradition was not inconsiderable is suggested by the verbal echoes of his pronouncement heard in the works of Ascham, Sidney, and Jonson.

In these judgments on classical, Biblical, and medieval literature may be said to be included the main elements of the Humanistic contribution to judicial criticism ; though remarks on contemporary activities, it is true, are also occasionally found and are worth noting. Erasmus, for instance, ridicules the extravagances of current complimentary verse, in which one writer is described as ' an absolute Alcaeus ', another as ' more learned than Plato '.[4] Elsewhere he censures the pulpit orators of his day ; their constant use of syllogisms, conclusions, new-found terms and prodigious words ; [5] their pride in rough speech, since ' mysteries are not to be cramped by narrow rules of gram-

---

[1] Vives, *De corruptis artibus*, II. vi. 109 : also F. Watson, *Vives and the Renascence Education of Women*, p. 61.
[2] *In. Christ. Matrim.* (1526), pp. 152 ff.   [3] *Opera*, iv. 587.
[4] *Praise of Folly*, p. 110.   [5] *ibid.* p. 122.

mar ' ; [1] their delight in insipid fables ; [2] or again, their fondness for ' pricking in a jest here and there ',[3] since Quintilian had discoursed on laughter in his treatise on eloquence. For the rest, Vives has but little comment to make, though he praises More for his wit, and Erasmus, he states, ' is like Horace, as he would wish to be '.[4] As yet, however, contemporary English writers, such as Hawes and Skelton, receive no attention ; the claims of the vernacular had yet to be recognized.

This then was the advance made in literary judgment and appreciation at this date ; and not without their interest are the critical standards and methods now brought to light. It is clear, to begin with, that literary judgment as yet was subject to no arbitrary standards, no authoritative system of rules, still less to the criterion of age, as Vives, recalling a passage in Horace (*virtutem aestimat annis*), incidentally explains.[5] Equally evident, however, is the confusion of thought that prevailed, due partly to preoccupation with educational matters, partly also to the borrowed nature of many of the judgments ; so that literary merit is assigned mainly to style and edifying subject-matter. Yet glimpses of more adequate criteria at the same time also appear ; and already it was being suggested that greatness in literature was ultimately bound up with aesthetic effect and the permanent delight afforded. Thus Erasmus, alluding to the works of great writers, maintains that ' when read a thousand times they please more and more (*millies relecta magis magisque placeant*), ever revealing to the reader some new wonder '.[6] And this same standard is also implied when Vives prescribes the test of universality and time. ' Books ', he states,[7] ' are deserving of respect when they have satisfied thinkers for many ages, and the consensus of so many minds for so long a period has confirmed the judgment, so that there is substantially only one opinion offered concerning the writers ' ; and here was suggested none other than the *quod semper, quod ubique, quod ab omnibus* principle of ' Longinus ', the one ever-valid test of greatness in literature.

Nor as regards methods of appreciation was guidance entirely lacking, despite the practice of adopting ready-made judgments of Quintilian and others. It is true that the allegorical method of interpretation was generally maintained ; though the application of the ' four senses ' to Biblical literature at least had been

---

[1] *Praise of Folly*, p. 125.   [2] *ibid.* pp. 134–5.
[3] *ibid.* p. 136.   [4] Watson, *op. cit.* p. 160.
[5] *ibid.* p. 294 : cf. Hor. *Epist.* II. i. 48.
[6] Woodward, *op. cit.* p. 225.   [7] Watson, *op. cit.* p. 294.

challenged by that historical approach which had increased the capacity to understand and enjoy. Moreover, prime importance was still being attached to ethical values and to the moral teaching of a literary work. On the other hand, hints were also given relating to sounder methods. Thus stress was laid by Erasmus on the importance of considering a given work as a whole, the general sense first, and then its broader significance ; [1] while Vives was equally emphatic in discountenancing a pedantic concern with non-essential details. ' It is no crime ', he asserts,[2] ' if one does not know every myth and trifle ' ; thereby adapting Quintilian's dictum that ' there are some things which it is a merit in a teacher of literature not to know '. At the same time it is recognized that obscurities which hindered a true understanding would sometimes occur ; and Vives (following Servius) wisely recommends that such passages should be explained in the light of similar but clearer passages of the same author or his contemporaries.[3] Then, too, both Erasmus and Vives recognize that literary appreciation is not a matter of mere rules. Erasmus, for instance, held that qualities of style had to be felt and absorbed in reading, that they could not be imparted by precept ; while Vives maintained that ' in eloquence the rules are not defined in every case '.[4] Most suggestive, however, is Erasmus's advice as to the method of appreciating literary work, though still subject to limitations. ' When anything has delighted you ', he writes,[5] ' ask the reason why (abs te ipso rationem exige quare tantopere sis ea oratione delectatus). You will find that it is due to some device or subtlety or harmony of expression, to some ingenious use of proverb, fable, simile and the like.' It is true that his outlook is here limited to rhetorical devices, though he also recommends some consideration of the author's plan and design ; but it was helpful counsel at the time, suggesting methods calculated to lead ultimately to a reasoned appreciation of literature in the concrete.

Such then were the main features of the contributions made to literary criticism during the opening decades of the 16th Century by Humanists who were not without their influence on English thought at the time ; and altogether it may be said that sound foundations had thereby been laid for future developments in both literary theory and judgment. As yet, it is true, no coherent body of doctrine was forthcoming, and not a little

[1] Woodward, op. cit. pp. 174, 224.
[2] Watson, op. cit. pp. 102, 235 ; cf. Quintilian, Inst. Or. I. viii. 21.
[3] ibid. p. 106.
[4] ibid. p. 194.   [5] Woodward, op. cit. p. 224.

confusion of thought still prevailed. The break with post-classical and medieval ideas, for instance, was by no means complete ; and the conception of imaginative literature with its various forms was still inadequate. Moreover, the preoccupation with ancient literature had led to a neglect of the vernacular and vernacular literature ; in the revived study of rhetoric undue attention was still paid to such matters as ' amplification ', figures and the like ; and as for poetry, medieval vagueness concerning its nature still persisted, so that poetry in general was regarded as little more than fanciful trifling, while allegorical interpretation and moral standards were still being applied.

On the other hand, highly significant is the fact that it was now that the need for literary criticism was first recognized and its practice established. And at the same time a deliberate break (as Vives [1] expressly stated) had been made with earlier pedantic and pedestrian treatises by attempts at a clearer and more attractive treatment of literary matters. Inspired by Italian Humanists, and drawing freely on the teaching of Cicero and Quintilian, to a lesser degree on Aristotle and Plutarch as well, successful efforts were now made, with reason or Nature as guide, to expound the literary principles of classical antiquity and to inculcate the value of literature as a means of culture. With the ancient conception of rhetoric restored and accepted as the main study, valuable advice was now given relating to prose style ; attention was called to such matters as ' that other harmony of prose ' or the element of personality in style ; and at the same time new and vitalizing ideas concerning the nature of poetry were also being suggested. Then, too, fresh light had been thrown on the classical literatures of Greece and Rome ; glimpses had been caught of the ultimate test of greatness in literature ; the historical method of interpretation had been applied to Biblical literature with illuminating results ; and further hints had been given on methods of literary appreciation. Most significant of all, however, was the enlightened attitude adopted at this stage towards classical antiquity, from whence, it was generally allowed, sound guidance in literary matters could alone be looked for. A question of fundamental import-ance had been raised by the Ciceronian controversy, though dis-cussion as yet was limited to matters of prose style. What had actually been broached, however, was the far wider problem of how best a modern age might profit by the artistic achievements of the ancients. And in face of determined opponents who advocated a close and even slavish imitation, a definite stand

[1] Watson, op. cit. p. 6.

was now made for a free assimilation of ancient art, for an adaptation of classical technique in accordance with modern needs and in keeping with individual and national geniuses. The ancients were in fact to be leaders, not dictators ; their artistic processes were to be studied with the view of adapting them for use in work of an original kind. Here then were laid down sound lines of artistic advance. It was doctrine of a timely and enlightened kind, embodying principles which, had they been followed, would have changed the whole course of later literary criticism in Europe.

CHAPTER IV

THE RHETORIC TRADITION: JEWEL, WILSON, AND ASCHAM

I N order to understand the true significance of the critical contribution made by Englishmen during the first half of the 16th Century it has been necessary to recall by way of preliminary the achievements of the Humanists, not only in 15th-Century Italy, but also in England during the opening decades of the 16th Century, for it was from those varied activities that both inspiration and direction ultimately came. That critical movement, it has been seen, was full of promise. It had opened up fresh vistas of the possibilities of literature ; had given access for the first time to much that was valuable in ancient classical theory ; had thrown fresh light on the classical literatures themselves as well as on methods of appreciation ; and last, but not least, it had indicated the lines along which those literatures might best be utilized, for educational purposes primarily, but also for a better understanding of literature and literary methods in general. In England, however, the immediate sequel can only be described as disappointing. Up to a date well beyond the middle of the 16th Century but few works of critical interest were forthcoming. In fact the poverty of the output is only realized fully when compared with the lively interest betrayed in literary questions, and in poetry more particularly, by contemporaries belonging to both Italy and France. From the third decade onwards, the poetic doctrines of Aristotle and Horace were being discussed by an imposing array of Italian scholars, including Vida (1527), Daniello (1536), Robortelli (1548), Cinthio (1554), Minturno (1559), Scaliger (1561), and Castelvetro (1570).[1] And, as a result, systematic theories of the nature and art of poetry, of the drama and epic in particular, were elaborated, attention being thus called to the Horatian doctrine of the civilizing function of poetry, as well as to Aristotle's philosophical justification of imaginative literature, which, while superseding the unconvincing medieval attempts at vindication, also gave to poetry a new status, dignity, and value. Likewise in France the middle of the century witnessed the enthusiastic efforts of Du Bellay (1549), Ronsard (1565),

---

[1] See G. Saintsbury, *History of Criticism*, II. chs. ii and iii : J. E. Spingarn, *Literary Criticism in the Renaissance*, pp. 1–167.

and others to set forth a new and exalted conception of the poetic art ; [1] after which none could doubt the grandeur and moral dignity of poetry, as the product of gifted and inspired souls, with a technique based on the teaching of classical antiquity and yet adapted to the requirements of the national genius. Of neither the philosophical treatment of literature characteristic of Italy, nor again of the enthusiastic yet practical manifestos of the contemporary French school, are any traces to be found in England at this particular date. Such treatment of literature as occurs is concerned for the most part with rhetorical matters, with preliminary questions relating to the vernacular and the literary language, and only occasionally with poetry and with literary theory in general. The few substantial pronouncements of the time are to be found in Bishop Jewel's *Oratio contra Rhetoricam* (1548), Thomas Wilson's *Arte of Rhetorique* (1560), and Roger Ascham's *Scholemaster* (1570) ; and for the rest we must take into consideration sporadic remarks on a variety of topics scattered throughout works of different kinds.

To account for this tardy and restricted beginning of critical activities in 16th-Century England we must look to the conditions which then prevailed. In the first place, a marked decline in scholarship had set in after the great days of Colet, Linacre, More, and others, when Erasmus had praised English learning in glowing terms, and Aldus had looked to England to reduce the ' barbarism ' of the time. The truth was that the intellectual promise of the early years of the reign of Henry VIII was never fulfilled. The hostility to Greek learning revealed by the obscurantist ' Trojans ' at Oxford (1518), the temper displayed in the dissolution of the monasteries (1535-9),or again, in the wholesale ejection of scholars at Cambridge by religious fanaticism (1553), all point to a serious decline from the generous intellectual outlook of those early English Humanists. Then, too, matters other than literary were soon absorbing all attention, for English Humanism was modified, and even opposed, by the zeal for religious reform. The main interests became those of a political, social, religious kind. Educational treatises, translations of the Bible, books of devotion, controversial tracts and the like were increasingly in demand ; and literary discussion for the time being was practically crowded out. Concerning literature itself, moreover, there existed much confusion of thought, for the new Humanistic teaching had clashed with those medieval traditions which still held their ground in the works of Hawes and Skelton, in popular romances, interludes, pulpit

[1] Saintsbury, *op. cit.* ii. ch. iv ; Spingarn, *op. cit.* pp. 171-250.

oratory and the like ; and, in addition, the first effect of printing had been to prolong those earlier traditions, since the main output of English printing-presses up to 1530 consisted of works characteristically medieval. Such confused conditions were not conducive to serious inquiries concerning literature as such. It was, in short, by scholars primarily interested in the transmission of Renascence culture that questions regarding literature were discussed at this date. Literature was valued, not so much for its aesthetic qualities, as for its ethical teaching, its usefulness as an instrument of higher education ; and while the claims of rhetoric in the first place were generally conceded, attention was incidentally given to the constitution of the vernacular, and in a lesser degree to the nature and art of poetry.

Of the causes which led to the prominent position thus assumed by rhetoric in contemporary studies something has already been said. They were causes which had been operative among the earlier Humanists, and were mainly the outcome of the predominant influence of Cicero and Quintilian, now and in the century preceding. Other contributory factors undoubtedly there were, such as the urgent desire for the correction of those strange notions of rhetoric which had persisted throughout the Middle Ages ; or again, there was the timely appearance of the *Rhetores Graeci* (1508–9) from the Aldine press, while a revival of interest in rhetoric had already made itself felt in 15th-Century England. Nevertheless it was from the undisputed prestige of Cicero and Quintilian that inspiration and direction ultimately came. Both had written at length on matters of oratory ; and their teaching had definitely assigned to rhetoric the leading place among intellectual studies. To them rhetoric was not merely a valuable scholastic discipline ; it was also an instrument indispensable for the welfare of the state. Oratory, in fact, was the queen of the literary ' kinds ', with poetry as its handmaid ; and, as Cicero had somewhat patronizingly declared, the poet was ' closely akin to the orator, . . . his rival and almost his equal in some respects '.[1] This then largely accounts not only for the priority now given to rhetoric in the field of literary studies, but also for the comparatively slight interest taken in poetry by contemporary English scholars.

For an adequate appreciation, however, of what was now achieved in rhetorical studies the character and position of rhetoric in the centuries preceding must first be recalled. Throughout the medieval period all literary theory had been coloured by ' rhetorical ' doctrine ; though apart from Alcuin's

[1] *De oratore*, i. 70.

elementary treatise no systematic treatment of the subject had so far appeared. The conception underlying this pervasive medieval ' rhetoric ', however, differed vitally from that of classical antiquity. Based as it was mainly on pre-Ciceronian doctrine, and influenced more especially by the New Sophistic, that morbid revival of Asiatic tendencies in rhetoric which had marked the opening centuries of the Christian era, it was subsequently developed by post-classical theorists, by the Encyclopaedists Capella, Isidore and others, until finally it came to mean little more than ornate and grandiloquent speech, amplified by various devices, including countless figures ; and so far from being an independent discipline, concerned as in classical antiquity with oratory and the writing of prose, it now became merged in the medieval arts of poetry (*poetria*) and letter-writing (*dictamen*), to which it gave both form and substance. This then was the conception of rhetoric expounded in the 15th-Century *Court of Sapience* as well as in Hawes's *Pastime of Pleasure* (1506) ; and from both it is clear that rhetoric and poetic were still being confused and that poetic was regarded as little more than versified rhetoric. In the meantime signs of a reversion to the classical tradition were being revealed in the *Nova Rhetorica* (1478) of Traversagni, an Italian Franciscan then lecturing at Cambridge ; and his treatise, which embodied some amount of classical doctrine, thus representing a departure from the medieval tradition, was the earliest Rhetoric to be printed in England, first by Caxton in 1479 and then by the ' St, Alban's Scholemayster ' in the following year. From Caxton, too, came further evidence of this change of outlook. In a passage treating of rhetoric in his translation, *The Mirror of the World* (1481) [1] he gives some sound advice on eloquence, condemning all superfluous expression and too much ' amplification '. Thus was heralded the larger conception of rhetoric characteristic of classical times, with its more definite scope and its illuminating doctrine ; and it was mainly along these lines that the rhetorical studies of the 16th Century were to develop.

The earliest stage of the development was marked by the appearance of certain school-books, of which Cox's *Arte or Crafte of Rhethoryke* (1524) came first and was followed by Sherry's *Schemes and Tropes* (1550). Both were manuals written by schoolmasters for their English pupils ; and despite obvious limitations they are not without historical interest, as pointing to a newly-felt need for guidance in vernacular expression and for the application of ancient teaching made available by the

[1] D. ii. r.

Humanists. Neither, however, represents original work ; and neither can be said to afford an adequate treatment of the subject. Cox, for instance, deals solely with *inventio*, with the development of a theme, the finding and arranging of argument ; and while his material is drawn largely from Melanchthon's *Institutiones Rhetoricae* (1521), his examples are taken mainly from Cicero's orations. Sherry, on the other hand, confines himself to matters of diction and style, on the ground that a knowledge of figures was needed for a correct reading of both pagan and Biblical literature ; and, influenced apparently by Erasmus's *De copia* he treats mainly of ' garnished words ', methods of amplification, and the use of figures and tropes. Moreover, both contain elements of post-classical and medieval teaching. Cox, for instance, retains not a little of Sophistic doctrine ; Sherry, again, preserves the medieval tradition of rhetoric in his exclusive treatment of ornate and figurative language. It is therefore clear that such works, summary in treatment, schematic in form and lacking in freshness and vitality, did but little to commend the study to wider circles of readers. And the same holds true of the series of school-manuals by which they were followed, works including P. Rainolde's *Foundations of Rhetoric* (1563), H. Peacham's *Garden of Eloquence* (1577), and A. Fraunce's *Arcadian Rhetorike* (1584), in which the rules of rhetoric were illustrated from Sidney's *Arcadia* ; while the medieval *ars dictaminis* was continued in works on letter-writing, such as A. Fleming's *Panoply of Epistles* (1576) and A. Day's *English Secretary* (1586). The main significance of such works lay in the indication they gave of the persistent desire for ' fine writing ', encouraged no doubt by influential manuals which had appeared abroad, notably, Susenbrotus's *Epitome Troporum ac Schematum* (1540) and Talaeus's *Rhetoric* (1547). But something more than mere text-books were needed for courtly readers ; and this was forthcoming in Wilson's *Arte of Rhetorique* and other courtly expositions.

Meanwhile the development of rhetorical studies was not allowed to pass without comment. And viewed apart from its scholastic uses and as an instrument of wider culture, the study of rhetoric was strongly advocated, on the one hand, by Sir Thomas Elyot (*c.* 1490–1546) in his *Boke named the Governour* (1531),[1] a popular and attractive treatise which dealt with the education of statesmen. On the other hand, strangely enough, it was as fiercely condemned by John Jewel (1522–71), Praelector of Humanity or Rhetoric at Oxford and later Bishop of Salisbury,

[1] ed. H. H. S. Croft (1883).

in his *Oratio contra Rhetoricam* [1] (*c.* 1548) ; and neither pronouncement is without its significance. Animated by the desire to
render accessible to English readers the wisdom of the ancients,
Elyot, in the first place, unreservedly recommends the new study,
suggesting as guides Quintilian and Hermogenes, and as models
the works of Isocrates, Demosthenes, and Cicero.[2] In support
of his position he then recalls that commonplace much used in
classical antiquity, according to which eloquence was the first
civilizing agency. ' In the first infancy of the world ', he writes,[3]
' men wandered like beasts in woods and mountains until
Mercury (as Plato [4] supposes) or some other . . . assembled them
and persuaded to them what commodity there was in mutual
conversation and honest manners.' Concerning eloquence
itself he also has something to say, in reminding his readers of
some of the ancient precepts. He insists, to begin with, on the
importance of sound subject-matter, recalling that Cicero had
required for the orator an acquaintance with many branches of
knowledge ; and he further recommends the use of words ' clean,
proper and comely ', arranged so as to ' affect the minds of the
hearers and to persuade, move and delight '. In addition, he
utters a warning against the excessive pursuit of elaborate
expression. Eloquence, he states, ' is more than words and
colours of rhetoric ', while a mere stylist is ' no more to be
praised than a popinjay or a pye . . . when they speak featly '.[5]
He is also alive to the pedantic character of much of the rhetorical
teaching of his day ; and such teachers he condemns as de-
claimers or *logodedali* [6] (artificial speakers), the term used by
Plato and later by Cicero and Quintilian.[7] Thus in judicious
fashion and in general terms does Elyot commend the study of
rhetoric to contemporary readers as a valuable and necessary
part of the new culture.

More contentious, and also more heated, was the treatment
of rhetoric in Jewel's *Oratio,* which constituted a direct challenge
to the whole movement. Originally inspired, it may be sur-
mised, by the threat of Ciceronianism, and the heavy fighting
in which Politian and Bembo, Erasmus and Vives, Longolius
and Scaliger had all previously engaged,[8] the attack on that
heresy was now extended so as to include an assault on rhetoric

---

[1] See *Works of J. Jewel*, 4th Portion, ed. J. Ayre (Parker Soc. 1850),
pp. 1283 ff.
[2] *Governour*, p. 117.   [3] *ibid.*   [4] cf. *Protagoras*, xii ; *Laws*, iii. *ad init.*
[5] *Governour*, p. 116.   [6] *ibid.* pp. 119–20.
[7] cf. Plato, *Phaedrus*, 266 ; Cicero, *Orator*, c. 12. Quin. *Inst. Or.*, III. i. 11.
[8] See pp. 22, 46 *supra*.

itself. Concerning Jewel's fierce hostility to Ciceronianism, in the first place, there can be no doubt in view of the unmeasured scorn which he pours on the cult and all its votaries, those ' fine writers ' (*elegantiusculi*) who followed Cicero alone and that in slavish fashion.[1] Equipped with a lavish supply of choicest words they are said ' to polish and hesitate, to correct and torture, now rejecting a word, now seeking another ', while at the same time they ' imitate Cicero's most trifling features, stuffing them into every chink ; and, as if they had no sense of their own, they feel nothing but what Cicero had felt before them, so that their standard of taste is Cicero's and not their own '.   Moreover, it is added, they read no other books, no poet, historian, or philosopher. ' In Cicero alone they place their tabernaculum, and in him they seek neither knowledge nor judgment, but only words, ornaments, particles, elegancies of style and abundance of words.'   As for the results of all these labours, nothing, so it is urged, was more distasteful. To imitate him adequately was by no means easy on account of his inconsistencies ; since ' no one was ever so unlike others as Cicero was to himself '.   And, besides, Cicero himself had not been perfect.   His oratory had in fact been censured by his contemporaries as ' loose, nerveless and Asiatic ', and had won the approval of the ignorant crowd alone.

Justifiable in the main as this attack on Ciceronianism un-doubtedly was, the same cannot be said of Jewel's censure of rhetoric itself ; and this is seen from the specious character of most of his arguments, in denouncing first eloquence, and then rhetorical studies in general.   In the first place he has some-thing to say on the nature and effects of eloquence.   He argues,[2] for instance, that since men speak to be understood, there is no better way of speaking than that of plain utterance (*aperte, plane, dilucide*) ; and that truth, which has no need of eloquence, is only obscured and distorted by polished phrases.   Thus it was, he adds, that Protagoras was able *deteriorem causam dicendo facere superiorem* ; that Carneades at Rome was successful in pleading against justice ; and whereas Mercury, the god and patron of orators, was held to be responsible for deceits and frauds, from him came naturally many oratorical devices (*illae orationis figurae, formae, schemata, et quae illi lumina vocant (tenebrae potius)*), as well as a host of false tricks of delivery, gesture and the like.   But while eloquence is thus shown to be of deceit and falsehood all compact—and orators, it was also noted, conceal their art [3]—no less serious are said to have been the injuries wrought on great states down through the ages.[4]   Rome, for

1 *Works*, p. 1287.   2 *ibid*. pp. 1285–6.   3 *ibid*. p. 1290.   4 *ibid*. p. 1288.

instance, fell, so we are told, through the eloquence of Cicero—that proud Rome which ' neither Gracchus, nor Marius, nor Sylla, nor the anger of Catiline could wholly destroy '. Again, it is stated, men are wont to attribute the downfall of states to avarice and luxury ; whereas, in truth, ' the plague and pest of states is eloquence, which wherever it alights brings fires and tempests '. And for this reason orators from the earliest times had been condemned ; had in fact been banished from Rome, ' while actors and flute-players had been allowed to remain '.[1] Nor were its evil effects wanting in a later age, when Scotus and other acute philosophers reigned supreme. For when Cicero, ' like some Cerberus, was cast back from darkness into light, then literary studies were quenched and intellectual ardour languished '.

With this as the main substance of Jewel's remarks on the value of eloquence, there was obviously but little to be said for rhetoric itself. That art, in short, he declared to be a waste of time ; and the quest for *venustatem quandam in dicendo* to be unworthy of serious minds.[2] More dignified, he asserts, were the long silences of the Pythagoreans, or the brief utterances of Spartans ; while Homer's epithet in ' winged words ' (πτερόεντα) was said to imply the flimsiness of all speech. Then, too, an art of rhetoric he described as unnecessary, as absurd as an art of hearing or walking would be ; for speech came naturally to every man, and men had discussed great matters before Demosthenes and Cicero saw the light. Moreover, with more justice, it was claimed that among the teachers of rhetoric there had never been any sort of agreement, any definite standards.[3] Corax and Tisias, Theophrastus, Demetrius and Hermagoras, he points out, had all been at variance ; Aristotle, again, ' lest he might seem to know too little, had condemned the precepts of all his predecessors ' ; and to-day, added the Praelector, ' there are more than six hundred rhetors, all in disagreement '.

Such then was Jewel's disquisition on rhetoric before his erudite Oxford audience ; and in spite of its obvious perversity, it is not without its significance in critical history. That it was a piece of special pleading, in which was displayed considerable learning, along with garbled history and shallow sophistical arguments, this much, to begin with, will be conceded. Yet it is also something more than a plea for anarchy in expression, even though its argument is mainly of a destructive kind. It is perhaps best interpreted as an overstatement of Jewel's real intention, which was to condemn the prevailing rhetorical

[1] *Works*, p. 1289.   [2] *ibid.* p. 1284.   [3] *ibid.* p. 1286.

instruction—an over-statement occasioned by strong feeling against the arrogant claims of the Ciceronians, and by youthful impatience with the infinite complications of current scholastic doctrine. At any rate it is not wholly devoid of positive value ; for it supplies an interesting sidelight on contemporary perplexities regarding literature. Besides being the most definite and outspoken attack by an Englishman against the Ciceronian heresy, as well as a timely protest against the pursuit of ' fine writing ', it is indirectly a plea in an age of confused thinking for that plain unadorned speech which had been intermittently advocated by English writers from the time of Bede onwards.

Despite the limitations imposed by scholastic text-books and the doubts expressed by academic theorists, rhetorical studies, however, still retained much of their appeal to wider scholarly circles ; and with the appearance of the *Arte of Rhetorique* [1] (1553, completed 1560) by Thomas Wilson (*c.* 1525–81), something of the larger conception of rhetoric, the rhetoric of Cicero and Quintilian, was for the first time recaptured and presented to English readers. The work was one of the first-fruits of the Cambridge school of scholarship ; for Wilson as an undergraduate of King's (1541) had come under the influence of both Cheke and Ascham. It was actually designed, however, for those about to enter public life, and, in 1558, before the complete edition had appeared, it had involved its author, then an exile in Rome, in a charge of heresy brought by the Inquisition, from whose clutches he narrowly escaped, *tanquam per ignem*, as he himself put it. Recalled to England in 1559 he subsequently played a great part in political and diplomatic affairs, became Secretary of State (1579), and one of the most influential men of the time. Meanwhile his *Arte* had attained considerable popularity, having been frequently reprinted before 1588 ; and of its value there can be no doubt. Warton in the 18th Century described it as ' the first system of criticism in our language ' ; and as the first ordered attempt to set forth the guiding principles of effective speech (and writing) in English, it calls for something more than passing notice.

At first sight the plan of the work, which consists of three Books, has but little to distinguish it from that of earlier school-rhetorics. Thus Bk. I (pp. 1–99), after some preliminary remarks, provides explanations of such technical matters as the five elements of oratory, the seven divisions of an oration, the three kinds of oratory and the rest ; and then concerns itself with Invention (or the finding of suitable subject-matter) in connexion

[1] ed. G. H. Mair (1909).

with the different kinds of oratory. Bk. II (pp. 99–160) deals with Disposition (or the arranging of subject-matter) and adds some remarks on methods of Amplification; while Bk. III (pp. 160–222) is mainly devoted to Elocution (or style), with a lengthy exposition of colours and ornaments, followed by a summary treatment of Memory and Pronunciation (or delivery). All this was on the lines of earlier school-texts from the *Rhetorica ad Herennium* onwards, with their schematic form, their divisions and sub-divisions; while post-classical and medieval influences are seen in the stress laid on such matters as ' amplification ' and the figures as elements of style. Yet into this traditional form Wilson has breathed new life, basing his teaching throughout on Nature or reason, explaining technicalities, adding illustrations and anecdotes to enliven the way, and presenting his doctrine, if discursively, yet often in lively and conversational style. What is more, he has recalled for his readers that more generous conception of rhetoric characteristic of classical authorities from Plato to Quintilian. He has also avoided the formal, dogmatic, scholastic manner, and has aimed at suggesting principles rather than fixed rules. Thus he succeeds in throwing light on some at least of the fundamental principles that govern effective expression in prose; and since his ultimate object was to bring ancient teaching to bear on writing in the vernacular, his work forms a valuable introduction to the critical study of English prose-style—a timely achievement in an age of much formless prose-writing.

Not without their interest, to begin with, are his preliminary remarks on eloquence in general; and at the outset he is at pains to explain that what he has in mind is expression in words generally, that is, not merely oral speech, but written prose as well.[1] Most of his remarks, it is true, consist of ancient commonplaces. Yet they have considerable importance for 16th-Century readers; and, apart from the conventional claim (denied by Quintilian)[2] that eloquence had first been instrumental in civilizing man and organizing society,[3] they are reminders of elementary truths reiterated throughout antiquity. Thus eloquence, in the first place, he explains as the outcome of trained skill and a knowledge of art; and art, he adds, consists of no arbitrary precepts but of laws based on observation of existing oratory, since ' eloquence came not up first by the art but the art rather was gathered upon eloquence '.[4] That some men wrote well by the light of nature and without knowledge of art, this much he concedes. Yet art, he maintains, was a surer guide than

[1] *Arte*, p. 5.   [2] III. ii. 4.   [3] *Arte*, Preface.   [4] *ibid*. p. 5.

nature ; and whereas it added to the skill of genius, it also afforded
necessary help to those lacking in natural endowment. At the
same time he recognizes that something more than art is needed
for the attainment of eloquence. He therefore recalls the other
ancient requirements, namely, native endowment (*natura*), constant practice (*exercitatio*), and imitation of models (*imitatio*) ; [1]
though, like Cicero, he has but little to say on the much-vexed
question of ' imitation ', beyond stating that those who walk in
the sun generally become sunburnt.[2] As for the nature of eloquence itself, this he describes in terms of its effects. The skilful
orator (or writer), he holds, must ' teach, delight and persuade ',[3]
and his utterance must therefore be clear and intelligible, graceful and pleasing, and calculated to appeal to the emotions of
his hearers (or readers). Nothing, however, is more significant
than Wilson's freedom from pedantry and dogmatism in expounding his doctrine ; as when, for example, he recognizes that no
absolute rules could be laid down, that all circumstances should
be taken into account, and that expression should necessarily
vary with time and place, with the nature of the theme and the
character of the hearers (or readers).[4] ' The wise man ', he
states,[5] ' will not be bound by any precise rules, . . . but such
only as by reason he shall think best to use, being master over
art, rather than art should be master over him.' This was wise
and enlightened advice for his contemporaries ; and, as he adds,
' what mattereth whether we follow our book or no, if we follow
wit and appoint ourself an order such as may declare the truth
more plainly ? '

The main body of Wilson's theorizing, however, is concerned
with the specific details of the art of eloquence ; and not least
important is the fact that he realizes from the first, as the ancients
from Plato onwards had realized before him, that eloquence is
something more than a mere matter of words, and that much
would depend, first, on clear thinking and the choice of adequate
and appropriate subject-matter, and, secondly, on the orderly
and effective arrangement of the thought expressed. To the need
for sound subject-matter, in the first place, he has devoted considerable attention ; [6] though the treatment here, following the
traditional lines of earlier rhetorics, confines itself to the subject-
matter of orations in particular—orations for use on ceremonial
occasions (demonstrative or epideictic), for great assemblies
(deliberative), or for the law-courts (judicial), and is thus highly

---

[1] *Arte*, pp. 4–5.   [2] cf. Cicero, *De oratore*, ii. ch. xiv.
[3] *Arte*, p. 2 : cf. Cicero and Quin., *docere, delectare, movere*.
[4] *ibid*. pp. 8, 158–9.   [5] *ibid*. p. 159.   [6] *ibid*. pp. 11–99.

technical in character and of limited application. He treats, for instance, at great length of ' causes ', of ' places ', of ' issues ' and the rest ; and then illustrates his teaching by full-length orations characteristic of the three kinds of oratory—i.e ' On Comfort ', ' On David's slaying of Goliath ', ' On a legal offence committed by a soldier '—mostly of his own composition, though one, ' On persuading a young friend to marriage ', is a translation of one of Erasmus's epistles. The illustrations, though not without their interest, are, however, not very illuminating. Yet this section has at least this merit, that in discussing the necessity for sound and clear thinking as a preliminary to impressive speaking or writing, it has emphasized the intimate relation existing between subject-matter and effective utterance, and has thus recalled a stylistic principle of the first importance and of universal application.

Equally valuable, however, is his insistence on the need for an orderly arrangement of subject-matter in artistic compositions ; [1] and this, he suggests, is required by a law of Nature. ' All things stand by order ', he asserts,[2] ' and without order nothing can be.' Nature herself, for instance, every realm and government, craftsmen with their tools and armies in the field, all are said to obey the law of order ; and the same law is held to apply also in artistic matters. To ignore it, in short, is to be ineffective ; it is to lose direction, to grope and stumble, to repeat unnecessarily or else to omit. And in this connexion Wilson is even more explicit. He recalls, for instance, the seven-fold division traditionally assigned to an oration [3]—introduction, narration, proposition and the rest—and explains the reasons formerly given for such divisions. But while he thus submits the current doctrine he does not recommend a slavish adherence to any stereotyped formula. On the contrary he recognizes that form must vary with circumstances, that the speaker (or writer) must adopt methods in accordance with Nature or reason ; and with this idea in mind he has certain practical injunctions to offer. Thus he commends an Introduction in which a given theme is approached, either directly or indirectly, with a view to winning the attention and co-operation of the hearer (or reader) ; then a plain and intelligible statement with parts carefully articulated, to be followed by a Conclusion summing up the whole matter. Elsewhere he gives further advice as to the placing of arguments ; the strongest arguments first, with some reserved for an impressive ending.[4] Moreover,

[1] *Arte*, pp. 99–160.
[2] *ibid.* p. 156.
[3] *ibid.* pp. 7, 99 ff.
[4] *ibid.* p. 158.

he recognizes the value of some amount of amplification,[1] such
as the skilful introduction of occasional ' sentences ' or proverbs
to enforce an argument, or of amusing passages to lighten the
narrative ; while by no means irrelevant is his remark (drawn
from Plato) that ' the measuring of an oration standeth not in
the speaker but in the hearers '.[2]

So far eloquence has been shown to result from the employment of clear ideas skilfully arranged ; and now Wilson proceeds
to discuss the treatment of the medium, that is, words, by means
of which the thought expressed is commended to the hearers (or
readers). By the use of an attractive style, he states, ' reason
seemeth to be clad in purple, walking afore both bare and naked ' ;
and of the urgent need for the cultivation of style he is firmly
convinced. Many of his contemporaries, he explains,[3] can ' tell
their minds ' in English, yet few with any charm. Others, again,
seeking only knowledge, are said to be lacking in effective utterance ; they are like ' wealthy men who go with their hose out at
heels ' ; and such barbarous clerks he describes as ' slovens with
good gear who neither can nor will wear it cleanly '. To the
exposition of style he therefore devotes considerable attention,
as being the means necessary for winning and retaining attention,
and for presenting wisdom in attractive fashion ; and in his treatment he draws freely on ancient teaching, at the same time
making constant reference to English needs. He treats, first,
of words singly, then of words in combination ; and in so doing
he lays down as the main requirements for an effective style,
plainness and aptness in the choice of words, skilful composition
(i.e. arrangement) and ' exornation ' in their use in sentence-
form.

In his demand, in the first place, for plainness and aptness
in the choice of words, Wilson is in line with classical tradition
from Plato and Aristotle onwards. Concerning aptness or propriety, it is true, he has not much to say, except that the words
chosen must be in keeping with the subject and the occasion ;
though the principle involved is applied throughout the discussion.
It is, however, on the necessity for choosing plain words, native
words, and words understood by all, that his main emphasis is
laid. He demands clearness of expression as the first essential ;
and as a necessary corollary he insists that style must be based
on the speech of ordinary life. An orator (or writer), he argues,
aims at being understood ; he should therefore ' utter his mind
in plain words, such as are usually received, and tell it orderly
without going about the bush '.[4] And in support of this precept

[1] *Arte*, pp. 116 ff.   [2] *ibid.* p. 137.   [3] *ibid.* p. 161.   [4] *ibid.* p. 2.

Wilson recalls the methods of Phavorinus the philosopher, who (according to Gellius) ' did hit a young man over the thumbs very handsomely for using over-old and over-strange words '. As a further authority he also quotes the familiar dictum of Caesar that ' a strange or unusual word should be avoided as one would a rock '.[1] This general principle he then applies to contemporary conditions, recalling first the crazy literary fashions of his day—the French-English and English-Italianate of the much-travelled Englishman, the endless Chaucerisms of the ' fine courtier ', the enigmatic utterances of ' poetical clerks ', the inkhorn terms and crude Latinisms of those who ' but smelt of learning '.[2] All such affectations, continued Wilson, were to be vigorously condemned ; and he illustrates the heights to which absurdity could reach in the letter of the Lincolnshire man, the speeches of the Cambridge townsman and the municipal official, all of whom, in their attempts to speak better than they knew how, had larded their utterances with grotesque Latinisms. At the same time he notes that Greek and Latin forms might well be employed to extend and enrich the native vocabulary, provided they were properly used and had been approved by custom. For the rest, however, literary English was to be attained, not by overfine or outlandish diction, but by using the language of ordinary men and words that all could understand.

Turning then to the use of words in combination, or in sentence-form, he lays stress once again on the principles of clearness and fitness ; though he also alludes in passing to the harmonies underlying all good prose, but without enlarging on those subtle rhythmical effects expounded by both Cicero and Quintilian. His main object is thus limited to the correction of the more glaring faults in contemporary prose, those defects arising out of its sheer formlessness ; and with these he deals in detailed fashion.[3] He decries, for instance, those long unwieldy sentences with their hordes of clauses, of which the first parts were forgotten long before the ends were reached, and from which no clear thoughts could be said to emerge ; while on the other hand there were sentences much too short, so that an explanation of their meaning had necessarily to follow. Then, too, there were the misty oracular utterances of ' poetical ' writers, the disordered effusions of mere babblers, the preciosity of those who indulged in tedious repetitions of a word or an idea, or again in alliterative and rhyming effects ; while obscurity, ' dark as hell ', was said to result from the use of endless parentheses and

[1] Aulus Gellius, *Noctes Atticae*, i. 10, 4.   [2] *Arte*, p. 162.
[3] *ibid.* pp. 166–9.

digressions. Here, again, an attempt was made by condemning current excesses to introduce order and good sense into English prose and to induce men to write well knowingly by exercising their judgments. As Wilson explained, in connexion with the use of rhyming sentences, ' certes there is a mean, and no reason to use any one thing at all times, seeing that nothing delighteth (be it never so good) that is always used '.

Yet clearness and fitness, he adds, are not the only qualities to be aimed at in employing words in combination. For an effective style an element of ' exornation ' or beauty was said to be needed ;[1] and this, he maintains, was provided by the ' goodly colours ' of rhetoric, by tropes and schemes (i.e. figures) which had come down from antiquity, all representing departures from the normal usage in speech (' vices used with propriety ', as Isidore had called them), and consisting originally of devices calculated to relieve tedium, to confer elegance and to add to expression elements of novelty and surprise. Already in antiquity, however, such ' ornaments ' had assumed a multitudinous character, with numerous divisions and sub-divisions ; and this multiplicity and confusion had been greatly increased by post-classical and later rhetoricians. Their importance also had been much exaggerated ; while they had often been represented as mere technical artifices to be mechanically applied. It is therefore not surprising to find that something of the same attitude as well as the earlier complications are still present in Wilson's treatment ; though he endeavours in some measure to rationalize for his countrymen the current teaching. Thus, on the one hand, he perpetuates the endless distinctions, the confusion of terms, tropes, colours, and the like ; and in general, his treatment is eclectic, with reminiscences of *Ad Herennium*, Cicero, Quintilian, and others. On the other hand, he gives to many of the devices English interpretations by way of simplifying his treatment ; he recognizes that many Latin artifices are not applicable to English, an uninflected language ; and he prides himself in places on his moderation in curtailing his list.

Of the actual details of Wilson's treatment of these figurative devices it is perhaps sufficient here to say that they follow the conventional lines. He submits, for instance, the usual groups, giving lists (with useful examples) of thirteen tropes,[2] twenty-seven figures of thought (or colours),[3] and nineteen figures of speech ;[4] and thus preserves in the main the earlier distinctions, according to which tropes involved changes of meaning, whereas

[1] *Arte*. pp. 169 ff.   [2] *ibid*. pp. 170–6.
[3] *ibid*. pp. 176–200.   [4] *ibid*. pp. 200–9.

figures (or schemes) consisted of artificial and ingenious patterns of thought and speech. In this way he explains the effects of many of the devices by which human emotion has always found artistic expression, the metaphor (or ' translation '), for instance, the simile, the hyperbole and the like ; he also throws light on the uses of other important figures such as antithesis, periphrasis, understatement, digression, apt repetition, or the rhetorical question ; while he also discusses more trivial devices, such as the addition or omission of syllables, as well as a host of subtle tricks of oratory which have but little bearing on literary work. He further makes mention of the traditional three style (high, middle, and low),[1] recommends a free use of figures in the ' high ' style and their omission from the ' low ' ; and, demanding that one style should be maintained throughout a given composition, he adds that ' comeliness ' should ever be the aim of the writer.

Such then is the main outline of Wilson's teaching on eloquence ; and as the first attempt in English to treat of style in its broader sense, it has a place of its own in English critical literature. Yet this by no means exhausts the interest of the work for modern readers. Scattered throughout its pages are numerous comments bearing on literary matters ; and these are of value for the light they throw on contemporary ideas of literature or on later literary developments. Not without its significance, for instance, is Wilson's exposition of the nature of the comic and the effects of wit and humour in literary expression ;[2] for here, as if recognizing that characteristic feature of the English genius, its deep-seated sense of the need for mingling the serious and the humorous, he has incidentally revealed some of the elements of comedy in general. Of the nature of laughter itself he wisely has but little to say. He recognizes that it may be invoked by a look, a gesture, or a foolish word aptly spoken ; but, as he is careful to add, ' to tell in plain words what laughter is . . . passeth my cunning '.[3] Its general causes he attributes (following Cicero [4]) to some deformity or defect in others, which may be either mental or physical in character ; though neither great vice nor yet great misery, he states, is a fit subject for ridicule. Folly or a lack of natural intelligence, on the other hand, he describes as fruitful sources of humour ; and in any event ridicule should be employed in the proper place and should be properly directed, moderation being always necessary, for crude jesting was distasteful. It is with wit in its modern sense, however, that he is specially concerned, with the mirth that

[1] *Arte*, pp. 169–70. [2] *ibid.* pp. 134–56.
[3] *ibid.* p. 135. [4] cf. Cicero *De orat.* ii. 236 ; Quin., *Inst. Or.* vi. 3.

arises from a distortion of the meaning of words. Thus wit, he
explains,[1] is occasioned by various devices ; by ambiguous
speech, by things said contrary to expectation, by puns and play
upon words, by understatement and overstatement, or again by
irony, as when a merry saying conceals a serious thought.
' Those jests are bitter ', he adds, ' which have a hidden meaning ' ; and in this form of wit Socrates and Sir Thomas More are
said to have excelled—the latter being described as ' a wonder
to all the world '.[2]

Then, too, not without its literary interest is the new conception of character-drawing which he submits in place of the
stereotyped methods of the medieval ' description '. According
to the medieval theory [3] a given personality was best described
by enumerating in a fixed order his moral and physical attributes,
including the smallest details of face, body, and dress. Now,
however, freer and more realistic methods are advocated, consisting not of a catalogue of qualities but of a vivid and animated
representation of significant details, the method involved, in
short, in the classical device, *enargeia*,[4] commended by both
Cicero and Quintilian. At the same time, it is true, Wilson
suggests that increased verisimilitude would result from the
observance of ' types ' ; and he therefore recalls the stock distinctions associated with differences of nationality, age, sex, and
vocation.[5] Yet, even so, he is conscious of the existence of
individual traits in human personality ; and the short sketches
he submits of the characters of Henry VI and Richard III [6] are
not only free from the limitations of types, they also point the
way to a definite advance in character appreciation. In addition,
he shows that there need be nothing mechanical or stereotyped
in the treatment even of types. In his brief but delightful
sketch of ' the covetous man ' [7] he indicates yet another method
of character delineation ; and in this sense he anticipates that
character-literature of the 17th Century, of which Overbury and
Earle were the main exponents.

Nor are these the only places in Wilson's work that have
a wider literary bearing. The later Euphuistic fashion, for
instance, is already foreshadowed when he recommends the use
of similes and metaphors drawn from natural history to amplify,
to beautify, and to illuminate normal expression. ' Brute
beasts ', he explains,[8] ' minister great occasion of right good

[1] *Arte*, pp. 139 ff.   [2] *ibid*. p. 147.
[3] See Atkins, *Engl. Lit. Crit. Med.*, pp. 103–4, 199.
[4] *Arte*, p. 178.   [5] *ibid*. p. 179.   [6] *ibid*.
[7] *ibid*. p. 187.   [8] *ibid*. p. 191.

matter, considering many of them have shewed unto us the patterns and images of divers virtues '; and his teaching is illustrated by examples culled from stories of 'doves, cranes, lions, dragons, and the rest. Equally interesting, however, are the views he expresses concerning poetry. It is clear, for one thing, that he still cherishes the medieval conception of that art as essentially allegorical and esoteric in kind. 'There is no one tale among all the poets ', he writes, ' but under the same is comprehended something that pertains to the amendment of manners, to the knowledge of the truth and to the setting forth of Nature's work ' ;[1] and he further explains that poets wrote in this allegorical fashion for the initiated alone, ' so that none might understand but those unto whom they pleased to utter their meaning '. Then, too, worth noting in this connexion is the fact that he shares in the common Humanistic prejudice against rhyme ; and this, apparently, for reasons of his own. He rightly condemns its excessive use in contemporary prose, particularly in pulpit oratory, as is shown by his remarks on the figures *similiter desinens* and *similiter cadens* ;[2] though he also recalls St. Augustine's successful use of such devices. But what is of special interest is the account he gives of its nature and history. To him rhyme was nothing more than a wanton and specious device. It was part of the ' minstrel's elocution ', fostered by such ' minstrel makers ' as Apuleius, Ausonius, and others, until finally ' the Popes (seeing the people's folly to be such) made all our hymns and anthems in rhyme, that with the singing of men, playing of organs, ringing of bells and rhyming of hymns and sequences, the poor ignorant might think the harmony to be heavenly '.[3] Such an explanation differed vastly from those of Ascham and others ; and Marston, it might be added, later on ridiculed this prejudice against bell-ringing when he wrote of

> The bells profane and not to be endured
> Because to Popish rites they were inured.[4]

And lastly, not without its significance is the light Wilson throws on the disrepute into which the earlier romances had fallen. That later on they had become subject to popular ridicule is nowadays well known. But on Wilson's evidence the decline had already begun ; allusions to the Arthurian story, he states, were in his day fruitful sources of merriment, and ' to dub a man a knight of the Round Table ' afforded excellent sport.[5]

Of the many-sided interest of Wilson's *Arte of Rhetorique*

[1] *Arte*, p. 195. [2] *ibid*. pp. 202–3. [3] *ibid*. p. 203.
[4] Marston, *Works*, ed. Bullen, iii. 282. [5] *Arte*, p. 145.

there can therefore be no doubt ; and its claim to be reckoned among the more significant of Elizabethan critical works cannot well be challenged. In the revival of rhetorical studies in 16th-Century England it occupies the central position. It was an attempt to correct the current notion that ' rhetoric stood wholly upon dark words ', and, further, to introduce form and comeliness into English prose, not only by insisting on the purity of written English but also by revealing some of the broader principles of all good writing ; and in these tasks Wilson was eminently successful. He makes use where possible of the teaching of the ancients ; but his ultimate guide throughout is Nature or reason. Apart from this, the work is something more than a mere formal Rhetoric. Despite its somewhat lengthy and discursive treatment, it was calculated to appeal to cultured readers by reason of its good sense, its rich humanity, its abundant classical lore, and the wit and wisdom enshrined in those apophthegms, proverbs, and anecdotes in which the age delighted. And if we may judge from the numerous editions which subsequently appeared, the work was widely circulated and was not without its influence, more especially as it represented the teaching of a well-known and distinguished scholar-statesman of the time.

Nor is it altogether fanciful to add that Shakespeare in all probability knew the work well and was indebted to its pages for stray suggestions and ideas.[1] It is not only that he frequently tilts at the pedantry of rhetoricians. The pleasantries underlying Holofernes's use of technical terms,[2] for instance, or again, the string of questions in Don Armado's letter to Jacquenetta,[3] these and similar jests might well have been Shakespeare's reaction to any one of the contemporary rhetorical hand-books. What, however, is significant are the number and variety of details in his works which are reminiscent of passages in Wilson's treatise. Thus Dogberry is foreshadowed in Wilson's town-official and his blundering interview with ' the yngrame and vacation knave ' ;[4] while certain aspects of Falstaff are suggested by Wilson's roystering gentleman, ' a man of good years and much authority.[5] Then, too, those Sonnets (1–17) of Shakespeare which treat of persuasion to marriage, his famous speech on Order (*T. and C.* i. iii. 84 ff.), his enumeration of national characteristics (*M. of V.* i. ii. 39 ff.), his choice of Timon as the subject of one of his plays, or again, his reference to grafting (*W.T.* iv. iii. 88 ff.) and his use of the antithesis between the

---

[1] See Mair, *op. cit.* xxxiii–iv.   [2] *L.L.L.* iv. ii.
[3] *ibid.* iv. i. 61 ff. ; cf. *Arte*, p. 22.   [4] *Arte*, p. 164.   [5] *ibid.* pp. 122–3.

ploughman's happy state and the cares of a king (*Hen. V.* IV.
i. 257), suggestions for all these details may be found in Wilson's
work ;[1] and their evidence, which is cumulative in kind, points
with some likelihood to Shakespeare's indebtedness, whether
conscious or unconscious, and to his appreciation of some of the
good things in what is after all not the least readable and suggestive of Elizabethan writings.

Less direct as a contribution to rhetorical studies, but nevertheless of first-rate importance, is the *Scholemaster* [2] (1570) of
Roger Ascham (1515–68), a work on education primarily (Bk. I),
but which also treated of sound methods of writing (Bk. II),
and thus represents a contribution to the theory of style in
general. Written towards the close of the author's life but left
uncompleted, the treatise was intended for courtly circles (*aulus
non academicus*), as Ascham himself explained to Sturm,[3] and
has since become more or less familiar to modern readers, not
only by its sound pedagogy, but also by its vivid reminiscences
of contemporary life and its autobiographical details. A distinguished member of Cheke's circle at Cambridge and Public
Orator (1546), Ascham afterwards became tutor to Princess
Elizabeth (1548–9), travelled in Germany and Italy as Secretary
to the English ambassador (1550–3), was appointed Latin Secretary by Queen Mary (1553–8), while under Elizabeth he retained
his position at court as Secretary and tutor ; and many of these
experiences are reflected in his ' sweet remembrances ' of his
Cambridge days, in the gracious vignettes of Lady Jane Grey
and Elizabeth as scholars, or again, in his sweeping condemnation
of Italian influences and the Italianate Englishman. For our
present purpose, however, the work is chiefly notable for its
judgments on literary matters ; for its comments on rhetorical
theory, its considered views on the best methods of imitating the
writers of antiquity, for sundry remarks on medieval romances
and current methods of versifying and for occasional attempts
at literary appreciation. Latin style, it is true, is the subject
discussed throughout ; but the discussion has also its wider
bearings, and Ascham's interest in the writing of English is
everywhere apparent. His deliberate use of the vernacular, for
instance, in *Toxophilus* (1545) and in the *Scholemaster* was highly
significant ; while his confidence in its future was shown when in
writing to Sir William Cecil in 1548 he urged him to cultivate
the English tongue, ' so that men might understand that even

[1] cf. pp. 39, 157, 179, 55, 48, 178
[2] *Works of R. Ascham*, ed. Giles, iii. pp. 63 ff.
[3] See *Works*, ii. p. 176 (*Letter*, 1568).

7

our language allows a man to write in it with beauty and eloquence '.

For Ascham's contribution to rhetorical theory, in the first place, we must look to various remarks scattered throughout his works, rather than for the systematic treatment of a formal Rhetoric ; and in this casual fashion he will be found to recall not a few of the elementary principles bound up with the classical conception of eloquence. Thus he notes, for instance, the preliminary requirements for success in any art ; and in prescribing in *Toxophilus* ' aptness, knowledge, and use ' he is renewing the familiar demands of the Platonic trinity, namely, *natura, ars*, and *exercitatio*. Then, too, in opposition to the medieval conception of eloquence as merely ornate language, he now emphasizes the basic need for having clear ideas and something definite to say. He refers to both Plato and Horace for support of his teaching ; and adds, later on, that in ancient classical literature ' wisdom and eloquence, good matter and good utterance, were never or seldom asunder '.[1] Elsewhere he is found insisting on the need for ' the right choice of words ' and ' the right framing of sentences '; and concerning a proper vocabulary he, like most of his contemporaries, has rather more to say. Thus he reminds his readers of Cicero's statement that ' a right choice of words (according to Caesar) is the foundation of eloquence ' ; [2] in *Toxophilus* he asserts that ' he that will write well in any tongue must follow the counsel of Aristotle, to speak as the common people do, to think as wise men do ' ; [3] and, further, observing that ' many English writers, using strange words as Latin, French and Italian, do make all things dark and hard ', he condemns the result, as he would a nauseating mixture of wines, as ' neither easy to be known, nor yet wholesome for the body '. In yet another place he calls attention to the need for the observance of fitness or *decorum* as all-embracing. ' To understand what . . . is *nimium, satis, parum* ', he allows, ' is the hardest point in all learning ' ; but this, he adds, should be the aim of all writers.[4]

Not less interesting, however, are his remarks of a more particular and practical kind, which reveal by their soundness the wise judgment of the experienced tutor. The exercise of

[1] *Works* iii. p. 211.
[2] *ibid.* p. 88 ; cf. Cicero, *Brutus*, lxxvii. 253.
[3] *ibid.* ii. p. 7, also iii. p. 265, *Loquendum ut multi, sapiendum ut pauci ;* cf. Roger Bacon, *opus Majus*, i. 4. *Quare Philosophus dicit in secundo Topicorum, quod sentiendum est ut pauci, licet loquendum sit ut plures,—* probably a generalization of Aristotle : cf. *Topica*, ii. 110, as suggested by W. Aldis Wright in his edition of the *Advancement of Learning*, p. 308.
[4] *ibid.* iii. p. 185.

paraphrase, for instance, he definitely condemns. 'A matter well-expressed ', he states,[1] ' was not to be altered '; and to attempt a fresh rendering of some utterance already perfect was, in the words of the younger Pliny, *audax contentio*. On the other hand he urges a plentiful use of the file, and recalls Virgil's practice (according to Donatus) of polishing his daily output of forty or fifty verses until he had reduced them to the number of ten or twelve.[2] ' Twenty to one ', he maintained, ' offend more in writing too much than too little '; and ready speakers, he added, were not usually the plainest and wisest of writers, since they did not trouble to judge or weigh their words. At the same time exuberant and over-elaborate expression was to be condoned in youth, though discretion should come later ; [3] and here Ascham was repeating the earlier advice of both Cicero and Quintilian. Finally, as if conscious of the limitations of all artistic precepts, he supplies a suggestive note on beauty as a by-product of all activities. ' Comeliness ', he states,[4] ' can never be taught by any art or craft ', adding further that what is most effectively done in all matters is also ' most comely done '. And here once again he is reiterating the teaching of Cicero, to the effect that ' those things which have the greatest utility have also the greatest dignity and beauty '.[5]

It is, however, with one particular rhetorical doctrine, namely, that of ' imitation ' as an aid to good writing, that Ascham's most valuable work was done. It had been lightly touched upon by Wilson ; and Ascham's discussion of that much-debated, much-distorted theory is important as representing the English contribution to the European controversy then raging. The doctrine itself was nothing new. Isocrates had been the first to suggest the importance of example or model for acquiring skill in writing ; and subsequently at Rome the process had become generally recognized in both theory and practice. By later Humanists, however, it had been seriously narrowed and perverted ; and the merits of Ascham's performance lay in his modification of current conceptions by attaching to the doctrine something at least of its earlier meaning and vitality. For the theory in its original form we must look to critics of 1st-Century Rome—to Cicero and Horace, to Dionysius of Halicarnassus, ' Longinus ' and Quintilian [6]—by whom the process was conceived of in no narrow or constricting sense. To Dionysius, for instance, ' imitation ' was an activity of the soul inspired by the

---

[1] *ibid.* pp. 182 ff. [2] *ibid.* pp. 207 ff.
[3] *ibid.* p. 203. [4] *Works*, ii. p. 139. [5] cf. Cicero, *De orat.* iii. 178.
[6] See Atkins, *Lit. Crit. in Antiquity*, ii *passim*.

spectacle of the seemingly beautiful ; to ' Longinus ', again, it was a process of the spirit, the outcome of an imaginative stimulus derived from works of genius ; while all were agreed that it was something more than a slavish or mechanical copying of words or technical details. What it stood for was an attempt to recapture the spirit of earlier models, to assimilate their details, to adapt and develop their artistic methods ; and while the best writers alone were to be imitated, they were also to be imitated with judgment and discernment. Nor was such ' imitation ' merely an end in itself. It was intended to assist in the development of a writer's native powers, to help in the discovery of fresh effects, and to evolve something new out of the old by adapting earlier methods. It was, in short, neither mere borrowing nor mere copying, but a sort of re-creation, a process calculated to lead ultimately to originality of expression.

Such then was the sane and inspiring conception of ' imitation ' formulated in ancient Rome ; and Ascham's interest in the doctrine is shown by the fact that he devotes one-fourth of his treatise to the discussion, while at the same time corresponding with his friend Sturm, the Strasburg Humanist, for advice on the subject. He himself was convinced that in Greek and Latin classics alone could be found the true patterns of eloquence, ' if in any other mother tongue we look to attain either to perfect utterance of it ourselves or skilful judgment of it in others '.[1] On the other hand he was conscious of perplexity as to the best methods of utilizing those patterns. As ' a looker-on in the cock-pit of learning ', so he explains,[2] ' he had noted that many men had written with much diversity ' on the subject, and latterly, ' with some stomach among themselves ' ; and he now submits his views in tentative and imperfect (inchoate) fashion, views still unformed and somewhat confused, but not without their definite value. Moreover, his urgency in the matter he also explains to his friend Sturm. Considerable opposition to the idea of thus utilizing the classics, he states, had come recently from those who wished to rely on the guidance of Nature alone. But that, he argues,[3] was to deprive Nature of the most valuable assistance, to make a discord between Nature and art ; and besides, it was significant that many famous teachers of old— ' Demetrius, Halicarnassus, Hermogenes, Cicero and Quintilian ' —had unanimously commended the process with the utmost zeal and confidence.

In therefore submitting his views on the problem Ascham begins by reminding his readers not only of the teaching of

[1] *Works*, iii. p. 239.   [2] *ibid.* p. 219.   [3] *ibid.* p. 184.

the ancients, but also of the varied pronouncements of later Humanists, including Erasmus, Longolius, Budaeus, Melanchthon, Cortesi, Bembo, Ricci, and Sturm ; and in addition, he recalls the assistance rendered in other ways by Henri Estienne, Victorius, and Hessus. His list though not complete is sufficient to show the widespread interest aroused by the matter in Italy, France, and Germany ; it also suggests the confusion in which the whole question was enveloped at that date. Then, by way of clarifying the issue, Ascham distinguishes between the 'imitation' which implied 'a following of the best authors', and that other doctrine of 'imitation' bound up with Cicero's definition of comedy as an imitation or reflexion of human life.[1] With this latter doctrine, however, he states that he was not concerned. He merely notes that it had been treated by Plato in his *Republic* ; and it is significant that neither here nor elsewhere does Ascham show any acquaintance with Aristotle's more philosophical interpretation of the term as the creative process by which the poet is enabled to reveal truth of an ideal or universal kind. At the same time he is puzzled by a further use made by Plato of the term 'imitation'. When Socrates in the *Republic*, for instance, transforms the Homeric speech of Chryses into elegant prose,[2] Plato describes it as an example of μίμησις ; though this, in Ascham's opinion, involved further technical confusion and was merely an instance of the process known as metaphrasis.[3]

With 'imitation' thus defined as 'a following of the best authors', Ascham proceeds with his criticism of earlier Humanistic expositions of the doctrine. In the first place he notes that recent writers had concentrated mostly on one point only, namely, whether one or more models were to be adopted in cultivating a correct style—an obvious reference to the absorbing interest betrayed in the question of Ciceronianism. In general he maintains that the best authors alone were to be followed ; and 'in eloquence', he adds, 'you must follow choicely a few and chiefly some one'.[4] And as an example of the successful imitation of several models he observes how Cicero had reproduced the varied stylistic excellences of Plato and Xenophon, Demosthenes, Isocrates and Aristotle.[5] At the same time he held strongly to the notion of an ideal classical period, from which period alone Latin models might safely be drawn. He quotes Velleius Paterculus to the effect that perfection in art endures but for a time

---

[1] *Works*, iii. p. 213. [2] *Iliad*, i. 12–42 : *Republic*, 393.
[3] *Works*, iii. pp. 193–4. [4] *ibid.* pp. 238–9.
[5] *ibid.* p. 227.

and is inevitably followed by a period of decline and decay.[1] And in the light of this theory he maintains that Latin eloquence in its purity lasted for scarcely a hundred years, that is, 'from the time of the last Scipio Africanus to the empire of Augustus'. On reviewing the writings of that particular period, however, he is forced to the conclusion that one author alone afforded fit models for imitation in prose. In the styles of Plautus and Terence, in Varro, Sallust, and Caesar he finds faults and short-comings of various kinds; [2] and in commending Cicero alone as the one suitable model he conforms with the orthodox teaching of his time, though not with the narrow interpretation insisted on by the Ciceronians.

Of greater significance, however, and of first-rate importance, is Ascham's discussion of the wider possibilities of 'imitation', when, suggesting that, so far from being limited to style alone, it had also a bearing on literary creation in general, he further insists on the necessity for understanding its true nature and methods. He points out, to begin with, that the process had been employed by most of the great Latin writers; that Virgil, for instance, had been indebted to Homer, Cicero to Demosthenes, Horace to Pindar, Terence to Menander, while Seneca and Livy also owed much to Euripides and Polybius respectively.[3] More-over, this indebtedness, he adds, had not escaped the notice of scholars; for Macrobius long ago had detected Virgil's borrow-ings, more recently Ricci and Hessus had contributed to the same studies, and Victorius in his *Variae Lectiones* (1553) had collected a vast number of parallel passages taken from Greek and Latin authors.[4] For a true appreciation of the process of 'imitation', however, this was not enough. It was necessary, Ascham con-tended, to understand how 'imitation' was effected. And this, he suggested, was best achieved by a study of Virgil's methods in following Homer; by noting first what Homeric details he had borrowed, his omissions and additions, his modifications and re-orderings of Homeric material; and then considering the reason for each step in his procedure.[5] From this it would be seen that 'imitation' in the true sense consisted not in the indiscriminate borrowing of incidents, phrases or diction; still less in the slavish and mechanical copying of verbal or structural details. Its essence lay rather in the considered and rational use of a given model, in a process in which artistic instincts and artistic judgment were constantly at work; and its nature, he

---

[1] *Works*, iii. pp. 244-5.   [2] *ibid*. pp. 246 ff.
[3] *ibid*. pp. 214 *et passim*.   [4] *ibid*. p. 228.
[5] *ibid*. p. 215; see also Letter to Sturm.

states more than once, would more fitly be described as reproduction or refashioning (*exprimere* or *effingere*) rather than as
mere copying (*imitari*).[1] The doctrine thus outlined was due to
Sturm, as Ascham gratefully acknowledged. By Sturm 'imitation' was defined as 'a vehement and artistic application of the
mind', which judiciously used and transfigured all that it
imitated ; and a full and reasoned account appeared later in his
De imitatione (1574).[2] A similar work by Ascham was un-
happily forestalled by his death ; but in the meantime he had
succeeded in recalling something of the ancient process commended by Roman critics which had produced enduring results
in Latin literature.

Apart from these remarks on rhetorical theory, and on
'imitation' in particular, of interest too are Ascham's occasional
comments on literature in general for the light they throw upon
ideas and standards current in English scholarly circles well into
the second half of the 16th Century. Significant, in the first
place, is Ascham's classification of literature, derived from Sir
John Cheke, according to which the differentiae of the traditional
'kinds'—poetry, history, philosophy, and oratory—lay in their
differences of style (*per diversa genera dicendi*), that is, in differences of vocabulary, in their use of figures and the rest ; while
further differences of style were said to distinguish the various
sub-divisions of each 'kind'—comedy, tragedy, epic, and lyric,
for instance, the several sub-divisions or 'species' of poetry.[3]
Such a classification points clearly to the strength of the rhetorical
tradition at this date. Reminiscent in one sense of the pre-
Aristotelian classification of poetry on a basis of verse-form, it
also suggests how slight was the influence on English scholars
of the new Aristotelian theory that was being expounded at the
time in Italy.

Equally interesting, however, are Ascham's stray remarks
on poetry, and the indication they give of the imperfect grasp
of Humanists on the true nature and status of that art. It is
true that his object in writing his *Scholemaster* was 'to teach a
young scholar to go, not to dance, to speak, not to sing' ; the
singing and dancing school, he suggests, should come later.[4]
Yet there is also something of disparagement and patronage in
his attitude to poetry, as a pursuit hardly suited for more serious
minds. 'Quick wits' he describes as superficial rather than

---

[1] *ibid.* p. 227.
[2] See also Sturm, *Nobilitas Literata*, translated by T. B. Gent (1570),
as *A Rich Storehouse or Treasury*.
[3] *Works*, iii. p. 240.   [4] *ibid.* p. 259.

profound, with restless minds that found delight in easy and pleasant studies ; and these, he adds, ' may commonly prove the best poets.'[1] Apart from this, he confesses that he himself had no head for poetry ;[2] while his approval of Galen's dictum that ' much music marreth men's manners '[3] is highly suggestive in itself. Nevertheless, despite these disabilities, what he has to say on poetry, though slight, is of interest ; and, for one thing, it is noteworthy that he, like Wilson, subscribes to the medieval conception of poetry as essentially allegorical in kind. Thus in defending archery in *Toxophilus* by an appeal to the authority of ancient poets he maintains that ' poets oftentimes under the covering of a fable do hide and wrap in goodly precepts of philosophy ' ;[4] though he is at fault in his further assertion that Plato and Aristotle ' through all their works had determined all controversies ' by references to Homer, Euripides, and others. Of the different forms of poetry he has but little to say ; yet his remarks on tragedy and comedy are of interest as showing that with him the medieval conceptions of those forms were being supplanted by those of antiquity—a development which will be more conveniently considered at a later stage.[5]

On certain questions relating to the vernacular literature he also has definite and characteristic views. Thus he shares, for instance, in the Humanistic blindness to the merits of the medieval romances, those ' books of chivalry, as some say, made in monasteries by idle monks and wanton canons '. In such books, he asserts, ' those be counted the noblest knights that do kill most men without any quarrel and commit foulest adulteries by subtlest shifts ' ; and in Malory's *Morte Arthur* he can see little else than ' open manslaughter and bold bawdry '.[6] Then, too, he joins Wilson in his attack on the ' rude beggarly rhyming ' verse which had persisted from medieval times. Unlike Wilson, however, he vaguely attributes it to the Goths and Huns who are said to have introduced it into Italy during the Dark Ages, from whence it spread to France, then to Germany and finally to England [7]—a flight of fancy even more remote from the truth than Wilson's account had been. His scorn for rhyme, he asserts, was no new thing ; it was said to have been characteristic of ancient times, though Ascham is unfortunate in the instances he cites. Thus he recalls a book of so-called rhyming Greek verse, entitled ᾠόν (the egg) which had been written by Simmias of Rhodes and was assigned to the great age of Greece.[8] This book,

---

[1] *Works*, iii. p. 98.   [2] *ibid.* p. 172.   [3] *ibid.* p. 180.
[4] *Works*, ii. pp. 32–3.   [5] See pp. 222 *infra*.
[6] *Works*, iii. p. 159.   [7] *ibid* .p. 249.   [8] *ibid.* p. 253.

he states, had been read by few, while none was found to imitate its eccentric verses, until the folly was repeated by the Goths and the Huns. The work thus referred to was, however, no product of classical Greece ; it belonged to the Hellenistic age, was not written in rhyming verses, but represented one of those fantastic figure-poems in which that ingenious age delighted. Nor is Ascham more convincing in his statement concerning Quintilian, who is said to have ' inveighed against all rhyming '.[1] In the passage in question, however, Quintilian is discussing oratory and censures the use of successive sentences ending in similar cadences, terminations or inflexions ; in other words, he is merely condemning an excessive use of rhyming sentences in prose, as Wilson after him had done. The truth is that Ascham's attack on rhyming verse was inspired solely by Humanistic prejudice and by his zeal for the newly-recovered glories of ancient literature. He therefore recommends the abandonment of ' rude and barbarous rhyming ' and the adoption of the ancient classical system of versification. To do otherwise, he states, was to continue ' to eat acorns with swine when we might freely eat wheat bread amongst men '.[2]

Concerning this ' true order of versifying ', however, Ascham has something more to say. He concedes that Chaucer, Surrey, Wyatt, and others had achieved all that could be effected by rhyme ; but he regrets that they had not chosen the better way of his Cambridge friend, Watson, who in his unpublished translation of the *Odyssey* (1540–50) had shown how the hexameter might be employed in English. He further quotes by way of illustration the doggerel lines.

All travellers do gladly report great praise of Ulysses,
For that he knew many men's manners and saw many cities.[3]

and unwisely challenges comparison with their Greek and Latin equivalents. From the first he shrewdly recognizes that the hexameter presented some difficulties in English (a fact borne out by later experience) owing to the prevalence of monosyllables in that language and the rarity of the dactyl, ' the aptest foot for that verse '.[4] But while realizing that hexameter verse ' doth rather trot and hobble than run smoothly in English ', he was also confident that *carmen iambicum* might successfully be naturalized, provided that ' just measure in every metre and true quantity in every foot and syllable ' were duly observed.[5]

[1] *ibid.* p. 250 ; cf. Quintilian *Inst. Or.* ix. 4, 42.
[2] *ibid.* p. 250 ; cf. Cicero, *Orator*, ix. 31.
[3] *ibid.* p. 150.   [4] *ibid.* p. 250.   [5] *ibid.* p. 252.

This then was the ' new versifying ' recommended by Ascham.
The old fourteener line and the ballad measure with their ' lewd
and rude ' rhymes were to be abandoned for verse of a quantitative
kind, just as Virgil had adopted Greek metres in place of the
old measures of Ennius and Plautus. What Ascham failed to
recognize was that in the blank verse of Surrey's translation of
the *Aeneid* (1557) such innovation as the genius of the language
permitted had already been made—an innovation, moreover,
which time was ultimately to confirm. In that verse, as Ascham
allowed, the fault of rhyming had been avoided, just number
and even feet had been observed, but not true quantity of
syllables ; and without such observance of quantity the verse
to him was ' deformed, unnatural and lame '.[1] Such was the
gist of Ascham's proposals for the improvement of English verse ;
and it is perhaps worth noting that they formed part of a wider
European movement. Ascham, it is true, rejoices that ' even
poor England had prevented Italy ' [2] in this matter ; but already
in 1539 an organized attempt to introduce classical metres into
the vernacular had been made by Tolomei in Italy, and before
1570 Sibilet, Ramus, J. de la Taille, and Baïf had also been at
work in France.[3] While therefore Ascham as the first champion
of the cause in England doubtless gave a lead to later English
theorists, the influence of foreign advocates cannot altogether
be overlooked.

In the discussions on rhetoric, ' imitation ', and versifying
which have now been outlined, may be said to be comprised
Ascham's main contribution to critical activities. At the same
time brief reference must finally be made to certain judicial
comments in his works which have the merit of reflecting contemporary literary taste and methods of appreciation. Not
without its interest, for example, is his comparison of the values
of Greek and Latin tragedy. ' Sophocles and Euripides ', he
writes,[4] ' far overmatch our Seneca in Latin, namely in οἰκονομία
et decoro ; though Seneca's elocution and verse be very commendable for his time.' On the other hand his limitations as
a judicial critic are seen in his pronouncement on contemporary
tragedy, to the effect that Watson's *Absalon* and Buchanan's
Jephthe alone ' were able to abide the true touch of Aristotle's
precepts and Euripides's examples '.[5] In his somewhat shrewd
judgment on Erasmus's achievement, which was said to be
satirical rather than constructive, he is more successful. ' More

---

[1] *Works*, iii. p. 254.   [2] *ibid*. p. 255.
[3] See Spingarn, *Lit. Crit. in the Renaissance*, pp. 222, 298, &c.
[4] *Works*, iii. p. 228.   [5] *ibid*. p. 241.

occupied ', states Ascham,[1] ' in spying other men's faults than declaring his own advice, he is mistaken of many, to the great hurt of his study. For he writeth rightly, rightly understanded.' Then, too, his remarks on Chaucer are also worth noting. To the old English poet he offers the conventional praise due to the ' English Homer ',[2] adding that ' I ever thought his sayings to have as much authority as either Sophocles or Euripides '. As yet, however, it is evident that Chaucer's real qualities are not adequately appreciated. He is valued primarily for his moral teaching, his warning against gambling, for instance, in the *Pardoner's Tale* ; [3] though elsewhere he is also praised for his skill in character-drawing. In his lively descriptions of persons, so states Ascham,[4] he revealed not merely external or physical attributes but ' the inward disposition of the mind ' as well— a judgment which marked a notable advance in Chaucer-criticism at this date.

It is from Cheke, however, that Ascham derives his most illuminating judgment, one of the first-fruits of that Cambridge teaching which had aimed at understanding and appreciating literature, rather than at a mere cultivation of style. And Cheke's appreciation of Sallust, preserved in the *Scholemaster*,[5] is notable for its enlightened methods which carry on the earlier tradition of Colet and Erasmus in their Biblical criticisms. Cheke's treatment, it is true, is limited to Sallust's style alone, which is described with illustrative detail as artificial, obscure, replete with archaisms, coinages and Greek idioms, and characterized generally by ' an uncontented care to write better than he could '. What distinguishes the criticism, however, is the attempt at explaining the facts psychologically by an analysis of the historical causes—a process possibly suggested by Sallust's own philosophical approach to history. Thus the obscurity and artificiality of Sallust's style is ascribed partly to the influence of Thucydides and Cato, but partly also to the conditions under which he wrote. Removed in Africa from the common haunts and speech of Roman life, he is said to have developed in consequence a bookish style which lacked the common touch as well as the naturalness and perspicuity needed for success in the Forum. The appreciation is by no means complete ; but it is highly suggestive and represents something new in literary judgment. Nor does Ascham fail to apply such methods in pointing out for instance the merits of More's *History*

[1] *ibid.* p. 221. [2] *Works*, ii. p. 42.
[3] ll. 263 ff.: see. [4] *Letter to J. Astley* (1552) ; see *Works*, iii. 6.
[5] *Works*, iii. pp. 264 ff.

of Richard III.[1]   He explains that he had learnt from his reading of Livy the qualities necessary for success in writing history. They included a regard for truth, vivid characterization, a style varying with the subject-matter, but ' ever open and plain ', and in addition, a philosophical approach involving inquiries into the causes of things, ' after the example of Polybius in Greek and Philip Comines in French '. And Sir Thomas More, he maintains, in ' that pamphlet of Richard the Third doth in most part . . . of all these points content all men '.

Such then were the contributions of Wilson and Ascham to those rhetorical studies which represented the main body of critical work at this date.   It yet remains, however, to recall sundry remarks of other writers of this early Tudor period which go to supplement this performance by occasional comments on what at the time were very real and urgent problems, namely, the claims of the vernacular to recognition as the literary medium and how best to improve its power of expression, or again, the need for a better understanding of the nature and value of poetry. In the first place, of the reality of the vernacular problem at this date there can be no doubt.   It is true that, from pre-Conquest times onwards, English had been employed, and successfully employed, for literary purposes.   But it was not before the 14th Century that it had triumphed over medieval Latin as the accepted medium, when a standard dialect emerged from the dialects of the medieval period,—a triumph that had been instinctive rather than the outcome of explicit reasoning!   Then at the later Revival of Learning the challenge of Latin was once more renewed for obvious reasons, and now with added force. According to Bishop Gardiner, for instance, all religious works were to be written in either Greek or Latin, languages well established, whereas ' English had not continued in one form of understanding for two hundred years '.   Again, ' our learned men hold opinion ', so wrote Sir Thomas Hoby,[2] ' that to have the sciences in the mother-tongue hurteth memory and hindereth learning '.   And while Ascham was not alone in thinking that to have written the *Scholemaster* in Latin would have been more ' honest ' for his good name, Bacon, years later, was still lamenting that ' these modern languages would play the bankrupt with books '.   The truth was that throughout the first half of the 16th Century Latin was still generally regarded as the sole vehicle of deeper thought and therefore the literary language of all learned men.   At the same time with the rapid growth of

---

[1] *Letter to J. Astley* (1552) ; see *Works*, iv. p. 6.
[2] Preface to his translation of *The Courtier* (1561).

national consciousness the claims of the vernacular were becoming more definite and insistent ; and the clash of values gave rise to critical comment. The case for the vernaculars had been presented two centuries previously by Dante in his *De vulgari eloquentia*, later on by Bembo and others in Italy and by the Pléiade in France. Now, however, the problem was being seriously faced for the first time in England ; and the results, so far from being empty platitudes, were a significant contribution to literary theorizing at a critical stage in the development of English literature.

Of the characteristic Humanistic attitude to the vernacular question something has already been said ; [1] and for the treatment of the matter by English scholars we must look mainly to discussions that arose in connexion with the work of translation. Already in the Prologue to the translation of Terence's *Andria* (1520) attributed to John Rastell, friend of Sir Thomas More, direct reference is made to the development of the English language and its use in literature ; and at the same time confidence is expressed in its high destiny as a literary medium.[2] It was in connexion with Biblical translation, however, that the question was more widely and strenuously debated ; and Tyndale, following Colet and Erasmus, became the leading advocate of a Bible in the vernacular. For this he claimed ample authority, seeing that the Old Testament had first been written in the language of the Hebrews, that the Apostles had also preached in their native language, while Jerome later on had translated the Bible into Latin, his mother tongue.[3] In addition, he urged, not without some daring, that English, so far from being a barbarous dialect, had qualities of its own, qualities indeed that challenged comparison even with those of Latin. Moreover, as he explained, ' the Greek tongue agreeth more with the English than with Latin, and the properties of the Hebrew tongue agreeth a thousand times more with English than with the Latin '. The manner of speaking, he adds, is much the same in both Hebrew and English, so that ' in a thousand places thou needst not but to translate it into the English word for word, when thou must seek a compass in the Latin '. And these were no idle comments but a reasoned statement of some of the properties of English as they appeared to one with a keen and critical sense of the genius of language. Nor were the objections raised by Sir Thomas More against Tyndale's translation of the *New Testament*

[1] See pp. 53 ff. *supra*.
[2] See E. J. Sweeting, *Early Tudor Criticism*, pp. 132–3.
[3] *Obedience of a Christian Man* (1528), pp. 144 ff.

(1525) concerned with the merits of the vernacular as such. His scruples were rather of a theological kind. His contention was that Tyndale in translating ' priests ' as ' seniors ', ' church ' as ' congregation ', ' charity ' as ' love ', had inadequately rendered certain words to which, by ecclesiastical authority, definite meanings had become attached ; and that in thus failing to adopt the vocabulary of common usage he had distorted the meaning of the passages in question.[1] For the rest, however, More was strongly convinced of the possibilities of English as a literary language ; and he replies in convincing fashion to current objections concerning its crudity and inadequacy. To describe English as ' barbarous ', he retorts,[2] ' is but a fantasy ; for so is . . . every strange language to other '. Nor again could it be said to be deficient in vocabulary, since ' it was plenteous enough to express our minds ' on any subject. And this testimony of More was not without its influence on later scholars.

Meanwhile the problem of fitting the vernacular for its rôle as the literary medium was also being considered. When Elyot, for instance, declared that in writing his *Governour* he had aimed at ' augmenting our English tongue ', he was but voicing the ambition of many of his contemporaries and continuing in a sense the tradition of Lydgate and his aureate diction. Now, however, with the closer acquaintance with classical and other literatures the medieval passion for fine diction became somewhat modified ; though various attempts were still made at enriching the language by Latin borrowings, often coupled with their English equivalents,[3] as well as by the use of ' inkhorn ' terms, such as archaisms, coinages, Latin-English, English-Italianate and other mongrel forms. At the same time there were those who doubted the wisdom of this indiscriminate borrowing and who wished to preserve the language in its purity ; and of these Cheke was the leading exponent. Following the earlier example of Pecock in his use of native compounds, such as ' out-draught ' (extract), and ' before-crier ' (herald), Cheke avoids in his translation of St. Matthew's Gospel all Latin derivatives, and substitutes instead such artificial ' Saxon-English ' forms as ' tollers ' (publicans), ' crossed ' (crucified), and ' hundreder ' (centurion). These then were the prevailing tendencies, and the contemporary comments on the confusion that resulted are not without their interest. A similar situation, it might be noted, had arisen in Augustan Rome when the ' neoteric ' poets had indulged in excessive Greek borrowings,

---

[1] *Dialogue concerning Heresies* (1529), iii. cap. xvi.   [2] *ibid.*
[3] cf. Elyot's pairs : ' obfuscate or hyd ', ' adminiculation or aid '.

while the antiquarians stood for the preservation of words of an archaic kind. Horace had then provided the common-sense solution in maintaining the right of judicious borrowing, with *usus* or custom as the sole criterion ; and the same compromise between innovation and conservatism now suggested itself to English minds. Moreover this attitude was not altogether new ; for in earlier England, from the time of Bede onwards, protests had been raised against the use of affected and eccentric vocabularies.[1] Now, however, it was the considered policy of the leading authorities, Cheke, Wilson, and Ascham ; and in Cheke's famous letter to Sir Thomas Hoby [2] will be found the most judicious statement of that policy. In the main he contended that ' our tongue should be written clear, pure, unmixed and unmangled with borrowings of other tongues ', and that reliance should be placed primarily on native resources. At the same time he does not rule out borrowing altogether ; he recognizes that the language was imperfect and should be improved in various ways. Yet such borrowing, he urged, should be undertaken with ' bashfulness ', and preference given to words formed ' in the mould of our own tongue ' and to ' old-denizened words ' of the language, before resorting to the use of unknown words. It was, in short, a condemnation of contemporary licence, and a plea for judicious borrowing together with a vocabulary based primarily on words in common use.

Of the remaining incidental remarks of a critical kind the most significant are those which throw light on the inadequacy of the current conceptions of poetry and the poetic art. As has been already stated, to Wilson and Ascham alike poetry was little more than an allegorical and an esoteric way of writing ; and this limited medieval conception was more or less characteristic of the early Tudor period. A more notable treatment had, however, come from Sir Thomas Elyot who in his *Governour* had already handled the subject with greater sympathy and at greater length. In the first place he attempted to counteract the prevailing prejudice against poets and poetry, after which he added what is one of the earliest defences of poetry written by an Englishman during this Renascence period. Symptomatic, for instance, of the low esteem in which the poet was held at this date was the loose use of the terms ' poet ' and ' poetry '. Thus More's imaginary prose dialogue, the *Dialogue concerning Heresies* (1529), was described by opponents as so much ' poetry ' ; its author was derisively labelled a ' poet ' ; while Tyndale, in

---

[1] See Atkins, *Eng. Lit. Crit. Med.* p. 188 *et passim*.
[2] See Hoby, *Translation of the Courtier*, ed. Raleigh, pp. 12–13.

particular, spoke scornfully of its ' painted poetry, its babbling eloquence '.[1] And this was the position which Elyot set out to rectify. Recalling the fact, to begin with, that in ancient times the poet had been highly thought of, he frankly admits that ' men now (especially in this realm) have such indignation . . . that they use only poets in the contempt of eloquence ' ; [2] and he then reminds his readers of that pre-Socratic teaching, according to which all wisdom was supposed to be included in poetry, from which, as ' the first philosophy ', men acquired not only moral instruction but also knowledge of ' the wonderful works of Nature ', of ' science mystical and inspired '. He further adds, by way of support, that Plato and Aristotle had ' frequently alleged the authority of poets '.

Not content, however, with this general statement, Elyot proceeds to formulate his Apology on lines calculated to appeal to contemporary readers. In order to restore something of the lost prestige of poetry he begins by distinguishing between poets and mere versifiers, those whose verses ' express nothing but the craft of versifying ' ; [3] and on the authority of Plato and Cicero he claims for poetry an element of ' celestial instinction ' or inspiration. He then faces the main current objection, namely, that poetry contained ' nothing but bawdry and unprofitable leasings ',[4]—those charges of immorality and untruth which had persisted from Plato's day. The charge of untruth had already been met by the claims advanced for the moral and philosophical teaching of poetry ; though reference is also made to Horace's definition of the poet's function as ' the giving of precepts, the rebuking of wrath and envy and the providing of virtuous examples '. Elyot therefore now concentrates on the charge of immoral influences, the contention being that ' in Terence, . . . in Ovid, Martial, Catullus and other lascivious poets that wrote epistles and ditties of love—*elegiae* and *epigrammata*—there was nothing but incitations to lechery '.[5] In reply he points out that comedy, so far from being ' a doctrinal of ribaldry ', was rather (in Cicero's phrase) a picture or mirror of human life, wherein evil was not taught but only revealed. It enabled men, for instance, to see ' the promptness of youth to vice, the snares of harlots, the deceits of servants, the chances of Fortune ', thus giving them warning and preparing them to resist. Moreover, it was added that in comedies, and even in Ovid and Martial ' wise counsels and profitable " sentences " ' were often found ; and if it should be argued that the exhibition of vice was in

[1] *Expositions*, ed. Walker, p. 100.   [2] *Governour* I. ch. xiii.
[3] *Governour*, I. xiii.   [4] *ibid*.   [5] *ibid*.

itself evil, then there was danger in interludes and even in some sermons. Elyot's advice is therefore that of Plutarch, namely, that in the reading of poetry discrimination and a wise selection were necessary. 'No wise man,' he argues,[1] 'entereth a garden but he soon espies good herbs and nettles ; the nettles he treadeth under his feet, while he gathers the good herbs.' And therefore, he adds, no man 'should be prohibited from entering a fair garden lest the scent of sweet herbs and flowers should move him to wantonness, or lest in gathering wholesome herbs he may be stung by a nettle '. It is further noted that among the Jews certain parts of the Old Testament were forbidden to children ; and Elyot finally concludes that all ancient poets were worth reading, and if read discreetly were capable of yielding fruit. Such then was this early Tudor Apology for poetry, obviously traditional and limited in its advocacy. As yet, it will be noted, no acquaintance is shown with Aristotle's philosophical defence ; while comedy (not tragedy) together with love-poetry engage the main attention. Ethical considerations, too, are as yet uppermost ; but under Plutarchian influence, the medieval line of defence, that of allegorical interpretation, is to some extent being modified.

[1] *Governour*, I. xiii.

8

CHAPTER V

THE DEFENCE OF POETRY : WILLIS, LODGE, AND SIDNEY

I T was comparatively late in the 16th Century that critical activities in England first concentrated on what was subsequently to become their main preoccupation, namely, the understanding and appreciation of poetry. That the earlier interest in rhetorical matters was to be continued until the close of the century, as were also discussions relating to the literary language, classical metres and the like, later developments were to show. These, however, were but preliminary studies, a useful though limited introduction to literature in general ; and now, after 1570, new and more far-reaching problems urgently presented themselves, and serious efforts for the first time were made to expound the nature and art of poetry. To this change of direction in critical interest many causes had contributed. Something, to begin with, was undoubtedly due to the growth of Puritan feeling, which, having revived the earlier distrust of art, and of the drama in particular, now challenged anew the status and value of poetry. Nor was this challenge confined to English Puritanism alone. Savonarola in Italy, for instance, had previously raised the same questions ; an attack on poetry had also been made by that eccentric German philosopher, Cornelius Agrippa, in his work *De vanitate et incertitudine scientiarum* (1527), which, translated by J. Sandford (1569), was not without its influence on Sidney ; while in 1537 had also appeared Berni's *Dialogo contra i Poeti*.

Apart from this, however, there were incentives of a more positive kind which led men at this date to inquire more seriously into the meaning and significance of poetry and to claim for it a worthier place in the intellectual life. With the new courtly ideals, for instance, which now animated society, there had come a livelier sense of the value of the poetic art, even though as yet that sense was inarticulate. ' One of the courtier's most necessary gifts ', so wrote Castiglione,[1] ' is that of writing both in rime and prose, especially in this our vulgar tongue ' ; and already the works of those ' courtly makers ', Wyatt and Surrey, published in *Tottel's Miscellany* (1557), had been attracting attention ; while elsewhere a host of experiments in epitaphs, epigrams, eclogues, songs, sonnets and the like was being made by lesser

[1] See Hoby's trans. of *The Courtier* (1561), ed. Raleigh, p. 85.

versifiers. Then, too, not without its significance was the fact that already in Italy and France concerted efforts had been made to throw light on the whole subject of poetry. With the epoch-making re-discovery of Aristotle's *Poetics* in Italy at the beginning of the century had come a series of illuminating commentaries and discussions on poetry in general ; by the middle of the century, moreover, the Pléiade in France were proclaiming a rebirth of poetry with infectious enthusiasm ; and these activities were not wholly without their influence on English readers. As for the urgent contemporary need for some guidance in the matter, of that there can be no doubt ; more especially in view of the vague and confused conceptions then current, the suspicion and even the scorn with which the poetic art was generally regarded. Medieval traditions, for instance, with their fragments of post-classical and patristic doctrine still survived, and altogether they were more than puzzling in their variety. Thus poetry, according to that teaching, was but the handmaid of theology or philosophy, it was a branch of logic, it was ' versified rhetoric ', it was no real art but merely vain trifling, a ' spice ', a plaything ; or again, and here was the generally accepted idea at this later date, it was an esoteric art based on allegory, laden with hidden meaning and adorned with verse and fine diction. Of the imperfect sympathies and limited insight of Humanists something has already been said. Their regard for poetry as part of classical culture was tempered by their distrust of its immoral influences ; and altogether they shared in the perplexities of their contemporaries. What therefore emerged in the Apologies that followed were no pedantic disquisitions or idle speculations, but definite attempts to respond to a very real and widely-felt contemporary need ; and English criticism in those works, if it failed to solve finally the immediate problem, was at least successful in raising poetry on to a higher platform.

What men were thinking about poetry at this date may to some extent be gathered, in the first place, from *De re poetica disputatio* (1573) of Richard Willis, a short Latin treatise which must be hailed as the earliest of Elizabethan Apologies. The *disputatio* was appended to his *Poematum Liber*,[1] a curious collection of Latin poems composed for Winchester scholars with a view to commending ' a new and more subtle (*abstrusius*) form of verse not hitherto made known ' ; and incidentally, the collection which consists of a hundred poems, each representing a distinct verse-form, is in itself a lively illustration of the confusion which then prevailed. It included, for instance, along with

[1] See G. Gregory Smith, *Elizabethan Critical Essays*, i. pp. 46–7 fn.

scholia, such forms as epitaph, epigram, eclogue, epithalamium and encomium, others less familiar such as palinodia, epicedium, pasquinus, and threnus, while figure-poems (e.g. altar, egg, sword, a pair of wings, and such-like) also formed a notable part of this quaint Alexandrian collection.[1] Of the *Poematum Liber* (and the *disputatio*), it might be added, four copies are recorded, and these are to be found, one in the British Museum, the others in the Bodleian, Cambridge University, and the Huntington Libraries. Concerning Willis himself but little is known, though he seems to have been a man of wide interests and culture. Gabriel Harvey in one place described him as ' a great traveller, very well learned ' ;[2] and to him have been ascribed *The History of Travayle in the West and East Indies* (1557) as well as certain contributions to the famous volume of *Hakluyt's Voyages* (1582). Moreover, his effort to commend ' a new and more subtle form of verse ' seems to have attracted some attention at the time. Abraham Fraunce, for instance, in his *Arcadian Rhetorick*[3] (1588) refers to his ' conceited verses, . . . the grace and delicacy of which proceedeth from the figures ' ; whereas Harvey, on the other hand, in denouncing such subtleties claims that at the date of writing his opinion was shared by the author himself. His statement in his *Letter-Book* is that he had heard ' one Mr. Willes, now of riper years and sounder judgment . . . call such verses mere fooleries, . . . apish devices, frivolous boyish grammar-school tricks '.[4]

It is with the *Disputatio*, however, that we are here concerned ; and in that work Willis undertakes some explanation of poetry along with its defence, being conscious, as he explains, of the manifold hindrances to its proper appreciation in his day, as well as of the ignorance and caprice of critics which caused men to publish their works anonymously. The treatise consists of three main sections ; first, some remarks on the nature and origin of poetry, secondly, three theses maintaining the excellence, the usefulness, and the delight of the poetic art, and thirdly, an enumeration of the current objections and his replies to those objections. All three sections are of definite interest ; and not least, to begin with, is his concluding argument, his treatment of the charges brought against poetry by the ἀμοῦσοι and the malicious of his day.

The main objections are said to be two-fold ; poetry was

---

[1] For a similarly extensive variety of verse-forms see Scaliger, *Poetice*, Bk. I.
[2] Smith, *op. cit.* i. p. 126.
[3] fol. D7.V⁰ : see Smith, *op. cit.* i. p. 305.   [4] Smith, *op. cit.* i. p. 126.

condemned as being worthless by nature and its influence was described as definitely harmful. Its worthlessness, in the first place, was said to be shown by its appeal to the senses, an appeal shared by the brute beasts, according to the old story of Orpheus, and therefore degrading. Moreover, its themes were held to be devoid of value. Stories of immoral gods and of men made in their likeness, accounts of wanderings, battles and crimes, of cruel heroes and deceitful counsellors, all these were described as nothing more than old wives' tales. As for its harmful influences, these were even more strenuously exposed. First, there was the lascivious love-poetry, commended with all the devices of art, and eagerly employed by lovers for their own evil ends. There was also the fact that poetry was mere fiction (*fingendo*) and therefore the handmaid of lies, not truth. Had not Aristotle, for instance, described poetry as ' the art of lying ' ? Moreover, Lucan and Virgil (in his *Georgics*) had been denied the name of poet because they, forsooth, had dealt with facts alone. Then, too, there was the degradation which from the beginning had accompanied poetry on the stage. At first comedy had consisted of mere personal invective ; later on, its stories became impersonal in kind and all was turned to ridicule. The resulting themes were stories of lovers, of harlots and panders, of fierce and violent soldiers ; all stories which polluted the morals of spectators. In addition, it was notorious that Plato long ago had banished poets from his ideal state ; and apart from this, history had shown that many poets, inspired by Bacchus, were wine-bibbers and evil-livers. If perchance they wrote something of an elevating kind, yet such was the discord between their way of life and their utterances that their writing became merely a source of laughter. And, finally, on the authority of Democritus, all poets were insane, so that poetry was far removed from reason and good sense.

To all these charges Willis more or less directly replies. Against the alleged worthlessness of poetry, to begin with, he urges that the primary aim of poetry was not to titillate the senses but to inculcate virtue, and that the attack on the themes treated in antiquity was really an attack on ancient religion rather than on poetry itself. Nor was it true to say that poets dealt only with lust, cruelty, and crime. For the penalties of evil were amply displayed ; the virtues of good men were celebrated ; and in representing cruel heroes and deceitful counsellors Homer and the later satirists were more true to life than many historians and orators, who were wont to pass over in silence human defects. As for the harm attributed to poetry, Willis points

out, first, that all men everywhere had praised poets, and that
honours and affection had been showered on them from ancient
times.   It was true that there had been obscene poets, Ovid and
the Roman elegiac poets among their number; but not all poets
were of that character.   Moreover, the vicious elements in plays
were not intended to provoke vice but to deter men from evil-
doing.   Poetry, in short, was no encouragement to vice, though
discretion had always to be exercised in reading ; and to condemn the whole craft for the abuses of the few was both unreasonable and unjust.   Nor, again, were poets harmful because they
dealt often with mere imaginings ; any more than the mathemat-
icians who imagined in the heavens circular paths (*circulos*)
which did not exist.   And as for Plato's rejection of poets, it
was important to note that what he had rejected were bad poets
only ;   while the ' madness ' attributed to poets did not necessarily carry with it any pathological suggestion—an important
point on which Willis enlarges elsewhere in his work.

Significant, however, as was this attempt of Willis to reply
to current censures, equally interesting historically are the views
he puts forward concerning the value of poetry and its worth
to the community.   Despite the primary position assigned to
rhetoric by the earlier Humanists, he now categorically declares
poetry to be the most excellent (*praestens*), the most profitable
(*fructuosa*), and the most delightful (*jucunda*) of the arts ; though
he also concedes that, from its very nature, it was the most
difficult of all the arts of expression in words.[1]   Its excellence.
in the first place, was due partly to its nature.   The poet (according to Cicero) derived his strength from inborn genius, whence
the saying *oratores fieri et poetae nasci* ; and what sprang from
Nature was more excellent than what was due to art alone.
Then, too, there was its element of inspiration, which enabled
the poet to sing of great and mysterious matters.   And apart
from this, no art had been held in greater honour by the ancients.
Plato, on his deathbed, for instance, had cherished the works
of Homer ;   Alexander had spared the house of Pindar ;   while
seven cities had contended for the birthplace of Homer.   Nor
had heathen writers been alone in testifying to its excellence ;
for many of the early Fathers—Augustine, Jerome, Lactantius,
and St. Paul himself—had made use of poetry in support of
truth.   Jerome, indeed, had commanded men ' to spoil the
Egyptians ' ;   Christian poets such as Prudentius, Prosper,
Sedulius, and Juvencus, had commended Christian doctrine with
their writings in verse ; the Bible itself was full of poetry, and

[1] *Dedicatory Epistle* to the scholars of Winchester, *ad. init.*

Christian hymns and songs had long been instrumental in chanting the glories of God. That poetry, in the second place, was the
most profitable of the arts, this he maintains by recalling Strabo's
description of it as 'the first philosophy',[1] which taught the
principles of right living and sound knowledge in pleasing fashion.
The poet, in fact, had been the earliest teacher, as Horace had
testified ;[2] and within his works, it was maintained, had existed
seeds of all arts and sciences. Then, too, the poet was useful
to both orators and philosophers in giving authoritative support and power to their arguments and in softening the asperity
of their utterances. Moreover, at great festivals he fostered
courage by singing the praises of illustrious heroes—a form of
poetry which even Plato had allowed—and there was also the
fact that thoughts in verse were more easily remembered than
thoughts in prose form. As for his third claim, the element
of delight bound up with poetry, that was said to result mainly
from the music and rhythm of the verse, which charmed the ears
and soothed the minds of hearers in virtue of the harmony existing between music and the human soul. It was this charm of
numbers, greater than that of oratory, that explained the attraction of vernacular poetry for even the uncultured populace.

It is in the remaining section of the *Disputatio* when he
enlarges on the origin and nature of poetry that Willis's remarks
assume something more than conventional form, though his
treatment in part is still on the lines of earlier medieval and post-
classical teaching. Thus after emphasizing the value of speech
in making civilized life possible, he recalls the gradual development of a refined oratory and adds that poetry at length emerged
as a more ornate form of expression ; though he is also aware
of Strabo's more correct pronouncement, that poetry had come
before prose in the matter of time.[3] Then he traces its development from the *vates*, who told of things superhuman, to the poet,
so called because of his skill in creating (παρά τὸ ποιεῖν) ; from
versificatores or mere versifiers to poets inspired by the Muses,
'the interpreters and ministers of the gods', as Plato called them.
He also distinguishes three kinds of poets ; first, the religious
poets, Orpheus and Amphion, secondly, philosophical poets,
such as Empedocles, Nicander and Lucretius, who treated of
natural philosophy, thirdly, moral and economic poets, including
Solon, Tyrtaeus, and Hesiod ;[4] and finally he recalls the Hellenistic distinction of *poema, poesis*, and *poeta*. Concerning metrical
form, which he accepts as an integral part of poetry, he also has

[1] *Geographia*, I. ii. 8.   [2] cf. *Ep.* II, i. 126.
[3] *Geogr.* I. ii. 6.   [4] cf. Scaliger's classification in his *Poetice*, i. 2.

something to say. From the earliest times, he states, rhythmical
tendencies (*vis numerosa*) had formed part of human nature ;
but metre itself was ultimately of divine origin, since all things
had been created by a certain measure, and, according to Pythagoras, there existed a harmony between things celestial and things
terrestrial. Such harmonious expression, moreover, was first
used by the Hebrews of old ; and here Willis follows the earlier
teaching of Josephus, Eusebius, and Jerome. Thus Moses is said
to have written in hexameter verse, David in various metres,
while, according to Jerome, the *Psalms* embodied Alcaic and
Sapphic measures, the Books of *Deuteronomy*, *Isaiah* and *Job*,
hexameter and pentameter verse ; after which came the Greeks
with Orpheus, Homer, and Hesiod.

Nevertheless, despite so much post-classical and patristic
theory, his survey is not without some glimpses of the new
Renascence thought ; and of special interest, for one thing, is
his reference to that ' ideal imitation ' which formed so important a part of Aristotelian theory. Thus he explains that poetry
is an art of imitation, and that it is so called ' because it imitates
in words not only existing things, but also things non-existent,
just as if they existed, and represents them moreover as they
might be or ought to be '.[1] It is true that he does not develop
the point further, so as to bring out the essential truth of
poetry. Yet he is the first to present to English readers something of the Aristotelian conception of ' imitation ', a conception
distinct from the idea of a mere reflexion or representation of
human life, distinct also from the Humanistic process of copying
the best models ; and this doctrine, it might be added, was
apparently not fully understood by some of the contemporary
Italian theorists.

Then, too, on the doctrine of ' poetic inspiration ' he also
throws new light ; and this is perhaps his most valuable contribution to critical thought. Thus he states, to begin with,
the current version of the doctrine, then comments on Plato's
meaning, and supplies further a rational interpretation of his
own which has much to commend it. ' Of all the arts conceived
by human genius ', he writes in the first place, ' poetry alone is
deemed to proceed from divine frenzy. For poets, inspired by
a sort of divine breath, sing of matters worthy of wonder and
amazement ; and without this frenzy and inspiration Democritus
(according to Cicero) says there are no great poets, since they are

---

[1] Poesis dicitur propterea quod non solum vocibus res ipsas imitaretur
quae essent, verum etiam quae non essent, quasi essent, et quomodo esse
vel possent vel deberent, repraesentaret. (§. *de poeticae natura, ad init.*)

only true *vates* in a state of frenzy.   Wherefore Plato calls poetry a divine madness.'[1]   Then follows his illuminating commentary on Plato's meaning.

By this divine frenzy or madness [he suggests] Plato understands in one place a withdrawal of the soul from the body and a sort of compulsion by which the soul is drawn aloft, striving vehemently after higher things ; while elsewhere he interprets it as a kind of possession by the Muses, which selects a suitable soul, awakens it and arouses it by means of songs, and begets poetry for the moral instruction of mankind.   To this he adds that that man is vain and truly ridiculous who attempts poetry without this poetic madness, since poetry is of so great a value that apart from the will of God it cannot be produced very abundantly.[2]

Still more valuable, however, is Willis's attempt to rationalize Plato's doctrine and to expound it in terms understandable by all.   Thus poets, so inspired, he explains, are distracted,

not because they are out of their minds, but because they so apply their minds to things and assume the emotions they describe, that, as if stimulated by passion or roused by the divine breath, they seem to be transported hither and thither ; which often happens to us when contemplating something seriously, not to understand in a measure what we are doing.[3]

And to this our author adds a further comment of considerable interest.

This madness, nevertheless, [so he explains] is not to be understood in such a way . . . that we should venture to urge that no poet could

---

[1] Ex omnibus artibus quae ab humani ingenii vi percipiuntur sola poetice a divino furore proficisci putatur.   Nam poetae quodam spiritu divino afflati, res admiratione et stupore dignas canunt, sine quo furore ac spiritu magnos esse poetas, apud Ciceronem Democritus negat, quippe qui tum demum veri sint vates cum insaniunt.   Quare Plato poesim insaniam divinam appellat. (*Thesis* I.)

[2] Divini autem furoris insaniaeque nomine Plato nunc animae abstractionem a corpore et nexum quendam intelligit, quo anima ad superos trahatur et vehementius adnitatur ; nunc poeticum furorem esse statuit quandam a Musis occupationem, quae facilem sortita animam excitet, ac per cantilenas exagitet, alatque poesin ad humanum genus recte instituendum.   Ad haec adjungit, inanem esse hominem ac prorsus irridendum, qui absque Musarum furore poeticen tractet, quippe quae tanti est, ut sine Dei numine valde prolixo comparari nequeat. (*Thesis* I.)

[3] Non quia mente carent, sed quoniam ita mentem rebus applicant, ita affectus quos describunt, induunt, ut quasi furore perciti, aut divino afflati spiritu, huc illuc rapi videantur : quod saepe nobis evenit serio quippiam contemplantibus, non animadvertere quodammodo illud quod agamus. (*Disputatio*, ad. fin.)

be successful unless he were wholly insane, even if we understand
' insanity ' in Plato's sense.   This was the error of the ancients. . . .
But we make use of this testimony of antiquity so that in the light of
their judgment you may clearly realize that the nature of poets is
divine and their art of the greatest excellence.[1]

Such then is Willis's interesting account of ' poetic inspiration ' ; and it might further be noted that he does not omit
to mention as additional evidence of the mysterious power of
poetry the hint given by Plato of its inexhaustible vitality,
and its faculty of communicating this ' inspiration ' to the
reader.[2]
    The substantial value of this contribution of Willis to Eliza-
bethan criticism therefore admits of no question ; though,
written in Latin and academic in form, its influence would seem
to have been limited in kind.   It is true that its formal defence
of poetry embodies elements that are conventional, unhistorical,
and, to modern minds, irrelevant ; for quibbles have a way of
begetting quibbles.   Its arguments, moreover, are largely drawn
from earlier authorities, and treat, as was perhaps inevitable, of
ancient poetry alone, of Orpheus as well as Homer ; while it also
fails to reply to the fundamental objections, those relating to
Plato's much-quoted rejection of poets and the alleged untruth
of poetry.   Yet not without its significance is the fact that he
writes in defence of poetry at all.   For in view of the comparative
neglect of the subject by earlier Humanists, it points to an
awakening of interest in matters of poetry and a desire to re-
establish it in a new and a fairer light.   Part of its merit lies
in the information it gives concerning the current conceptions
of poetry in England.   They were conceptions based largely,
as in medieval times, on patristic and post-classical teaching,
on doctrines of Eusebius, Jerome, Cicero, Strabo, and others ;
altogether a confused medley, well illustrated by the place given
to figure-poems in the collection of verse bound up with the
treatise.   But what gives to the work its outstanding value is its

    [1] Tametsi quae de hoc . . . spiritu poetico ab istis auctoribus dicuntur
non ita accipi volumus . . . ut persuadere conemur non futurum poetam
bonum nisi plane fuerit insanus, etiamsi insaniam intelligamus eo modo
ac sensu quo Plato eam significabat.   Fuit is antiquorum error. . . .
Sed iccirco ha-ec veterum testimonia usurpamus ut eorum judicio divina
esse poetarum ingenia praestantissimamque ipsorum artem clare per-
spiciatis.   (*Thesis* I.)
    [2] Immo vero, inquit apud Platonem Socrates, musa divino instinctu
concitat poetas, conciti poetae alios furore corripiunt.   (*Thesis* I.)
cf. Plato, *Ion*, 533.

original outlook in places and the introduction it affords to some
of the basic doctrines of Aristotle and of Plato in particular.
At a time when rhetorical studies firmly held the field, it represents poetry, among other things, as the most excellent and
most difficult of all the arts—a strange hearing doubtless for
many contemporaries. It also conveys something of the
mysterious processes of poetry; and these matters it makes
intelligible by its somewhat surprising treatment of a psychological kind. The work may lack the finish and charm of later
courtly writings; but it is sensible, scholarly, and above all
enlightening.

Meanwhile Puritan hostility to art in all its forms would
seem to have been gathering head; and a series of attacks were
made, on the stage primarily, but partly on poetry as well,
beginning with a treatise by John Northbrooke (c. 1577) and
continuing well into the following century.[1] Of these the best
known perhaps, and one more or less representative of all that
followed, was *The School of Abuse* (1579), a 'pleasant invective'
by one Stephen Gosson (1554–1624), a young Oxford man who
had previously written plays which he had since regretted, pleading human infirmity and that *semel insanavimus omnes*. Dedicated, significantly enough, to 'Master Philip Sidney' and
written in the pretentious Euphuistic style, the work classes
poets along with 'pipers and jesters',[2] denounces poetry, music,
and the drama all alike as 'caterpillars of the commonwealth',
and adopts to that end the exhaustive method of contemporary
controversialists, that of overwhelming the reader with 'authorities, similitudes and examples' drawn from ancient stories,
legends, proverbs, natural and unnatural history. Of substantial
argument there is little or nothing; and the interest of the work
lies mainly in the fierce animus displayed against poetry and the
sister arts. Poets, Gosson allows, are 'whetstones of wit'; but
that wit he regards as too dearly bought. Plato, for instance,
had given to all poets 'Drummes entertainment'; music was
debilitating; and the drama again was an incitement to popular
debauchery. All alike, added Gosson, were enemies to virtue;
and 'he that goeth to sea must smell of the ship'.

To this venomous attack a reply was immediately forthcoming

[1] See J. Northbrooke, *Treatise wherein vain Plays or Interludes are
reproved* (1577) : S. Gosson, *School of Abuse* (1579) : H. Denham, *Second
and Third Blast of Retreat from Plays* (1580) : S. Gosson, *Plays Confuted
in Five Actions* (1581–2) : P. Stubbes, *Anatomy of Abuses* (1583) : J. Rain-
oldes, *Overthrow of Stage Plays* (1599) : W. Prynne, *Histriomastix* (1633).

[2] cf. Erasmus, p. 48 *supra*.

from Thomas Lodge in his *Defence of Poetry* [1] (1579), a pamphlet devoted to the defence of poetry in general, and interesting mainly as illustrating the degree to which the post-classical and patristic ideas of medieval times still persisted. Thus he adopts as his first line of defence the allegorical theory, explaining, with abundant illustration, the significance of that theory, and how ' under the shadow of birds, beasts and trees the follies of the world were deciphered '.[2]   At the same time he is aware that Aristotle had declared that *Poetae multa mentiuntur*,[3] and that Cato had held that *admiranda canunt, sed non credenda, poetae*. But such objections, he maintained, had been fairly met by Lactantius, who, in condemning a literal reading of Scripture, had also urged the necessity for weighing the poet's hidden meaning, not merely his words.   Moreover, he recalls that Plato had indeed wished to banish poets from his ideal commonwealth ; though ' the wisest ', he adds, ' were not of that opinion '.[4] Jerome, however, he points out, had since replied to that detraction in making ' Plato's exiles honest men, and his pestiferous poets good preachers '.[5]   Then, too, he attaches considerable importance to the place occupied by poetry among the ' precise ' Jews.   Thus Josephus, Origen, and Jerome were called to witness to the use made of metrical forms by David and others ; reference was made to St. Paul's use of the Greek poets, Epimenides and Aratus ; Cassiodorus, it was noted, had held that all poetry proceeded from the Scriptures ; and the venerable Bede himself had not disdained the art of poetry.   Nor was reference wanting to the dignity of poetry as the fruit of ' inspiration ', and therefore of divine origin.   Ennius sleeping on Mount Parnassus, for instance, was said to have received the soul of Homer ; and if poetry was sometimes abused by men like Ovid, then discretion in reading was all that was necessary.   ' Those of judgment ', he maintains, ' can from the same flower suck honey with the bees, from whence the spiders take their poison.'   Concerning the drama in particular he has something further to say.   He points out, to begin with, its honourable antiquity, its original function being (according to Donatus [6]) that of praising God for the harvest ; and while he briefly dismisses tragedy as consisting of instructive stories of the falls of princes, he directs his attention

---

[1] Its actual title is uncertain, the title-page having been lost : but it has been identified with *Honest Excuses*, to which Gosson later on refers.   For text see G. Gregory Smith, *Elizabethan Critical Essays*, i. pp. 61–86.

[2] Smith, *op. cit.* i. p. 65.   [3] *ibid.* i. p. 73.

[4] *ibid.* i. p. 67.   [5] *ibid.* i. p. 75.

[6] *ibid.* i. p. 80 : see Donatus, *De tragoedia et comoedia, ad. init.*

mainly to a defence of comedy. Thus in tracing its development
from Eupolis and Aristophanes onwards, he recalls Cicero's
familiar definition of comedy as *imitatio vitae, speculum consue-
tudinis, et imago veritatis*,[1] and notes the part it had played in
censuring vice, *quodam lepore*, by means of that pleasure-giving
device of imitation approved of by Aristotle.[2] He regrets, moreover, that in his day writers of comedy had applied ' this writing
to the people's vein ' ; yet Germans, he adds, when forbidden to
preach, had used comedies for the purpose of correction.
Altogether, then, for comedy he claims great and positive value,
not only on account of its antiquity, but also because of its
usefulness and its pleasure-giving qualities. Finally, to all
these arguments, medieval for the most part, in defence of poetry,
he adds others rather more characteristic of Renascence times,
notably, Horace's tribute to its civilizing value, its work in
founding cities and in providing ' footpaths to knowledge '.
But all this was nothing more than the conventional appeal to
ancient authorities ; and however convincing to Lodge's contemporaries, it threw but little light on the nature of poetry
itself.

It was not long, however, before there appeared a more
adequate defence of poetry, a defence possibly occasioned by
Gosson's rude challenge, but more certainly inspired by a desire
to explain to an age, confused and perplexed, what poetry really
was, and what it stood for in the life of the community. These
at least are the main questions to which Sir Philip Sidney (1554–86)
addresses himself in his *Apology for Poetry*. The actual date of
the work is somewhat uncertain, though a letter (Oct. 1580)
addressed to his brother Robert,[3] contains allusions to matters
discussed in the *Apology* and thus suggests that the latter was
possibly written about that date. In view of Sidney's apparent
acquaintance with Gosson's *Plays Confuted* (1851–2),[4] however,
a slightly later date seems more probable, so that the work is
perhaps best assigned to the year 1582–3. As is well known the
volume was published posthumously in 1595, after being circulated in manuscript form ; and then in two separate versions
which were based apparently on different manuscripts and with
different titles. The edition submitted by Henry Olney was
entitled *Apologie for Poetrie*, that of William Ponsonby being
The Defence of Poesie ; and of the two versions the former on the
whole provides the better text. That Sidney's effort was inspired
by a genuine concern at the slow awakening of his fellow-country-

---

[1] *ibid*. i. p. 81.   [2] *ibid*. i. p. 83.
[3] See Shuckburgh's ed. of the *Apology*, p. xxxiii.   [4] See pp. 227–8 *infra*.

men to a sense of the greatness of poetry is evident throughout. When, for instance, he laments that poetry in his day was but ' the laughing-stock of children ' and that England had proved ' a hard step-mother to poets ', or again, when he suggests that it was dangerously near sacrilege to apply to the much-loved *Psalms* the despised name of poetry,[1] such places, however strange-sounding at first to modern ears, are nevertheless to be interpreted in no merely figurative sense, but rather as statements of hard fact which throw light on actual conditions and the urgency of the situation. For this task of enlightenment, however, Sidney was specially well equipped. Himself a poet, a courtier, and a scholar, imbued with much that was best in classical and Italian thought, he yet carries his learning lightly, fuses it into some sort of unity ; and the result is a surprising performance for a young man of twenty-seven or thereabouts, a work unique in contemporary literature, and one rare at any time, with its wide scholarship, its good sense, and its enduring charm.

Not the least admirable feature, to begin with, is its general planning and the well-devised scheme with which the main argument unfolds itself. First comes a section in which conventional reasons are given why poetry should be specially valued ; and this is followed by arguments of a more ' palpable ' or convincing kind, based on an exposition of the nature and usefulness of poetry itself. After thus fortifying the reader with positive ideas on the subject, Sidney then proceeds to discuss the current objections to poetry ; and the work is brought to a close with remarks on the state of English poetry in Sidney's own day. These then are the four main divisions of the *Apology* ; though at no stage does the work assume the severity of a formal or impersonal treatise. Writing as he does for courtly circles, Sidney from first to last discards the rôle of schoolmaster and adopts the method formerly advocated by Vives, of writing on learned matters ' spontaneously and clearly . . . so that knowledge might be gained with a certain delight '.[2] Thus he winds his way into his subject with an amusing ironical prologue, takes farewell of the reader in the same ironical vein ; and over every page there lingers the spell of a humane and gracious personality.

The first plea advanced by Sidney for the recognition of poetry is based on its antiquity, its universality, and the high esteem in which it had been held from the earliest times,[3]—

[1] Smith, *op. cit.* i. p. 155.
[2] *De tradendis disciplinis*, Pref. : see Watson, *op. cit.* p. 7.
[3] Smith, *op. cit.* i. pp. 150–5.

stock arguments all, utilized by most of the contemporary critics. Thus poets were described as 'the first light-bringers to ignorance'; the earliest Greek philosophers and historians, it was claimed, had really been poets; and, moreover, poets from the first had flourished in all quarters of the world, among the Turks and American Indians, for instance, as well as among the early Irish and ancient Britons nearer home. Of special value in this connexion, however, was held to be the testimony of those peoples of antiquity from whom Western civilization had ultimately sprung. And Sidney therefore, with the help of etymology, calls attention to the reverence paid to the poet, first, by the Romans who had called him *vates*, a 'prophet' or 'seer' (a description, it is added, that might with special force be applied to the writer of the *Psalms*), and, secondly, by the Greeks who had honoured him with the name of 'poet', that is, 'maker' or 'creator', a description suggestive of divinity and therefore above all others. Such then is the witness of antiquity in the matter; and the argument from authority was not without its influence at the time.

It is when Sidney submits his views on the nature of poetry itself, however, that he comes really to grips with his problem, and presents something more than a *prima facie* case on its behalf. He treats first of poetry in general, then of its different forms; and his teaching consists of ideas gathered from various sources, ideas which are not always blended into a consistent whole, though they are successful in giving to poetry an added dignity and meaning. Worthy of note, to begin with, is the fact that under the head of poetry in general he includes apparently all imaginative literature, that is, literature into which the element of fiction entered, whether written in prose or verse. On this score, for instance, he claims that Herodotus had all the qualities of a poet,[1] that Xenophon's political romance of Cyrus, as well as Heliodorus's romance, *Aethiopica*, were really 'heroical poems' or epics;[2] while those, he added, who failed to see in Plato's prose *Dialogues* 'flowers of poetry, did never walk into Apollo's garden'.[3] Furthermore, he categorically declares that 'it is not rhyming and versing that maketh a poet, no more than a long gown maketh an advocate';[4] in short, verse to him is but 'an ornament and no cause to poetry'. At the same time there is an element of inconsistency in the position he thus assumes. For elsewhere he allows that 'the exquisite observing of number and measure in words . . . did seem to have some divine force in

[1] *ibid*. i. p. 153.
[3] *ibid*. i. p. 152.
[2] *ibid*. i. p. 160.
[4] *ibid*. i. p. 160.

it ' ; [1] and in treating later of contemporary poetry, it is to compositions in verse, significantly enough, that he confines his attention. The truth would seem to be that in denying verse to be the essential element in poetry he was following the lead of Aristotle [2] and most of the Italian critics, Scaliger alone maintaining that verse constituted the ' matter ' of poetry, the raw material in which the poet worked. In practice, however, Sidney was conscious that verse, if not the essence, was at least a necessary and inseparable element of poetry. Poets, he stated, had chosen it as their ' fittest raiment ', as a form of expression which enabled them to speak in keeping with the dignity of the subject, and not loosely ' in table-talk fashion or like men in a dream '.[3] And this conception, based on experience and shared by Minturno and other Italians, probably represents Sidney's true position in the matter ; though his description of verse as an added ornament fails to suggest its organic character and the vital relation existing between poetic thought and rhythmical expression.

Of yet greater interest, however, is Sidney's attempt to represent what to him was the essential nature of poetry. That it was ultimately the fruit of inspiration and thus ' a divine gift ', of this he is apparently convinced ; though there seems at first sight some inconsistency in his remarks on the subject. Thus in more than one place he affirms the working of ' a divine breath ' ; [4] whereas elsewhere he finds himself unable to follow Plato in making a similar claim, definitely stating that Plato ' attributeth unto poetry more than myself do, namely, to be a very inspiring of a divine force '.[5] It may be that he discriminates between Plato's description of the process as the external working of a pagan Muse on man deprived of reason [6] and the influence of God raising to a higher power the inborn faculties of man ; and not without its significance is the fact that he nowhere discusses the actual nature of this divine influence. Indeed, such arguments, he rather curtly explains, ' will by few be understood and by fewer granted '.[7] On the other hand, he is at pains to define poetry in rational terms ; and his main doctrine, which is of an eclectic kind and is coloured throughout by Platonic teaching, is that poetry is essentially an art of ' imitation ' in accordance with Aristotelian theory, and that its function, as stated by Horace, is to teach and delight.[8] By this process of ' imitation ', in the first place, Sidney implies some-

---

[1] Smith, *op. cit.* i. p. 154.
[3] Smith, *op. cit.* i. p. 160.
[5] *ibid.* i. p. 192.
[7] Smith, *op. cit.* i. p. 157.

[2] *Poetics*, 1447 b, 14.
[4] *ibid.* i. pp. 157, 195.
[6] *Ion*, 534.
[8] *ibid.* i. p. 158.

thing more than mere copying or a reproduction of the facts of life. Representatives of other arts, he states, such as the astronomer, the physician, the historian and the philosopher, all treat solely of the works of Nature and the affairs of men ; but the poet, disdaining such limitations, ' borrows nothing of what is, hath been, or shall be '.[1] What he does is either to transmute the real and actual, or else to attempt an entirely new creation. ' Lifted up ', so Sidney declares,[2] ' by the vigour of his own invention, he doth grow in effect into another nature, in making things either better than Nature bringeth forth, or, quite anew, forms such as were never in Nature.' To Sidney, therefore, poetic ' imitation ' was really a heightening process, an exercise of the creative faculty ; and commenting on the ' high-flying liberty of conceit ' of the poet he states in lyrical strain that ' Nature never set forth the earth in so rich tapestry as divers poets have done. . . . Her world is brazen, the poets only deliver a golden ', while Nature, he adds, never produced ' so excellent a man as Virgil's Aeneas '. And in attributing to the poet this power of transcending Nature Sidney denies that he is making a presumptuous claim, since the creative force of the poet, he asserts, is due to inspiration derived from God Himself, who ' having made man to His own likeness set him . . . over all the works of that second Nature '.[3]

But having stated so far that the world thus created by the poet transcends Nature and represents something not found in actual life, Sidney proceeds to explain the significance of these poetic figments, that they are ' not wholly imaginative (i.e. fanciful) as we are wont to say by them that build castles in the air ' ; [4] in other words, they are something more than mere illusion. For the poet in his flight, he explains, ' ranges into the divine consideration of what may be and should be ' ; [5] so that the world thus conjured up is the world of the ideal, that world present in the mind of the Creator, but distorted in the phenomena of Nature and now made manifest by the creative activity of the poet. Elsewhere Sidney recalls Aristotle's testimony concerning the substantial nature of the poet's creation, how in dealing with the ' universal consideration (*katholou*) ' the poet reveals the unchanging characteristics of human life and thought, since ' the universal weighs what is fit to be said or done either in likelihood or necessity '.[6] It is therefore evident

---

[1] Smith, *op. cit.* i. p. 159.   [2] *ibid.* i. p. 156.
[3] *ibid.* i. p. 157.   [4] *ibid.*   [5] *ibid.* i. p. 159.
[6] *ibid.* i. 167. : cf. τὰ δυνατὰ κατὰ τὸ εἰκὸς ἢ τὸ ἀναγκαῖον. (Aristotle, *Poetics*, 1451 a, 39.)

9.

that Sidney's conception of the nature of poetry is not greatly
at variance with that of Aristotle ; though his terminology
differs in some respects, and he treats solely of ' things as they
ought to be ', omitting all consideration of ' things as they were
or are ', those particulars in which and through which the
universal was represented according to Aristotelian theory. For
in Aristotle's view the poet's material consisted of ' things as
they were or are, things as they are said or thought to be, or
things as they ought to be '.[1]   Apart from this, however, both
agree in seeing in poetry something more than mere fancy or a
bare transcript of life ; both maintain that it embodies elements
of real and permanent value.   But whereas, according to Sidney,
the poet inspired arrives intuitively at glimpses of an ideal and
perfect world, by Aristotle the poet is held to take a philosophical
view of things as they are, thus arriving at the universal through
the particular.   And in this way both discern in poetry truth of
the highest, that is, of an ideal or universal, kind, and thus
provide a vindication of poetry against the attacks of ' barking '
critics.

With this as his conception of the nature of poetry in general,
Sidney then notes briefly what he regards as the several kinds of
poetry.[2]   He adopts with some modification the traditional
classification, the grouping, for instance, employed by Scaliger [3]
and Minturno,[4] according to which the main classes were religious
poetry, philosophical poetry, and poetry which consisted of an
imaginary treatment of human life.   Of religious poets the stock
examples were said to be Orpheus and Amphion.   To these,
however, with their ' wrong divinity ', Sidney adds the more
notable Biblical poets, David and Solomon, the writer of *Job*,
' Moses and Deborah in their hymns ', all of whom had ' imitated
the inconceivable excellencies of God '.   The philosophical poets
Sidney takes over unchanged from earlier authorities, including
among their number Tyrtaeus, Phocilides, Lucretius, Manilius,
Lucan, and others.   These he commends for their ' delightful
teaching ' ; but since they had treated of ' things as they were
or are ', he is conscious of some inconsistency in his theorizing,
though he cheerfully sidesteps the difficulty by adding that
' whether they properly be poets or no, let grammarians dispute '.
It is to the third class of poets, however, ' right ' poets as he
terms them, those who had dealt ' imaginatively ' with life, that
Sidney calls special attention ; and of these he states that there

---

[1] *Poetics*, 1460 b, 10–11.
[2] Smith, *op. cit.* i. pp. 158–60.   [3] *Poetice*, I. ii.
[4] *De poeta*, pp. 53 ff. : cf. also Willis. p. 107 *supra*.

are various sub-divisions or 'kinds'—the heroic, lyric, tragic, comic, satiric, iambic, elegiac, pastoral, and others.[1] This conventional classification, as Sidney himself points out, was in some measure unsound, being based partly on subject-matter, partly on metrical considerations. Yet it was a timely reminder of poetic forms other than epigrams, epithalamia, figure-poems and the like, which mainly engaged the attention of his contemporaries; it was also an indication of the possibilities of poetry conceived on the lines of classical antiquity.

Having now submitted his views on the nature of poetry and its various 'kinds', Sidney proceeds to what is perhaps the main burden of his treatise, namely, a defence of the value of poetry in the intellectual life of the community. As before, he treats first of poetry in general, then of the different 'kinds'; though now he confines his treatment solely to poetry, as previously defined, of the third or 'imaginative' kind. His plan is to inquire into the efficacy of all arts and sciences, and by a comparison of their various effects on the human mind to assign to poetry its place in intellectual values. Concerning poetry in general, in the first place, the criterion he adopts is a sufficiently lofty one. All learning, he allows, is instrumental in 'lifting up the mind from the dungeon of the body to the enjoying of his own divine essence';[2] and not without its significance is his further definition of the effects of learning in general, described in terms of medieval Scholastic psychology, as the 'enriching of memory (i.e. history), enabling (or strengthening) of judgment (i.e. philosophy), and enlarging of conceit' (i.e. poetry).[3] Yet a knowledge of material Nature, of the stars and the causes of things, he asserts, has but little effect on man's inmost being. This, he maintains, is to be obtained only by means of the mistress-knowledge (*architectonike*),[4] that is, 'the knowledge of a man's self', and by an application of that knowledge to life and conduct. The ultimate end of all learning, Sidney contends, is 'virtuous action' or the good life; and he recalls the saying of Aristotle that the fruit of learning is not mere knowing (*gnosis*) but doing (*praxis*). So that with him the final test of value in connexion with the arts is not the conveying of knowledge, nor mere ethical teaching, but the imparting of an elevating influence, an uplifting power which should inspire in men the desire of

---

[1] Smith, *op. cit.* i. p. 159.   [2] *ibid.* i. p. 161.
[3] *ibid.* i. p. 160: cf. 'In cerebro sub craneo sunt tres cellulae; prima est ymaginaria, secunda rationalis, tertia memorialis'. John of Garland, *Dictionarius* (quoted by Spingarn, *Crit. Essays of the 17th Century*, i. p. 219).
[4] cf. Aristotle, *Ethics*, I. i.

well-doing. Furthermore, of all the traditional branches of learning there are four more especially which seem to Sidney to contribute to this mistress-knowledge. They are theology, law, philosophy, and history ; since the natural sciences, he has already explained, have but slight bearing on the study of humanity. Of these four, however, he would exclude theology and law from his inquiry ; theology as being concerned primarily with divine lore, law as being a corrective or deterrent rather than an inspiration to virtuous living. What he therefore proposes to show is that for poetry, no less than for the long-established studies of philosophy and history, serious claims of high cultural value might also be made.

He begins by stating that in the teaching of virtue, in the first place, both philosophy and history play their parts.[1] Philosophy, for instance, expounds its nature by means of analysis and definition, treating of its general categories and specific results, its private and public aspects, thus providing precepts of general validity in their bearing on human conduct. History, on the other hand, concerned with an ' active ', rather than a ' theoretical ', virtue, teaches not by precept or abstract argument, but by particular examples drawn from life which illustrate in concrete fashion what virtue really is. Both methods, however, are said to have their defects. Philosophy, dealing with abstractions, is ' hard of utterance and misty to be conceived ', is therefore a poor guide for youth and appeals only to those already learned. History, again, with its concrete examples, presents but a medley of empirical facts, from which general truths and the nature of virtue more especially but dimly and confusedly emerge. Poetry, however, is said to combine the merits of both. It represents the universal truths bound up with philosophy ; and this it does by means of particular examples which convey those truths in vivid and concrete fashion after the manner of history. Nor does it detract from the value of the teaching of poetry that its examples are fictitious, as contrasted with the facts of history. Sidney held that the world revealed by poetry was an ideal and a perfect world, a world more intelligible than the world of experience ; and that in that world were represented concrete and living embodiments of virtue, of ' what ought to be ', transcending Nature, it is true, but not contradicting her. The fictions of poetry, in short, transformed facts into truths, and presented virtue in a way intelligible to the plain man, so that its teaching became ' food for the tenderest stomachs '.

[1] Smith, *op. cit.* i. pp. 163–74.

Yet a knowledge of virtue in itself does not necessarily lead to virtuous action. As Sidney himself remarks, 'to be moved to do that which we know, *hoc opus, hic labor est*' ;[1] and for this is required a dynamic power which he finds pre-eminently in poetry and in its delightful teaching. Thus philosophy, he explains, scornful of pleasure, sternly abjures all emotional appeals ; whereas poetry attracts and holds the attention of all by its manifold delights. Of its essentially pictorial character he had written elsewhere in recalling Plutarch's description of poetry as ' a speaking picture '.[2] Now he notes further how poetry was wont to array its teaching in the fairest colours, resorting to the world of imagination 'from Dante's heaven to his hell ', and by making use of words ' set in delightful proportion ', often with the enchantment of music. Hence poetry, he maintains,[3] ' doth not only show the way, but giveth so sweet a prospect into the way as will entice any man to enter into it '. And further, he adds in unforgettable phrase, ' with a tale forsooth (it) cometh unto you, with a tale which holdeth children from play and old men from the chimney corner ; and pretending no more doth intend the winning of the mind from wickedness to virtue '. Such alluring methods, he argues, cannot fail to make their appeal, even to evil minds beguiled in spite of themselves, still more to men of goodwill, ' most of which ', he adds, ' are childish in the best things till they be cradled in their graves '. This, then, is the gist of Sidney's argument on behalf of poetry. With its lofty and effective teaching, its irresistible aesthetic charm, he claims for it no less than supremacy among the arts in virtue of its power of attuning the soul to high endeavour by means of glowing visions of the ideal.

Not content, however, with a vindication of poetry in general, Sidney also attempts to show what is valuable in its various ' kinds ' ;[4] though here he is less convincing, owing to his illogical classification and to the limitation of his test, for the time being, to moral instruction. Thus pastoral poetry, the lowliest of the ' kinds ', it is stated, treats of the evils of tyranny or the beauty of the simple life ; elegiac poetry, again, is said to arouse sympathy with weakness and misery. The function of iambic poetry, on the other hand, is described as the unmasking of the devices of villainy ; while satire is credited with laughing folly out of court. Then, too, comedy, described as an imitation of common errors in ridiculous fashion, is held to be effective in

---

[1] *ibid*. i. p. 172 : cf. Virgil, *Aeneid*, vi. 128.
[2] *ibid*. i. p. 158 : cf. Plutarch, *De aud. poetis*, 17 F.
[3] *ibid*. i. p. 172.   [4] *ibid*. i. pp. 175–81.

warning men against indulgence in such foibles ; whereas tragedy, with its ' sweet violence ' revealing wickedness in high places, is said to bring home to men the uncertainty of life. The lyric, again, with its abundance of moral precepts, is held to be instrumental in kindling courage in the hearts of men, while also hymning the praises of virtue and of God Himself. And, lastly, there was the epic or heroic poetry, significantly described as ' the best and most accomplished kind of poetry ' ; [1] in which form, Sidney asserts, heroic and moral goodness are most effectively portrayed. Thus all in different ways are said to provide illumination and guidance ; and so far from calling for scorn or censure they are held to be deserving of the highest praise and reverence. And as for the snarling critics, ' the poet-whippers ', adds Sidney in a parting shot, with them ' it falleth out as with some good women who often are sick but in faith they cannot say where '.

With this Sidney has concluded what he wished to say of a positive kind on behalf of poetry, having noted more particularly its idealizing nature, its essential truth, its uplifting and dynamic influence. He now turns, in his third section,[2] to consider the objections that were being raised by contemporary Philistines, captious and trifling though those objections were, lest, as he explains, being unanswered they might appear to some minds weighty and substantial. The first and most general complaint was that with poetry was bound up ' rhyming and versing ' ; and Sidney meets this objection by once more denying verse to be an essential. At the same time he is at pains to explain rationally something of what verse-form really meant to the poet. ' If Oratio next to Ratio, speech next to reason, be the greatest gift bestowed upon mortality ', then, argues Sidney, ' that cannot be praiseless which doth most polish that blessing of speech ' ; and he proceeds to enlarge on the advantages of metrical form, noting by the way that Scaliger had deemed it essential.[3] To expression in words, he points out, it brought a regulated verbal harmony ; and measure, order and proportion had ever been pleasing to men. Moreover, as ' the only fit speech for music ', it added to words a sensuous and emotional quality of which music was the supreme exponent. Or again, verse-form for obvious reasons lent itself easily to memorizing, and this had been shown by the use made of it by grammarians and others in compiling the rules of their crafts.

---

[1] Smith, op. cit. i. p. 179 : according to Aristotle tragedy was the higher form of art, see Poetics, 1462 b.

[2] ibid. i. pp. 181–93.   [3] ibid. i. p. 182.

There were, however, other and more serious charges, charges
advanced notably by Cornelius Agrippa and others, which called
for greater consideration. Cornelius Agrippa was an eccentric
German philosopher whose work, *De vanitate et incertitudine
scientiarum* (1527) embodied an attack upon poetry (cap. IV),
and having been translated by J. Sandford in 1569 was not
without its influence in England at the time. The main charges
Sidney enumerates as follows : first, that poetry was useless
and a waste of time ; secondly, that it was ' the mother of lies ',
a collection of falsehoods ; thirdly, that it gave rise to evil fancies
and had thus a degrading and enfeebling influence ; and lastly,
there was the tradition that Plato had banished poets from his
ideal state. The first of these charges Sidney briefly dismisses,[1]
claiming to have already refuted it in establishing the fact that
poetry stood supreme in conducing to virtue. The second, that
poetry dealt with things untrue, however, he stoutly denies.[2]
Astronomers, physicians, historians, and others, all these, he
concedes, inevitably make false statements. But the poet
' nothing affirms and therefore never lieth ' ; his aim being ' to
tell not what is or is not, but what should or should not be '.
So that what he offers is not fact but fiction ; yet fiction embodying truth of an ideal kind. Then, again, there was the objection
that poetry had a wanton and an effeminate influence on its
readers.[3] Comedy, the lyric, elegiac and heroic poetry, all alike
were said to be infected with the love-theme and its amorous
conceits, thus filling the minds of men with ' pestilent desires '.
For the sake of argument Sidney is prepared to grant that a
vicious treatment of love had not been altogether absent from
earlier poetry ; though at the same time he protested that the
love-theme in itself was not deserving of indiscriminate censure,
seeing that the gift of discerning beauty was a noble attribute
of all mankind. Yet, granted that such abuse really existed,
was the fault, he asks, inherent in poetry itself, or was it not
rather due to man's misuse of the same ? All arts and sciences
misused, he recalls, had evil effects ; but that did not detract
from their value when rightly employed ; and an abuse of poetry
should not be allowed to make ' its right use odious '. As for
its alleged debilitating influence its tendency to foster in men
an indulgence in fancy and a disinclination for action that
weakened the martial fibre of ancient days, to this charge Sidney
shrewdly retorts by asking when after all were those ancient
days, seeing that ' no memory is so ancient that hath the precedence of poetry ' ? The truth was, he explains with the

[1] *ibid.* i. p. 184.   [2] *ibid.*   [3] *ibid.* i. p. 186.

help of many instances, that poetry from the earliest times had been ' the companion of camps ', had been cherished above all by great men of action ; and he ventures to add that ' *Orlando Furioso* or honest king Arthur would never displease a soldier '.

It is to the last of the objections—Plato's rejection of poetry [1] —that Sidney finds the greatest difficulty in replying ; like many another before and since he is perplexed that the greatest and ' most poetical ' of philosophers should ' defile the fountain out of which his flowing streams had proceeded '. He reminds his readers, to begin with, of the ancient conflict between philosophy and poetry which had raged for two centuries before Plato's time ; [2] he also recounts how philosophers, having extracted their wisdom from ' the sweet mysteries of poetry ' and reduced it to a system, ' like ungrateful apprentices were not content to set up shop for themselves but sought all means to discredit their masters '. Nor, he added, was this hostility lessened at a later date by the high esteem in which poetry had continued to be held. Nevertheless, despite all this, Sidney refuses to think that Plato, although a philosopher, was therefore of necessity an enemy of poetry. On the contrary he urged that what Plato had really objected to were the false conceptions of the gods, the atheism and superstition which ancient poetry had fostered and sustained ; so that Plato's objection, he argued, was directed, not against poetry as such, but against current theological doctrines and the poetry which enshrined those doctrines. In other words, Plato in his view had banished the abuse of poetry and not poetry itself. [3] And this conclusion he supports by a reference to Plato's glowing description of the poet in *Ion* as ' a light and winged and sacred thing '. [4] This he suggests was valid testimony enough of Plato's real attitude to poetry ; though, as has been already stated, in attributing the poetic activity to ' the inspiring of a divine force far above man's wit ', Plato, he confesses, was making a claim which he for his part could not endorse. [5] This, then, was Sidney's solution of this much-vexed problem ; and if his argument fails to take into account all the relevant factors, it is nevertheless not without its interest. It provided a timely and reasoned reply to the age-long denunciation of poetry which had rested largely on Plato's authority ; and thus prepared the way for a truer appreciation of poetry and the poetic art.

By now Sidney has come to the end of his defence of poetry,

[1] Smith, *op. cit.* i. pp. 190 ff.   [2] See Plato, *Republic*, 607 B.
[3] See Atkins, *Lit. Crit. in Antiquity*, i. pp. 46 ff.
[4] *Ion*, 534.   [5] See p. 116 *supra*.

having discussed its nature, its value to the community and the well-worn arguments which still hindered a proper appreciation of the poetic art. And in so doing he not only gave to the ' poet-haters ' a crushing yet dignified reply, and this without recourse to the convenient but unsatisfying allegorical doctrine, he also flashed new light over the whole field, dispelling the mists which had gathered around poetry during the preceding centuries, those conceptions which made poetry out to be nothing more than a branch of theology, rhetoric, logic, and the rest ; and in addition he restored poetry once again to its place of honour among the great arts and claimed it as a serious and fruitful study for modern readers. Nor is his handling of this his main theme unworthy of the occasion. To it he has devoted the main part of his work, bringing to bear the results of wide and judicious reading, and fusing together ideas drawn from various quarters, from Plato and Aristotle chiefly, but from Horace, Cicero, and Plutarch, from patristic writings, from Italian and other sources as well. Of the debts to classical writers something has already been said. In addition, the comparison of poetry with philosophy, for instance, may well have been suggested by his reading of Daniello's *Poetica*. From Minturno he seems to have borrowed the terms ' admiration and commiseration '[1] as descriptive of tragic effects ; from Italian critics generally the term ' heroic poem ' in place of the ' epic ' ; as well as his conception of the supremacy of that poetic ' kind ' ; while his idea of tragedy, again, is reminiscent of medieval, rather than Aristotelian, doctrine.

Yet more notable, however, is the skill with which he has made his philosophical disquisition easy and attractive reading for courtly circles. To this end his liberal use of illustrations drawn from ancient and Biblical literature, from medieval romances and ballads alike, in some measure contributed. But more effective still is his concrete and picturesque treatment of an abstract theme, the humorous irony in which he has veiled his lively portraits of the philosopher and historian, and the charming simplicity of his account of the poet and his work. With pardonable malice aforethought, it may be, he prejudiced at the outset the case for both philosopher and historian, when he described the philosophers moving ' with a sullen gravity as though they could not abide vice by daylight, rudely clothed for to witness outwardly their contempt of outward things, with books in their hands against glory whereto they set their names, sophistically speaking against subtility and angry with any man

[1] See p. 128 *infra*.

in whom they see the foul fault of anger ' ; or again, the historian, ' laden with old mouse-eaten records, authorizing himself
(for the most part) upon other histories, whose greatest authorities are built upon the notable foundation of hearsay, having
much ado to accord different writers and to pick truth out of
partiality '.[1]   That there was an element of truth in these descriptions was what gave them their piquancy. From the earliest
times the pretensions of charlatan philosophers had been the
subject of ridicule, and two centuries previously they had been
derided in a well-known work by Boccaccio, to whom Sidney
indeed may have owed something in the way of suggestion ; [2]
whereas the limitations of contemporary historical studies, of
the uncritical chronicles more especially, are not altogether
unfaithfully represented here. By Sidney's courtly readers the
delightful irony of the treatment, with its concise epigrammatic
style, would doubtless have been appreciated ; and here, incidentally, was anticipated that later vogue of character-sketches,
which culminated, under Theophrastan influence,[3] in the 17th-
Century works of Overbury, Earle, and others.

Having now fulfilled his appointed task—the defence of
poetry—Sidney cannot help asking, before drawing to a close,
how it was that the prevailing contempt for poetry had come
about. He suspects, to begin with, that the peaceful years
(1558–81) immediately preceding, when ' an over-faint quietness '
seemed ' to strew the house for poets ', had in reality bred but a
tame and sluggish generation, devoid of the ardent and generous
spirits necessary for poetic creation ; so that poetry had come
to be represented by ' servile wits ', men uninspired and worldly,
in whose company finer souls had not deigned to range themselves.
Moreover, such ' bastard poets ', he explained, wrote in ignorance
of the poetic art, to the great hurt of poetry ; whereas its true
exponents should be gifted men who wrote well knowingly,
having first sought ' to know what they do and how to do it '.
For the attainment of such skill he deemed the old classical
prescription of the rhetoricians to be still valid, namely, a knowledge of art (ars), imitation of sound models (imitatio) and con-

---

[1] Smith, op. cit. i. p. 162.

[2] cf. Boccaccio, De genealogia deorum, xiv. v. : ' They go about with
downcast eye to appear inseparable from their thoughts. Their pace is
slow to make the uneducated think that they stagger under an excessive
weight of high speculation. They dress unpretentiously, not because
they are really modest, but only to mask themselves with sanctity '
(tr. C. G. Osgood, Boccaccio on Poetry, p. 34).

[3] See G. S. Gordon, English Literature and the Classics (essay on
' Theophrastus and his imitators ').

stant practice (*exercitatio*). But except for practice, and that of a misguided kind, such precepts, he contended, were everywhere neglected ; and ' the pitiful state of poor poetry ' he therefore attributed not only to contemporary activities of inferior and mercenary minds, but also to the widespread ignorance of the poetic art. This attempt of Sidney to explain causes in the light of prevailing conditions is by no means without its interest ; though there was more in the problem than emerges from his analysis—the confused and inadequate notions inherited from the Middle Ages, for instance, or again, the later side-tracking of poetry by the Humanists. What is of importance, however, is Sidney's clear recognition, despite all contemporary disparagement, of the need for a serious study of the poetic art ; and the rest of his work, a sort of appendix to his main theme, is a brief commentary on what he regards as defects in the native literature at the time of writing (c. 1582), together with some amount of discussion on points of literary art.

It is therefore as one of the earliest attempts to treat of the poetic art that this last section of Sidney's work is of value ; and here, once again, in characteristic fashion, he presents his teaching in no severe or pedantic form. Basing it on actual literature and on matters of topical interest, he submits his views on tragedy and comedy, the lyric, stylistic and metrical questions,[1] bringing to bear in the process his customary good sense and scholarship. Not without its significance, however, is the place given in the discussion to tragedy and in a lesser degree, to comedy ; whereas epic poetry, it might be added, he entirely ignores, though he had previously described it as ' the best and most accomplished kind '. He himself explains that the drama had already become the most popular of native forms, though characterized by many abuses which had given point to Philistine attack ; and in his treatment of tragedy and comedy Sidney is evidently submitting his reasoned reply. But apart from this, he was doubtless influenced by the importance attached to dramatic poetry by Italian critics in their expositions of Aristotle's *Poetics*. With their modifications of Aristotle's doctrine he was well acquainted ; and now for the first time new ideas concerning tragedy were submitted to English readers, though elsewhere dramatic theory concerned itself mainly with comedy, owing to long familiarity of scholars with the works of Plautus and Terence.

[1] His choice of subjects was possibly influenced by Minturno's *De poeta* (1559), in which Bk. III treats of tragedy, Bk. IV comedy, Bk. V lyric, Bk. VI diction and prosody.

When we turn to consider Sidney's conception of tragedy we shall find it˙to be somewhat indeterminate and composite in character, made up for the most part of ideas reminiscent of medieval tradition, together with fragments drawn from Aristotle as interpreted by Italian critics. Thus medieval doctrine still persists in his statement that tragedy treats mainly of the falls of tyrants and the uncertainty of life ; [1] but along with this are combined other elements. Following Scaliger, for instance, he maintains the necessity for stately speeches and moral teaching after the manner of Seneca ; [2] in describing the function of tragedy he adopts Minturno's terms, ' admiration and commiseration ',[3] in place of the Aristotelian ' pity and fear ' ; while most significant of all is his insistence on the need for the observance of the Unities,[4] Castelvetro's development of Aristotle's doctrine, for which (except for the unity of action, which Sidney fails to mention) there existed no actual warrant in Aristotle's work. At the same time he is not wanting in sound practical hints for the handling of the tragic plot, notably in his advice concerning the treatment of a given story for dramatic purposes. Thus tragedy, he explains, is subject, not to the laws of history, but to the laws of poetry [5]—a point seized upon by later dramatists to justify their ' romantic ' plays—so that the dramatist is free to modify or transform his material ' to the most tragical conveniency ', that is, with a view to obtaining the proper tragic effects. Furthermore, recalling Horace's advice, he recommends that the plot should open, not with a tedious account of the ultimate origin of the story (*gemino . . . ab ovo*),[6] but at some significant point which would bring the reader at once to the heart of things ; as Euripides, he adds, in his *Hecuba* had done. Then, too, in developing his plot the dramatist, he urges, was not to be bound by strict adherence to specific details or the chronological sequence of the original story ; he might, if necessary, invent fresh incidents and situations or freely change the order of events. And if there were details which for some reason or other could not well be represented on the stage, then such incidents could be reported (or described) [7] in accordance with the practice of the messenger in the plays of antiquity. Such advice was not without its bearing on the characteristic defects of the early Chronicle plays ; while it embodied valuable principles subsequently illustrated in the plays and critical remarks of later Elizabethan dramatists.

[1] Smith, *op. cit.* i. p. 177.   [2] *ibid.* i. pp. 196–7.   [3] *ibid.* i. p. 177.
[4] *ibid.* i. p. 197.   [5] *ibid.* i. p. 198.
[6] *ibid* : cf. Horace, *Ars Poetica*, 147.   [7] *ibid.*

Nor is this all that Sidney has to say concerning tragedy; for he calls attention to what he regards as two of the most serious defects of the contemporary drama, namely, the gross improbabilities caused by the neglect of the Unities of time and place, and the incongruous mingling of comic with tragic material. The first of these matters he treats at some length, claiming the support of Aristotle and ' common reason ',[1] asserting also that the Unities had been universally observed in antiquity, though Plautus and Terence had occasionally had lapses. His censure is made in characteristically picturesque and ironical fashion, and is couched in terms reminiscent of Vives's attack on the flagrant impossibilities of medieval romances,[2] terms which Whetstone had already adopted in his Dedication to *Promos and Cassandra* (1578),[3] in commenting on the improbable themes of the contemporary drama. That the stage should be deemed to represent now Asia, now Africa, now a garden, a rock, a cave, a battlefield; or again, that in two short hours the vicissitudes of a whole life-story could be fitly unfolded—all this was manifestly sheer absurdity, ' inartificially (i.e. inartistically) imagined '. Yet a closer acquaintance with Aristotle would have shown that he had nowhere insisted on the necessity for strict verisimilitude on the stage, and that to him the irrational, the incredible and even the impossible, were fit matters for poetry, provided that they were convincingly presented. His definite pronouncement had been that ' a likely impossibility is always preferable to an unconvincing possibility '; [4] and herein was formulated a defence long ago of that ' world of fine fabling ' which was to follow in later ' romantic ' literature. The truth of Aristotle's position was to be instinctively recognized by later Elizabethans; but the demand for verisimilitude here voiced by Sidney was to prove one of the stumbling-blocks of later dramatic theory.

Concerning the second of his censures relating to contemporary tragedy, namely, the incongruous mingling of comic with tragic material, Sidney has less to say; though if we may judge from the frequency of similar complaints,[5] the abuse was a very real one on the Elizabethan stage. Worthy of note, in the first place, is the fact that on the general question of blending comic and serious matter he makes no absolute or unqualified pronouncement. He is able to conceive of circumstances when the plot may require the presence of both kings and clowns, ' because the matter so carrieth it '; and with him the strict separation of

---

[1] *ibid.* i. p. 197.
[2] See p. 60 *supra.*
[3] See p. 232 *infra.*
[4] *Poetics*, 1460 a, 26–7.
[5] cf. Whetstone, Hall, Shakespeare, &c. pp. 232, 235, 249 *infra.*

serious and comic has not as yet become a fixed dogma. What he objects to is the ill-timed and indecorous mixing of tragic and comic elements, when clowns ' are thrust in by head and shoulders to play a part in majestical matters with neither decency nor discretion '.[1] The results, he suggests, are mere absurdity, scurrility, and vacant laughter ; whereas the ancients, he added, were careful ' never, or very daintily, to match horn-pipes with funerals ' ! And this same openness of mind is revealed in his attitude to tragi-comedy, which he recognizes as an acceptable blend of tragedy and comedy, on the ground that ' if severed they be good, the conjunction cannot be hurtful '.[2]

In the remarks on comedy itself that follow, the same method of commenting on current abuses is adopted in an attempt to point out a better way,   Sidney's chief complaint is the prevailing tendency to make comedy little more than rough farce, productive of empty and fleeting laughter, while his desire is for a more intellectual comedy resulting in delight of a satisfying and lasting kind.   His first endeavour is therefore to distinguish between ' laughter ' and that ' delight ' which he maintains to be ultimately the end of all true art ;   then, to confute the current notion that there could be no ' delight without laughter ' ;   and whatever may be thought of his analysis of these elusive matters, the attempt at a reasoned and psychological treatment at this date is at least noteworthy.   Thus ' delight ', he asserts,[3] implies a joy that is both ' permanent and present ', a joy arising from a sense of the ' conveniency ' (i.e. harmony) existing between specific subjects on the one hand and men and Nature on the other ; while ' laughter ' he defines as merely ' a scornful tickling ', momentary and superficial, caused by a sense of ' disproportion ' or incongruity between those subjects and men and Nature.   That there could be ' delight ' without ' laughter ', of that he is convinced ; and he instances the human response to a vision of feminine beauty.[4]   He is equally insistent that there could be ' laughter ' without ' delight ', as in the results produced by grotesque forms, the mad capers of ' antics ' or buffoons, or again, sudden and unexpected mischances.   At the same time he holds that ' delight ' and ' laughter ' could be effectively combined ; and this combination he regards as productive of comedy in the true sense.   As an instance of what he has in mind he recalls the situation of Hercules as described by Ovid, ' with his great beard and furious countenance, in woman's attire, spinning

---

[1] See Smith, *op. cit.* i. p. 199.
[2] *ibid.* i. p. 175.   [3] *ibid.* i. p. 199.
[4] cf. Trissino, *Poetica* (1563), ii. 127, to whom Sidney may be indebted.

at Omphale's commandment '.[1]   Here, he points out, over and
above the 'laughter' caused by an amazing and outrageous
spectacle is also the 'delight' arising from a realization of the
vagaries of love ; and in such a situation, he suggests, are to be
found the ingredients of genuine comedy, and 'that delightful
teaching which is the end of poesy '.

Having thus argued in favour of a more intellectual kind of
comedy, Sidney then proceeds to supply practical hints calculated to make such comedy effective.   In the first place,
recalling Aristotle's teaching,[2] he points out that comedy has
nothing to do with things evil or vicious ; such themes or
characters, he maintains, merely excite aversion and call for
stern treatment.   Nor again are painful human deformities to
be treated as comic material ; for such infirmities are grievous
to behold and give rise to pity rather than amusement.   The
proper material for comedy, he implies, is to be found in human
weaknesses and foibles of a harmless kind ; and he enumerates,
by way of illustration, certain characters which seem to him
appropriate, characters reminiscent of the stock figures of Roman
comedy, and including a fussy courtier, a cowardly boastful
soldier, a conceited pedant and an 'awry-transformed' (i.e.
affected) traveller.[3]   In suggesting such characters, however,
Sidney is not proposing to limit comedy to the use of these or
any other stereotyped figures or types.   To him they are merely
examples of human foibles ; and most significant of all is the
reason he submits for giving them his approval and for regarding them as likely to give rise to 'delightful laughter '.   Such
characters, he explains, are those 'which we play naturally ' ;
in other words, they are characters actually drawn from the
ordinary life of the time.   And here Sidney is suggesting a profound truth in connexion with comedy.   It was a truth which
Shakespeare seems to have first realized in his creations of
Bottom and his crew ; while not without its interest is the fact
that all the characters mentioned by Sidney are represented in
Shakespeare's plays.

Turning next to lyrical poetry, which, along with the drama,
had given clearest evidence of vitality amongst his contemporaries, Sidney is content with a brief but significant note.   'Other
sorts of poetry almost have we none,' he laments ; and his chief
complaint is the futility of the themes of contemporary efforts,
inadequate in his opinion to inspire true lyrical qualities.   Those
qualities, however, he finds in Biblical poetry, and more par-

[1] Smith, *op. cit.* i. p. 200 ; see Ovid, *Heroides*, 9, 75.
[2] *Poetics*, 1449 a, 32.   [3] Smith, *op. cit.* i. pp. 200–1.

ticularly in the *Psalms*, of which he himself had produced a
metrical version ; [1] and there, he maintains, the genuine lyrical
fire had been kindled, in chanting the praises of ' that unspeakable
and everlasting beauty to be seen by the eyes of the mind, only
cleared by faith '.[2]   Of the love-poetry of the time, and such
contemporary verse as came ' under the banner of unresistible
love ', he speaks with disapproval, censuring its insincerity and
lack of passion.[3]   Most of such poems, he notes, were made up
of borrowed and swelling phrases, loosely strung together and
ineffective because of their want of genuine force and feeling.
The obvious reference here is to the slavish following of the
Petrarchan tradition, from which Sidney, ' the English Petrarch ',
was by no means free ; as was abundantly shown by his *Astrophel
and Stella* sonnets (1580–4), which both in form and spirit betray
Italian influence.   Moreover, those poems are of the nature of
literary exercises, representing in accordance with the conventions of the time an idealized memory of a poetic courtship, and
therefore no utterance of actual passion, but rather of sentiments
fanciful and unreal.   Nevertheless his protest against insincerity
in the lyric is of no doubtful significance ; and in the sonnets
themselves he makes his views yet more clear.   He laments, for
instance, the fact that ' poor Petrarch's long-deceased woes '
were still being sung ' with new-born sighs and denizened wit ' ; [4]
elsewhere he claims to be ' no pickpurse of another's wit ' ; [5]
and above all, he recognizes for the first time the element of
personal feeling bound up with the lyric in the advice of his Muse
to ' look in thy heart and write '.[6]

With regard to the fourth subject on which Sidney dilates,
namely, diction and style, there he found defects yet more serious
and disturbing ; and consequently he calls attention to the
contemporary craze for ' fine writing '.[7]   Literary expression,
he asserts, was tending to become little more than a ' courtesan-
like painted affectation ', as a result of the use of far-fetched
inkhorn terms, obscure and grandiose, as well as devices such as
alliteration and other hackneyed figures.   Nor were these tricks,
he adds, confined to versifiers alone ; they coloured ordinary
prose, even the prose of scholarly men, while they also formed
part of pulpit oratory.   The origin of these vicious practices he
attributes to the earlier rhetorical studies, and more especially
to the use in schools of ' Nizolian paper-books ',[8] those collections

[1] ed. later by Ruskin as *Rock Honey*.   [2] Smith, *op. cit.* i. p. 155.
[3] *ibid.* i. p. 201.   [4] *Sonnet*, xv.   [5] *Sonnet*, lxxiv.
[6] *Sonnet*, i.   [7] Smith, *op. cit.* i. p. 202.
[8] cf. M. Nizolius, *Thesaurus Ciceronianus* (1535).

of Ciceronian phrases and figures employed in the teaching of
Latin ; whereas a better way, he rightly suggests, of acquiring
classical style would be to abandon such note-books and to recapture the methods and spirit of the great classics by ' devour-
ing them whole ',—advice reminiscent of the teaching of the
Pléiade, according to which the essence of the classical languages
was to be converted into ' blood and nourishment ' of other
tongues. As it was, however, rhetorical devices were used
without discretion, in season and out of season, so that ' sugar
and spice were cast upon every dish ' ; and this ' seeming fine-
ness ', this tawdry eloquence, failed completely in its true function,
which was that of persuasion. Among all these abuses, however,
one more especially claimed Sidney's attention, namely, the
inordinate use of similes drawn from unnatural history which had
already become the fashion, as was seen, for instance, in Lyly's
Euphues (1578) and Gosson's *School of Abuse* (1579). This craze
of Euphuism he strongly denounces both here and elsewhere ;
as when, for instance, he derides those poets who

> With strange similes enriched each line,
> Of herbs or beasts, which Ind or Afric hold.[1]

Similes, he points out, contributed not at all to the task of persuasion ; they proved nothing, but only illustrated ; and illustration overdone was both tedious and distracting. ' To win
credit of popular ears ', he urged, ' plain sensibleness ' alone
was necessary. And he recalls in this connexion Cicero's
testimony concerning the famous Roman orator, M. Antonius
(143–87 B.C.) who claimed to know nothing of the subtleties of
art.[2] A sparing use of similes and other devices he therefore
commends, at the same time maintaining that the man who
employed them indiscriminately was ' more careful to speak
curiously than to speak truly ', and was ' but dancing to his own
music '.

Having thus pronounced judgment on the meretricious
literary ornaments of his day, Sidney goes on to remark, with
keen critical insight, how, strangely enough, he had found in the
writings of courtiers of no great learning a sounder and more
effective style than in the works of certain of the ' professors of
learning '. This, however, he ventures to suggest, was due to
the fact that the courtier, guided by natural instincts of good

---

[1] *Astrophel and Stella*, Sonnet iii.
[2] Smith, *op. cit.* i. p. 203 : cf. Cicero, *De orat.* ii, i. 4 : also Shakespeare,
Julius Caesar, iii. ii. 233, where the statement is assigned to the later
Mark Antony.
10

taste and tact, had unknowingly written in accordance with the dictates of art ; whereas the scholar, ostentatiously displaying the rules of art, had written in unnatural, and therefore inartistic, fashion. Hence the methods of art, so Sidney implies, were in reality prescribed by the laws of Nature,[1] while for their effective working the devices employed were to be deftly concealed— fundamental precepts both, characteristic of ancient teaching from Aristotle onwards. He then explains that while treating of current stylistic abuses, he had been conscious of sharing in the ' common infection ' and of ' being sick among the rest '— a handsome confession and a piece of self-criticism suggested possibly by his experiments in his *Arcadia* (1580), with its word-jingles, its excessive use of *prosopopeia, oxymoron* and the rest. Moreover, he adds that he too had felt the need for restraint in these matters, more especially in view of the potentialities of English as a literary medium. That it was a language with many foreign elements but without inflexions, was no doubt true ; but these features, he maintained, only added to its wealth and ease of expression ; while in its faculty of forming compounds, ' one of the greatest beauties in a language ', it rivalled Greek and surpassed Latin. The truth was, added Sidney, that ' for the uttering sweetly and properly the conceits of the mind, . . . English hath equally with any other tongue in the world ' ;[2] and with Latin still strongly entrenched as the literary medium of scholars, this unequivocal pronouncement on the vernacular was without doubt both timely and reassuring.

The last matter treated by Sidney was the question, much debated at the time, concerning the possibility of reforming English prosody along classical lines. Of the widespread character of the inquiry and the suggestion originally made by Ascham [3] something has already been said ; and in the meantime the idea had been taken up seriously, not to say laboriously, by a mixed coterie consisting of the redoubtable Cambridge scholar, Gabriel Harvey, and one Master Drant, together with those ' diamonds of the court ', Sidney himself and his friends Dyer, Fulke Greville, and Spenser as well. In 1579 Spenser had stated that ' Sidney and Dyer had proclaimed a general surceasing and silence of bald rhymers and also of the very best too ' ;[4] that inspired by Drant, they had also ' prescribed certain laws and rules of quantities for English verse ' ; and in addition it was said that a rival programme was in contemplation by Harvey. That Sidney was attracted by the project is also made clear by

[1] Smith, *op. cit.* i. p. 203.   [2] *ibid.* i. p. 204.
[3] See p. 93 *supra*.   [4] Smith, *op. cit.* i. pp. 89, 99.

his inclusion in the *Arcadia* of verses in hexameteis, elegiacs, sapphics, anacreontics and the rest, incidentally the most solid residuum of the reforming movement. At the date of the *Apology*, however, Sidney was still doubtful as to the wisdom of the change ; in judicial mood he states that the relative merits of the ancient or quantitative and the modern or accented and rhyming systems was a matter that ' would bear many speeches '. Each, he maintained, had a ' sweetness ' of its own, and neither was wanting in ' majesty ' ; while the English language, he added, ' was fit for both sorts '.[1] His judgment, which is thus one of compromise, is notable however, for its method of approach. Refraining from giving a decisive verdict in favour of the quantitative system on the authority of the ancients alone, he bases his pronouncement on the charactcristic features of the vernacular as compared with other languages. What is also significant is that the earlier unreasoning prejudices against rhyme are with him no longer apparent, while the accentual nature of English is duly noted ; and with this more balanced judgment the way was prepared for a juster appreciation of the problem of English versification.

By now Sidney has brought his *Apology* to a close ; but a word must still be added concerning his achievement as a judicial critic, and the extent to which, in the course of his abstract and technical theorizing, he has contributed to the appreciation of literature in the concrete. Of the accuracy with which he has arraigned the outstanding defects of the literature of his day— the drama, the lyric and style generally—some indication has already been given ; though within a decade or so those breaches of the Unities which he deplores were to be vindicated in practice. And the same independent judgment is likewise revealed in his refusal to accept some of the older literary traditions. Thus the *Sortes Virgilianae*, for instance, he describes as ' a vain and godless superstition ' ; and in place of the wild conjectures that had come down concerning the metrical character of the *Psalms*, he holds, rightly, that the rules governing Hebrew verse had not hitherto been ' fully found '.[2] On the other hand, it is true, he accepts the tradition according to which the mysterious Dares Phrygius [3] had provided an authentic story of Acneas in his *History of the Trojan War*.

Of greater importance, however, is his work as a constructive critic, seen in scattered remarks which contribute to a better understanding and appreciation of literary values. A just appraisal of contemporary literature is notoriously chancy ; but

[1] Smith, *op. cit.* i. p. 205.   [2] *ibid.* i. p. 155.   [3] *ibid.* i. p. 168.

Sidney's selection of the *Mirror for Magistrates*, Surrey's lyrics, *Gorboduc* and the *Shepherd's Calendar* [1] as worthy of praise, gives evidence of discrimination, which is by no means invalidated by the reservations he makes, namely, that the plot of *Gorboduc* was somewhat faulty and unconvincing, or again, that no precedent existed in the practice of the ancients for Spenser's use of dialect and archaic forms.[2] Apart from this he calls attention to literary excellences of more than one kind. Not without its significance, for instance, in his enthusiasm for Biblical literature ; as when he notes the beauty of the penitential *Psalm*,[3] the compelling suggestion of the sublime ' majesty ' of God elsewhere in the *Psalms*, when the mountains, awe-struck, are said to leap at his presence,[4] or again, the wonderful narratives contained in the parables of Dives, the prodigal son, as well as in Nathan's parable of the ewe lamb.[5] Then, too, unlike the Humanists, he can discern merit in medieval literature. In one place, for instance, he refers to the excellences of Chaucer's *Troilus and Criseyde*, adding that ' I know not whether to marvel more, either that he in that misty time could see so clearly, or that we in this clear age walk so stumblingly after him '.[6] Moreover, he can conceive of inspiring effects resulting from a reading of *Amadis of Gaul*,[7] one of the despised romances ; while in connexion with the old ballads, reduced in his day to pot-house fare, he has to confess, not without some bewilderment, that he never heard the old song of Percy and Douglas that he ' found not his heart moved more than with a trumpet '.[8] To contemporary readers such comments were calculated to bring both illumination and guidance ; and in the critical development they are no less noteworthy. Sidney's standards, it is true, were ostensibly those of the ancient classics. Thus *Amadis of Gaul* he recognizes is not ' perfect poesy ' ; the *Ballad of Chevy Chace*, again, he points out, falls short of ' the gorgeous eloquence of Pindar ' ; while the *Shepherd's Calendar*, for all its ' poetic sinews ', fails to conform with the traditions of Theocritus and Virgil. Nevertheless, what is important to note is the fact that, apart from his strictures on the neglect of the Unities, his judgments are nowhere determined in accordance with rules or theories. His ultimate test is of an aesthetic kind, that is, the ' moving ' or emotional

---

[1] Smith, *op. cit.* i. p. 196.

[2] *ibid* : cf. however Theocritus's use of rustic Doric, the use of which Dryden likens to ' a fair shepherdess in her country russet, talking in a Yorkshire tone ' (Ker. *Essays of Dryden*, i. 265).

[3] *ibid*. i. p. 174 (*Psalm* 51).   [4] *ibid*. i. p. 155 (*Psalm* 114).

[5] *ibid*. i. pp. 166, 174.   [6] *ibid*. i. p. 196.

[7] *ibid*. i. p. 173.   [8] *ibid*. i. p. 178.

effects produced, with their bracing and uplifting results; and these dynamic qualities in literature he is prepared to commend wherever he finds them. For a detailed analysis of these emotional effects it would be folly to look at this date; and indeed, for some time to come, later critics were not always able to give clear and definite reasons for the faith that was in them. The first sign of literary appreciation is to feel; and not the least of Sidney's achievements as a critic was the early recognition of that fact.

Such then are the main contents of Sidney's *Apology for Poetry*, a work which has rightly been valued as one of the outstanding performances in English criticism and one which inaugurated a new phase in critical history. It has been described as an epitome of Renascence theory; but this description can be misleading if it is taken to mean nothing more than a summary reproduction of classical and Italian doctrine. What gives to the work its undoubted value is its originality, the skill with which Sidney has drawn on earlier teaching, selecting, adapting and fusing together ideas gathered from many sources, in order to set forth ultimately his own conception of poetry, independently arrived at. Thus apart from the Italians, he makes use of Plato and Aristotle, Horace and Plutarch; but, like Horace, he subscribes to the authority of no one school of thought. His treatment throughout is of an eclectic kind; his conclusions are the result of personal reflexion as well as wide reading; and upon them is stamped the impress of a lofty personality. At the same time it cannot be doubted that Platonic influence played a considerable, perhaps a predominant, part in shaping his views, owing to some affinity of spirit. To him poetry was a natural human activity enabling men to sing of beauty and truth, and to satisfy their longings for a world transformed, thus nurturing in them what was good and noble. Moreover, so far from being merely an instrument for moral teaching, it was a concrete and inspiring revelation of human ideals, and thus, in a sense, a criticism of life. This, then, with its element of permanent truth, was the substance of Sidney's message to an age perplexed and even hostile. With the traditional objections boldly faced, with claims put forward for a place for poetry in the intellectual and social life, and with attempts made at a serious treatment of the poetic art, that message constituted a vindication of poetry, individual and unique in kind, which restored to poetry something of its ancient prestige and meaning, and was calculated to bring enlightenment and reassurance to his own generation.

Nor was the originality of the work confined solely to its

subject-matter ; in the manner of presentation, too, will be found a freshness and vigour characteristic of Sidney alone. Writing for courtly circles and in a vein far removed from the fantastic and pedestrian styles of contemporary pamphlets and disputations, he achieved a form of expression unsurpassed even in an age of daring experiments in prose. Nowhere else do we find the same happy mingling of the ideal and the practical, the same blend of dignity and humour, of sincerity and irony, of controlled enthusiasms and racy colloquialisms ; or again, that unstudied simplicity and grace which everywhere pervade the work. And over and above all this was the realistic presentment of his abstract theme in concrete terms. In antiquity the vivid representation of things by means of word-pictures (i.e. ἐνάργεια) had been strongly commended ; but to the Elizabethans the device seems to have come naturally and inevitably in the absence of abstract and philosophical terms. This accounts in a large measure for the appeal of much of Elizabethan prose ; and in Sidney's *Apology* it gives to the work much of its simple charm and effectiveness. It is therefore as the first piece of literary criticism in English that is literature itself that the *Apology* figures in critical history ; and appearing as it did in the dawn of the great efflorescence, it forms a worthy prelude to what was to follow. Of its actual influence on contemporaries one can but conjecture ; though circulated in manuscript as it was among Sidney's friends up to the date of publication (1595) its effects can scarcely have been slight. On Ben Jonson its influence is abundantly clear ; the same is also true in connexion with Shakespeare and other dramatists ; while Shelley later on was not alone in deriving inspiration from its pages when he wrote his *Defence of Poetry*. As a fitting legacy of one of England's noblest and gentlest souls the work will continue to charm modern readers with its idealism, its sanity, its humour, and its grace. And nothing is surely more characteristic of the spirit of its author than the delightful irony with which he takes leave of his readers in uttering his direful threat to all those ' earth-creeping minds ' who, despite the claims he had made so eagerly and convincingly, still remained deaf to ' the planet-like music of poetry '.

CHAPTER VI

THE ART OF POETRY: GASCOIGNE, HARVEY, 'E. K.', WEBBE, PUTTENHAM

MEANWHILE, along with the vindication of poetry in general, some treatment of the poetic art, apart from Sidney's comments, now for the first time becomes perceptible; and this activity, though tentative and occasional to begin with, produced ultimately one systematic treatise of considerable value, in fact, one of the outstanding works in Elizabethan criticism. Concerning the causes which led to this new interest in the poetic art and to the changed direction thus given to literary discussion, something has already been said. From the Humanists, as we have seen, had come no sort of guidance in the matter; and from the early Tudor period nothing more than casual remarks on poetic technique confined mainly to the academic Latin drama, which however had but slight bearing on vernacular literature. And in the meantime the vague and confused ideas of the art of poetry then current are amply illustrated in the *Miscellanies* which from time to time appeared; or, again, by Willis's strange collection of poetic forms, and the technical defects of contemporaries with which Sidney had dealt. With the recognition, however, of the claims of poetry to be regarded as a serious factor in the national life, a growing need was felt for some consideration of those principles and methods which should govern its practice; and soon after 1570 efforts of various kinds were made to treat of matters relating to the technique of English poetry.

Not that matters of poetic technique alone engaged the attention at this date. For one thing, the influence of the earlier rhetorical tradition was still alive and vigorous; as was shown not only by the appearance of Abraham Fraunce's *Arcadian Rhetorike* (1588), but also by the popularity which had attended the lectures of Gabriel Harvey (1545–1630) on rhetoric at Cambridge (1576), and by the production of his works *Rhetor* and *Ciceronianus* [1] in 1577. In the former of those works Harvey had described Eloquence, in terms reminiscent of Martianus Capella's fantastic description of Rhetorica in *De nuptiis*, as a divine creature of great physical beauty, gloriously arrayed in colours of all kinds, and with Honour, Glory, and Magnificence

[1] See Grosart, *Works of Gabriel Harvey*, i. xvii–xviii.

in her train ; whereas in the more judicious *Ciceronianus* he had renounced his earlier creed of Ciceronianism, explaining how, taught by Ramus, Sturm, and others, he had learned to appreciate the independent attitude of Pico, Erasmus, and Politian, to look for personality as the source of style and not to the mere surface polish of the writer's language, adding finally, in his authoritative fashion, ' let any man learn to be not a Roman, but a Frenchman, German, Briton, or Italian '. Then, too, the nature of poetry itself, as distinct from the art, had by now become a subject of lively interest, as when Spenser in his *English Poet* (unpublished) emphasized the element of inspiration in poetry, described it as ' no art, but a divine gift and heavenly instinct, not to be gotten by labour and learning, but adorned with both, and poured into the wit by a certain ενθουσιασμὸς and celestial inspiration '.[1] Nevertheless, amidst the various signs of an awakening interest in critical matters at this date, an outstanding feature is the distinct trend towards a more detailed study of poetic technique, and of prosody in particular. Already in a prose passage of the *Mirror for Magistrates* (1559) passing reference had been made to the irregularities of native versification, when excerpts from 15th-Century verse, with their broken rhythm, were discussed, ' misliked ', and excused for historical reasons. And now with the contributions of Gascoigne, Harvey, ' E. K.', and others, in spite of their sporadic character and the various forms they assumed, a serious beginning of technical inquiries was successfully made. Their contributions were followed by the more ambitious but disappointing effort of Webbe in his *Discourse of English Poetrie* (1586), an attempt at a treatment of a more comprehensive and systematic kind. After which came the more interesting and suggestive treatise, Puttenham's *Arte of English Poesy* (1589) ; and from now on, poetry and the poetic art were to occupy the main attention in critical inquiries.

The first, and the most valuable, of these preliminary contributions came from George Gascoigne (1542–77), that versatile man of letters, who now added to his list of pioneering ventures in the masque, the satire and prose comedy, a short treatise on prosody. His work, *Notes of Instruction concerning the making of verse or rhyme in English*,[2] first appeared as an addition to his collected poems, the *Posies* (1575), and is notable for its sound and practical guidance, clearly and tersely expressed, with an

---

[1] See ' E. K.'s ' *Argument* to the October Eclogue of *Shepherd's Calendar*.

[2] See Smith, *op. cit.* i. pp. 46–57.

intimate bearing on contemporary verse. Thus in view of the artificiality and vapidity of much of the contemporary output he emphasizes, as a fundamental requirement, the selection of some worth-while theme, adding that mere praise of 'crystal eyes' or 'cherry lips' was not enough, any more than the mere use of pleasing words, neat epithets, or 'Rym, Ram, Ruff' alliterations derided by Chaucer.[1] As to the choice of themes he makes no definite suggestion, except that 'the uncomely customs of common writers' should be avoided. This much, however, he adds in terms reminiscent of Horace, that a suitable theme having been found, 'pleasant words would follow . . . fast enough'.[2] He then urges the need for retaining one verse-form throughout a poem, and for avoiding redundant words or meaningless tags to make up a rhyme—rhyme without reason, as he terms it. In the matter of diction, again, he recommends that the words employed should be those in ordinary use, that polysyllabic words 'smelling of the inkhorn', as well as all strange (obsoleta et inusitata) forms should be avoided unless the theme required them ; otherwise, he explains, their effect would be to 'cloy the verse'. At the same time he shrewdly recognizes that 'in some places a strange word doth draw attentive reading' ;[3] yet discretion in this matter, he adds, was everywhere necessary. Then, too, he demands that native idioms should be preserved, that inversion, for instance, should be sparingly used, and to each word should be given its ordinary pronunciation (e.g. treásure not treasúre). There was thus to be no wrenching of word-accent for metrical purposes ; though some allowance, he notes, should be made for that 'shrewd fellow, poetical licence ',[4] with its conventional liberties of making words shorter or longer, ydone for done, tane for taken, heavn for heaven. Concerning the use of figurative devices he advises further that the distinction drawn by 16th-Century rhetoricians between figures of prose and figures of poetry should be disregarded,[5] and that figures of prose should all be at the poet's service, seeing that they produced in poetry most effective results. Here, again, he adds his usual caveat of ne quid nimis, deploring more especially the excessive use of alliteration by his contemporaries ; and his good sense is once more apparent when he counsels that poetic style in general should be clear and sensible, devoid of 'superfineness' or 'obscure and dark phrases', since high-flying obscure utterance provided but little delight.

[1] Smith, op. cit. i. p. 47 : cf. Chaucer, Parson's Prol., l. 43.
[2] Ars Poetica, l. 40.   [3] Smith, op. cit. i. p. 53.
[4] ibid.   [5] ibid. i. p. 52.

Of equal interest, however, are his remarks on verse-forms, the first of their kind in English. Thus he treats in general of the main stanza-forms available ; [1] the rhyme royal, for instance, consisting of seven-line stanzas (*ababbcc*) with decasyllabic lines, well suited for ' grave discourses ' ; the ballad made up of six-line stanzas (*ababcc*), each line consisting of eight or six syllables, and employed for ' dances or light matters ' ; or again, the sonnet, consisting, not as was sometimes said, of any short poem, but of fourteen decasyllabic lines ending in a rhyming couplet, and commonly used for love-themes ; and in addition he mentions such forms as dizaines, sixaines and virelayes. Specially worthy of note, however, is his description of the sonnet, for he describes what was to be the characteristic Elizabethan form. In it, he explains, ' the first twelve lines do rhyme in staves (i.e. stanzas) of four lines by cross metre, and the last two rhyming do conclude the whole '. Of interest, too, are his remarks on current practices. The most commonly used form, he states, was the ' Poulter's measure ', with lines of twelve and fourteen syllables alternately ; while the omission of any mention of the two verse-forms which were to predominate in later literature is highly significant at this date. Thus no reference is made to the blank verse already introduced by Surrey, or to the heroic couplet so successfully used by Chaucer in his *Canterbury Tales*. The truth was that the secret of Chaucer's versification had been lost at this date ; and Gascoigne's description of the verse in Chaucer's ' merry tales ' was that of ' riding rhyme ', that is, a sort of free verse based on accent and not on a regular iambic measure.

Apart from this he laments the limitations imposed on contemporary verse by the exclusive use of the iambic measure and the neglect of anapaestic and other trisyllabic feet. For this, however, he sees no remedy, his advice being ' let us take the ford as we find it '. Chaucer in time past, he implies, had used such trisyllabic measures ; and incidentally he illustrates the confused ideas that prevailed concerning that poet's verse when he states, strangely enough, that ' our father Chaucer hath used the same liberty in feet and measures that the Latinists do use '.[2] His lines, Gascoigne explains, had not always the same number of syllables ; yet ' being read by one that hath understanding, . . . the longest verse will fall (to the ear) corresponding with that which hath fewest syllables in it '. Then, too, he notes the part played by the caesura in verse ; [3] and recommends that it should come in the middle of an octosyllabic line, after the sixth in an Alexandrine, and after the eighth in

[1] Smith, *op. cit.* i. pp. 54–6.   [2] *ibid.* i. p. 50.   [3] *ibid.* i. p. 54.

the fourteener line. He further discountenances the use of run-on lines, and complains of writers who failed to conclude their sense at the end of a stanza or couplet, thus ' making an end at latter Lammas '. But what above all were to be avoided were ' prolixity and tediousness '. ' Knit up your sentences ', he urges, ' as compendiously as you may ; since brevity (so that it be not drowned in obscurity) is most commendable '—and so thought Pope and others a century or so later.

Such then are the main elements of Gascoigne's teaching ; and despite obvious limitations, it is not without its value as an introduction to English prosody. Much of it may seem trite to modern readers ; indeed the writer himself apologizes more than once for its elementary character. Yet a reminder of basic principles was what was needed at the time ; and Gascoigne throughout has in mind the prosodic vagaries of his generation. The work is in fact the product of good sense and some feeling for poetry ; it is also free from pedantry and dogmatism ; and in tentatively submitting his views on the matter Gascoigne recalls the old saying, *Quot homines, tot sententiae*, as being specially true where poetry was concerned. Nor was his work without its influence on the generation that followed, if we may judge from later tributes. ' Master Gascoigne ', wrote Nashe in his Preface to Greene's *Menaphon* (1589), ' first beat the path to that perfection which our best poets have aspired to since his departure ' ; and he was not alone in testifying to Gascoigne's worth.

In the meantime Gascoigne's concern for English versification was being shared by others ; and further aspects of prosody were being considered by Gabriel Harvey and his circle ; the main question discussed being the possibility of substituting for English rhyming verse a system based on classical metres, though some attention was also given to the status and value of the quaint figure-poems then popular. Of the part played by Sidney in the controversy relating to the ' new versifying '—his active sympathy and indeterminate position—something has already been said ; while reference has also been made to the activities of Archdeacon Drant, Dyer, and others, in what at the time was a serious movement. At the centre of things, however, stood Gabriel Harvey, whose acknowledged eminence as a scholar added weight to the movement, and whose views are preserved in *Four Letters* (1580),[1] representing correspondence which passed between him and Spenser in the years 1579–80. From these *Letters* Harvey's position becomes plain. Following Ascham he

[1] *ibid*. i. pp. 87–126.

continues the attack on ' beggarly rhyming ', maintaining that
hexameters and pentameters would ' fairly yield themselves to
our mother tongue ', and that the exchange would be one of
' pure and fine gold ' for ' counterfeit and ill-favoured copper '.[1]
To this view Spenser for a time was strongly attracted ; though
from the first he saw difficulties in the native word-accent,
which, he held, would inevitably clash with a quantitative
system [2] and give rise to halting and limping movements, like
those of ' a lame gosling that draweth one leg after her '. At
the same time he suggests that some way of overcoming the
difficulty should not be impossible. Like the Greeks of old,
Englishmen, he claimed, should have control of their language ;
and he looks to Harvey for guidance in the matter.

    To this problem Harvey therefore addresses himself ; and the
first need, he asserts, is for some agreement on a standard
orthography,[3] in view of the chaos that prevailed in contemporary
writings, with their glaring discrepancies between spelling and
pronunciation. Sir Thomas Smith in his *De recta et emendata
Linguae Anglicae Scriptione* (1568) had previously dealt with
the question ; but Harvey is not convinced that he had solved
the problem. Moreover, he illustrates at some length the
absurdities resulting from all such pseudographies, in their
attempts at reconciling spelling and pronunciation, thus giving
rise to such forms as *yrne* (for *iron*), *heavn* (for *heaven*), and
Godd hys wrath (for *Goddes wrath*). Apart from the orthographical
difficulty, however, Harvey also recognizes the problem presented
by the native word-accent ; and despite his confidence in the
future of the ' new versifying ', he confesses his perplexity as to
the means of adapting the vernacular to the quantitative system
involved. With arbitrary attempts to tamper with the natural
quantities of English syllables he will have nothing to do ; and
he ridicules such fantastic pronunciations as *majéstie, excéllent,
follówing*, and the like.[4] ' It is not either position . . . or any
like Grammar school device ', he explains,[5] ' that can make
long or short ' ; and he refuses ' in despite of custom, forcibly
to usurp and tyrannize upon a quiet company of words that
have . . . so peaceably enjoyed their several privileges and
liberties without any disturbance '. Then, recalling Horace's
dictum that contemporary usage or custom was the ultimate
criterion in linguistic matters,[6] he stoutly maintains that it was
' petty treason ' to revolt from ' ordinary use and custom, and,

[1] Smith, *op. cit.* i. p. 101.   [2] *ibid.* i. pp. 98–9.   [3] *ibid.* i. p. 102.
[4] *ibid.* i. p. 118.   [5] *ibid.* i. pp. 121, 117.
[6] *ibid.* i. pp. 117, 119, 121 : cf. Horace, *Ars Poetica*, 72.

as it were, from the majesty of our speech ', which he accounted
' the only infallible and sovereign rule of all rules '; and thus
holding witĥ Gascoigne that ' we must take the ford as we find
it ', he looks to ' the vulgar and natural Mother prosody ' alone
for such adjustments as were necessary.

This, however, is as far as Harvey goes ; his good sense [1]
prevented him from suggesting any definite plan such as that
associated with Drant. And in the meantime the problem was
being approached in a more venturesome spirit by the eccentric
Richard Stanyhurst (1547–1618), who, inspired by Ascham,
influenced also by Harvey, turned into English hexamcters the
first four Books of Virgil's *Aeneid* (1582), explaining his system
of prosody in the Dedication and Preface to that work.[2] Disregarding Harvey's remarks concerning orthographical difficulties
he indulges in linguistic experiments of the most fantastic kind,
which ' stript Virgil out of a velvet gown into a fool's coat ',
and made of the translation one of the curiosities of English
literature. In the matter of prosody, however, he displays a
more rational temper, influenced, it would seem, by Harvey's
teaching. Thus he realizes, for one thing, that too close a following of the Latin rules of quantity prescribed by ' grammarian
precisians ' would not do. He argues, for example, that since
the Latins had handled Greek precepts freely the same liberty
should be granted to Englishmen ; [3] that moreover the nature
of English itself forbade a slavish adherence to their rules of long
and short, that ' nothing may be done or spoken against Nature,
and that Art is bound to shape itself by all imitation to Nature '.
' Every country ', he concludes,[4] ' hath its peculiar law ; and
every country must be permitted to use its particular lore.'
With this sound doctrine in mind he submits a system of his own
devising, according to which every syllable has its proper quantity, but with its length varied according to its termination and
the consonant or vowel that followed. Even so, however, these
suggestions he puts forward tentatively. He proposes ' to chalk
out no lines or rules for others ' ; and he therefore leaves the
matter much as he had found it.

Such, then, were the fruitless attempts at this stage to grapple
with the difficulties raised by the ' new versifying ' ; and while
the discussion was to be renewed at a later date, comments on
the futility of the idea were to come from more than one quarter.

---

[1] See G. M. Young, *A Word for Gabriel Harvey*, in *English Critical
Essays, 20th Cent.* (World's Classics), pp. 284–90.
[2] Smith, *op. cit.* i. pp. 135–47.
[3] *ibid.* i. p. 142.   [4] *ibid.* i. p. 144.

To the end, however, Harvey remained convinced that a way would be found, that appropriate rules would ultimately be devised ; añd at this earlier stage he had desired to be ' epitaphed ' as ' the inventor of the English hexameter '.[1] Nor was he alone in his confidence in the future of the hexameter in English. An anonymous writer, in his Address to the Reader prefixed to *The First Book of the Preservation of King Henry the VII* (1599) in hexameter verses, argued strongly in favour of the new versification, describing contemporary verse as a sort of ' prose-rhythm which every fiddler or piper could make on a given theme '.[2] He allowed that many good poets, Spenser above all, had written in that less desirable form ; but he did so regretting that they had not adopted true hexameters, thus beautifying the language. Neither his hopes, nor those of Harvey, were however to be realized ; and Harvey's reputation was subsequently to suffer, somewhat unduly, in wordy conflict with the more sprightly Nashe.[3] Nevertheless his part in the metrical discussion had not been without its value ; in spite of his obsession with classical metres he had at least recognized one important principle, namely, that English verse-forms must ultimately conform, not with alien rules, but with the genius of the English language.

While the main interest of the sporadic theorizing at this stage thus gathered round the ' new versifying ', not without their value in clarifying the conception of the poetic art were the comments made on those figure-poems (*carmina figurata*) which, commended by some authorities, were becoming common in England, after the example of French and Italian writers. The use of symbolic verse-forms (i.e. verses with their lines so arranged as to form definite shapes) dated from ancient times,[4] probably from the Hellenistic age, when Alexandrian poets with their love for the ingenious in art, influenced also by Oriental example, devised poems of this kind, trifles generally known as τεχνοπαίγνια. Among the Hellenistic poets traditionally associated with these figure-poems was Simmias of Rhodes (wrongly described by Ascham as the originator of rhyme [5]) whose experiments in this vein led to a revival at this later date and to an acceptance of such verse as a desirable poetic form. The new vogue was illustrated, for instance, by the *Poemata* (1538, 1549) of Pierius

[1] See Grosart, *op. cit.* i. 182.
[2] Smith, *op. cit.* i. p. 377   [3] See p. 185 *infra*.
[4] For their medieval vogue, see Atkins, *English Literary Criticism, Medieval*, p. 167.
[5] See p. 92 *supra*.

Valerianus, and again, by Willis's strange collection in his *Poematum Liber* (1573) ; while Scaliger in his *Poetics* [1] had also duly noted the form. It is therefore not without its significance that Harvey in his *Letter-book* [2] (1573–80) decried this particular practice in no uncertain terms, referring to ' an invective against Simmias Rhodius ', a poet whom he described as ' foolish, idle and fantastical ', one who ' first devised . . . trifling and childish toys to make verses, that should . . . represent the form and figure of an egg, an ape, a wing, and such ridiculous and mad gewgaws and crotchets '. He then notes with regret that this form of verse had of late been revived ' by some not otherwise unlearned, as Pierius, Scaliger . . . and the rest of that crew ', adding, in caustic vein, that ' nothing so absurd and fruitless, but being once taken up, shall have some imitators ' ; and he further notes that Willis had since denounced the fashion. It is true that Nashe later on charged Harvey with having indulged in freaks of the same sort, and of being guilty of verses in the forms of ' a pair of gloves, a painter's easel, a trumpet, an anchor ' [3] and the like. But this charge, if justified, possibly applied to Harvey's salad days ; and in any case his pronouncement at this date is not without its interest. Not that it was successful in altogether discouraging the fashion. Figure-poems were to be seriously discussed by Puttenham in his *Art of English Poesy* ; and in the early 17th Century their popularity was to increase, examples being forthcoming from Sir John Davies, Sylvester, Herbert, Wither, and others. On the other hand they were to be ridiculed by Ben Jonson, and later on by Dryden and Addison ; and in this saner counsel Harvey led the way.

So far comment on the poetic art had been of an occasional character, concerned mainly with versification ; and to the contributions already mentioned might be added the *Reulis and Cautelis* (1584) [4] of the youthful King James I, a work by no means devoid of interest, embodying notes reminiscent of the teaching of Ronsard, Gascoigne, and others, and doubtless inspired by his tutor, the famous Latin scholar, Buchanan. In the meantime, however, fresh light from different angles and by different means, had been thrown on the poetic art by ' E. K.' [5] in his *Gloss* on the *Shepherd's Calendar* (1579), the first critical

[1] ii. 25.
[2] ed. E. J. L. Scott (Camden Soc.), pp. 100–101 : see also Smith, *op. cit.* i. p. 126.
[3] *Have with you to Saffron Walden* (1596), ed. Grosart, iii. 98.
[4] Smith, *op. cit.* i. pp. 208 ff.
[5] Probably Edward Kirke, a Cambridge friend of Spenser.

' Introduction ' in English.   It was a notable attempt at editing
which represented an adaptation of the marginal notes or *scholia*
of ancient grammarians on classical texts, and an innovation
which its author recognized would seem ' strange and rare ' to
English readers, though not without precedent in Italian works.
Confident of the outstanding merits of the work of his friend,
the ' new poet ', he endeavours to perform the highest function
of the critic, that of helping others to understand and appreciate ;
and in discussing actual details of literature in the concrete he
supplemented the abstract theories of his contemporaries, and
thus rendered to criticism a service worthy of more attention
than it has usually received.

But while the elucidation of the art underlying one particular
poem was thus his main object, of interest, in the first place, are
his casual comments on the nature of poetry in general, though
some, it is true, are but echoes of familiar commonplaces current
at the time.   The honour paid to poetry in antiquity, for
instance, is illustrated by Scipio's regard for Ennius, by Alexander's sparing of Thebes, the birth-place of Pindar, and his cherish-
ing of the books of Homer found in Darius's coffers ; [1] while poetry
itself is defined as ' a divine instinct and unnatural rage passing
the reach of reason ', and its works are said to be immortal in
character.[2]   Less familiar, however, is his account of the origin
of poetry, which he explains (ascribing the explanation to Plato)
as having first come into being in the verses sung by *vates* in praise
of virtue and immortality at solemn feasts (*panegyrica*) ; verses
which were subsequently adapted to lighter themes of love or
satire or were chanted for mere pleasure by men to whom the
name ' poet ' was ultimately given.[3]   Or again, there is his
explanation of the transporting or ecstatic effect of music (or
poetry), due to the harmony existing in human souls (according
to Pythagoras and Plato), an effect which he illustrates by the
passionate results of Timotheus's playing to Alexander, exciting
him first to fury by Phrygian melodies, then calming him by soft
Lydian airs.[4]

It is, however, in the light he throws on one special form
of poetry, the pastoral, and on Spenser's treatment of that form,
that ' E. K.'s ' *Gloss* is of prime importance.   Recognizing, to
begin with, that for an intelligent reading a clear understanding
of the text was needed, he supplies explanations of unfamiliar
or archaic words,[5] as well as of classical allusions ; and along

---

[1] *October Eclogue.*   [2] *December Ecl.*   [3] *October Ecl.*
[4] *ibid.* : cf. Dryden's *Alexander's Feast.*
[5] e.g. *fon* (fool), *meynt* (mingled), *yfere* (together), *greete* (weep).

with these he discusses something of the art underlying the poem. Thus he explains, in the first place, what he regards as characteristic features of pastoral poetry. It was, for instance, a convenient form for discussing great matters covertly ; it was also an unambitious form of verse suitable for the trial flights of young poets ; and a brief sketch of its development from Theocritus to Marot provides a sort of historical setting.[1] In addition he calls attention to the structure of Spenser's poem, claiming for it unity of a kind in its revelation of the folly of love, ' proportionate to the state ' of the various months ; though he also notes that the eclogues varied in form and tone, some being complaints, others complimentary or personal poems, while some again were of a moral or satirical character. Then, too, he points out the classical colouring which pervades the poem, and is seen more especially in the imitation of Theocritus (*Idyll* xvi) in the *October* eclogue, but also in passages and phrases elsewhere reminiscent of Theognis, Virgil, Ovid, Seneca, and others. Nor are his comments on the artistic devices employed without their significance, as illustrating the conception of the poetic art then current. Thus he notes the observance of ' decorum ' maintained throughout the poem, ' in personages, in seasons, in speech and generally in all seemly simplicity of handling ' ; [2] and for the rest he is at pains to point out the rhetorical devices employed, the various uses, for instance, of syncope, epanorthosis (correction), paronomasia (play upon words), periphrasis, epiphonema (moral), and the like. On the other hand he has but little to say on versification or the newly-invented harmonies of Spenser's verse ; though he implies its excellence in comparison with that of the ' rakehelly rout of ragged rhymers ' whom he fiercely derides, with their ' loose and ungirt ' form of expression, their wild ravings, and their excessive use of the alliterative device.

But while matters of versification concern ' E. K.' but slightly, on another vexed question of the time, that of the literary language, he has some suggestive remarks to make,[3] thus continuing the discussion begun by Cheke, Ascham, and others. Conscious of the challenge thrown out by Spenser in making free use of archaic and dialect forms in his poem, he attempts a defence of that innovation, by way of anticipating objections of judicious readers, among whom were to be included Sidney and Jonson. That such forms were ' hard and of most men unused ', this much he concedes, claiming however that they were nevertheless of good English stock, had been used by earlier native poets, and that Spenser ' having walked in the sun must needs

[1] *Intro. Epistle.*   [2] *ibid.*   [3] *ibid.*

11

be sunburnt '.[1]   In such terms, he added, had Cicero [2] acknowledged his indebtedness to earlier influences ;   and likewise
Spenser, 'with the sound of those ancient poets still ringing in
his ears, must needs hit out some of their tunes '.   But he does
not rest his case solely on native precedents.   In pastoral poetry
more especially, he maintains, an element of 'rustical rudeness ',
resulting from the use of obsolete and dialect words such as
countrymen employed, was calculated to add a touch of realism,
even 'grace and authority ', to expression.   It was true, he
recalls, that L. Valla in commenting on Livy had objected to
that historian's excessive 'affecting of antiquity ' ;   and that
Cheke for much the same reasons had commented adversely on
the style of Sallust.[3]   Nevertheless, he added, he was not alone
in thinking that their use of ancient forms had brought something of value to expression ;   and, besides, there was Cicero's
authority for holding that 'oft-times an ancient word maketh
the style seem grave . . . and reverend '.   But there was even
more to be said than this ;   and 'E. K.' maintains further that
provided such 'old and unwonted words ' were used with discretion, they were capable of aesthetic effects and of adding fresh
beauty to normal expression.   As in painting, he explains, where
dainty forms are effectively depicted against a background of
'rude thickets and craggy cliffs ', or again in music where 'oftentimes a discord maketh a comely concordance ' ;   so also in
poetry, he urges, the occasional use of 'rough and harsh terms
. . . illumines the brightness of brave and glorious words '.   And
in this connexion he gives striking utterance to a 'romantic '
doctrine, in confessing, not without perplexity, that 'oft-times
we find ourselves, I know not how, singularly delighted with the
show of such natural rudeness, and take great pleasure in that
disorderly order '.[4]

Such then was 'E. K.'s ' defence of Spenser's attempt to
form a poetic diction on Chaucer's model, the only source to
which Spenser makes acknowledgment.   And so far from
apologizing for this revival of old and unfamiliar forms, 'E. K.'
boldly claims as calling for special praise the effort 'to restore,
as to their rightful heritage, such good and natural English
words as have been long time out of use and almost clean dis-
herited '.[5]   To the neglect of such resources he attributed the
poverty of the literary language at that date ;   and he deplored
the attempts of others to supply the deficiencies with 'pieces

[1] *Intro. Epistle* :   cf. p. 76 *supra.*   [2] *De oratore*, ii, ch. xiv.
[3] See p. 95 *supra.*   [4] *Intro. Epistle.*
[5] *ibid.*

and rags of other languages ', thus making of English ' a galli-maufray or hodge-podge ' of Latin, French, and Italian tongues. Those who objected to Spenser's innovations, he declared, were animated by none other than ignorance, prejudice or deficient patriotism ; and that there was a place for both archaic and dialect forms in literature later native developments were ultimately to show.

Of less intrinsic value, though still of interest as witnessing to the growing concern with poetry and the poetic art, was William Webbe's *Discourse of English Poetrie* [1] (1586), the most extensive treatise on the subject that had as yet been published. Concerning the author himself little is known, except that he was tutor to the sons of an Essex squire, Edward Sulyard, and that, imbued with a genuine love of poetry, he endeavoured in the leisure of ' summer evenings ' to commend that art to his country-men, by providing ' a simple judgment of English poetry ', in the hope, *instar cotis*, of inducing others more gifted to discuss literary standards and the ' right practice ' of the art. To that ampler task, he complains, English scholars were still not attracted, the subject being one ' which men of great learning had no leisure to handle, or at least, having to do with more serious matters, did least regard '. And more than once in his work Webbe laments that ' poetry had found few friends to amend it ', at the same time claiming for poetry the same atten-tion as was being given to rhetorical matters. But while a review of English poetry is all that Webbe modestly proposes, his actual treatise contains much else besides ; for to treat of that subject in isolation, he not unreasonably explains, would be ' like drawing one's picture without a head ', and he therefore ' has recourse to those times and writers whereon English poetry taketh as it were the descent and propriety '. His main topics are, briefly, the development of English poetry, its subject-matter and its forms ; but his treatment ranges over wider fields in a laudable attempt to provide a historical setting. For this task, however, he was inadequately equipped ; and his work suffers in consequence, being marred by scraps of learning gathered from various sources, often ill-digested and imperfectly set forth.

The first section of his *Discourse* [2] treats of the development of poetry ; and except for his review of existing English poetry—the first yet attempted—it is largely made up of oft-repeated commonplaces and familiar lists. Beginning with a revealing

[1] Smith, *op. cit.* i. pp. 226–302.
[2] *ibid.* i. pp. 230–47.

derivation of the word ' poetry ' from the ghost-word ποετρια,[1] an impossible form, he follows ' E. K.' in supplying Plato's explanation of the origin of poetry as being due to the activities of vates and ' poets ' at the panegyrica,[2] remarks subsequently on its civilizing influence, its element of inspiration referred to by Cicero and Ovid,[3] as well as on the honour in which it had been held by Alexander and Scipio,[4] and then proceeds to sketch the history of poetry in antiquity. His list of Greek poets begins as usual with Orpheus, Amphion, and Tyrtaeus, includes Homer (placed strangely enough after Pindar), the writers of comedy, Eupolis, Cratinus, and Aristophanes, the tragedians, Aeschylus, Sophocles, and Euripides (whose value, he states, ' hath been long in controversy '), and finally, the pastoral poets, Hesiod and Theocritus, of whose salutary influence he has less doubt. Latin poetry also he treats in some detail, beginning with Ennius. Virgil he describes as following in the steps of Homer, Theocritus, and Hesiod ; Propertius, Tibullus, and Catullus as writers of epigrams and elegies ; Lucan and Silius Italicus as famous historians. After them he places Ovid, and still later Horace (' about the same time as Juvenal and Persius '), followed by Martial and Seneca, and finally, with a characteristic disregard of chronology, Boethius, Lucretius, Statius, Manilius, Ausonius, and others.

For his survey of English poetry [5] rather more independence may be claimed. It is a pioneering effort at a historical approach to the subject, though little more than a mere catalogue and a somewhat superficial sketch of earlier native activities. Gower, to begin with, is mentioned with respect as ' the first English poet '; whereas greater praise is accorded to Chaucer, ' the god of English poets ', whose style, it is true, ' seemed blunt and coarse to many fine English ears ', but who had boldly and successfully satirized abuses in delightsome vein. Then came Lydgate, notable for ' the good proportion of his verse '; and after him Langland, ' a pithy writer, somewhat harsh and obscure ', yet ' the first . . . that observed the quantity of our verse without the curiosity of rhyme'. Skelton followed, ' a sharp wit and exceeding bold '; then Gascoigne, ' the chief of our late rhymers ', as well as a goodly company, including the Earl of Surrey, Lord Vaux, Norton, Tusser, Whetstone, Church-

---

[1] Possibly suggested by the medieval Latin poetria (= ars poetica), though more probably a fabrication of Webbe's : cf. his λοητεια for Plato's γοητεία (enchantment).
[2] See p. 148 supra.   [3] Tusc. i. 26 : Fasti, vi. 5.
[4] See pp. 106, 148 supra.   [5] Smith, op. cit. i. pp. 239–47.

yard, and sundry others. Due note is also taken of translators, such as Phaer, Twyne, and Golding, with the addition of Barnaby Googe, that ' painful furtherer of learning '. But the greatest praise is reserved for Spenser, ' the rightest English poet ', with his rare gift of verse ; while the customary scorn is expressed for the rabble of senseless sonneteers and ballad makers, and all ale-house poets who ' with an A to make a jerk at the end of their lines ' snatched at the garlands due to poets.

In the second section of his work [1] Webbe deals with the subject-matter and the different ' sorts ' of poetry ; but the result is not very helpful and is chiefly of interest as illustrating the vague ideas of poetry still current. He begins by recalling what he describes as the themes of ancient tragedy and comedy, and the distinction ultimately drawn between the two ' kinds '. Tragedy, he states, had dealt with the calamities that had over-whelmed exalted personages, whereas comedy had consisted of stories which, ' beginning doubtfully, drew to some trouble, yet ended joyfully '. These distinctions, however, were none other than the post-classical and medieval conceptions ; and Webbe's suggestion (' as some hold opinion ') that they were based on an imitation of Homer is without foundation. Aristotle, it is true, had noted that in Homer's epics the elements of classical Greek tragedy and comedy had been present ; [2] and this idea, referred to by Scaliger,[3] probably accounts for Webbe's tentative state-ment. After this he suggests that all poetry might conveniently be described as of three ' sorts ' or ' kinds ' ; [4] first, the comical, including epigrams, elegies, and songs of delight ; secondly, the tragical, including complaints and sad stories ; and thirdly, the historical, including chronicles and complimentary poems. This, however, does not preclude him from mentioning three other ' kinds ' which fell outside his general classification. Thus he proceeds, somewhat inconsequently, to refer to the epic as ' the sum and ground of all poetry, . . . and incomparably the best of all other ' ; and while regretting that in English hitherto there was nothing of the sort to show apart from ' our ancient chroniclers ', he nevertheless maintains that Phaer in his *Trans-lation of Virgil* had shown that English writers were capable of attaining excellence in that particular ' kind '. Then there was also the pastoral ' kind ', with its varied subject-matter, in which Spenser was said to have imitated and even rivalled Virgil ; and finally, the poetry of husbandry, such as Virgil's

---

[1] *ibid.* i. pp. 248–66.
[2] *Poetics*, 1448 b, 12.   [3] *Poetice*, i. 4.
[4] cf. the classification of plays in Shakespeare's First Folio.

Georgics, in which Tusser and Googe were said to have deserved commendation.

Having endeavoured so far to sketch the development and the ' kinds ' of poetry, Webbe in his final section [1] proceeds to treat of versification. Rhyming verse, a ' barbarian ' form, he recognizes in the first place to be everywhere prevalent ; but while (following Ascham) he ascribes its origin to Simmias Rhodius and latterly to the ' Hunnes and Gothians ',[2] he nevertheless refrains from the customary attack, noting that it had been ' engrafted by custom ', had produced excellent results in the hands of the more skilful poets, and that in English perhaps it was more effective than in any other language. He therefore (with Gascoigne's aid) submits some advice concerning the treatment of such verse.[3] Thus, for example, one type of verse was to be employed throughout a poem ; while the wresting of word-accent or undue distortion of word-order for the sake of rhyme was to be sedulously avoided. As for the variety of verses and stanzas, they were said to be infinite ; and he illustrates from the *Shepherd's Calendar* some of the possible variations, including the ten-syllabled line, the lighter line of seven syllables and the roundelay, as well as the more intricate stanzas with lines of unequal length. At the same time he calls attention to ' the rare devices and pretty inventions ' [4] which were held to contribute to the poetic effect. And among them were mentioned ' the clerkly conveying of contraries ' (antithesis), the skilful use of repetition, when significant words repeated at intervals added emphasis to the main thought of a poem, or again, the echo device, when words at the beginning or end of each line were so arranged as to form an independent and significant thought in themselves. But while devoting thus much attention to popular verse-forms, Webbe is nevertheless of opinion that ' the reformed kind of English verse ' represented a finer poetic medium and should therefore be cultivated ; [5] though to the debate on this much-vexed question he has little or nothing to add. He recognizes that native words presented serious difficulties in any attempt to adopt the quantitative system ; yet he looks forward to the devising of some process of adaptation, just as the Latins of old had modified the Greek tradition in accordance with the genius of their language. Of the classical metres he held that the hexameter and sapphic measures could best be naturalized ; of the elegiac measure he

[1] Smith, *op. cit.* i. pp. 266–90.   [2] See p. 92 *supra.*
[3] Smith, *op. cit.* i. p. 268.
[4] *ibid.* i. p. 276.   [5] *ibid.* i. p. 278.

is less certain. But neither his approval of Watson's ' sweet
and gallant hexameter ',[1] nor yet the English hexameters and
sapphics he himself provides, can be said to be convincing. In
those unhappy experiments he merely succeeded in depriving
Virgil's and Spenser's Eclogues of all their subtle charm ; and
he therefore leaves the problem where he found it—a pious wish
which was not to be realized in actual practice.

This then represents the main substance of Webbe's *Discourse
of English Poetrie*. It is seen to consist largely of ideas drawn
from earlier English writers ; and to those already mentioned
might be added the passage where, in defending poetry from the
charge of immorality, he reproduces Elyot's plea for discrimination in reading on the ground that those who read amiss were
like ' foolish folk who, coming into a garden, . . . tread down
the fairest flowers and wilfully thrust their fingers among the
nettles '.[2] To Horace as well he is specially indebted, quoting,
for instance, his doctrine of ' delightful teaching ' (*prodesse,
delectare*),[3] his demand for verisimilitude in fiction (*ficta voluptatis
causa sint proxima veris*),[4] while also supplying in an Appendix
some 54 rules based on Horace's *Ars Poetica* and extracted by
the German scholar, Georg. Fabricius (1516–71). Less conventional in kind, however, are certain occasional pronouncements
which either point to some sense of the range and liberty required
for the poetic activity, or else represent judgments on English
writers. Thus in contrast with his crude attempts at distinguishing the ' kinds ' is Webbe's statement that ' poetry is not debarred
from any matter ' ;[5] or again, that ' we must prescribe to no
writer (much less to poets) in what sort they should utter their
conceits '.[6] And, maintaining that the ' new versifying ' should
be developed ' without any prescription of rules ', he also recalls
the fact that poetry was originally written without the aid of
rules, and that rules were subsequently based on the works of
the earliest poets.[7] Of his stray comments on English writers
the most interesting are those on Chaucer, Spenser, and Lyly.
Chaucer, for instance, is praised for giving to his fictions ' the
near resemblance of truth ',[8] for his skill in teaching wisdom
under cover of a merry tale ; though less obvious is the claim
that many of his poems are of a pastoral kind.[9] Spenser, on the
other hand, is acclaimed as England's supreme pastoral poet,

---

[1] *ibid*. i. p. 283.   [2] *ibid*. i. p. 252 : cf. p. 101 *supra*.
[3] *ibid*. i. p. 250 : cf. *Ars Poetica*, 333–4.
[4] *ibid*. i. p. 251 : cf. *A.P.* 338.
[5] *ibid*. i. p. 249.   [6] *ibid*. i. p. 265.
[7] *ibid*. i. p. 279.   [8] *ibid*. i. p. 251.   [9] *ibid*. i. p. 263.

comparable to Theocritus and Virgil, both of whom, it is added, he might well have surpassed, had he written in a more cultured tongue.[1] Nor are Webbe's remarks on Lyly's *Euphues* without their significance ; for, judged by rhetorical standards, that work is said to have attained the height of eloquence in English, with ' its apt words and sentences, its fit phrases and gallant tropes, its flowing speech and plain sense '.[2] Its style, in short, is said to combine the qualities of both Demosthenes and Cicero as described by Quintilian,[3] so that from it nothing might be taken away and to it nothing might be added. It was extravagant praise characteristic of critical judgment in its infancy, but it has its bearing on literary opinion at the time.

Of the intrinsic value of this work of Webbe there is little to be said. A mere compilation of ideas drawn from Elyot and Ascham, Gascoigne, ' E. K.', and Harvey, it gives little evidence of original thinking, or of any real insight into poetry or the poetic art. Written, moreover, in a pedestrian style and in loose and discursive fashion, it is wholly lacking in any sort of distinction ; and whereas its scholarship in places is seen to be woefully defective, its judgments are mostly superficial when they are not ill-founded. That an attempt for the first time was made at a survey of native poetry, this might be held to mark some advance in critical activities. Yet the work is best regarded as the uninspired and uninspiring effort of a genuine lover of poetry, who, with no special gifts and with a limited outlook, submitted his views on poetry tentatively and with a disarming modesty. Of sound doctrine or helpful judgment the work has little to offer ; and to modern readers the *Discourse* is mainly of historical interest, as witnessing to the confusion and poverty of ideas concerning poetry which prevailed in England even towards the close of the 16th Century.

Of far greater value, in fact, one of the outstanding contributions to Elizabethan criticism, was the *Arte of English Poesie* published anonymously in 1589 ; a work, it is true, not without its difficulties, but one which, strangely enough, has failed until quite recently to receive adequate appreciation. The main problems connected with the work relate to its authorship and date of actual composition. That the *Arte*, in the first place, may reasonably be assigned to George Puttenham (*c.* 1529–90), nephew of Sir Thomas Elyot, would now seem to be tolerably certain, though other names have been submitted in this connexion, notably those of Richard Puttenham [4] (elder brother of

---

[1] Smith, *op. cit.* i. p. 263.   [2] *ibid.* i. p. 256.   [3] *Inst. Or.* x. i. 106.
[4] See Elyot, *Governour*, ed. Croft, i. clxxxii–clxxxix.

George) and Lord Lumley.[1] The case for Lord Lumley, however, is far from convincing, while early definite evidence of the association of the work with a ' Putnam ' or Puttenham comes from Harington (1591), Carew (1614), and Bolton (1616) ; and of the two brothers George, rather than Richard, would seem to have been more likely as author, and this, by reason of his more pronounced activities of an intellectual and literary kind. Of those literary activities, unfortunately, the only extant remains definitely ascribed to him is a prose pamphlet, *A Justificacion of Queen Elizabeth* ; whereas the author of the *Arte* claims to have written *Partheniades*, a collection of complimentary poems addressed to Elizabeth, as well as numerous other works including *De decoro*, a treatise entitled *The English Tongue*, and verse of various kinds. Yet in the *Justificacion*, on the one hand, and in the *Arte* and *Partheniades* on the other, there exist many striking common features of thought, style and treatment, all of which go to suggest a common authorship, and to warrant the ascription of the *Arte* to the writer of the *Justificacion*. So that in the light of what is known of George Puttenham's career, together with the contemporary references to a Puttenham as author, such evidence would seem to be fairly conclusive.

But, granted that George Puttenham was in all probability the author, for an intelligent reading of the *Arte* some explanation of further difficulties is also needed ; difficulties as to the date of actual composition, arising from apparent inconsistencies and from certain characteristic features of outlook and treatment which distinguish it from other contemporary critical writings. Thus Puttenham's claim, some fourteen years after Gascoigne and others had written, to have been ' the first deviser ' of English prosody and an original theorist ($\alpha\dot{\upsilon}\tau o\delta\iota\delta\dot{\alpha}\varkappa\tau o\varsigma$) [2] at that, sounds somewhat strange, to begin with. But equally strange at that date (1589) is also the inordinate consideration given to rhetorical figures in a treatment of the poetic art, the range of his illustrations, most of which are taken from *Tottel's Miscellany* (1557), or again, the absence of concern with those Puritan attacks which had begun with Gosson and others. All these features, which go to determine the essential character of the *Arte*, would have been consistent with one writing before 1570. On the other hand, some acquaintance is occasionally shown with

---

[1] See B. M. Ward, article in *Review of English Studies*, 1925, pp. 284–308. For a full discussion see Puttenham, *Arte of English Poesie*, ed. G. D. Willcock and A. Walker, Intro. pp. xi–xliv, to which admirable edition I am indebted both here and elsewhere.

[2] Smith, *op. cit.* ii. p. 61.

developments after 1570, with the ' new versifying ', for instance ; while references are also made to Gascoigne and Sidney, as well as to the verses of Dyer, Spenser, and Raleigh. The only possible explanation is that the work was first drafted prior to 1570, and was afterwards revised, with certain material interpolated, before being published anonymously by Field in 1589. And this hypothesis derives support from Drummond's statement in 1619, that the *Arte* had been ' kept long in wrytt (i.e. manuscript) as a secret '.[1] These facts, however, only add to the interest and value of the work. They make it clear that, despite the predominating influence of the rhetoric tradition during the earlier generation of Cheke and Ascham, there had been at work an original mind concerned with the future of poetry ; and that Puttenham's claim to be a pioneer in this respect was not altogether unfounded. In an age busied with the cultivation of Latin prose and verse, he not only threw light on the vernacular achievements of early Tudor poets, but was also the first to proclaim a future for English poetry generally. ' Why should not poesy be a vulgar art with us as well as with the Greeks and Latins ? ' [2] he confidently asks ; and proceeds to give reasons for the faith that was in him.

When we turn to consider the substance of Puttenham's doctrine, not without its relevance, to begin with, is the account he gives of the disabilities under which poetry laboured in his day. For one thing, he explains, poets were generally regarded with a withering contempt. ' A light-headed or phantastical man ', he writes,[3] ' they call a poet ' ; while poetry itself was viewed as little more than ' monstrous imaginations '. Then, too, contemporary conditions were said to militate against the production of poetry. Not only had patronage ceased in its gracious work of encouragement, but in ' an iron and malicious age ', obsessed with political affairs, there was ' scarce any leisure to think one good thought in perfect and godly contemplation ' ;[4] and, moreover, he complains, gifted writers ' were loath to be known of their skill ', and either suppressed their work or sought the protection of anonymity.[5] These then were the conditions which induced Puttenham to write his *Arte* ; and in estimating its value no slight importance in the first place must be attached to the method and plan of his treatise. From the outset it becomes plain that his inquiry is to be based on first

---

[1] B. Jonson's *Conversations*, xvi : see Spingarn, *Critical Essays of the 17th Century*, i. p. 214.

[2] Smith, *op. cit.* ii. p. 5.   [3] *ibid.* ii. p. 19.
[4] *ibid.* ii. p. 22.   [5] *ibid.*

principles—a point of some significance. He relies, not on ancient authorities, but on the critical instrument provided by the law of Nature or the dictates of ' right reason ', an instrument forged anew at the Renascence ; so that his methods throughout are consequently of a rational and psychological kind. It is true that he is by no means unheedful of the historical development of the art ; yet he is bound by no tradition as such, and his approach to poetry is in the light of the unchanging needs of human nature. Nor does he altogether neglect those earlier teachings of the ' best clerks ', the fruits of his wide and judicious reading ; though for the most part he contrives to adapt them successfully to his main scheme. And, again, writing as he does primarily for courtly readers, he claims to have omitted ' all nice and scholastical curiosities ', while providing many lively anecdotes to lighten the way. Hence the orderly simplicity of his general plan, which is divided into three Books ; Book I, ' Of Poets and Poesy ', consisting of general remarks on poetry and its various forms, Book II, ' Of Proportion ', treating of prosody as an indispensable formal element of the poetic art, and Book III, ' Of Ornament ', dealing with the means of rendering poetic utterance attractive to both mind and ear.

Of definite interest, in the first place, are his remarks in Book I on the nature of poetry, which already give promise of an original treatment. He recalls, it is true, some of the oft-quoted arguments in favour of poetry—its civilizing influence on primitive society, the honours bestowed on poets from Homer onwards, and the like—but more characteristic and also more significant, are his illuminating comments on the nature of poetry as he himself conceives it. Thus for the poet he claims the God-given faculty of creation, which gives him ' pre-eminence above all other artificers ' ; [1] at the same time adding that it was no disparagement to describe him also as an imitator, reproducing in vivid fashion the world around him. So that poetry was therefore the product of some or all of certain factors, namely, a divine instinct (the Platonic *furor* or inspiration), and natural gifts, as well as experience and observation of the world of men. Then, too, in poetic creation he calls attention to the workings of an ' imaginative ' or image-forming faculty, in accordance with medieval psychology.[2] It was the faculty known as ' phantasy ' or ' fancy ', the true meaning of which, he complains, was commonly misunderstood by his fellow-countrymen ; and to this cause he attributes largely the derision in which poetry was held. A wild and disordered fancy, he concedes, ' doth

[1] *ibid.* ii. p. 3. [2] See p. 119 *supra*, fn.

breed Chimeras and monsters in men's imaginations '; yet there was nothing disorderly in the make-up of the true poet. Poetic fancy, he maintains, represented ' the best, most comely and beautiful images . . . of things to the soul, and according to their very truth '.[1] By its aid, moreover, originality in creation was fostered, ' new and rare things being devised '; it was also most needful for ' sound and true judgment '; and it played a valuable part in all intellectual activities. The distinction thus drawn between sound and disordered ' fancy ' was something more than a reply to contemporary traducers. In representing ' phantasy ' as a means of revealing the beauty of things ' according to their very truth ', Puttenham was hinting at something like the workings of ' imagination ' in its modern sense.

But apart from his conception of the creative process, Puttenham has also some significant remarks to make on the subject-matter and function of poetry in general. The subject-matter of poetry he broadly defines as ' any witty or delicate conceit of man '; [2] but elsewhere he enlarges on the element of fiction in poetry, for the poet, he maintains, is by no means confined to actual fact. Fiction, he explains,[3] besides being more pleasing, is often more effective than historical truth, because capable of freer treatment ; and by means of fiction more excellent examples were provided in a single day than in many ages in actual life. In poetry (as in prose narratives), he adds, the subject-matter might be of three sorts ; the ' wholly true and wholly false and a third holding part of either '. Here he was recalling the teaching of Alexandrian theorists, according to which the themes of poetry might consist of (i) the actual or true (ἱστορία), (ii) the fabulous or absurd (μῦθος), and (iii) the probable (πλάσμα),[4] though his actual source may have been Plutarch,[5] who in similar terms had emphasized the value of fiction in poetry. And all three kinds of subject-matter Puttenham declares to be in practice both useful and effective.

Then, again, of interest is his conception of the function of poetry. In the main he adopts the conventional position, namely, that its aim was to afford both instruction and delight. But his independence is shown by the stress he lays on the *dulce*, rather than on the *utile*, as opposed to the prevailing doctrine, according to which poetry was primarily didactic and moralistic, conducing above all to the formation of character. That he attaches value to poetry for its ethical teaching is clear

---

[1] Smith, *op. cit.* ii. p. 20.   [2] *ibid.* ii. p. 25.   [3] *ibid.* ii. p. 42.
[4] See Atkins, *Lit. Crit. in Antiquity*, i. 174.
[5] *De audiendis poetis*, 16 B : see Atkins, *op. cit.* ii. 313.

when, for instance, he describes historical poetry, next to divine, as the most honourable and beneficial and the best guide to conduct.[1] Yet his main emphasis throughout is laid on the aesthetic side of poetry and on those qualities affording ' solace and recreation '. Poetry, for example, he defines as ' a pleasant manner of utterance . . . to refresh the mind by the ear's delight ' ;[2] ' merry matters (not unhonest) ', he adds, ' may also be well allowed ' ; while the poet he describes as treating of ' pleasant and lovely causes ' which ' dispose the hearers to mirth and solace '.[3] In thus presenting poetry as something primarily delightful Puttenham broke away from the ranks of the graver scholars and rendered a distinct service to his courtly readers. With Dryden he would have agreed that ' delight· is the chief, if not the only, end of poesy ' ; and, in passing, he hints at the nature of this poetic charm, representing it as something subtle and alluring that wove its spell by ' inveigling ' words and harmonies.

Equally interesting and independent (if also less convincing) is his treatment of the various ' kinds ' or forms of poetry. What he has in mind is an art of poetry designed for Englishmen ; yet he refers to the works of antiquity, not, be it noted, for purposes of imitation, but for comparison with what had already been achieved in English. He therefore submits the orthodox list of the classical ' kinds ', along with representative poets, a list including the heroic, lyric and elegiac ' kinds ', together with comedy, tragedy, the pastoral, satire, and the epigram ;[4] and then, approaching the subject from a new angle, he endeavours to trace what he regards as the rational development of poetry in the past, and to show how it had sprung from, first, the social, and secondly, the emotional, needs of men. Thus the earliest needs of primitive society were said to have been met by hymns in praise of the gods, then the necessity to reprove vice brought forth comedy, tragedy, and satire ; or again, the need for praising famous men resulted in heroic poetry, *encomia* and epitaphs [5]— altogether an account which, unfortunately, was somewhat lacking in historical truth. Apart from these responses to the demands of society, however, other ' kinds ', he explains, were evolved later in accordance with the emotional demands of individual men. Thus love, the concern of all, had given rise to odes and ballads, songs and sonnets ; human rejoicings had inspired marriage odes (*epithalamia*) and birthday verses (*genethliaca*) ; human sorrows had found expression in elegies, funeral songs (*epicedia*),

[1] Smith, *op. cit.* ii. p. 41.   [2] *ibid.* ii. p. 24.
[3] *ibid.* ii. p. 160.   [4] *ibid.* ii. p. 26.   [5] *ibid.* ii. pp. 28–45.

and epitaphs ; the epigram was the medium for uttering ' witty scoffs and sharp conceits ' ; [1] and all these ' kinds ', he maintains, were duly represented in English verse.

Defective as was this account of the development of the different forms of poetry, it is nevertheless of interest, owing to the light it sheds on the conception of poetic forms then current, while it also embodies some shrewd casual comments on the nature of poetry generally.   Thus not without its significance is the attention given to the multitude of minor forms (epigrams, epithalamia, and the rest), among which comedy, tragedy, and the epic are mentioned, but without any special consideration. To Puttenham tragedies were still merely narratives of the doleful falls of princes ; comedies, amusing tales of ordinary life ; [2] and no trace is seen of the more intensive studies of those particular ' kinds ', in which were engaged many Italian critics, who, under Aristotelian influence, regarded them as the most important of all the ' kinds '.   On the other hand, there are not wanting occasional remarks of a more notable sort, which give evidence of some amount of independent thinking.   The pastoral, for instance, Puttenham refused to regard as the earliest poetic form ; [3] he sees in it a device for treating of matters more important than those bound up with shepherd life.   Then, too, of love-poetry, so frequently condemned by Humanists, he warmly approves ; [4] to him it is a form of poetry enshrining a multitude of moods and ' a thousand delicate devices '.   Or again, he has a word to say on behalf of the despised romances, *Arthur and his Knights, Bevis of Southampton* and *Guy of Warwick* ; his comment being that there are ' sundry forms of poetry and not all one '.[5]   Most interesting of all, however, is his psychological explanation of elegiac effects, when he states that elegies and laments act as an alleviation of sorrow, by allowing the grief-stricken mind to pour forth its griefs, thus making ' the very grief itself (in part) cure of the disease '.[6]   The followers of Galen, he notes, were wont to cure by medicaments of a contrary kind, those of Paracelsus by medicines of a similar kind ; and the methods of the latter, he suggests, are those that are at work in elegiac verse.   The homoeopathic process he thus describes is reminiscent of the Aristotelian *catharsis* ; but the suggestion here is obviously drawn from another source.

These, then, are the main points of interest in Puttenham's disquisition on ' Poets and Poesy '.   But with English poetry

[1] Smith, *op. cit.* ii. p. 60.   [2] *ibid.* ii. pp. 33–6.
[3] *ibid.* ii. p. 40.   [4] *ibid.* ii. pp. 46–7.
[5] *ibid.* ii. p. 44.   [6] *ibid.* ii. pp. 49–50.

ever in mind he cannot refrain from recalling briefly what had already been achieved by native writers; and he therefore attempts at this stage the first reasoned estimate of English poetry from Chaucer to the Elizabethans, claiming it to be 'nothing inferior' to that of either Italy or France.[1] Thus Chaucer, 'the most renowned of them all', he praises more especially for his *Canterbury Tales* with their original plan, their 'pleasant wit', their perfect similes and descriptions, their 'decent' characterization and delightful use of 'riding rhyme'. Of Chaucer's contemporaries and followers he has less to say. There was first the moral Gower, with his homely verses and defective rhymes; the writer of *Piers Plowman* with his satirical themes, his loose versification and obscure vocabulary, affording but little pleasure; Lydgate, again, described as 'a translator only', yet a competent versifier; and finally Skelton, 'a sharp satirist, but with more raillery and scoffery than became a Poet Laureate'. Then came Wyatt and Surrey, 'the two chief lanterns of light to all who followed', and the first of the 'courtly makers'. They were commended for their lofty ideas, their stateliness of style, their appropriate diction and well-devised measures, both successful imitators of their master, Petrarch. These in due course were followed by another courtly company, of whom Sidney and 'that other gentleman who wrote the late *Shepherd's Calendar*' are said to have excelled in the pastoral vein; Phaer and Golding are also mentioned as successful translators, while special praise is accorded to the love-poetry of Raleigh, with 'its vein most lofty, insolent (i.e. rare)[2] and passionate'.

So far Puttenham has been treating of the nature and development of poetry by way of introduction to his main theme; and from now on he devotes his attention solely to matters of technique, to that art of poetry for Englishmen, which, undeveloped as yet, he confidently predicted, owing to the excellence of the English genius and the potentialities of the native language. That art, he explains, would have many points in common with Greek and Latin principles; though it would also differ in some respects owing to differences in language. And what he pro-

[1] *ibid*. ii. pp. 61–6.
[2] The Elizabethan term 'insolent' (Lat. *insolens*), explained in *N.E.D.* as (?) 'swelling, exulting, in a good sense', is perhaps best interpreted here as 'rare'. The meaning is applicable to Seneca's *insolenti Graeciae* (*Controv.* i. pref. § 6) and consequently to Jonson's 'insolent Greece': while with *Doctor insolens*, the description applied to an eminent 15th Century Spaniard (see Weiss, *Humanism in England*, p. 76) might be compared the familiar epitaph of 'rare Ben Jonson'.

posed to do was not to formulate any rigid system, but merely
' to fashion an art, not to finish it, which time only and custom
had authority to do '.[1] At this point, however, it is worth
noting that Puttenham uses the term ' art ' in more senses than
one. Thus early in the work he defines ' art ' as a body of ' rules
prescribed by reason and gathered by experience ' ; [2] for, as he
states elsewhere, ' all arts grew first by observation of Nature's
proceeding and custom '.[3] And the definition is one which
incidentally throws light on the basis of his critical theorizing.
Elsewhere,[4] however, he employs the term in a less restricted
sense, when it stands for the skill derived from a knowledge and
practice of those artistic rules or principles.   In Books II and III
he therefore provides rules of prosody and figurative expression
in accordance with his opening definition ; while scattered
throughout the work are his more illuminating remarks on art in
its wider and more general sense.   And if his main treatment of
the latter occurs somewhat casually at the close of the treatise,
it is in deference to his courtly readers, and because of his desire
to afford them easy reading by minimising ' all nice and
scholastical curiosities '.

It is, however, in the light of his conception of art as something more than a body of rules that the doctrine contained in
Books II and III is best appreciated ; for it becomes evident at
once that what he has in mind in formulating his teaching is
something more than the inculcating of purely mechanical
processes.   Highly significant, to begin with, is his description
of ' art ' in general, as ' an aid . . . to nature and a furtherer of
her actions to good effect, . . . or a means to supply her wants
by reinforcing the causes wherein she is impotent and defective '.[5]
This is none other than the Aristotelian conception (most clearly
illustrated by the ' useful ' arts), according to which art is designed
' to supply the deficiencies of Nature by imitating Nature's
methods ' ; [6] and Puttenham, it is worth noting, draws his
illustrations from the art of the physician (as Aristotle had done),
while also adding the art of gardening on his own.   Then, too,
besides hinting at those proportions of Nature and artifice that
exist in artistic processes, he proceeds to point out the various
effects of art in its treatment of the world of Nature.   In the

---

[1] Smith, *op. cit.* ii. p. 130.   [2] *ibid.* ii. p. 5.
[3] *ibid.* ii. p. 133.   [4] *ibid.* ii. pp. 182 ff.   [5] *ibid.* ii. p. 187.
[6] cf. Aristotle, *Pol.* iv. (vii.), 17, 1337 a 1–2 : πᾶσα γὰρ τέχνη . . . τὸ
προσλεῖπον βούλεται τῆς φύσεως ἀναπληροῦν, and *Phys.* ii. 2, 194a, 21, ἡ
τέχνη μιμεῖται τὴν φύσιν : see Butcher, *Aristotle's Theory of Poetry and
Fine Art*, pp. 113 ff. for a full discussion.

first place, he explains, art may merely imitate or reproduce
Nature's works, by ' following and counterfeiting her actions
and effects ' ; and of this, the arts of painting and sculpture are
said to afford examples. Again, the effect of art may be to
transform or improve on Nature's achievements by enhancing her
beauty or rendering her ' more strange and miraculous ', thus
completing her unfulfilled intentions ; and this he illustrates by
the art of the gardener which succeeds in making ' the single
gillyflower or marigold or daisy, double '.[1] And, thirdly, art
may produce effects contrary to Nature, effects ' of such form
and quality as she never would or could have done of herself '.

Having thus submitted his conception of art, Puttenham
then treats of the part it should play in human activities, and
more especially in the work of poetic creation.[2] In certain
activities, he explains, such as music and dancing which are
the result of study and practice, art is everything ; but there
are also activities which come more naturally to men, where
artifice becomes ludicrous, as when a man with good 'hearing
makes use of an ear-trumpet. Utterance in words, however, he
states to be more or less natural ; and more praise is consequently due to the poet who creates by natural instinct than to
one who writes laboriously by art and precepts. At the same
time something is undoubtedly added to natural expression by
means of art ; and this is specially true of poetic utterance.
Such creation, he points out, is a complicated process. An
appropriate theme has first to be devised ; it must then be
presented in orderly and effective fashion ; a fitting verse-form
has also to be found ; and expression made attractive by means
of style and figures. For such processes, he states, Nature
unaided is unable to prescribe ; and some knowledge of the
necessary craft or art is therefore needed. Nevertheless, while
the poet may be said to employ art in its various senses, imitating
the actions of men, heightening natural effects, or producing
something new and strange, his highest glory, adds Puttenham,
is not derived from art, but rather from original and lively
invention, from the play of ' phantasy and imagination ' and
from natural eloquence ; and he is most admired when most
natural and least artificial.

Nor must we omit to notice Puttenham's further injunctions
concerning the employment of art by the poet, when he urges
the need for a skilful concealment of artistic devices as well as
for ' decency ' or a sense of fitness. Of the need for concealment
of art, in the first place, he has not much to say, though he

---

[1] cf. Shakespeare, *Winter's Tale* IV. iii. 89 ff.   [2] Smith, *op. cit.* ii. p. 189.

12

recognizes it as one of the fundamental requirements. Dissembling in general he describes as ' the great art at court ' ; but the poet, he adds, dissembles only in the subtleties of his art.[1] And this he does so that his devices may not be obvious, ostentatiously displayed and thus ineffective ; and that when he is most ' artificial ', the result may appear natural and not the outcome of labour and rules. On the importance of fitness or ' seemliness ', however, he dilates at considerable length. He notes, to begin with, that this demand was no arbitrary requirement. It had been valued, it is true, by both Greeks and Romans, with whom the respective terms had been $\tau\grave{o}$ $\pi\varrho\acute{e}\pi o\nu$ and *decorum* ; but his advocacy of the principle he significantly rested, not on classical authority, but on a law of Nature. ' The conformity of things and circumstances ', he describes as a quality which Nature had observed in all her works, and a desire for which she had implanted in all men's minds ; [2] so that it was in reality one of the laws of life, a law which applied to human conduct in general (to court-life in particular) and to all forms of human activity, including that of poetic creation. What this ' decency ' or *decorum* was precisely he found difficult to say, in view of the infinitude of human actions and circumstances. To him it was a matter of discretion, a matter on which all men of good taste would generally agree ; and here his position is that of Quintilian who, faced with the same problem, had held that ' we must rely on feeling and take Nature for our guide '.[3] At the same time he endeavours to throw light by various anecdotes and examples on what this ' decency ' or *decorum* was not ; and his illustrations refer to such things as untimely speeches, vulgar utterances and laughter out of place. Moreover, he prescribes fitting conduct for all sorts and conditions of men ; as when he demands that a priest should be ' sober and sad ', a judge, ' uncorrupt and solitary ', a courtier, ' lofty and curious in countenance, and sometimes a creeper ' ; while not without interest are his suggestions that ' a man should be a lamb in the house, a lion in the field ', and ' a woman, a shrew in the kitchen, a saint in the church '.[4] Here, however, he is making for that false *decorum*, according to which all characters might be divided into fixed types, a doctrine which vitiated the judgment of later artists and theorists. To *decorum* in its true sense he attached great importance in view of his courtly readers, as his work, *De decoro*, goes to show. And he is on sounder ground when he describes it as

---

[1] Smith, *op. cit.* ii. pp. 186–7.
[2] See *Arte*, ed. Willcock and Walker, p. 262.
[3] *Inst. Or.* ix. 4, 120.   [4] *Arte*, ed. Willcock and Walker, p. 293.

'that only that giveth everything its good grace, . . . without which nothing in man's speech could seem good and gracious ', and therefore as ' the line and level for all good makers '.[1]

With this conception of art in mind Puttenham proceeds in Book II to deal with ' Proportion poetical ' or versification, as one of the essential components of poetry. And here, again, in assuming the indispensability of verse he relies, as before, not on ancient authority (modified by Aristotle), but on what he regards as a fundamental law of Nature. According to current philosophy ' God had made the world by number, measure and weight (or tune) ' ; [2] and ' without proportion nothing could be good or beautiful '. Hence the basic need in poetry, which was none other than ' the skill to speak and write harmonically ', for that congruity of sounds found in verse or musical utterance. Apart from this he argues that expression in verse was more effective than expression in prose.[3] Language, he explains, had been given by Nature to men for purposes of persuasion ; and it was significant that the earliest philosophers, historians, and orators, as well as David and the Hebrew prophets, had spoken in verse. This was because metrical speech was melodious and pleasing, compendious, easily remembered, eloquent and ' inveigling ', whereas utterance in prose was looser in form, lacking in colour, and made up of ordinary words. In short, he added, ' poets from the beginning were the best persuaders and their eloquence the first rhetoric of the world '.

But while he thus regards verse on philosophical grounds as an essential part of poetry, equally significant is the fact that he concerns himself almost solely with verse of a rhyming kind, as being the only kind suitable for English poets ; and this in spite of the persistent calumnies inspired by Ascham and others. Early in his work he explained that the beauty of classical verse had depended on metrical quantity, in which the English language by its very nature was deficient. Yet he confidently claims for rhyme no less effective qualities which were unknown to the ancients, and upon which, he maintained, an art of English verse should necessarily be based.[4] ' The chief grace of our vulgar poetry ', he definitely states, ' consisteth in the symphony (i.e. rhyme),' provided the poet ' be not too licentious in his concords '.[5] Moreover, in view of Humanistic prejudices so freely and fiercely expressed, he is at some pains to dispel the current

---

[1] Smith, *op. cit.* ii. p. 173.
[2] *ibid.* ii. p. 67 ; cf. Pico, p. 29 *supra.*
[3] *ibid.* ii. p. 8.
[4] *ibid.* ii. p. 6.   [5] *ibid.* ii. p. 85.

notions of its history, pointing out that it was something more than a cunning Papal device or a barbarous legacy of the Huns and the Goths. Thus rhyming verse, he maintains (on dubious grounds) had existed prior to the Greeks and the Romans, being ' due to the instinct of Nature which was before art ' ;[1] and it had been employed, he asserts, by the Hebrews and Chaldees, as well as by primitive peoples such as the ' Americans, Perusines and even the cannibals '. Then, after the decline of Rome, Latin poetry was modified by rhyming verse, and rhyming sentences became fashionable among orators and preachers. In Charlemagne's time,[2] moreover, rhyming verse was commonly used by learned monks ; and he recalls the rhyming verses of a work on medicine [3] dedicated by the School of Salerno to the son of William the Conqueror (*c.* 1100), the subsequent use of rhyme by medieval Latinists for themes political and trivial, as well as the many ' pretty inventions ' inspired by this new device, such as ' retrograde verse ', or again, the fantastic poem of the 9th-Century monk, Hucbald, dedicated to Carolus Calvus in praise of bald heads, a veritable *tour de force* in which every word began with the letter ' c '.

Having thus assured his readers that rhyming verse was something more than a barbarous invention, that it was also the form best suited for English writers, Puttenham proceeds to discuss its technique in practical and sensible fashion with the help of occasional illustrative passages. The basis of classical verse, he recalls, had been the metrical foot (iambic, trochaic, dactylic, anapaestic, and the rest), whereas in English it was the number of syllables contained in a line ; and he comments, to begin with, on the effects of the varying lengths of lines in use.[4] Thus the line of six syllables he describes as ' sweet and delicate ', the line of ten syllables as ' stately and heroic ', the twelve-syllable line (the French Alexandrine, not used before Wyatt) as ' grave and stately ', while the fourteener line was said to be often tedious, owing to its inordinate length ' keeping the ear too long from its delight, which was to hear the cadence at the end of the verse '. In all such lines, however, an important element was the caesura, that slight medial pause which made for clearness of utterance and was indeed necessitated by breathing require-ments ; and on this matter he has a word or two to say. In lines of six syllables, he notes,[5] no caesura was necessary ; but in the longer lines it was essential, and was to be observed

---

[1] Smith, *op. cit.* ii. pp. 10–11.   [2] *ibid.* ii. pp. 12 ff.
[3] i.e. *Conservandae bonae valetudinis praecepta.*
[4] Smith, *op. cit.* ii. pp. 70 ff.   [5] *ibid.* ii. pp. 73 ff.

precisely—after the fourth syllable, for instance, in lines of eight or ten syllables, and after the sixth in the twelve-syllable line. For the most part, it might be added, he has in mind lines of equal length ; but of significance too is his statement that an extra syllable in the line gives ' greater grace ' to expression, as in the acatalectic verses of the ancients.[1]

To the arrangement of such lines in stanzas, however, he devotes special attention, commenting first on the different varieties ;[2] the quatrain, for example, the stanza of six lines, the popular seven-line stanza used by Chaucer and Lydgate, the stanza of eight lines, ' very stately and heroic ', and the ten-line stanza, ' grave and graceful ', yet judged by some to be somewhat unwieldy. Groups of more than ten lines he described as ' ditties ' or poems in themselves ; while the couplet or distich he notes as useful for epigrams, epitaphs, and the like. At the same time he points out that there is also much art in arranging the stanza, in varying the length of the line and the position of the rhymes, thus producing ' a variable and strange harmony ', now grave, now gay, now passionate or pleasing to the ear, and, what is more, to the eye as well.[3] The most common arrangement he describes as that of the rhyming couplet, used by Chaucer in his *Canterbury Tales*, where the rhyming sounds are never lost ; but effective, too, are said to be alternate rhymes and arrangements that rhymed the first line with the fourth, the second with the third. With the longer stanzas, however, further complications were inevitable, examples of which were to be found in Petrarch's *Canzoni*. In such stanzas a vast number of arrangements was possible ; the rhymes might be interlaced at varying distances ; though then a danger existed lest the rhyming effects might in consequence be lost. Puttenham, however, adds that these more cunning patterns were intended only for delicate ears, and that they called for a more copious vocabulary. His main insistence is on the facts that every line in a stanza plays an organic part, and that the varying length of the line and the rhyming pattern are the keys to the music of the verse.

Having thus attached value to the formal or ' ocular ', as well as to the musical, effects of stanza-arrangements, Puttenham is now led in passing to give countenance to those figure-poems,[4] the main appeal of which was directed to the eye rather than to the ear. Such poems had been cultivated, and subsequently condemned, by Willis and Harvey ;[5] and Puttenham now commends them for their symmetry of form, their brevity and

[1] *ibid.* ii. p. 135.   [2] *ibid.* ii. pp. 68 ff.
[3] *ibid.* ii. pp. 88 ff.   [4] *ibid.* ii. pp. 95 ff.   [5] See pp. 104, 146–7 *supra*.

ingenuity, and the display of craft involved in working within such confined limits. He recognizes that the geometrical device had played no great part in Greek or Latin poetry ; though he had learnt in Italy that such forms had been common in Eastern countries. He therefore recommends them as an amusing pastime, suitable for ' pretty amourets in Court ' ; and supplies examples (with elaborate diagrams) of such forms as the rhombus, the triangle, the sphere, the oval, the cylinder, and the rest. Nor can he refrain from alluding to further courtly exercises of much the same kind; notably, the fashionable emblems and anagrams [1] recently introduced from abroad. Such trifles, he explains, were specially suitable for courtly ' makers ', embodying as they did in brief sententious form, ' high conceits and curious imaginations '.

All this, however, was of the nature of a digression ; and in connexion with his main theme, that of rhyming verse, Puttenham has something further to say concerning the rhymes themselves. He reminds his readers, to begin with, that while rhyme had been wanting in both Greek and Latin poetry, the device nevertheless had not been entirely unknown in antiquity, having been represented by the figure known as ὁμοιοτελεύτον, when clauses in orations or other prose compositions ended in similar terminations.[2] Concerning the actual treatment of rhyme he has some interesting advice to give. He maintains, for instance, that the rhyme which falls on the last syllable of a word is ' the most sweet and commendable ' ; that the double or feminine rhyme (e.g. trusty : lusty) is ' lighter and not so pleasant ' ; whereas triple rhyme (e.g. agility : facility) he describes as the least pleasing of all.[3] His preference is therefore plainly for strong masculine rhymes ; triple rhymes he describes as trivial, more suitable for epigrams and comic poetry than for poetry of a serious kind, while he also points out the difficulty of finding fit words for such rhymes. Then, too, he explains that in rhymes of a correct kind the rhyming syllables should not be identical (e.g. constrain : restrain), but should differ in the initial consonants (e.g. constrain : refrain) ; and that while wrenching the word-accent or distorting the orthography were foul faults in any rhyming poet, yet false spellings were sometimes permissible (e.g. dore : restore) to produce eye-rhymes and if necessary to avoid an unpleasant dissonance.[4] Moreover, he denounces the

---

[1] Smith, *op. cit.* pp. 105–16, note p. 417 : these remarks for some reason are omitted from all copies of the *Arte*, except from one formerly owned by Ben Jonson (now in the Brit. Mus.).

[2] *ibid.* ii. p. 81.   [3] *ibid.* ii. pp. 83–4.   [4] *ibid.* ii. p. 85.

use of inkhorn terms and words of foreign origin in the rhyming
position, describing them as more suitable for interludes where
less attention was paid to detail. And as for medial rhymes,
they were said to result in ' too speedy a return of the rhyming
sound, thus glutting the ear ' ; and as such, they were best
adapted for light and trifling themes, for use by tavern minstrels
and those who amused the common people at Christmas time
with old ballads and romances.[1]

Such, then, are Puttenham's ideas on ' Proportion poetical '
or versification ; and from first to last he remains convinced of
the suitability, as well as the possibilities, of rhyming verse for
English poetry. Yet he cannot altogether ignore the stir that
was being made by the ' new versifiers ' ; and ' for the information of young writers and the pleasure of all others who . . .
delighted in novelty ', he submits ' a few idle observations '[2] to
show that the proposed scheme was at least theoretically possible
for all but the most meticulous. Thus he distinguishes, first,
between what he regards as the genuine classical feet and the
multitude of additions resulting from the pedantry of grammarians. The essential feet, he states, were twelve in number,
four dissyllabic and eight trisyllabic ; and all, he asserts, were
provided by English words. Nor was any special difficulty
presented by trisyllabic feet such as the anapaest and dactyl,
the absence of which from native words had previously been
noted by Gascoigne.[3] The dactyl, indeed, Puttenham regarded
as the most suitable and pleasing in English. It had been
used effectively by Wyatt and Surrey ; though it needed to be
interlaced with dissyllabic feet to give it gravity and weight,
as otherwise it tended to produce a light and trivial effect.
These, then, briefly, are the lines along which Puttenham unfolds
his detailed plan, for which, not without pride, he claims ' some
small subtlety and originality of thought '. Yet he is far
from wishing the scheme to be put into actual practice. ' Wise
men ', he explains, ' do naturally mislike all sudden innovations,
especially of laws ' ; and moreover, he argues, ' it is somewhat
too late to admit a new invention of feet . . . that our fore-
fathers never used '[4]—a notable and significant recognition at
this date of the deference due to earlier native tradition. In
truth, the lack of seriousness with which Puttenham handles
the question is in itself illuminating. To him, and doubtless
to many of his contemporaries, the whole matter was but a
passing craze, a ' scholastical toy', and one of those things ' to be

[1] ibid. ii. p. 87.   [2] ibid. ii. pp. 117 ff.
[3] See p. 142 supra.   [4] Smith, op. cit. ii. pp. 117, 124.

pleasantly scanned upon, as are all novelties so frivolous and ridiculous '.

This then brings Puttenham to the third section of his work, to Book III ' On Ornament ', where he deals with the means of rendering attractive the language and style of the poet, by giving to expression a certain pleasing novelty and strangeness ; and this, he maintains, is done chiefly by a judicious use of figures which give delight to both ear and mind of the reader. But first he treats of the language and style appropriate to the poet ; and his remarks on language,[1] to begin with, are worthy of note. With a commendable knowledge of the history of the English language and its mixed ancestry of Celtic, ' Angle-saxon ' and French elements,[2] he is apparently the first to recognize the existence of a standard dialect as the literary language, which had evolved from the several dialects of medieval times. And that literary language he defines as the speech current in and around London, at the Court and among educated men generally ; adding further, that this and this alone was the proper language for cultured poets. Hence all departures from that standard English were in general to be avoided, including archaisms, foreign words, inkhorn terms, and colloquialisms. Nor, again, were dialect forms any more suitable, though he concedes that the purest ' Saxon-English ' was being spoken in remote northern, western and southern districts. Moreover, the language of ' learned clerks ' was also open to objection, seeing that scholars at the Universities were wont ' to use much peevish affectation of words out of primitive languages '.[3] On the other hand, he recognizes that additions to the standard vocabulary from all these sources could with advantage be made, provided they added something to the range or power of expression. And he quotes Horace [4] in support of his contention that a living language was subject to no conventional limits but must ever be in a constant state of flux.

What he has to say on poetic style is interesting mainly because of its mixture of classical and medieval ideas. He is on sound ground, for instance, in maintaining along with Plato and Cicero, ' Longinus ', Quintilian and others, that style is necessarily a reflexion of the writer's personality [5] (mentis character) ; also in demanding an observance of ' decency ' or decorum, so that expression should be in keeping with the subject-

[1] Smith, op. cit. ii. pp. 149 ff.
[2] cf. his work, Originals and Pedigree of the English Tongue.
[3] Smith, op. cit. ii. p. 150.
[4] ibid. ii. p. 153 : cf. Hor. Ars Poetica, 70 ff.   [5] ibid. ii. p. 154.

matter treated.   Thus obscure or frivolous words, he held, were
unsuited for treating of grave or weighty matters ; while a lofty
style was ruined by an affected manner, the effect of which was
likened to that of ugly giants in a London midsummer pageant.
Then, too, he makes use of the ancient distinctions of style, high,
middle, and low ; but those distinctions he interprets in an
arbitrary sense characteristic of medieval theorists, that is, in
accordance with the social dignity of the personages or subject-
matter concerned.[1]   Thus the high style was said to be employed
in treating of the affairs of princes or great men, the middle style
in treating of the deeds of honourable citizens, while the low
style was concerned with the affairs of common artificers,
shepherds, and the like.   It therefore followed that histories and
tragedies required the high style, comedies and love-poetry the
middle style, pastoral poetry the low style ; and with each style
were associated certain distinctive verse-forms, words, and
figures.

It is to the use of figures, however, that Puttenham looks
mainly for ' the ornamentation of poetry ' ; and in this he
betrays the influence of the earlier rhetoric tradition, which he
now brings to bear on poetic theory.   He notes, to begin with,
that figures had long been recognized as ' the instruments of
ornamentation in every language ' ;[2] though at the same time
they were really departures from the normal mode of expression,
in fact, so many ' vices in speech ' (as Isidore[3] long ago had
termed them), designed to ' inveigle ' the mind of the reader.
In Athenian law-courts, he added, their use had been forbidden
as being calculated to pervert judgment.   Yet the poet, he
urged, was no pleader before severe judges, but an advocate of
' pleasant and lovely causes ', who aimed at ' moving his readers
to mirth and solace ' ; and provided that they were used discreetly, with special regard to circumstances of person, place,
time, and purpose, these ' vices of speech ', he maintains, were
capable of adding much grace to poetic expression.   Then, too,
on their historical development he has also something to say ;
though he is inaccurate in stating that the formulation of the
figures had been preceded by the enunciation of certain basic
principles of style—the need for orderly structure, for forceful,
rhythmical and concise expression—by Greek theorists.[4]   Already
in the 5th Century B.C. Gorgias had recommended certain figures

[1] ibid. ii. p. 158 : see Atkins, Eng. Lit. Crit. Med. pp. 107-8.
[2] ibid. ii. p. 159.
[3] Etymologiae, i. 35, 7, vitia cum rationi (vices used with propriety).
[4] Smith, op. cit. ii. pp. 161-2.

of speech which had persisted with various modifications and additions until Roman times, when, as Puttenham explains, Cicero, Quintilian, and others had substituted for the Greek terms others of Latin origin.[1] Encouraged by their example, Puttenham now proposes to make use of a more intelligible English terminology along with the unfamiliar Greek, and the inadequate Latin, terms ; and he submits his scheme, not without some scruples, as being free from pedantry and tedious doctrine, and as a new and picturesque list more suitable for courtiers.

When we turn to consider more closely his treatment of the figures we shall find that his claim to independence is justified, quite apart from his quaint attempt to simplify the traditional terminology by employing such descriptions as ' the loud liar or over-reacher ' (*hyperbole*), ' the wonderer ' (*paradoxon*), ' the like-loose ' (*omoioteleuton* or rhyme), ' the insertor ' (*parenthesis*), or again, ' the qualifier ' (*epitheton*). Much of his material was obviously of a stock character, made up of details gathered apparently from no one source, and including many trifling devices advocated by the zeal and ingenuity of earlier pedantic grammarians. But what was original was his attempt to present a more rational classification of the figures, his use of illustrations drawn from contemporary poetry as well as from earlier text-books, and his success not only in explaining their emotional value, but also in applying them to a reasoned appreciation of literature in the concrete. Thus, to begin with, he breaks away from current methods by discarding the traditional divisions of tropes, figures of thought and figures of speech.[2] He first submits as his general principle that grace is added to ordinary expression by figurative devices consisting of alterations in the form, the sound and the sense of words and sentences ; alterations which give delight to both ear and mind. And then he explains that such effects are obtained in general by means of additions or omissions, sometimes by re-arrangement or even disorder, or again, by amplifications and abridgements which render expression more copious, pithy, subtle, and lively, thus adding to the effect an element of pleasant surprise.[3] After this comes his classification of the figures, grouped in accordance with the nature of their appeal. First he treats of those figures that affect the ear, alterations designed for formal or rhythmical purposes, and described as ' orthographical ' by earlier grammarians, but for which he proposed the name ' auricular '.

[1] Smith, *op. cit.* ii. p. 163. [2] See p. 80 *supra*.
[3] Smith, *op. cit.* ii. p. 165.

Secondly, there were those that affect the mind, consisting of alterations in sense ; they were the earlier ' syntactical ' figures, which he now described as ' sensable '. And thirdly came those that affect both ear and mind, the earlier ' rhetorical ' figures, for which he suggests the term ' sententious '. Under these three heads he then discusses his selection of figures (numbering 105 all told), noting that ' learned clerks ' had held that ' auricular ' figures (21) concerned only the poet, that the ' sensable ' kind (24) applied to both poet and orator alike, while the ' sententious ' sort (60) was intended for use by the orator alone.[1] These divisions he therefore adopts with one important difference, namely, that since the poet was the earliest orator, all the different kinds, he maintains, belonged rightly to the province of poetry ;[2] though he also recognizes that some figures, common in Latin, were impossible in an uninflected language such as English, while others again were useful only in oratory of a forensic kind.

Concerning the actual details of this somewhat formidable collection of figures this much may be said, that they are of interest nowadays chiefly as illustrating the main lines of the Elizabethan approach to literature, and the technical apparatus available. Modern readers, for instance, find no great delight, as the Elizabethans undoubtedly did, in the fine distinctions prescribed by such figures as *antiphrasis* (broad flout) and *charientismus* (privy nip), or again, in the abstruse workings of *symploche, anadiplosis, aposiopesis,* and the rest. Nevertheless, apart from supplying a key to the understanding of much in Tudor and early Elizabethan verse, Puttenham's treatment is still of value in that it provides some elementary teaching, some shrewd remarks on the poetic craft, together with occasional comments of a contemporary on the actual verse-productions of the time. Of interest, for example, are his remarks on the ' vivid ' metaphor, ' the most commendable and common ' of the figures, on the ' gallant ' figure, periphrasis, and the simile which added beauty and emphasis to expression ; or again, on the skilful use of the repetition and interlacing of words, the relief supplied by the apostrophe or exclamation, the graceful effect of a refrain or of a closing epigram, the virtuosity of a neat play upon words, as well as the effects of the medieval devices of ' amplification ' and ' description '.[3] Of yet greater significance

[1] *ibid.* ii. p. 166.   [2] Willcock and Walker, *op. cit.* p. 196.
[3] See Atkins, *Eng. Lit. Crit. Med.* pp. 102 ff. Noteworthy also is the fact that the ' description ' of the Queen in *Partheniades* (Willcock and Walker, ed. p. 244) is in accordance with medieval theory.

are his occasional penetrating remarks on poetic craft ; his comment, for instance, on the use of the ' epithet ', that ' sometimes words suffered to go single do give greater sense and grace than words qualified by attributions do ' ;[1] or his statement that more cunning is needed to describe convincingly ' what never was nor is like to be, . . . than to describe things that be true '.[2]   Then, too, there are his wise counsels that parentheses must not be too frequent or lengthy lest they confuse the main theme,[3] that ' in praising we must be allowed now and then to over-reach a little ',[4] and that in fiction reported speech must always be in character.[5]   Of all these figures illustrations are given, illustrations taken from ancient, medieval and contemporary poets, and comprising passages from such writers as Virgil and Juvenal, Petrarch and Chaucer, Wyatt and Surrey, Sidney, Raleigh, and Dyer.   And, in addition, the more common defects of contemporary versifiers are also noted, namely, the resort to affected speech (*cacozelia*) and bombast (*bomphiologia*), or again, the excessive use of alliteration, epithets, periphrasis, antithesis, and the like.

This then is the main substance of Puttenham's *Arte of English Poesie* ; and despite its length and its formidable array of prosodic and rhetorical details, it is, next to Sidney's, perhaps the most valuable contribution to literary criticism at this date. That it lacks the many-sided charm of Sidney's work is of course true.   Concerned largely with matters of an elementary and a technical kind, it is written in a style that lacks distinction and is often tiresomely discursive with its loose involved sentences. At the same time it is free from the studied mannerisms of much of the contemporary prose ; and through its pages there peers a live and an engaging personality, with a shrewd, well-stored mind and an independent outlook on life and letters.   To look for definite sources is a somewhat fruitless task.   Many of his anecdotes, it is true, are taken from Erasmus's *Apophthegmata* ; his figures have much in common with those of Susenbrotus's *Epitome Troporum ac Schematum*, as well as with those of other text-books ; while traces of classical, post-classical, and medieval doctrines are scattered here and there throughout the work, in occasional reminiscences of Aristotle, Quintilian, Plutarch, Pico, and others.   On the other hand he is apparently uninfluenced by 16th-Century Italian critics ; and this is suggested by the limitation of his treatment to the minor forms of poetry, and his

[1] Smith, *op. cit.* ii. p. 169.
[2] Willcock and Walker, *op. cit.* p. 238.   [3] Smith, *op. cit.* ii. p. 169.
[4] Willcock and Walker, *op. cit.* p. 192.   [5] *ibid.* p. 235.

lack of concern with those theories of tragedy and the epic which were being propounded in Italy in the light of Aristotle's *Poetics*. The work would therefore seem to be the fruit of considerable reading within certain limits, of ideas digested and adapted to a new and original treatment, and dependent on no earlier authority for either plan or guidance. Arguing throughout from first principles Puttenham commends poetry to his generation on rational and psychological grounds, treating with deference the practice of antiquity, scorning such doctrines as the ' mystical theories ' of the Cabalists, who claimed to have ' received the same . . . from the first parent Adam '—theories, he added, which ' I will give them leave alone both to say and believe for me '.[1]

Of the merits of his teaching, however, there can be no question. In commending poetry as something worthy of the attention of cultured minds, his argument has been seen to differ somewhat from that of Sidney. For whereas Sidney had beheld in poetry an inspiring revelation of human ideals and universal truth, Puttenham, no less convincingly, emphasizes the relation between life and letters, representing poetry as an exalted form of intellectual activity, a valuable addition to the joys of life, and a natural response to human needs, both social and individual. Of poetry, more especially as an art, he is the first to treat in adequate and coherent fashion ; and not least illuminating is the general conception of art that he submits, more particularly in its relations to ' Nature ' and the life of men. In his treatment the necessity for inspiration and the workings of ' phantasy and imagination ' are duly noted ; but his main emphasis is laid on the poetic art as a craft, a rational business, though subject to no fixed or final rules—a treatment which called forth from Harington later his somewhat caustic and unfair remark.[2] Thus Puttenham points out as fundamental the need for a sense of form and fitness ; the need also for an artistic concealment of the devices of art ; while in connexion with diction, he is the first to give a reasoned account of the standard dialect or literary English. Moreover, unlike Sidney, he definitely regards verse as an integral part of poetry, explains something of the mysteries of lines, stanzas, and figures, as well as their effects on mind and ear ; and accepting rhyme without question as the native verse-form, he helps in some measure to dispel the mists of unreasoning doubts and prejudices, though he fails to see the significance of the current developments in the sonnet and blank verse. Altogether his treatise may thus be said to have opened up new

[1] Smith, *op. cit.* ii. p. 123.   [2] See p. 188 *infra*.

possibilities in the critical sphere. He ignores entirely, for instance, the allegorical and moralistic theories of poetry ; he gives examples of that detailed examination of literature in the concrete, essential for a proper appreciation of its aesthetic qualities ; while, as his main message, he proclaims to his generation that, in spite of linguistic and other difficulties, there was possible ' an art in our English poetry as well as there is of the Latin and Greek '.   And this he does in the genuine Renascence spirit ; not by a mere appeal to the texts and authorities of antiquity, but by free inquiry, by argument based on ' the law of Nature or reason ', that unwritten law, universal in its bearing, which constituted for many of his contemporaries the ultimate and infallible guide in matters intellectual.

CHAPTER VII

CRITICAL DEVELOPMENTS : NASHE, HARINGTON, DANIEL, MERES, HALL

IT was in the nineties, however, that a marked change became perceptible in the nature and scope of the critical effort, when the Humanistic approach to literature, latterly modified by courtly ambitions, was superseded by a more popular, less conventional, treatment. From now on, rhetorical studies were to be consigned to the schools ; and the vindication of poetry, together with some exposition of its art, ceased to be the all-absorbing topics. A more varied criticism, in short, was being generated, a phase less concerned with formal treatises and abstract questions, and one which, in different forms, gave evidence of the growth of an artistic consciousness, a tendency to judge and appreciate, as well as a closer concern with literature in the concrete and with contemporary literature in particular. In other words, the age now became critically, as well as poetically, minded.

To this development many causes contributed, awakening latent energies and giving fresh impetus and a new direction to the critical movement. For one thing, after the fall of Antwerp (1576) London had become the capital of European commerce ; and added prosperity gave rise to a new race of city wits and men of letters, to a reading public no longer confined to the Universities and the Court, and to wider intellectual interests which led to the production of a literature of observation and comment on many aspects of contemporary life, including literary activities. Then, too, not without their effect in critical history were those spacious days immediately preceding, which had witnessed the rout of the Armada and the exploits of Eliza bethan seamen recorded in Hakluyt's *Divers Voyages* (1582). Having infused men's minds with fresh ambitions and enthusiasms, they also rendered men more alert and enterprising ; and the results are seen in the new spirit of adventure reflected in the sudden outburst of literary activities, in the rise of the popular drama more particularly, and in a poetic development no longer fettered by the uncertainty of design and the limitation of form of the earlier period. Harvey, for instance, writing in 1593, was not alone in hailing the glorious efflorescence of literature which marked the nineties, when he declared that ' the wind had changed ', that ' there was a busier pageant on the stage ', and that Sidney and Spenser were but the harbingers of Spring, ' the violets of March or the primroses of May '.[1] At the same time a certain liveliness was added to the critical movement by a revival of the taste for satire and invective, which fanned into new life the old spirit of contention represented in the fierce exchanges of earlier Humanists and Reformers, thus adding to ' the curiosity of these nicer times '. So that altogether the discussion, as well as the creation, of literature became of interest as never before ; while the critical works produced were of a varied character, suggestive of changes in the critical atmosphere.

Of the critical contributions at this stage those of Nashe, to begin with, point most clearly to new popular forces at work, thus marking a distinct departure from the earlier scholarly and courtly methods. His themes are mainly the defects of contemporary prose and verse, along with some original ideas regarding style ; and these he treats in spirited fashion, at times with a boisterous vigour that culminates in his famous feud with Gabriel Harvey. In the works of Harington, Campion, and Daniel, again, which treat of old problems in the earlier and more cultured manner, there is also much that distinguishes them from the formalities of earlier *Arts* and *Apologies* ; so that they are something more than belated contributions to unfinished controversies. Campion in attacking rhyme, for instance, has a new suggestion to offer ; while in the works of Harington and Daniel may be detected a new range and freedom of treatment. Of popular tendencies, it is true, they have little or nothing to show ; but in Harington will be found a directness and an urbanity unrivalled except by Sidney, in Daniel an originality of thought and a sustained eloquence that were something new. Their works represent the most substantial contribution to criticism at this stage ; and they must also be reckoned among the most interesting and attractive of all Elizabethan writings. Then, too, not without its interest is the work of Meres. It took the form of a commonplace book, embodying a curious collection of extracts from various authorities, a crude attempt at comparative criticism, as well as some remarks of historical value on contemporary literature. Nor must the sporadic criticism of certain aspects of contemporary poetry be overlooked at this date ; for it points to a growing concern with the literature of the day and to a freer expression of literary taste. Its subjects were chiefly the sonnet sequences and amatory poetry so popular at

[1] Smith, *op. cit.* ii. pp. 261, 249.

the time ; and the satirist, Hall, is a prominent, but by no means the only, commentator in this field.

For the critical work of the freelance, Thomas Nashe (1567–1601), we must turn first to his *Preface to Greene's Menaphon* (1589) and his *Anatomy of Absurdity* (1589), and then to the pamphlet entitled *Strange News* (1592), a reply to certain unkind remarks concerning Greene made by Harvey in his *Four Letters* of the same date. Already at the age of twenty-five Nashe by his invective had won for himself the title of ' the English Juvenal ' ; and it is not strange to find that most of his critical work is severely judicial in character, though not without their interest are his occasional remarks of a more positive and constructive kind. In the first place his judgments are directed against contemporary prose-writers, and against abusive pamphleteers in particular, those authors of words without matter, the ' fountains of our finer phrase ', as he calls them. Yet it is against ' fine writing ' in general that his attack is really directed ; and he begins by diagnosing the causes of that prevailing disease. Contempt of the simple vernacular, the influence of bombastic playwrights and pedantic grammarians, and the slavish imitation of ancient and Italian models, to these causes he ascribes the fantastic styles of the writers of his day, whose one slogan, he adds, was apparently, *nil dictum quod non dictum prius*.[1] His remedy for all this artificiality was both sane and characteristic. In the quest for a more natural style he urges men to adopt ' the remedy of contraries ', to turn to the realistic expressions of ordinary life, just as the Sabeans of old (according to Strabo), when sated with the sweet spices of their country, were wont to refresh their jaded senses with the slime of the Euphrates.[2] It was, in short, by utilizing what was valuable in everyday speech that overdone rhetoric and the grotesque in style would be most effectively eliminated. Yet he sees many hindrances, not the least being the disordered taste of the day, worthless matter being valued and genius attributed to ' privy slanderers '. The truth was, he significantly adds, that the plain man is ' often more judicial in matters of conceit than our quadrant crepundios '[3] (academic chatterboxes).

With the defects of poetry, however, Nashe is also in some measure concerned ; and he proceeds to censure what he regards as trivial or faulty in the verse productions of previous years. First he notes the spate of shoddy translations made by men ill-qualified for the task. Apparently he had Kyd primarily in

[1] *ibid.* i. p. 309.   [2] *ibid.* i. p. 310.
[3] *ibid.* i. p. 311.

13

mind, though his reference includes also *Seneca and his Ten Tragedies* (1581), to which several pens had contributed. On the other hand the efforts of Erasmus and Elyot, Cheke, and Ascham are duly commended ; and there are words of praise for Turberville, Phaer, and Golding. Stanyhurst's *Translation of the Aeneid* (1592), however, evokes Nashe's choicest invective ; that pioneer's ' hexameter fury ' is said to recall to life ' the hissed barbarisms ' of past ages, and to represent a style ' scorned by any ploughman '.[1] Apart from this he complains of the absence of serious poetry. Writers of epitaphs and figure-poems, he stated, ' swarmed like crows to a dead carcase ' ; as did also writers of invective who revived stock complaints to make a show of learning—' small ships ', as he described them, ' in shallow waters '. Then, too, there was much trivial love-poetry, designed to ' enchant chaste minds with amorous discourses '.[2] In such poetry, he remarks, the slender praises of feminine perfection were sung, regardless of the fact that along with your loyal Lucretia the light-o'-love Lais was also to be found. Or again, there were the romances which aimed at reviving ' the legendary licence of lying ' by imitating afresh ' the fantastical dreams of those abbey-lubbers, who had perpetuated the feigned nowhere acts of Arthur, Sir Tristram '[3] and the rest. And with them went the ballads, the new songs and sonnets familiar to ' every red-nosed fiddler and ale-knight ' ; the poetry, so it was said, formerly banished by Plato and Augustine,[4] and productions which alienated the sympathy of every thinking man. At the same time he is aware that this was not the whole story ; and he claims that Chaucer (as well as Gower and Lydgate) in an age of ignorance had rivalled Ariosto in his poetic achievement. Moreover, Spenser, he added, might confidently challenge all Europe ; and he was ' not the only swallow of our summer ', for other London wits, among them Peele and Warner, were said to be exalting poetry to something of its former glory.

Such then is Nashe's critical survey of the literary productions prior to 1590 ; and of no less interest are his views on literary theory in general, on the principles underlying good prose, or again, on the nature of poetry. In the first place, despite his praise of Greene's ' extemporal vein ', and his own daring stylistic practices as well, he has yet some sound advice to give on the cultivation of eloquence or style. For one thing, he maintains the existence of definite standards of excellence ; for to adopt

[1] Smith, *op. cit.* i. p. 315.
[2] *ibid.* i. p. 323 : see also pp. 211–12 *infra.*
[3] *ibid.*   [4] *ibid.* i. p. 328.

CRITICAL DEVELOPMENTS 183

the rude methods of ' the strutting Hortensius ' in prose would be as fatal as to follow Horace's Choerilus [1] in poetry. There was therefore, he added, a definite need for the study of rhetoric, ' without which all the other arts are naked ' ; though at the same time its principles should be applied with discretion and without affectation. Apart from this he has some practical advice to give which, besides being timely, is reminiscent of certain suggestive doctrines of classical antiquity. Not the least important (and it may be added, surprising) is his injunction ' to speak many things in few ' ; [2] though at the same time he urges that conciseness should not be overdone. And closely bound up with this precept was the warning against irrelevance in expression, that most common and tedious of errors. Thus writers, he explains, ought not ' to speak all things which to their purpose they may speak, lest those things be less profitably spoken which they ought to speak ' ; and this principle of economy and artistic selection, later on emphasized by Dryden,[3] had been expounded even more fully by Theophrastus and Demetrius [4] in ancient times. Then, too, he urges the need for sincerity of expression ; ' that which we think let us speak, and that which we speak let us think ' —a precept which he more clearly follows in actual practice. Or again, he insists on the ancient rule enjoining constant exercise. ' Add unto art experience,' he writes, ' experience more profitable void of art than art which hath not experience ' ; and explains further that ' of itself art is unprofitable without experience, and experience rash without art '. Nor should his remark on the art of reading (or study) be overlooked, when, following the younger Seneca and Quintilian,[5] he recommends concentration on essential details and decries idle curiosity concerning futile matters, such as those relating to Homer's birthplace, whether Lucan was poet or historian and the like.

Then there are his views on poetry and the poetic art ; for he notes that many men ' meddle with poets that know nothing of the art ', adding that ' he that will seek for a pearl must first learn to know it when he sees it '. He begins by stating that he is no enemy to that art, though that he harbours some doubts as to its real value is at least suggested by his advice elsewhere that ' we should not dwell so long in poetry that we become pagans '.[6] Nevertheless he proceeds to describe it as ' a more hidden and divine kind of philosophy, enwrapped in blind fables

---

[1] *ibid.* i. p. 334 : cf. Hor. *Ars Poet.* 357.   [2] *ibid.* i. p. 335.
[3] *Essays of J. Dryden,* ed. Ker, ii. 265.
[4] See Atkins, *Lit. Crit. in Antiquity,* i. 158, ii. 206–7.
[5] *ibid.* ii. 167, 259.   [6] Smith, *op. cit.* i. p. 337.

and dark stories, wherein the principles of more excellent arts and moral precepts . . . are contained'; [1] and this allegorical conception he defends on conventional lines with the help of Cicero [2] and Plutarch. The earliest Greek philosophers, he points out, had been poets, and poets from the first had allured men to wisdom by the sweetness of their verse and the variety of their stories; so that poetry was said to be 'the very same with philosophy', there being scarcely any poetic figment that had not a deeper meaning relating to physics, ethics, history, and the like. And to this defence are added Plutarch's description of poetry as 'the Muses' vine' [3] with ripe fruit under the leaves, as well as Erasmus's conception, that of 'a dainty dish seasoned with delights of every kind of discipline'. On the question of rhyming he adopts a non-committal attitude, and is content to suggest that no subtle effects at least resulted from the monotonous rhyming of the old romances.[4] Concerning the lack of serious poetry in his day, however, he feels more strongly, and ascribes the deficiency to the influence of Puritans, who 'in senseless Stoical austerity accounted poetry impiety and wit folly'.[5] Emotional values, he recognizes, had been debated and denounced from the earliest times; but he, for his part, belonged to the Peripatetic persuasion, and thus approved of the pleasure which poetry provided. Moreover, in condemning poetry on the scores of immorality and futility the Puritans, he asserted, were 'casting away the nut because they disliked the shell'; and he reminds his readers of the bees that gather honey from the bitterest flowers whereas spiders suck poison even from the honeycomb. In his opposition to the Puritan temper he adds, in characteristic vein, that there was something to be said for the inspiration of Bacchus; and then quotes the saying, *qui bene vult ποιεῖν debet ante πίνειν*, at the same time allowing that it would be folly to say that no man could write well 'except he took counsel of the cup'.[6]

This then was Nashe's contribution to critical thought in his writings of 1589; and it is supplemented by certain views on literature which emerge in the course of his quarrel with Harvey some three years later. The quarrel, it is true, was largely one of personalities; but it is also of special critical interest as throwing a vivid light on the clash of literary ideals at this date. In his remarks on English hexameters, in the first place, the prime interest arises from the lively illustration of Nashe's

[1] Smith, *op. cit.* i. p. 328.   [2] Cicero, *Tusc. Orat. ad init.*
[3] *De aud. poetis*, 15 E.   [4] Smith, *op. cit.* i. p. 329.
[5] *ibid.* i. p. 330.   [6] *ibid.* i. p. 317.

temper and style ; for his arguments were nothing new, though they reflect in some measure a sense of historical values. Harvey had previously lamented the flouting of hexameter verse in English, protesting that it was a verse of which ' neither Homer nor Virgil had been ashamed '.[1] And to this Nashe replies in a well-known passage :

the hexameter verse I grant to be a gentleman of an ancient house (as is many an English beggar) ; yet this clime of ours he cannot thrive in. Our speech is too craggy for him to set his plough in ; he goes twitching and hopping in our language like a man running upon quagmires, . . . retaining no part of that stately smooth gait, which he vaunts himself with amongst the Greeks and Latins.[2]

Moreover he points out that it did not necessarily follow that because Homer and Virgil had employed that verse-form, therefore Chaucer and Spenser were bound by their examples.

It is, however, on the question of prose style that the clash of literary ideals is more clearly revealed, with Harvey the protagonist of the earlier scholarly tradition, and Nashe the exponent of new and more popular methods. Harvey, so far from being the hide-bound pedant he is sometimes made out to be,[3] was not wholly unconscious of the inevitability of change and development in literature. ' Hope is a transcendent ', he writes,[4] ' and will not easily be imprisoned . . . in any predicament of ancient or modern perfection ; which it may honour with due reverence but will not serve with base homage. Excellency hath in all ages affected singularity.' At the same time he stands for methods of ancient culture, for ' the perfectest art with most perfect industry '. ' A snatch and away with Neoptolemus ', he adds,[5] ' may please a little but profiteth nothing ' ; and then explains further that ' right artificiality (i.e. artistry) is not mad-brained or ridiculous but pleasurable, delicate and gracious '.[6] What he therefore objects to is Nashe's defiance of old traditions in his robustious eloquence, with its unconventionalities, its lack of restraint, its coarse epithets and noisy exclamations ; while he fails to see that Nashe was really blazing a new trail with his daring expressions, his raciness, and his English of colloquial discourse. Hence his provocative descriptions of Nashe as ' the brave Columbus of terms ', ' the thunder-bolt of humanity ', and one who by his ' ruffian rhetoric '

[1] *ibid.* ii. p. 230.   [2] *ibid.* ii. p. 240.
[3] See p. 145 *supra.*   [4] Smith, *op. cit.* ii. p. 283.
[5] *ibid.* ii. p. 237 : Neoptolemus is Ennius's shallow philosopher : cf. Cicero, *De orat.* ii. 156.
[6] *ibid.* ii. p. 234.

surpassed even Aretino himself, who was 'a mere hyperbole incarnate '.[1]

Nashe in reply makes a spirited defence of his unconventional style, first attacking Harvey in return, and then explaining in part his own position. Thus he arraigns Harvey for what he describes as ' the new engendered foam of English ',[2] that is, for his use of inkhorn terms and Latinized diction, as well as for his many archaisms ; and concerning the latter he has something of interest to say. He concedes that such archaic words had Chaucer's authority ; but adds that had Chaucer lived he would have discarded half of them. As it was he himself regarded them as the raw products of a time when ' art like young grass in the spring of Chaucer's flourishing was glad to peep up through any slime of corruption '.[3] That time however had passed ; and there was no reason, he added, that poetry, ' a banished queen into this barren soil . . . should still be constrained . . . to jet it in her old rags, when she is wedded to new prosperity '. Then, reverting to his own defence, he explains that he had outlived those tricks of Euphuism which he had admired when ' a little ape at Cambridge '. Moreover, he had since come to realize that his natural vein was the impassioned style of the *tragicus orator*, and that the ' demure and soft *mediocre genus*—like wine and water mixed ' [4]—was alien to his temperament ; so that while he followed in the train of Aretino, his style was nevertheless personal and ' of his own begetting, calling no man father in England '.[5] It was thus a notable plea for the development of originality in style and for the free expression of personality, as against the fixed and formal precepts of the rhetoricians. He had previously recommended a recourse to the colloquial English of ordinary life and had recalled the advice of Caius Caesar in the *Noctes Atticae* of Aulus Gellius, namely *utere moribus praeteritis, loquere verbis praesentibus* ; [6] and now he emphasizes the importance of originality and personality in style as legitimate and essential ingredients in successful writing.

From these various pronouncements of Nashe some idea may now be gathered of the place he occupies in critical history. Of orthodox judgments and doctrines he provides ample traces ; yet the most striking feature of his work is the divorce existing between his earlier orthodoxy and his later general practice. In other words, the development in his ideas concerning literature

---

[1] Smith, *op. cit.* ii. pp. 246–52.
[2] *ibid.* ii. p. 242.   [3] *ibid.*
[4] *Works of Thos. Nashe*, ed. R. B. McKerrow, iii. 152.
[5] Smith, *op. cit.* ii. p. 243.   [6] *ibid.* ii. p. 243.

and literary expression in particular. In matters of poetry he shares the limited views of many of his contemporaries ; but in treating of style he is an individualist, announcing confidently the changes that seemed to him inevitable. And in so doing he reflected the changing ideals of his age, those principles of realism and individualism that were breathing fresh life into the popular drama. Herein then lies his most valuable contribution to critical doctrine. Something more than a mere voice from the underworld of letters, he presents his views in enthusiastic and forcible fashion, thereby sounding an alarm against fixed rules and standards, and claiming for natural instincts their due place in literary ventures.

Meanwhile a contribution of a different kind had come from Sir John Harington (1561–1612), courtier, wit, and liveliest of epigrammatists, the purpose of whose critical essay is indicated by its title, *A Preface or rather a brief Apology of poetry and of the author and translator*, prefixed to his translation of *Orlando Furioso* (1591). The work was in fact an attempt to commend his translation to that courtly favour which he had forfeited by an earlier version of a certain episode in Ariosto's famous epic.[1] For that experiment, designed merely for light amusement, he had been soundly rated by the Queen, his godmother, had been banished from Court on moral grounds, and ordered, curiously enough, to complete his version of the Italian poem. This was duly accomplished in 1591, when he published his translation with the additional support of a defence of poetry in general, of Ariosto and his own translation in particular ; and while his comments on Ariosto and the translation are not without their value, the main interest is undoubtedly attached to what he has to say on behalf of poetry.

To the defence of poetry, in the first place, he devotes the greater part of his work ; and in his treatment nothing is more conspicuous than the critical tact with which he avoids the reiteration of hackneyed arguments which had proved so tedious in earlier works of the kind. He is indeed doubtful, to begin with, whether at the date of writing any sort of apology was really called for, since poetry, he significantly explains, was no longer being challenged save by a weak faction. Yet, recalling the existence of ' envious teeth ' and of the ' Zoilus at every street corner ', he allows himself to think that a further effort at defence might not be altogether unnecessary. And in the same understanding spirit he proceeds with his task, dismissing with brief, if not scornful, reference those well-known arguments of his pre-

[1] The episode of Giocondo (Canto 28).

decessors which he regarded as trifling or unconvincing. Thus he devotes but few words to the tributes paid to poetry by the Alexanders, the Caesars, and the Scipios ; he refuses to trouble his readers with definitions of poetry, or 'subtle distinctions of the kinds ' ; he refrains from harping on the creative processes of 'makers ' ; and proposes to waste no time on such futile questions as whether the prose dialogues of Plato and Erasmus constituted poetry, whether Lucan was to be described as historian or poet, or whether translators were anything more than mere versifiers. All this was a shrewd commentary on earlier theorizing. The matters mentioned, he concedes, had been handled 'right learnedly ' by both Sidney and *Ignoto* [1] (i.e. Puttenham) ; yet he cannot forgo a somewhat unworthy jibe against the author of the *Arte of English Poesie*, on account of the 'receit of poetry ' prescribed in that work. 'The poor gentleman ', he remarks, 'laboureth greatly to prove poetry an art ' ; yet in the light of 'parcels of his own poetry . . . he doth prove nothing more plainly . . . than that it is a gift and not an art '.

He then turns to his main business, his advocacy of the value of poetry, and accepting for the time being the plain man's belief that 'all that is written in verse is poetry ', [2] he holds that even rhymers and ballad-makers had their uses. As his test of values he adopts the highest of standards, that of spiritual effects ; and judged by that criterion, he allows (perhaps too readily) that poetry contributes nothing to 'the health of our souls ', and was therefore 'in a manner vain and superfluous '. At the same time he is also conscious of human limitations and of the mysteries in divine lore ; and he argues that men should be led gradually to the study of such mysteries, just as Moses was instructed in Egyptian, Daniel in Chaldean, learning. This he implies is performed by the poet. 'Poetry ', he asserts,[3] 'with her sweet stateliness doth erect the mind . . . to the consideration of the highest matters ' ; that therefore it was of use as a preliminary study leading up to the truths of divinity, and that in that function lay its ultimate value. And this contention he supports by a reference to Tasso's simile of the 'gilded pill ',[4] in which poetry is likened to the 'sugared ' physic given to children when they are sick. For this conception of poetry as a preparatory school for the sterner studies of divinity Harington was ultimately indebted to Plutarch, while the idea of the gilded pill was common

---

[1] Smith, *op. cit.* ii. p. 196 : the earliest reference to Puttenham's *Arte* (1589), as yet anonymous.
  [2] *ibid.* ii. p. 197.   [3] *ibid.* ii. p. 198.
  [4] *ibid.* ii. p. 199 : cf. Tasso, *Gerusalemme Liberata*, canto i. 3.

during the Renascence period. Plutarch had described poetry as a preparation for philosophical studies, as a kind of twilight enabling men to face without flinching the blazing and bewildering light of the mistress-study, philosophy ; [1] and Harington has adopted this doctrine, while substituting divinity for philosophy as the mistress-study. Nor should his significant remark on the analogy of the ' gilded pill ' pass unnoticed. That conception of poetry, he notes, involved some amount of artistic deceit, ' honest fraud ' as he termed it ; and this element he justifies, once more with the help of Plutarch. According to that authority poetry was designed for sensitive souls alone, to whom such illusion was both intelligible and acceptable ; and in support Plutarch had quoted the earlier profound statement of Gorgias, to the effect that tragedy indeed deceived by myths and the display of fictitious passions ; but even as the tragic poet in his deceptions was juster than the poet who practised no illusions, so the man who was thus deceived was wiser than the one who was not deceived. [2] This, then, was the defence submitted by Harington ; and it anticipates in a sense Coleridge's later plea for that ' willing suspension of disbelief . . . which constitutes poetic faith '.

Not content, however, with vindicating poetry as a preparatory school for the study of divinity, Harington proceeds to challenge the objections that from time to time had been urged against it. And, following Sidney, he singles out Cornelius Agrippa [3] for attention, as having embodied in his invective ' all that could with any probability be said against poetry ', at the same time adding that Agrippa was by nature ' a general libeller ', one who made absurd and indiscriminate attacks on kings and priests, lawyers, doctors, and the like. Yet for purposes of argument he is prepared to deal with Agrippa's charges, namely, that poetry was the nurse of lies, that it pleased fools, bred errors and had wanton effects ; though it is only the first of these objections that in his opinion called for serious attention.

With regard to the allegation that poetry dealt with falsehood and not with truth, this, he claims to begin with, might reasonably be met by the plea of poetic licence, seeing that poets were everywhere recognized as a privileged class. Moreover, he adds, Aristotle had defined their art as an art of imitation, thus allowing them to ' feign what they list ' [4]—an interesting allusion that

[1] cf. Plutarch, De aud. poetis, 14 E, 36 E.
[2] cf. Plutarch, De aud. poetis, 15 D, De gloria Atheniensium, 348 C : see also Atkins, Lit. Crit. in Antiquity, i. 18 : ii. 314.
[3] See p. 123 supra.   [4] Smith, op. cit. ii. p. 200.

reveals but scant knowledge of Aristotle's actual doctrine. But there was also more to be said than this ; and Harington goes on to argue that poets, least of all men, were guilty of lying. Other writers, he points out, might stumble and make false statements ; but not so with poets who were incapable of false-hood, since they never affirmed anything as true but were content with presenting stories and fables. Nor was this all ; for, granted that poets did not lie, equally true was it to say that what they conveyed was truth in manifold form. This fact Harington demonstrates from the practice of ancient poets, who, he claims, had wrapped up in their poetry sundry senses or mysteries ; and here he is relying on patristic and post-classical teaching con-cerning the three-fold or four-fold methods of interpretation.[1] First there was the literal or historical sense (' the outer bark or rind ' [2]) of the story or fable, which recounted the actions of men ; then the moral sense (' nearer to the pith ') which revealed the moral truths underlying ; and thirdly, the allegorical sense which embodied truths of a theological, political or philosophical kind. And, remarking on the skill required for so complicated a process, he illustrates from the story of Perseus's slaying of Medusa the historical, moral and theological meanings to be read into that story.

Having thus established to his own satisfaction the thesis that poetry dealt with truth, both various and profound, Harington proceeds to justify the particular methods adopted by poets in conveying their truths ; and here again he is indebted to patristic and post-classical theory. He explains, for instance, that the mysterious truths of poetry were deliberately concealed in esoteric fashion to protect them from the profane by whom they might be abused ; [3] that they were written in verse so as to be the more easily remembered ; while the complexity of the method, again, served a very real purpose in providing matter of various kinds, the story and verse pleasing weaker capacities, the moral sense appealing to ' stronger stomachs ', the allegory to more ' conceited ' or imaginative minds. Such methods, he added, conduced to the preservation of learning, which, he held, had much decayed since poets had abandoned ' that mystical way of writing '. At the same time he is conscious that such allegorical

[1] Smith, op. cit. ii. pp. 201–2 : see Atkins, Eng. Lit. Crit. Med. pp. 22, 79.
[2] cf. Bede's description of the process of allegorical interpretation as ' a stripping off the bark of the letter to find a deeper . . . meaning in the pith of spiritual sense '. (Pref. to Commentary on Ezra (Giles, viii. 360).)
[3] Smith, op. cit. ii. p. 203 : see Atkins, Eng. Lit. Crit. Med. pp. 20, 30.

methods had been denounced by both Plato and Aristotle.[1] And in reply he suggests, somewhat lamely, it is true, that devices intended for ordinary men would naturally not appeal to those 'princes of philosophy'. Moreover, he points out that in spite of their objections, both philosophers had made partial use of the methods involved ; fables by Plato in his *Dialogues*, the esoteric style by Aristotle in his treatises. And, for the rest, it was well to remember that Plato was in reality no enemy to poetry,[2] even though he had rightly censured comic poets for their strange religious teachings. It was significant, for instance, that he had retained in his writings the two main elements of poetry, namely, ' fiction and imitation ' ; and if apparently he had abjured all verse, there was on the other hand the example of his master, Socrates, who, according to Plutarch, wrote verse in his old age.

Yet some might still demur to the element of fiction (or ' lying ' as it was sometimes called) in poetry, as well as to the verse-form in which that fiction was clothed ; and Harington has a word more to say on both these subjects.[3] Fiction, he contends, was not only permissible but was also a valuable and helpful component in poetry ; and he illustrates the effect of its oblique method of teaching by reference to Demosthenes's success in persuading the Athenians and to the Biblical use of many parables. As for verse-form, he maintains that it not only aided the memory, but with its orderly and forceful phrase it far excelled prose in effectiveness, while its persuasive sweetness was wont to commend matters ' harsh and unacceptable '. It was in addition of greater antiquity than prose and had Scriptural sanction for its use, having been employed in the *Psalms* and elsewhere in the Bible ; though the exact nature of Hebrew verse, he cautiously remarks, was still in dispute.

Such then is Harington's reply to the first of Agrippa's charges ; and the three remaining objections he treats in more summary fashion [4] as hardly worth answering. That poetry pleased fools, for instance, he gladly concedes ; but this, he argues, was surely to its credit, since it made fools wise by presenting them with ' tales able to keep a child from play and an old man from the chimney corner '. On the other hand he denies outright that poetry bred errors, since poetry dealt only with fictions which were not confined to their literal senses ; so that here again the charge was unfounded. To the complaint of wantonness he attaches greater weight, recalling that Sidney had confessed that ' Cupido had crept even into heroical poems '. Yet an honest

1 *ibid.*
3 *ibid.* ii. pp. 204-7.
2 *ibid.* ii. p. 204.
4 *ibid.* ii. pp. 207-9.

inquiry, he suggests, would show that the evil was more imaginary than real, and at any rate was not inherent in poetry itself.   Thus he holds that heroical poetry, ' the chief form of poetry by general consent ', was least affected by vicious tendencies ; tragedy with its stories of lawless princes aroused pity or abhorrence ; comedy ridiculed vice and satire reproved it ; while elegiac verse again was for ever mourning.   The pastoral, the sonnet and the epigram alone, he allowed, sometimes savoured of wanton love ; yet those works, he added, were ' all too delightful ', and he quotes with a malicious joy Martial's pungent epigram, that ' men praise other works but these they read ' (*laudant illa sed ista legunt*).[1]   With this his defence of poetry is complete ; and he concludes that all poetry may be read with pleasure and profit.

Less revealing though still of interest is his treatment of the second of his main themes—the defence of *Orlando Furioso*.[2] Beginning with a superficial comparison of that poem with Virgil's *Aeneid*, he points out that both poets had begun and ended in much the same fashion, that Virgil had written in praise of Augustus, Ariosto in praise of the house of Este, that Ariosto, in addition, had successfully imitated most of Virgil's felicities ; and in view of these parallels he claims for Ariosto some measure of Virgil's greatness, more especially as in the Italian poem there were elevating Christian elements of which Virgil had been ignorant.   At the same time he is aware that Ariosto had been censured for lascivious passages in his poem ; but such places, he explains, were intended ' to breed detestation not delight '. Besides, Virgil had handled similar matters, with decorum and covertly, it was true ; while Chaucer, again, had frequently been guilty of ' flat scurrility '.

Apart from this, however, there was also the charge that Ariosto had ' wanted art ',[3] which meant, as Harington explains, that he had not conformed with the methods of Homer and the precepts of Aristotle.   To this he replies that what was praiseworthy in Homer's day would be thought otherwise at that later date, the times being changed, so that ' both in phrase and in fashions the world grows more curious each day than other '. Nor, he maintains, was it true to say that Ariosto was entirely at variance with Homer ; for certain charges brought against Ariosto applied also to the Greek poet—the inartistic introduction of certain episodes, for instance, or again, the failure to name his poem after the epic hero.   Equally unjust was also said to be the complaint that Ariosto had flouted Aristotle's rules relating

---

[1] *Epigr*. iv. 49, 10.   [2] Smith, *op. cit*. ii. pp. 211 ff.
[3] *ibid*. ii. pp. 215 ff.

to the ' *Epopeia* or heroical poem '.[1] In the first place he had taken for his theme, as those rules were said to demand, a historical narrative of Charlemagne's days and had limited the time-duration of his story to a year or thereabouts. He had likewise avoided incredible incidents ; for his enchantments and miracles had full ecclesiastical support. In addition, his poem was said to be ' full of *Peripeteia*, that is, the agnition (or recognition) of some unlooked-for fortune either good or bad ' ; and as for apt similes, they were lavishly scattered throughout the work. Yet some readers, continued Harington, might perhaps object to the abrupt endings of some of his narrative passages. But this had been a feature of Sidney's treatment in his *Arcadia* and was not altogether inartistic, as it excited curiosity and compelled the reader to continue to the end of the work when things were cleared up. Nor, again, should serious objection be taken to the moralizing digressions which he had woven into his narrative ; though the practice had been condemned by some on the ground that ' neither Homer nor Virgil doth it '. For Harington, however, it was enough to say that ' Ariosto doth it ' ; and such moralizings he commended as both profitable and delightful, besides providing breathing-spaces for the reader.

As a vindication of Ariosto it is obvious that these arguments of Harington leave much to be desired ; though at the same time they are of considerable interest historically, as embodying the first discussion of the epic (still an unfamiliar term) in English, as well as an early application of the comparative and historical methods of criticism. Harington's use of trifling parallels in his comparison, it is true, is far from convincing ; whereas his claims that the epic laws of ancient Greece were not necessarily binding on modern writers, and that Ariosoto was therefore justified in his innovations, were declarations of first-rate importance. Here no doubt was an echo of that earlier Italian controversy in which Cinthio in his *Discorsi* (1554), Pigna in *I Romanzi* (1554) and Minturno in his *Arte Poetica* (1563) had engaged concerning the *romanzi* in general and *Orlando Furioso* in particular, and which had culminated in Tasso's *Gerusalemme Liberata*, 1581. Harington's line of defence is that of Cinthio, Pigna and Tasso, who had maintained that Ariosto's poem was of a correct and an independent kind, though at the same time they endeavoured to reconcile it with the so-called rules of Aristotle. And of the distorted Aristotelianism of some of the Italian critics Harington also reveals traces, in implying that Aristotle had required for the epic subject-matter of a historical kind, also an avoidance of all

[1] *ibid.* ii. p. 216.

' marvellous ' details ; while his vague reference to the much-debated *Peripeteia* points to no very profound acquaintance with Aristotle's real teaching.

Finally, in his third section, Harington briefly defends his own translation,[1] shrewdly depreciating his workmanship for the sake of *captatio benevolentiae*, and at the same time claiming for translation in general a dignity often denied it by those who, according to the proverb, were said to ' correct *Magnificat* without knowing *quid significat* '. Fault, for example, had been found with his use of two-syllable and three-syllable rhymes, while he himself confessed to having been responsible for certain omissions and additions in his treatment of Ariosto's text ; and to these matters he accordingly directs his attention. With regard to his rhyming endings, in the first place, he protests that to have preserved single rhymes throughout would have been easier but less effective ; that much would have been lost by the neglect of double or feminine rhymes with their sweet falling cadences, rhymes much in favour among the French and adopted by Sidney himself. The best results in rhyming, he asserts, were won by means of variety, by a judicious mixture of masculine, feminine, and triple rhymes ; and he recalls in this connexion the ancient advice of Corinna to the young Pindar (as recorded by Plutarch [2]), ' to sow with the hand and not with the whole sack '. As for his treatment of Ariosto's text, this he defends in accordance with native tradition. Earlier English writers had translated with some amount of freedom ; and this same liberty of treatment Harington now claims for himself, while denouncing the futility of a word-for-word translation.

Such then is the many-sided interest of Harington's *Apology of Poetry* which includes the first English study of an Italian poet together with some slight treatment of epic theory. In it a maturing of the critical spirit becomes visible, not only in the discriminating treatment of stock arguments or in the tentative use made of comparative and historical methods, but also, and above all, in the claim for the recognition of relative standards in poetry and in the freedom with which Aristotle, Puttenham, and others are discussed. For his arguments the author has drawn on a wide culture, having gone mainly to Sidney and Plutarch and to patristic and post-classical authorities, while he is also influenced by earlier Italian critics. Throughout the work echoes of Sidney are heard, and Plutarch's influence is seen in his adoption of the allegorical theory as his main line of defence ; though the stress thus laid on the didactic function of poetry may have

---

[1] Smith, *op. cit.* ii. pp. 217 ff.   [2] *De gloria Atheniensium*, 348 A.

been partly due to a courtier's desire to placate an offended Queen. Nor is the value of the work confined to its theorizing. It commends itself also by qualities of style somewhat rare in contemporary writings, while sacrificing nothing of Elizabethan colour and charm. Its easy familiar manner, its urbane and courtly wit, like so many arguments in the work, are reminiscent of Sidney, though Sidney's high-seriousness is obviously wanting. But it has also attractive qualities of its own ; its neat planning, its lucid and controlled argument, its freedom from Euphuistic tricks on the one hand and from formless writing on the other, these are qualities that render the work more than acceptable to modern readers. In the Epistle Dedicatory to the Queen Harington had stated ' I desire to be brief because I love to be plain ' ; and a delightful brevity and plainness are among the main features of this most readable work.

Yet more significant of changes in the critical atmosphere were the contributions of Samuel Daniel (1562–1619), Humanist, poet, and courtier, who now brought to bear on current problems a judicious and an original mind, besides wide learning and an eloquence admired by all his contemporaries. His best-known work is his *Defence of Rhyme* (1603), a reply to Thomas Campion's *Observations in the Art of English Poesy* (1602), in which rhyme, strangely enough, had been condemned by one who had already endued with fresh charm that particular lyrical device ;[1] and ' whose commendable rhymes ', as Daniel himself put it, ' had given hitherto . . . the best notice of his worth '. To this attack, as well as to those of earlier assailants, Daniel replied in convincing and final fashion ; and his *Defence* is one of the great achievements in Elizabethan criticism, a work remarkable alike for its profound and judicial treatment and for its grace and courtesy in developing its argument. Nor should his lesser contribution be overlooked. In his poem, *Musophilus* (1602), he wrote in defence of literature generally, a theme which had engaged the attention of Humanists from the time of John of Salisbury onwards ; and in that poem he revives once again the spirit of the Quattrocento, the enthusiasm for letters of 15th-century Italian Humanists, shorn, however, of its later pedantries.

Something, however, must first be said of Campion's *Observations*, which, so far from being an exclusive attack on rhyme, contains also positive and original suggestions concerning English versifying. That he was influenced in some measure by the previous outcry against rhyme is seen by his adoption of certain

[1] cf. the lyrics, ' When thou must home ' (1601), and ' The man of life upright ' (1601).

earlier arguments.   Rhyme to him is still originally a product
of the Middle Ages and ' barbarized Italy ', those ' lack-learning
times ' when ' learning lay most pitifully deformed till the time
of Erasmus, Reuchlin and Sir Thomas More ' ; [1] it was moreover
a product since established by ' the consent of many nations '.
In essence it was described as nothing more than a rhetorical figure
of speech (*similiter desinentia*),[2] like the foolish and much-abused
device of alliteration ; and, as such, it was to be used sparingly,
' lest it should offend the ear with tedious affectation '.   Then,
too, in practice it often led to sense being sacrificed to sound ;
and not without its significance was the censuring of Ovid for an
isolated lapse into rhyme, or again, its use by Sir Thomas More
for burlesque purposes.   With these strictures in mind, conscious
too of the ordered beauty of classical verse with its symmetry
and proportion, qualities which were said to characterize all
Creation and music as well, Campion therefore suggests a new
form of versifying which might ultimately dispense with ' the
childish titillation of rhyming ', and thus rival the perfection of
the poets of ancient Greece and Rome.

In the main his proposal is of the nature of a compromise.
What he aims at is a rhymeless verse based on classical feet as
far as the nature of the vernacular rendered it possible.   The
essential classical feet, he maintains, were the dactyl, the trochee,
and the iambus ; whereas the anapaest, spondee, and tribrach
($\smile \smile \smile$) he describes as subsidiary forms, as were also the endless
varieties of the grammarians.   Of the essential feet, the iambus,
he asserts, comes naturally to English speech ; the trochee, again,
is in full accord with English syllables.   The dactyl alone is said
to be unfit for native use ; and therefore the hexameter, in which
that foot played a conspicuous part, was impossible in English,
as indeed had been shown by ' the passing pitiful success ' which
had attended earlier attempts at that verse-form.   What he
advocates therefore is a system of versification based on iambic
and trochaic measures alone ; for he fails to notice the possibilities
of the anapaest in English.   And he proceeds to discuss, with
examples, eight kinds of rhymeless verse, including the regular
Iambic, the ' licentiate ' Iambic, the Iambic Dimeter and Trochaic
verse with various modifications.[3]   His ' licentiate ' Iambic
differs from the regular Iambic in imitating more nearly the
ordinary speech-rhythm, and was practically a form of blank
verse.   The Iambic Dimeter he describes as the most natural and
ancient of English verses, and as a sort of Anacreontic verse
well suited for madrigals and the like, while Trochaic verse with

[1] Smith, *op. cit.* ii. p. 329.   [2] *ibid.* ii. p. 330.   [3] *ibid.* ii. pp. 332 ff.

its various modifications was represented as most effective in epigrams and elegies.   This then, roughly, was Campion's scheme ; and he notes incidentally that Latin verses of six feet have the same sound-duration as English verses of five feet.   Apart from this he requires that the native word-accent should everywhere be observed, that elisions should be employed to avoid ' gapings in our verse ', and he suggests certain rules concerning the quantitative value of English syllables ; though, in general, he adds that no fixed rules were possible, and that others would doubtless suggest themselves since ' no Art was begun and perfected in one enterprise '.   That his proposal was not without its merit is shown by the excellence of at least two of the rhymeless poems provided as examples, namely, the charming *Rose-cheeked Laura* and *Constant to None*.[1]   Whether such lyrics would have been improved with rhyme, however, is another question ; and at any rate it is interesting to note that, despite his theory, most of his later lyrics are of the rhyming kind.

Such then was the work which proved to be the immediate occasion of Daniel's *Defence of Rhyme*.   Coming as it did from ' a man of fair parts and good reputation ', it seemed to Daniel to call for a considered reply, especially in its strictures on rhyme ;   and although the status of rhyme he had hitherto regarded as a closed question, he nevertheless undertakes the task, recalling Horace's wise saying that ' what is derided is more easily learnt and more readily remembered than what is approved and respected '.[2]   Concerning Campion's positive scheme he has something to say ; but his main attention is given to the vindication of rhyme, and above all to the treatment of certain fundamental questions which arise in the course of the discussion. This it is that removes the work from the plane of a mere quarrel concerning a literary device, and gives to it its wide outlook and permanent value.   Already in his preamble traces of Daniel's wise and generous spirit are seen when he regrets that Campion had not been content to submit his scheme on its own merits and without an attack on rhyme.   Moreover he concedes that new ways of writing poetry were not inconceivable and were deserving of consideration, seeing that ' evermore of one science another may be born ' ; [3] and as he adds further, ' to set a limit on the work of another is the mark of an unbecoming and grudging spirit '.

On the question of rhyme, however, he takes up from the first an uncompromising attitude ;   and the original character of his

---

[1] *ibid.* ii. pp. 344, 348.   [2] Hor. *Epist.* ii. 1, 262–3.
[3] Smith, *op. cit.* ii. p. 359.

procedure is seen at once in the nature of the tests he applies in the defence of that device. So far from relying on mere authoritative pronouncements of others, he attempts first to show that rhyme was in accordance with the law of Nature, the guiding-star of contemporary thinkers ; secondly, that it had been ' universally received and confirmed by Time ' ; and thirdly, that it discharged certain valuable aesthetic functions. Thus he begins by defining verse in general as an arrangement of words in measured form, differing from ordinary speech and designed to express more effectively the thoughts of men. Such arrangements, he explains, varied in accordance with the language, the particular age and the individuality of the writer ; and that originally they had been based on rhythm and metre alone. In English, however, rhyme was of the nature of an added harmony, naturalized by custom, and ' happier than any proportion antiquity could show us ' ; and its justification lay in the fact that it contributed further to the grace of expression, in ' giving to the ear an echo of a delightful report and to memory a deeper impression ' of the thought conveyed. Thus does Daniel claim that rhyme is in accordance with the law of Nature or reason ; though he is less happy in his speculation that the term itself was derived from *rhythmus* or ' romance ', or the Italian form *remensi*.[1]

But if there were rational grounds for recognizing rhyme, its universality and its functional values, suggested Daniel, were also arguments in its favour. Aristotle, he recalled, had noted in all men a natural instinct for *rhythmi*,[2] and the resort to rhyme right down through the ages would seem to point to the existence of a similar instinct for rhyme. Thus he claims (on slender grounds) that it had appealed to civilized and uncivilized peoples alike ; [3] to Turks and Arabs, Poles and Hungarians, to Germans, Italians, and Spaniards, as well as to the Irish, the Scots, the Danes, and Saxons nearer home. Some of these races, he ventures to add, had used " no other harmony of words ' ; it was as if Latin verse, despite its excellences, had failed to satisfy ' the ear of the world '. Nor had it been wanting in medieval times ; as the verses of the *Schola Salerna* [4] and of the popular *Carmina Proverbalia* went to show. Then, too, there were its functional values in inspiring the poet and giving added delight to the reader. ' In an eminent spirit ', wrote Daniel,[5] ' rhyme is no impediment to his conceit, but rather gives him wings to mount, and carries him, not out of

---

[1] Smith, *op. cit.* ii. p. 360 : for Cinthio's use of this term see Smith's note.
[2] *ibid* : cf. Arist. *Poetics*, 1448 b, 20.   [3] *ibid*. ii. p. 361.
[4] See p. 168 *supra*.   [5] Smith, *op. cit.* ii. p. 365.

his course, but as it were beyond his power to a far happier flight.' And as for its effects upon the reader, Daniel's contention was that ' it delighted the ear, stirred the heart, and satisfied the judgment . . . as I doubt whether ever single numbers will do in our climate '.[1] In these arguments, the main body of his actual defence, Daniel had applied sound methods in adopting as his tests those of reason, universality and aesthetic function. On the other hand, his treatment obviously suffers from a lack of authentic historical knowledge, as well as from a blindness to the evidence existing in the vernacular efforts of Chaucer and others. Of the depth of his conviction as to the value of rhyme for English verse there can, however, be no doubt ; and this is seen in his impassioned reference to ' the sacred monuments erected therein, which contain the honour of the dead, the fame of the living, . . . and the best power of our speech, and wherein so many honourable spirits have sacrificed to Memory their dearest passions, showing by what divine influence they have been moved and under what stars they lived '.[2]

But Daniel is not content to leave the matter there. Proposals for a new versification, those of Campion and others, called for a reply ; and Daniel discusses, first, the general question, and then the particular scheme submitted by Campion. He points out, to begin with, that any new system would need time for its proper development ; and meanwhile to ordinary readers the ' laboured measures ' of innovators would appear as nothing more than an orderly prose. Nor could the ' tyrannical rules of idle rhetoric ' be allowed to dictate in the face of established custom ; and as for those who aimed at getting rid of the fetters of rhyme, they were merely proposing to substitute fetters of another kind.[3] Indeed, so far is he from submitting to any system of rules that what he proposes is that popular taste should be decisive in the matter—a most notable suggestion at this particular date. He had previously discussed the aesthetic effects of rhyme ; and his advice now is ' to suffer the world to enjoy that which it knows and what it likes, seeing that whatsoever force of words doth move, delight and sway the affections of men . . . is true number, measure, eloquence, and the perfection of speech '.[4] Then, too, in Campion's scheme he finds nothing to commend : he rather condemns it outright as being inconsistent in itself and the mere fruit of a desire to say something new. In the first place, he argues, the reader is urged to imitate the ancients, and then is shown how to disobey them in the matter of quantities ; or

[1] *ibid.* ii. p. 362.
[3] *ibid.* ii. pp. 362–3.
[2] *ibid.* ii. p. 381.
[4] *ibid.* ii. p. 363.

again, the scheme represented as a perfect art of versifying is later on described as open to improvement. The intricacy of the rules proposed is also noted, though, as Daniel recalls, *in pessima republica plurimae leges* ; and, moreover, there was no certainty that another law-giver would not soon arise. As for Campion's eight kinds of rhymeless verse, they are briefly dismissed as nothing new, being merely verses ' used amongst us time out of mind, . . . only now apparelled in foreign titles '.[1] Here, however, it would seem that Daniel is less than fair to Campion. He fails to consider the essential point of Campion's proposal, namely, the positive merits of unrhymed verse, especially in the lyric ; and whereas its possibilities had already been shown in *Rose-cheeked Laura*, later on they were to be amply illustrated by Collins in his *Ode to Evening*.

With this Daniel has completed his task of defending rhyme and of parrying the threat which he had discerned in Campion's tract ; and in so doing he had made an interesting contribution to contemporary criticism. Yet his discussion is not altogether limited to its primary object. Still more valuable, as seen in the perspective of time, are the digressions which supply his views on more general and far-reaching questions, the questions, for instance, of the relation of ancient literature to modern effort, of the attitude to be adopted to the much-maligned Middle Ages, or again, the line of true progress to be followed in literary matters ; so that what was begun as an apology of a metrical device thus widens in scope and becomes a work of literary criticism in the larger sense of the term.

Of outstanding importance, to begin with, is his pronouncement on the current Humanistic doctrine which prescribed in literary affairs an imitation of the ancients. The doctrine, as is well known, was not confined to metrical matters. Definite models had from time to time been recommended for the various literary forms, Cicero for prose compositions, Seneca for tragedy, Plautus and Terence for comedy, Virgil for the epic, together with the rules of Aristotle and Horace ; and Daniel in writing his Senecan tragedy *Cleopatra* (1594) had so far conformed with the theory. Now, however, doubts arose as to its validity in the sphere of versification ; and Daniel proceeds to state his objections. For one thing, classical verse, he points out, had owed its felicity to the nature of the classical tongues, from which English differed in many vital respects, thus rendering imitation difficult, if not impossible. Then, too, he suggests (but here less happily) that the merits of classical verse lay in its subject-matter rather

---

[1] Smith, *op. cit.* ii. p. 377.

than in formal excellences ; and he takes particular objection to
its defiance of the natural word-order, to ' its dismembering of
words and disjoining such as should be married and march together '.[1]   Such verse, he maintains, ' is many times but a confused deliverer of their excellent conceits, whose scattered limbs
we are fain to look out and join together to discern the image of
what they represent unto us '.   Or again, he notes that imitation
as prescribed would involve much laborious toil and unnecessary
complexities, so that it would seem as if ' Art was ordained to
afflict Nature, and that we could not go but in fetters '.[2]   With
these thoughts in mind he is therefore disposed to doubt the
validity of the theory of imitation in general ; and he boldly
gives utterance to a yet higher law, all the more striking as
coming from so pronounced a Humanist as Daniel.   ' Methinks ',
he states in memorable phrase, ' we should not so soon yield our
consents captive to the authority of antiquity unless we saw more
reason ; all our understandings are not to be built up by the
square of Greece and Italy.   We are the children of nature as
well as they ; we are not so placed out of the way of judgment
but that the same sun of discretion shineth upon us '.[3]   And
here was being proposed a new charter of liberty for English
writers.

Equally significant and timely, however, is Daniel's attempt
to dispel those Humanistic prejudices concerning the Middle
Ages which, fostered by Ascham, had hitherto prevented any just
appreciation of the literary activities of that period.   The main
objection to rhyme had lain in its supposed origin as the product
of a dark and barbarous era ; and in removing the slur from the
age preceding Daniel prepared the way not only for a new sense
of the continuity of literature, but also for a better understanding
of the popular literature of his day, based as it was mainly on
earlier native tendencies.   He therefore discountenances forthwith as the mark of ' arrogant ignorance ' the practice of condemning ' this or that nation as barbarous, these or those times
as gross ' ; and this he does on the ground that ' this manifold
creature man . . . hath always some disposition of worth . . .
and is eminent in some one thing or other that fits his humour
and the times '.[4]   He also replies at some length to Campion's
charge concerning ' the lack-learning times ' before Erasmus and
Reuchlin had written.   He recalls, for instance the achievements
of Petrarch, Boccaccio, and the Quattrocento in Italy, the
contributions of Poggio, L. Valla, Chrysoloras, Trapezuntius,

[1] *ibid*. ii. p. 364.   [2] *ibid*. ii. p. 365.
[3] *ibid*. ii. p. 366.   [4] *ibid*. ii. p. 367.

Aeneas Sylvius, Politian, and Pico, ' the miracle and phoenix of the world '[1]—a long and significant list suggestive of sources whence inspiration was being derived even in Daniel's day. And, in addition, he directs attention to yet earlier literary activities in England, to the works of Aldhelm and Bede, Joseph of Exeter, Map and others, as well as to the political and legal triumphs which had brought England safely through troublous seas. For such a period, ' that rugged antiquity ' (*impexa illa antiquitas*)[2] as he terms it, he claims some measure of veneration ; and he concludes with another of his memorable passages. ' It is but the clouds ', he states,[3] ' gathered about our own judgment that makes us think all other ages wrapt up in mists and the great distance betwixt us that causes us to imagine men so far off to be so little in respect of ourselves. . . . The distribution of gifts are universal and all seasons have them in some sort.' It is true that Daniel, in thus writing, has in mind medieval Latinists only. But an important doctrine had been promulgated ; the barriers of prejudice had for sound reasons been broken down, and the way prepared for some consideration of medieval vernacular literature.

On yet one other general question does Daniel make a pronouncement, that is, on what he conceives to be the lines of true progress in creative literary methods. And at a date when ' imitation of the ancients ' was the dominant theory with scholars, with daring and original experimentation the general practice, his advice, though brief, was as timely as it is intelligible. Of the limitations of the method of mere imitation he had already spoken ; but he is also alive to the dangers of crazy and ill-judged novelties. And since at the time the greater threat seemed to come from an excessive and unbridled licence, his advice is therefore to aim at development along traditional lines, and to strive for perfection in accordance with the national genius. ' We shall never proceed ', he writes,[4] ' if we be ever beginning, nor arrive at any certain port, sailing with all winds that blow.' It was an early pronouncement on the secular conflict between Convention and Revolt ; and his counsel is to follow Convention, with, however, some reservations.

These then are the chief matters treated in Daniel's *Defence of Rhyme* ; though his interest is not confined to general questions, and this is shown by occasional comments on the actual literature of his time. Of special interest, for example, are his illuminating

---

[1] Smith, *op. cit.* ii. pp. 368–9.
[2] *ibid.* ii. p. 372 : cf. Tacitus, *Dialogus*, 20.
[3] *ibid.* ii. pp. 370–1.   [4] *ibid.* ii. p. 374.

remarks on the contemporary sonnet. Concerning its intricate rhyming system, in the first place, he had previously felt some doubts ; but he had since become convinced of the efficacy of its rhyming pattern. And if, as he explains, the multiplicity of rhymes presented some difficulties, yet ' all excellences were sold at the hard price of labour '. Of still greater interest is the light he throws on the peculiar merits of the sonnet form. So far from crippling expression by reason of its limited length, the sonnet is said to present thought in ' a just (i.e. appropriate) form, neither too long for the shortest project, nor too short for the longest, being . . . only employed for a present (i.e. passing) passion '.[1] Then, too, the psychological effects of this limitation of form are also explained. Our imaginings, he states, are at first a shapeless and ' unformed Chaos ' ; but being wrought into order they become ' more pleasing to Nature, that desires a certainty and comports not with that which is infinite '.[2] Moreover, he points out the excellence of thought conveyed ' in a small room ', the loss of beauty involved in expansion or contraction, the effects of the apt placing of the ' sentence ' where ' it might best stand to hit ', and ' the certain close of delight with the full body of a just period well carried '. These are effects, he concludes, to which neither the Greeks nor the Latins ' with their boundless running on ' ever attained. In the main idea underlying this commentary Daniel revealed a valuable secret of the poetic art ; and that idea, it is worth noting, is reminiscent of the ancient Greek doctrine, according to which the illimitable is naturally displeasing to men, being beyond human grasp, so that in all artistic expression a limiting principle is necessary—a doctrine endorsed by both Plato and Aristotle.[3] Moreover, by this commentary of Daniel, Wordsworth was probably influenced when he refers to ' the Sonnet's scanty plot of ground.' [4] He is known to have admired Daniel ; and in the *Excursion* [5] he quotes two of Daniel's lines.

Nor is Daniel without his practical suggestions as a poet ; and his advice throughout is based on the dictates of ' Nature and a judicial car ', though he repeats more than once that his remarks are merely tentative, since there was no absolute rule in things continually changing. Himself a conscious artist, he had elsewhere pleaded, in view of the careless workmanship of the time, for a plentiful use of the file ; and in his *Delia* sonnets (1592) had described his own practice of correcting ' as if there were no

---

[1] *ibid.* ii. p. 366.   [2] *ibid.*
[3] See Atkins, *Lit. Crit. in Antiquity*, i. 144–5.
[4] cf. sonnet, *Nuns fret not.*   [5] iv. 330–1.

sabaoth of the mind '.[1] Elsewhere he had pointed, without prejudice, to new and more realistic themes and methods. ' Let others sing ', he wrote,

> Of Knights and Paladins,
> In aged accents and untimely words ;
> Paint shadows in imaginary lines,
> Which well the reach of their high wits records.[2]

And now, in his *Defence* he adds further remarks on poetic technique,[3] suggesting, for instance, that rhyming couplets in long poems are apt to be tedious and surfeiting ; that run-on lines, on the other hand, have a grace of their own ; that blank verse, again, is best suited for tragedy, except where a ' sentence ' may call for a couplet ; and that while alternate rhymes added variety to expression, masculine and feminine rhymes should never be mingled. Apart from this he comments briefly on current questions, pouring renewed scorn on the new versification, as something alien to English writers, who ' owed fealty to no foreign invention ', especially when it ran counter to the dictates of Nature. Or again, he laments ' the forging of strange or unusual words ' ; and the arbitrary displacing of words which distorted the native idiom. What he advises is a recourse to natural expression and the use of the ordinary speech-rhythm. ' Our own accustomed phrase, set in due place,' he states, ' would express us more familiarly . . . than all this idle affectation of antiquity or novelty can ever do.'[4]   And as for rhyme, the attacks of innovators, he maintains, could but strengthen its position ; while he also ventures to prophesy that when ' after-times should make a quest of inquiry ' the best things of his day would be found in rhyme.[5]

Such then are the main contents of Daniel's *Defence*, in which he had attempted to correct what he regarded as a defect in the Humanistic outlook. At the same time he has been rightly described as ' one of the dwindling band of English Humanists ' ; and this becomes clear from his poem *Musophilus* (1599), in which the genuine spirit of Humanism is once more revived. Of the claims of that work to be included in a survey of contemporary literary theory there can be little doubt. In form a dialogue between a courtier (Philocosmus) and a man of letters (Musophilus), it constitutes a plea for the recognition of the refining and ennobling influence of literature in general ; that theme which had echoed throughout classical antiquity and had since

---

[1] *Delia*, To the Reader, l. 15.   [2] *ibid.*, sonnet XLVI.
[3] Smith, *op. cit.* ii. pp. 382–3.   [4] *ibid.* ii. p. 384.   [5] *ibid.* ii. p. 380.

been renewed from time to time. Castiglione had commended letters as a useful adjunct of the courtly life ; now Daniel presents them as an invaluable acquisition for life as a whole. And this he does with an eloquence and enthusiasm which raise his treatment to emotional levels and justify his use of verse for his particular purpose.

The main theme of *Musophilus* is that literature is primarily a means by which men may extend their own spiritual lives into the past and the future. ' O blessed letters ', writes Daniel,[1]

> that combine in one
> All ages past, and make one live with all,
> By you we do confer with who are gone,
> And the dead living unto council call ;
> By you th'unborn shall have communion
> Of what we feel, and what doth us befall.

And upon this theme he dilates at length, meeting current objections and moving on by stages to a splendid and eloquent close. First comes the objection that a busy age has no use for ' an ungainful art ', with its ' untimely music of neglected lays '. To this Daniel replies that in that art he finds delight and perhaps lasting fame. Even ' the words thou scornest now ', he adds, ' may live, the speaking picture of the mind ', for the poet is said ' to live two lives where others have but one '. Or again, the futility of all such effort is urged, in view of the factious opposition of ' viperous critics ', and of the ' many that so confusedly sing, whose divers discords have the music marred '. To the censures of the ' unnatural and wayward race ' of critics Daniel's answer is that ' a puff of folly never can deface the work a happy genius ' has framed ; while those presumptuous pedants, ' whose grace is not to work but to reprove ', he denounces with the brief comment that ' they others' virtues scorn that doubt their own '. And as for ' the disagreeing chords of interjangling ignorance ', these too might be safely ignored, as part of the discord of the age. Nor, again, should the neglect of the ignorant multitude deter the poet ; for him fit audience though few should suffice. And meanwhile Daniel proclaims the deathless quality of literature, recalling how nations with ' proud aspiring palaces ' had vanished ' since Chaucer lived, who yet lives and yet shall ', to ' the sacred relics of whose rhyme ' our reverence is due.

But, again, it is urged that the world's affairs call for action, not words, and that the world of letters is enervating, ' for who knows most, the more he knows to doubt ' ; so that ' eloquence

[1] ll. 189 ff.

and rhyme ' serve no real purpose. To this Daniel replies in the
spirit of the ancients extolling the power of Logos ;

> Power above powers, O heavenly Eloquence,
> That with the strong rein of commanding words,
> Dost manage, guide and master th'eminence
> Of men's affections, more than all their swords.
>
> . . . .
> Should we this ornament of glory then
> As th'unmaterial fruits of shades neglect ? [1]

And then with his thoughts reverting to England, he conjures
up, as in a prophetic vision, the glory that awaits the progress
of English verse and the world-wide mission English literature
was destined to serve :

> Or should we careless come behind the rest.
> In power of words, that go before in worth,
> Whenas our accents equal to the best
> Is able greater wonders to bring forth ;
> When all that ever hotter spirits exprest
> Comes bettered by the patience of the North ?
> And who in time knows whither we may vent
> The treasure of our tongue, to what strange shores
> This gain of our best glory shall be sent,
> T'enrich unknowing nations with our stores ?
> What worlds in th'yet unformèd Occident
> May come refin'd with th'accents that are ours ?
> Or who can tell for what great work in hand
> The greatness of our style is now ordain'd ?
> What powers it shall bring in, what spirits command,
> What thoughts let out, what humours keep restrain'd,
> What mischief it may powerfully withstand,
> And what fair ends may thereby be attain'd ? [2]

These are arresting lines ; though indeed the poem is full of good
things, with its recognition of the power of letters, its suggestions
of the immortality of literature and its civilizing effects ; or
again, its confidence in the vernacular, its daring challenge to
Italy, and, not least, its glowing vision of the glory that was to
be. Old arguments, maybe, are here repeated, though rarely
had they been presented in more spirited and persuasive form.
But what lingers in the memory is the concluding prophetic
utterance, embodying as nowhere else proud ambitions inspired
by new horizons then opening in the West ; while already the
greatest of poets had begun his triumphs which were to enrich
unknowing nations with the treasures of our tongue.

[1] ll. 939 ff.   [2] ll. 951 ff.

Of Daniel's place among the major Elizabethan critics there can therefore be no question; though what Coleridge said of his verse, that ' it had been most causelessly neglected ',[1] is to some extent true of his critical performance. To that work Renascence culture and idealism, good sense and poetic vision, all alike contributed; and with Nature as his guide he discussed with courtesy and insight a heated and much-vexed question of his day. Yet the least part of his achievement was his vindication of rhyme ; for he shares with ' Longinus ' the faculty of the great critic of penetrating to fundamental issues while ostensibly treating of minor matters alone. Thus he represents to his fellow-countrymen the true line of progress in literary affairs, not only by pointing to a higher law than that of ' imitation ', or by dispelling illusions concerning the Middle Ages, but also by recognizing the claims of the national genius and even of popular taste—all matters which were long to remain but imperfectly apprehended. That his historical statements are sometimes ill-founded, and that he is somewhat captious in his judgment of Latin verse, such things as these may be conceded. On the other hand there are his practical remarks on poetic technique, his illuminating comment on the Elizabethan sonnet, and not least, his timely reminder of the lasting power and influence of great literature. Moreover, all is communicated with a fervour and sincerity that free his expression from passing fashions and give to his style a dignity and elevation of its own. What Coleridge described as his ' neutral '[2] style of verse may have hindered a proper appreciation of his value as a poet ; but if it marred his verse, it invested his prose with fresh tones and imaginative colour. So that Daniel stands out as ' one of the golden writers of our golden Elizabethan age ', distinguished alike for his inspired eloquence and for the suggestive originality of his critical outlook.

Of far less importance, though still of interest, is that curious work, the *Palladis Tamia, Wit's Treasury* (1598) of the schoolmaster, Francis Meres (1565–1647) ; a sort of notebook or thesaurus embodying information concerning religion, philosophy, music, painting, and books, and in addition, a section on poetry and poets which is not without its bearing on critical history. The treatment throughout that section, it is true, is one of mere compilation, there being but few traces of independent judgment. What, however, is provided is a random collection of authoritative sayings concerning poetry, a survey as well of contemporary

[1] *Biographia Literaria*, ed. Shawcross, ii. 119.
[2] *ibid*. ii. 61, 280–1.

English writers and their work, all of which throw light on the literary ideas and opinions current at the time. Nowadays the work is primarily valued for one incidental feature, inasmuch as it represents the earliest reliable commentary on Shakespeare's literary activities. Of definite value, for instance, are the facts supplied concerning the puzzling chronology of his works. Thus at the date of writing (1598) Meres makes it clear that there had already appeared not only Shakespeare's *Venus and Adonis*, his *Lucrece*, and certain *Sonnets* then in circulation ' among his private friends ', but also his comedies, ' *Two Gentlemen of Verona*, his *Errors*, his *Love's Labour's Lost*, his *Love's Labour's Won* (possibly *All's Well that ends Well*), his *Midsummer Night's Dream*, his *Merchant of Venice*, as well as his tragedies, *Richard II*, *Richard III*, *Henry IV*, *King John*, *Titus Andronicus* and *Romeo and Juliet* '.[1] The list is a long one ; but it is first-hand evidence of what were undoubtedly Shakespeare's earliest plays. No order of sequence, it is true, is given ; yet trustworthy criteria are thereby provided for distinguishing between his earlier and later work, and on this as a solid foundation have been based all subsequent investigations into the dates and order of his plays.

Yet this does not exhaust the interest of the work ; for among other things it points to the importance attached at the time to Plutarch as an authority on poetry. The usual places in Cicero and Ovid are recalled in support of the doctrine of poetic inspiration ; Sidney, Webbe, and Harington are also quoted ; but it is Plutarch who supplies the main teaching. Thus poetry is described, for instance, as the first step towards the study of philosophy with its dazzling light : [2] it is also likened to the Muses' vine with clusters of grapes under the leaves.[3] Or again, there is Plutarch's explanation of the legitimate pleasure arising from poetry in which evil was depicted, namely, that it resulted from the artistic representation of things in themselves repellent, and that it was due to an appreciation of the artistic skill which imitated naturally and successfully.[4] Apart from this there is Meres's ' comparative discourse of English poets with Greek, Latin and Italian poets ',[5] which assumes the form of an undiscriminating catalogue of ancient and more recent writers. As an example of comparative criticism it must be described as worthless. Writers are brought together, not in order to dis-

---

[1] Smith, *op. cit.* ii. pp. 317–18.
[2] *ibid.* ii. p. 311 : cf. *De aud. poetis*, 14 E, 36 E.
[3] *ibid.* ii. p. 309 : cf. *De aud. poetis*, 15 E.
[4] *ibid.* ii. pp. 309, 312 : cf. *De aud. poetis*, 18 A–C.   [5] *ibid.* ii. pp. 314 ff.

engage their qualities by comparison or contrast, but simply by way of suggesting vague parallelisms between ancient and modern authors—a device common in ancient Rome when meaningless correspondences with representative Greek writings were frequently sought in Latin works. At the same time the list of English poets supplied is not without its value, including as it does writers of whom otherwise but little is known ; while an attempt is also made to classify them in accordance with the ' kinds ', namely, epic, lyric, tragedy, comedy, satire, elegy, pastoral, epigram, translation, emblems, and the rest. Certain of his comments, too, are worthy of note, though in stating that *Piers Plowman* was the first to observe ' true quantity ' without rhyme,[1] or again, in condemning outright the old romances, he was merely perpetuating imperfect judgments of his predecessors. Of greater significance is his estimate of Shakespeare as a dramatist, whom he describes as among the English ' the most excellent in both kinds for the stage ' ; [2] and (adapting a familiar commonplace handed down by Varro and Quintilian) [3] as one ' whose fine-filed phrase the Muses would speak if they would speak English '. Nor is he less happy in commenting on Shakespeare as a poet, and in suggesting Ovidian quality, if not Ovidian influence, in his *Venus and Adonis*, his *Lucrece*, and his sugared *Sonnets*.[4] The epithets ' fine-filed ' and ' sugared ' are not those which would suggest themselves to modern minds ; yet the passage supplies valuable first-hand evidence of the distinction already won by Shakespeare before the close of the century. It was a notable appreciation of one who at the time was catering for the popular stage ; and it represents the earliest attempt at that Shakespearean criticism which has since never ceased to engage the attention of later generations.

There yet remains to mention as belonging to this date certain occasional criticisms of contemporary poetry which come from other writers, and which point unmistakably to the increasing vitality of the critical temper, being not the least significant of the critical developments at this stage. At the time certain definite departures in poetry were being made, all of which excited comment ; and as a result an interesting sidelight is thrown on contemporary judgment and taste. Of these poetic developments the most striking was that of the sonnet-sequences ushered in by Sidney's *Astrophel and Stella* (1591), the vogue for which was at its height between 1590 and 1600 ; though, carried over into the years that followed, it was ended only in 1633, when Fulke

[1] *ibid.* ii. p. 314.　　　　[2] *ibid.* ii. p. 318.
[3] *Inst. Or.* x. i. 99.　　　　[4] Smith, *op. cit.* ii. p. 317.

Greville published his belated *Coelica*. Equally marked, though less enduring, was the fashion for voluptuous renderings of classical myth, reminiscent in their daring treatment and high colouring of Italian pictorial art. It was a vogue begun by Lodge's *Glaucus and Scilla* (1589) and Marlowe's fragment, *Hero and Leander* (before 1593) ; and its full development is seen in Shakespeare's *Venus and Adonis* (1593), Drayton's *Endimion and Phoebe* (1595), and Marston's *Metamorphosis of Pygmalion's Image* (1598). In addition, attempts were now made at poetry of a religious kind, partly by way of reaction against the immorality of the classical romances, partly also under the inspiration of Protestant influences. Its chief exponents at this date were Southwell and Markham ; but the appearance of Sylvester's translation of Du Bartas's *Semaines* (begun in 1592), and of numerous metrical paraphrases of Scripture, likewise gave evidence of the vitality of the movement. On these developments in poetry various judgments were now pronounced ; and from Hall and others came some significant comments.

It is as ' the first English satirist ' (to quote his own doubtful claim) that Joseph Hall (1574–1656), later bishop of Exeter and then of Norwich, figures in critical history. His contribution to criticism was made in his early *Virgidemiarum or Toothless Satires* (1597–8), a title subsequently ridiculed by Milton as a contradiction in terms : and of its six Books of satire in verse the first is definitely directed against the poetic taste of the day and includes some pungent remarks on the contemporary drama.[1] Hall's intention in general was to protest against what he regarded as the futilities and extravagances of the poetry then fashionable ; and although he has but few positive recommendations to make, he implies the need for themes and methods of a more realistic kind, and for a poetry more closely related to actual life. Deference, as was fitting, is paid to both Sidney and Spenser, the latter of whom is said to outdo Ariosto and ' the Sallust of France ' (i.e. Du Bartas). But in earlier efforts generally he finds much of which he disapproves, while concerning the reigning fashions he has some trenchant criticisms to make.

Of the poetry of his predecessors, to begin with, he holds up to ridicule those ' Complaints ', such as *The Mirror for Magistrates*, which found delight in ' rueful plaints ' and ' solemn tears ', while narrating ' the dreary fates of luckless peers ', whose misfortunes were bewailed by some ' whining ghost '.[2] Concerning the far-fetched themes of old-world romance he also harbours doubts, which, incidentally, he shares with Daniel ;

---

[1] See pp. 234–5 *infra*.   [2] *Virgidemiarum*, I. v. 1 ff.

those tales of ' elvish knights ' with their ' misty moral types ',
who fought with giants and monsters and by ' strange enchanted
sword and shield vanquished the foe and won the doubtful
field '.[1] Or again, it is to the pastoral convention that he objects,
when he decries the shepherds' contests and songs of the *Shepherd's
Calendar.*[2] Then, too, he deals faithfully with those who scorned
' the homespun thread of rhymes, matched with the lofty feet of
elder times '.[3] He likewise laments the widespread use of
strange diction, ' the forgéd mint that did create new coin of
words never articulate ' ; and while recognizing the grace of
compounds in the hands of Sidney (' sweet Philistides '), influenced by French poets, he also denounces their excess, and
epithets made by joining two words in one, as if adjectives were
unable to stand alone. It was, he added, as though one should
say of Bacchus that he was ' Semele-femori-genita '.[4]

Concerning more recent developments in poetry he also has
something to say, his attack being directed, in the first place,
against the rage for sonnet-sequences with their recurring love-
themes, to which so many writers of the time were contributing.
Love he allowed to be capable of inspiring noble thoughts. It
was the hackneyed and artificial Petrarchan sentiment, worn
threadbare at the time and often treated in trivial and fantastic
fashion, that seemed to him to call for censure ; and in one place
he makes plain the nature of his objection, ' The love-sick poet ',
he exclaims,

> whose importune prayer
> Repulséd is with resolute despair,
> Hopeth to conquer his disdainful dame
> With public plaints of his conceivéd flame.
> Then pours he forth in patchéd sonnetings
> His love, his lust, and loathsome flatterings ;
> As though the staring world hanged on his sleeve,
> When once he smiles, to laugh ; and when he sighs,
>   to grieve.
> Careth the world, thou love, thou live or die ?
> Careth the world how fair thy fair one be ?[5]

Then, too, he is not alone in his censure of what he regarded as
the lascivious and sensual element in those Italianate versions
of classical myth then popular. Formerly, he maintains, ' the
sisters nine were vestal maids ', whereas latterly, Cupid having

---

[1] *ibid.* Intro. *Defiance to Envy*, ll. 50 ff.
[2] *ibid.*   [3] *ibid.* I. vi. 1 ff.
[4] *ibid.* I. vi. 255 ff.   [5] *ibid.* I. vii. 7 ff.

joined the Muses, ' Parnassus was turned into a stews ' ; [1] and the licentiousness indulged in was said to surpass even that of the epigrammatists. Nor does the new religious poetry escape his rod. What he objects to is the incongruity that resulted from the mingling of Hebraic with pagan matter—Parnassus transformed to Sion-Hill, St. Peter weeping pure Helicon, Solomon singing in an 'English quire' [2]—so that his advice to poets is not to meddle with holy things.

In the light of such comments the limitations of Hall as a critic are tolerably plain. His object, to begin with, was satirical and therefore destructive, and his literary standards were non-aesthetic, mainly moralistic in kind. With an eye fixed on defects he is unable to see the finer qualities of the works he condemns, the artistry of the sonneteers, the glowing colour and freshness of Marlowe's and Shakespeare's art ; nor is he able to realize the possibilities in religious themes which a later generation was to reveal. That defects existed admits of no doubt ; and it is against the current trivialities and wantonness that his spirit reacts. His judgments are thus to that extent the product of prosaic good sense, though lacking in sensibility, imagination, and true literary insight. They are, however, presented in acceptable form, picturesque, concrete, no mere vague or declamatory pronouncements ; and at this date his was no negligible performance. To-day his comments may seem inadequate enough ; but then judgment of one's contemporaries has always proved to be a hazardous business.

Apart from the critical contribution of Hall, however, further scattered judgments of interest were at the time also forthcoming ; and these too call for some notice. They consist mostly of comments on current literary defects ; but not without their significance are the occasional attempts at criticism of a more constructive kind. Of the latter might be mentioned, for instance, Hall's notion (though misguided) concerning the nature of true satire. That form he regarded as essentially ' hard of conceit and harsh of style ' [3]—an idea, based on the practice of Persius and Juvenal, which was handed on to more than one later writer. Or, again, there is Harvey's less debatable statement concerning Lyly's style, namely, that ' Lyly merely hatched the eggs that his older friends laid '.[4] More significant,

---

[1] *Virg.* I. ii. 19–20.
[2] *ibid.* I. viii. I ff. The references are to Southwell's *St. Peter's Complaint* (1595) and Markham's *Sion's Muse* (1596).
[3] Hall, *Poems*, ed. Grosart, p. 186.
[4] Harvey, *Works*, ed. Grosart, ii. 124.

however, in view of the hackneyed Petrarchan sentiment then current, were the efforts made to recall the real merits of Petrarch's performance. Thus Harvey reminds his readers that Petrarch's theme had been ' pure love itself and his style pure beauty '.[1] He was said to have taught ' wit to be enamoured of beauty, and to have confined love within the limits of honour, wit within the bounds of discretion, and eloquence within the terms of civility '. Moreover, his Laura was hailed as ' a nymph of Diana, not a courtesan of Venus ' ; and in general he was said to have made art ' more excellent by contemplation of excellentest nature '. It was in fact a reminder of the lofty idealism that had animated Petrarch's verse ; and Harington subsequently added his testimony in noting that ' Petrarch seemed to have comprehended all the passions that men of that humour had felt '. Nor was evidence wanting concerning the extraordinary value attached to the work of Du Bartas at this date, despite its formlessness, its lack of taste, and its stylistic extravagances. He had previously been praised by both Sidney and Spenser, while Harvey in one place had held that ' Euripides was the wisest of poets, except now at length the divine Bartas '.[2] And from this same critic came now a yet more flattering estimate describing him as ' the treasurer of humanity, nothing inferior to Dante ',[3] a writer grave and profound, many of whose verses were oracles, and whose beauty of style was matched by his nobility of soul.

It was in efforts to correct current abuses, however, that this casual criticism was most commonly engaged ; and it was mainly concerned with those matters that had given rise to the censures of Hall. Marston in his *Scourge of Villainy* (1598-9), it is true, treated briefly of other things. He derided, for instance, such devices as invocations and dream-visions ;[4] he attacked critics themselves, ridiculing those who sought only for what would ' incend their lustful blood ', or who praised only that which they never understood ; and he also defended religious poetry, though his defence was little more than an attack upon Hall by whom he had been offended. For the rest, there was something like a general agreement as to what was wrong with poetry at the time. The main protests were directed against the excessive use of the love-theme, the wantonness of erotic stories of gods and goddesses, and above all against the artifices and affectations bound up with the sonnet fashion.

Amongst those, in the first place, who denounced the vicious

---

[1] Smith, *op. cit.* ii. p. 259.   [2] Marginal note in a copy of Quintilian.
[3] Smith, *op. cit.* ii. p. 265.   [4] Marston, *Works*, ed. Bullen, iii. 281-2.

15

erotic tendencies of the time was the poet Spenser. To him they stood for a degrading of chivalrous love ; and in *Colin Clout's come home again* (1595) he lashes the poets concerned,

> For with lewd speeches and licentious deeds
> His (i.e. Cupid's) mighty mysteries they do profane.[1]

Nor was he alone in his denunciation. Sylvester a few years later prays that he might turn Englishman ' from Ovid's heirs and their unhallowed spells '.[2] And significant, too, was Marston's handling of the situation ; for in his *Scourge of Villainy* he maintains (somewhat unconvincingly) that his *Pygmalion* had been written with satirical intention, and that it had aimed at noting the blemish that ' deformed the lineaments of modern poesy's habiliments '.[3] Yet more pronounced were the comments on the sonnet-convention, deriding its artificiality and vapidity in no uncertain terms. Its hackneyed sentiment had been ridiculed by Shakespeare in his *Two Gentlemen of Verona*, when Proteus submitted his recipe for ' wailful sonnets '.[4] Further ridicule came also from Drayton, when in his *Remedy against Love* [5] he describes a potent charm made up of the powder of a woman's heart, moistened in a woman's tears and boiled in a woman's sighs. And somewhat later Sir John Davies (1569–1626) declaimed against ' bastard sonnets ', and in his *Nine Gulling Sonnets* he ridiculed the current fashion of applying law-terms to affairs of the heart. Nor is Harington without his word of censure ; for he derides the inevitable epithet, ' sugared ', as applied to sonnets, and prays that his verse ' may have more salt to make it last '.[6]

Finally, not without their interest in critical history were the comments now made concerning the propriety of the borrowing that characterized much of this sonnet-writing. Watson's *Hecatompathia* (1583), for instance, had consisted largely of epigrams and phrases culled from ancient and modern poets ; he had even indicated his sources in prose introductions for the enlightenment of his readers. And now, fostered no doubt by the doctrine of ' imitation ', this process had become the common practice of sonneteers, ideas and phrases being conveyed wholesale from Petrarch, Ronsard, Desportes, and others, without any sort of acknowledgement. At the same time the justice of this proceeding was now being called in question. Puttenham had

---

[1] ll. 787–8.
[2] See his version of Du Bartas' *Second Week* (1598), *ad. init.*
[3] Marston, *Works*, ed. Bullen, iii. 340.   [4] III. ii. 68 ff. : see p. 247 *infra.*
[5] *Idea* (1594), Sonnet xv.   [6] *Epigrams*, i. 37.

previously denounced one Southern for ' pilfering ' from Ronsard while claiming originality of treatment ; and on this count, it was added, he had deserved ' to be indicted of petty larceny '.[1] In the decade that followed, further scruples were felt and expressed in connexion with this practice of literal and unacknow-ledged borrowing.   Thus Drayton, for one, charges such borrowers with the crime of ' filching ' ; [2] Daniel, again, is warned to make more sparing use of others' wit, seeing that he might well scorn ' base imitation '.[3]   And Harington gaily confesses that he too had been guilty of such borrowings, ' honest thefts ' as he calls them ; and addressing Daniel he exclaims :

> Then, fellow-thief, let's shake together hands,
> Sith both our wares are filcht from foreign lands.[4]

Such comments are not without their significance at this date. They witness in general to a reaction against the plagiarism that was rife, and mark the beginnings of something like a feeling for literary ethics.

---

[1] Smith, *op. cit.* ii. 171–2, 421.   [2] *Idea's Mirror*, dedication (1594).
[3] *Return from Parnassus*, Part II, ii. ii.   [4] *Epigrams*, ii. 30.

CHAPTER VIII

DRAMATIC CRITICISM: EARLY TUDOR CRITICS, GOSSON, WHETSTONE, LYLY, SHAKESPEARE, JONSON

so far the main concern of 16th-Century criticism would seem to have been poetry in general ; its aim being, first, the justifying of an innate feeling for poetry, despite the imperfect sympathies of Humanists, and, secondly, the establishing of the value of poetry by means of reasoned explanations of its nature and art. Meanwhile somewhat surprising at first sight is the slight amount of critical comment bestowed hitherto on that form of poetry which constitutes for us of to-day one of the glories of Elizabethan literature, namely, the drama. It was not that interest in the dramatic art had at any time been lacking. From the early Tudor period evidence had been forthcoming of the abounding vitality of the popular stage, with its miracles, moralities, and interludes, forms of medieval origin that gradually developed under classical and Italian influences into the more artistic creations of Lyly, Marlowe, and Kyd. Then, too, apart from the comedies of Plautus that were frequently acted, plays of an academic kind had been written, mainly in Latin ; and between Nicholas Grimald's *Christus Redivivus* (*c.* 1540) and the *Parnassus* trilogy (1598–1606) a variety of such works had appeared which betrayed classical influences and represented attempts to recapture the lost secrets of dramatic form. Throughout the century, in short, men had been groping confusedly for expression of a dramatic kind ; and yet, except for Sidney's comments of 1582–3, and the conventional statements of Webbe and Puttenham, we look almost in vain for remarks on the plays produced or for theorizing on the dramatic art itself.

The main explanation of this strange silence lay undoubtedly in the late flowering of the Elizabethan drama, which assumed its characteristic form only in the last decade of the century ; though it is also true that throughout the century stirring political events and heated religious questions had engaged for the most part the attention of serious minds. Not without its relevance, however, is the further fact that medieval tradition, which was still strong, provided neither precedent nor material for theorizing on the drama. Such conceptions of tragedy and comedy as had come down were indeed of a non-dramatic kind ; and, besides, no sort of theory had hitherto been formulated concerning the moralities and interludes of the popular stage. Nor was the gap filled by the teaching that was being expounded by Italian critics at the time. In the decline of classical scholarship, which followed the enthusiastic studies of the opening of the century, but slight interest was shown, even by University scholars, in Aristotelian doctrine or dramatic theory. Moreover, the main Italian treatises, Castelvetro's *Poetica* (1570), for instance, did not appear until late in the century. And as for the popular dramatists, to them it seemed that such works with their abstract theories had simply no bearing on the business in hand. The truth was that such advances as were made in dramatic development resulted mainly from the influence of models, both classical and Italian, rather than from the application of theories ; and in view of these empirical methods, dictated from the first by the national genius, an exposition of theory was neither looked for nor forthcoming. Nor must we forget the very definite obloquy attached to stage-plays at the time, an inherited prejudice which Humanistic reassurances were unable to remove ; for this too had the effect of discouraging discussion on the dramatic art. For an adequate realization of the violence of this prejudice something like an effort of the historical imagination is nowadays needed ; though it was made abundantly plain by the fiery onslaughts of divines delivered at ' Paul's Cross ', the persistent Puritan attacks after 1576, and the hostile measures of civic authorities against ' common players ' and play-houses from 1570 onwards. The early Reformers, it is true, were by no means hostile to the drama, while Elizabeth and her courtiers went some way towards countenancing the contemporary stage ; yet it was only in 1575 that the first theatre was opened, and about the same date a new status was granted to actors. Under such conditions of ignorance and prejudice, when a new national drama was slowly struggling into life, there was therefore little wonder that until the closing decade of the century comparatively little in the way of dramatic criticism was forthcoming.

Yet not without its interest is such critical material as has come down ; though it is significant that no single treatise on the drama appeared, nor was any attempt made to translate any of the great critical works of antiquity,[1] or to formulate a system of dramatic theory such as was being drawn up in Italy on the basis of Aristotle's teaching. The elements of dramatic criticism

[1] cf., however, Drant's trans. of Horace, *Ars Poetica* (1567), a clumsy paraphrase : also the trans. of Fabricius's prose summary of Horace's rules (mainly from *Ars Poetica*) appended to Webbe's *Discourse of Eng. Poetrie*.

at this stage consisted in fact of little more than sporadic remarks found in introductory Epistles to academic plays, in educational treatises, pamphlets, and latterly (and most important of all) in the plays themselves. Nevertheless from this material may be gathered some idea of the contemporary attitude to dramatic literature ; the reasoned experimentation that went on, the opposition to which dramatic works were then being subjected, the confusion of ideas that prevailed, and the gradual growth of some amount of insight and judgment. Nor in spite of its casual nature was the progress of this tentative criticism without its interest. Its earliest phase consisted of attempts to commend and recover the lost dramatic art ; this was followed by a challenge to its very existence ; and then, with the striking dramatic developments of the closing decade of the century, a marked increase in critical activities became apparent, which resulted in definite pronouncements on dramatists and their works, in Shakespeare's incidental but illuminating comments and in Ben Jonson's more deliberate theorizing on the dramatic art.

For the earliest contributions, which were concerned with inculcating the value of dramatic literature in general, we must look primarily to the Humanists, who accepted all ancient classics as a priceless legacy, though on educational grounds. Thus Erasmus in his *De ratione studii* [1] had commended to his readers as an elevating form of literature all Greek and Latin plays ; and in so doing he called special attention to the works of Plautus, Terence, and Seneca. He points out, for instance, their value as models of style and the moral lessons to be drawn from plot and character. He also recognizes their emotional effects, tragedy being said to appeal to the depths of human feelings, comedy to lighter emotions ; and worthy of note is his special tribute to Seneca, namely, that by him ' the mind of the reader was raised aloft (*in sublime*) from sordid cares '.[2] Rather more critical are the remarks of Vives who, while commending the dramatic works of antiquity as a whole does so with some reserve,[3] but supplies elsewhere a brief sketch of the history of comedy. He describes it, to begin with, as ' a picture of life ' (*imaginem quandam vitae*) and then explains how, corrupted at first by personal satire, it had subsequently been diverted to matters of ridicule and amorous intrigue, to stories of successful rascality (*ad fraudes meretricum, ad perjuria lenonis, ad militis ferociam et glorias*), which had led in due course to a decline in morality. To him was therefore preferable the

---

[1] §§ 3, 11, &c.   [2] *Opera*, iv. 92 B.
[3] Watson, *op. cit.* p. 136.

later development of *tragi-comoedia*, as seen in *Celestina* [1] (1499), in which evil had been suitably punished ; and he commends those of his contemporaries who, even in the vernacular, were adopting that more elevating form.. Meanwhile Sir Thomas Elyot in his *Governour* (1531), in the course of his defence of poetry, had something to say on behalf of the drama as well.[2] His conception of tragedy, it is true, was of the medieval kind ; though the comedy he has in mind was that of Plautus and Terence. Moreover he treated merely of their moral effects ; but his remarks are notable as being the earliest plea directed to English readers for recognition of work of a dramatic kind.

Of greater significance, however, are the remarks subsequently made in attempts to recover the dramatic technique of antiquity, attempts, for the most part in Latin, which marked the beginnings of the 16th-Century academic drama. As John Palsgrave explained,[3] educated men at this time had less skill in the vernacular than in Latin ; they could write an epistle ' right Latin-like ', and yet not be ' able to express their conceits in the vulgar tongue '. Worth noting, to begin with, is the casual remark made by Sir Thomas More on what was to prove an interesting point of dramatic technique. In his *Utopia* (1516) [4] he objects on the score of propriety to the mingling of comic and tragic affairs on the stage, pointing out how incongruous would be the reciting of a tragic passage from Seneca during a performance of one of Plautus's plays ; and such a ' tragical comedy ' he describes as ' mere gallimaufrey ', representing a violation of a universal principle. He is here possibly influenced by Cicero's earlier dictum, that *in tragoedia comicum vitiosum est et in comoedia turpe tragicum* ; [5] but the problem thus raised was to be keenly discussed for some time to come. Notable in another sense were the comments that accompanied Palsgrave's translation of *Acolastus* (1540), a Latin comedy on the Prodigal Son, written by the Dutch scholar Fullonius. Palsgrave's object was to point out the art underlying this imitation of Roman comedy ; and he therefore explains the rules that governed the use of various metres,[6] the effects of rhetorical figures, *exclamatio*, *dubitatio* and the like,[7] as well as the allegorical interpretation of the story involved. Such a commentary was characteristic of the mechanical methods of post-classical grammarians, such

---

[1] Adapted in interlude form in J. Rastell's *Calisto and Melibea* (1525).
[2] Sce p. 100 *supra*.   [3] See his trans. of *Acolastus*.
[4] See Robinson's trans. ed. J. H. Lupton, p. 98.
[5] *De optimo genere oratorum*, i. i.
[6] Note on Act i. i.   [7] Note on Act v. iv.

as Diomedes, Donatus, and Servius, whom indeed he quotes ; and it thus points to the survival of post-classical and medieval traditions at this date.

It is in the occasional remarks that accompany some of the academic plays, however, that more serious comments are found ; and of these plays the earliest surviving one is Nicholas Grimald's *Christus Redivivus* (c. 1540), a ' tragi-comedy ' in five acts, embodying a Senecan treatment of the Gospel story of the Resurrection, together with an underplot supplied by Roman soldiers. And in the Dedicatory Epistle [1] some interesting comments are made on dramatic technique, which give evidence not only of conscious craftsmanship and some knowledge of classical rules, but also, what is of greater importance, of independent judgment as well. In the first place the vitality of the rhetoric tradition is revealed by the importance attached to the need for observing *decorum* in style. Thus Grimald notes that in poetical composition, as in life and conduct, it was often difficult to perceive what was appropriate. At the same time he holds that the choice of diction should always be determined by the nature of the emotion to be expressed ; and that passages of plain narrative and scenes of boasting, soothing consolations, and complaints, voices from heaven and laments from hell, all required different styles of expression in order to be effective.[2] Of yet greater significance are his remarks on dramatic technique. In his play he had represented a story covering several days, thus neglecting the observance of the Unity of time. And now in his defence he maintains (quoting his tutor ' Aerius ', for that purpose) that such procedure was justified, since the scenes ' were not so far apart but they could easily be reduced to one stage-setting ',[3] and that, besides, in so doing he had followed the example of Plautus whose *Captivi* covered an interval of more than one day. Then, too, he is aware that his play embodied a mixture of comic and tragic elements in defiance of the rule prescribed by Cicero and others. Yet here, again, he defends this mingling on the ground of its successful results. Quoting once more his tutor he observes that in the play ' great things had been interwoven with the small, joyous with sad, . . . incredible with probable, . . . in order that variety might be opposed to satiety '.[4] And the argument is notable, not only for its defiance of the rule and its judgment by effects, but also for its early reference to the Unity of time, derived apparently

---

[1] See L. E. Merrill, *Life and Poems of N. Grimald* (Yale Studies in English, 169), pp. 95 ff : also E. Sweeting, *Early Tudor Criticism*, pp. 147 ff.
[2] See Merrill, *op. cit.* pp. 94–6.   [3] *ibid.* p. 110.   [4] *ibid.* p. 108.

from a reading of Aristotle before the chief Italian theorists had written.

Matters of a different kind are discussed by John Christopherson, later Master of Trinity College, Cambridge, in the *Carmina* following his dedicatory Epistle to *Jephtha* (1546), an academic drama in Greek, the only one to survive. He there explains what he conceives to be the true nature of tragedy; and obviously influenced by Seneca and medieval tradition, rather than by Aristotle, he states that tragedy's greatest glories were grandeur of style (*ornatum styli*) enlivened with *sententiae*, together with grave themes telling the sad stories of the falls of great men (*illustriun casus acerbos*).[1] Like Grimald, it might be added, he chooses for his theme a Scriptural subject, thus illustrating the influence of Reformers, Melanchthon among others, on the contemporary drama.

Still more clearly, however, is Protestant influence seen in the direct advocacy of Scriptural themes by Martin Bucer (1491–1551), a German Reformer and disciple of Melanchthon, who, invited to England by Cranmer in 1549, was in the same year appointed to the chair of Divinity at Cambridge. In his pamphlet *De ludis honestis* (*c.* 1550),[2] presented in 1551 as a New Year's gift to the young king, Edward VI, Bucer recommends the adoption of Biblical stories for both comedy and tragedy. Comedy, he notes, dealt with ordinary events and actions; and suggesting as matter suitable for such plays the quarrel between the shepherds of Abraham and Lot, he shows how the story divided itself naturally into six scenes, each with a moral. Of greater interest are his remarks on tragedy which he describes as treating of deeds more strange and wonderful (*majoris admirationis*) than those of comedy. He then points out that the Bible was full of suitable tragic material, of stories concerning divine and heroic beings, as well as of events and deeds which ' turn out unexpectedly in accordance with Aristotle's doctrine of περιπετεία'; [3] a passage that is noteworthy as providing one of the rare references to Aristotle's theory of tragedy. For the rest it is clear that his conceptions of both tragedy and comedy are somewhat vague and fluid. Classical and medieval ideas are loosely combined; and the dramatic purpose is limited to moral teaching. At the same time it is the only critical

---

[1] See F. S. Boas, *University Drama in the Tudor Age*, pp. 47–8 : also E. Sweeting, *op. cit.* p. 145.

[2] *Scripta Anglicana* (1577), cap. LIV. : see H. S. Symmes, *Les Débuts de la Critique Dramatique en Angleterre* (Paris, 1903), pp. 219–23.

[3] See Symmes, *op. cit.* p. 221 : cf. *Poetics*, 1452 a, 22.

attempt to justify plays based on Scripture ; while it also concedes the possibility of serious dramatic developments in the
vernacular as well as in Greek and Latin.

Somewhat clearer, though still confused, is the light shed by
Ascham on classical dramatic principles in the course of scattered
comments in his *Schoolmaster* [1]—the fruit, as he explains, of
many ' pleasant talks ' with Cheke and members of his Cambridge
circle.   For one thing, he submits definite views on both comedy
and tragedy.   His conception of comedy is that of Plautus and
Terence ;   and he states that its themes are taken from ordinary
life, that they treat of no weighty matters, and are confined to
stories concerning ' hard fathers, foolish mothers, unthrifty
young men, crafty servants, subtle bawds and wily harlots ',[1]
the conventional types of Roman comedy.   On matters of
tragedy he is yet more illuminating, his ideas being ostensibly
based on ' the precepts of Aristotle and Horace, with the examples
of Euripides, Sophocles, and Seneca ' [2] as standards and models.
Now for the first time, in accordance with Aristotle's teaching,
the supreme value of tragedy, as compared with the epic and
lyric, is urged.   It is declared to provide matter ' more profitable
than the works of Homer, Pindar, Virgil, and Horace ' ;   and
with a characteristic touch of Humanistic patronage where poetry
was concerned, it is said to be even ' comparable with the doctrine
of Aristotle, Plato, and Xenophon '.[3]   Then, too, Greek tragedy
is claimed to be superior to Roman tragedy.   Sophocles and
Euripides are said to ' far overmatch our Seneca, namely, in
οἰκονομίᾳ et decoro ' ;   though deference is also paid to Seneca,
his ' elocution (i.e. style) and verse ' being described as ' very
commendable for his time '.   Nevertheless, writing in 1570,
Ascham rightly complains that but few had hitherto attempted
to comply with these highest standards ; and adds that, except
for Buchanan and Watson, none in his opinion was able " to
abide the true touch of Aristotle's precepts and Euripides's
examples '.[4]   In thus assigning the primacy in poetry to tragedy,
as Aristotle before him had done, and in asserting the superiority
of Greek models as compared with Seneca's Latin tragedies,
Ascham made a definite and valuable contribution to dramatic
theory, though without practical result.   On the other hand his
acquaintance with Aristotle's actual teaching does not seem to
have been very profound.   For one thing, as has already been
noted, he differentiates tragedy from comedy primarily by considerations of style ; [5] he also looks to tragedy and comedy alike

1 *Works*, ed Giles, iii. p. 246.   2 *ibid*. iii. p. 241.
3 *ibid*. iii. p. 228.   4 *ibid*. iii. p. 241.   5 See p. 91 *supra*.

for moralistic, rather than aesthetic, effects ; and in describing both forms as in essence ' perfect imitations ', that is, ' fair lively painted pictures of the life of every degree of man ',[1] he falls far short of Aristotelian doctrine by his use of a Platonic and Ciceronian terminology in place of the more philosophical ' imitation ' expounded by Aristotle.

Such then were the fragmentary comments on dramatic theory made by various writers up to 1570 ; and all of them related solely to academic plays, little or nothing as yet being forthcoming in relation to the popular stage. From these comments it would at any rate appear that some conception of dramatic form, lost to the Middle Ages, was being gradually recovered ; that there was a growing tendency to discuss the drama as a separate literary form ; and that the position of Plautus, Terence, and Seneca as models was already established. On the other hand, not a little was wanting in the confused ideas that were being put forward, with marked results on later developments. Undue stress on stylistic *decorum* and moral teaching, for instance, was to affect in no slight measure later efforts ; and the adoption of religious themes was to be checked by the licensing of the drama in 1559 which brought all dramatic performances under civic control. Of considerable interest, again, was the early defiance of the Unity of time, as was also the advocacy by Grimald of the mingling of comic and tragic material, both of which were to make for realism and variety on the popular stage. As yet, however, though some of the elements of Roman comedy had been represented, no clear conception of tragedy had been formulated ; and this vagueness, which was to persist until a later date, is all the more surprising, in view of the various expositions of Aristotelian theory by Italian critics at this date. It would therefore appear that, in spite of isolated references, the authority of Aristotle in this field was as yet only partially and vaguely recognized. That it was not unchallenged abroad may incidentally be gathered from a passage in Casa's *Galateo* (an Italian work translated by R. Peterson under the title of *Galateo of Munners and Behaviours* (1576)), in which one of the rare allusions to Aristotle's *catharsis* occurs. There is recalled the theory that tragedies were made ' that they might draw forth tears out of their eyes that had need to spend them, and they were by their weeping healed of their infirmity '.[2] But the theory is here quoted only to be ridiculed, on the ground

---

[1] *Works*, iii. p. 213.

[2] Peterson's *Galateo of Manners and Behaviours*, p. 31 : quoted by Symmes, *op. cit.* p. 46.

that the same results would be obtained by simpler methods, by the use of strong mustard, for instance, or again a smoky dwelling. What at any rate is certain is that Aristotelian doctrine contributed little or nothing to dramatic theory before 1570.

Meanwhile a new critical phase was inaugurated by the Puritan opposition to all forms of dramatic work, an attack which raged most fiercely from 1577 to 1583, though echoes were to be heard right on to the middle of the following century. The attack, it should be noted, was not confined to English writers. The rise of the secular drama abroad had been viewed with some amount of doubt and hostility ; and this may have indirectly influenced Puritan activities. Moreover, strictly speaking, the Puritans were not the first to raise the question in England. A warning of the future controversy had been given when the first defence of plays in English had appeared in William Bavande's work, *The Good Ordering of a Common Weal* (1559), a translation of a Latin treatise written by the Italian, Ferrarius, in which it was held that plays were justified in any well-ordered state by reason of the moral lessons they supplied when interpreted allegorically. And this was followed by a defence of plays set forth by Lewis Wager in the Prologue to his interlude, *The Repentance of Mary Magdalene* (1566). There it is pointed out that plays had been sanctioned in antiquity and were being fostered at the Universities ; that they inculcated virtue, encouraged patriotism, were a solace to mankind ; and these claims Wager supports by an allegorical interpretation of his play. On the other hand, the first attack on the stage in England had come from William Alley, bishop of Exeter, who in his *Poor Man's Library* (1571) had condemned plays among other ' wanton books '. And this attitude was confirmed by Sandford's translation in 1569 of Cornelius Agrippa's work, *Of the Vanity of Arts and Sciences* ; also by Sir Geoffrey Fenton's *Form of Christian Policy* (1574), an English version of a work by an unknown French writer, which apparently supplied the Puritans with many of their arguments. In short, the Puritan attack was but the culmination of this wider movement, at a time when the liberal outlook of the early Reformers was degenerating into the narrow fanaticism of a sect, and when the popular stage, with its actors, was receiving for the first time some amount of official recognition.

Of one of the main protagonists, namely, Gosson, and of Lodge's reply to his onslaught of 1579, something has already been said.[1] Their interchange of pamphlets, however, had been

[1] See p. 111–12 *supra*.

preceded by John Northbrooke's *Treatise wherein Dicing, Dancing, vain Plays or Interludes . . . are reproved by . . . the Word of God and ancient writers* (1577), a work which thus represents the first systematic attack on the theatre in England. In it the stage was attacked along with other contemporary abuses, and a dialogue form was adopted, Age and Youth being the interlocutors. For the most part, however, its arguments are of a conventional kind. There are the customary citations from classical and patristic authorities, along with charges suggested in the Fenton translation just mentioned. Thus theatres are described as ' houses of Satan ' ; the treatment of religious themes in drama is said to be sacrilegious ; the evil effects of immodest scenes and songs are also censured ; though noteworthy is the fact that academic plays in Latin meet with Northbrooke's approval.

This work was followed by *The Second and Third Blast of Retreat from Plays and Theatres* (1580),[1] in which the attack was directed exclusively against stage-plays. It was a work compiled by ' Anglo-phile Eutheo ' and was arranged in two parts so as to reveal, first, ' the filthiness of plays in times past ', and secondly, the ' abominations ' of the contemporary stage, thus attempting to prove that God's curse rested on all commonwealths in which stage-plays were allowed. For the first part (i.e. *the Second Blast*) the writer supplies an English version of *De gubernatione Dei*, a treatise of Salvianus, a fifth-century bishop, who therein had exposed the vices of Romans and their plays, and had described such works as a mockery of religion, involving sins of the mind, the ear, and the eye. More original is the second section (i.e. the *Third Blast*) in which the writer, apparently a renegade playwright, ignores to some extent the teaching of ancient authorities and attempts to convince his readers by the light of ' logic and reason '. Thus the antiquity of plays, he argues, proves nothing except their pagan origin ; and, borrowing from Fenton, he describes them as enemies of virtue, a snare to the simple, a desecration of the Gospel and the Sabbath alike, and a source of disorder and corruption in any state. No sound teaching or healthy influence, he asserts, could possibly result from works of that kind. Nor is he content with vague generalities ; for he condemns outright the lascivious comedies written in imitation of *Celestina*, as well as the profanity and scurrility that accompanied moralities and Biblical plays. Most significant of all, however, is his censure of the wild and irrational fancies that formed the subject-matter of so many comedies.

[1] See W. C. Hazlitt, *English Drama and Stage*, pp. 96–155.

The notablest liar [he states] [1] has become the best poet, . . . for the strangest comedy brings the greatest delectation and pleasure. . . . The author . . . frames himself with novelties and strange trifles, . . . feigning countries never heard of, monsters and prodigious creatures that are not. . . . And if they write of histories that are known, such as the life of Pompey or the martial affairs of Caesar . . . they give them a new face and turn them out like counterfeits.

It was an objection shared by more than one of his contemporaries ; and for this and other reasons his work is of interest as illustrating the spirit of the time.

In the meantime the actors had replied in the *Play of Plays* (1581), a sort of morality (now lost) produced at *The Theatre*, in which it was maintained that plays provided an element of recreation and pleasure essential to life, and that Zeal (i.e. Puritanism) was useful only in company with Delight.[2] To this protest against purely moralistic standards Gosson retorted forthwith in *Plays confuted in Five Actions* [3] (1582), with each Action treating of a different aspect of the controversy. The main theme, as before, is that plays are intolerable in a Christian community ; and much of the work covers familiar ground, with the usual array of patristic and other citations. Thus in Action I plays are denounced because of their pagan origin and their treatment of pagan gods ; in Action III actors are condemned for their use of feminine attire, their mimicry of feminine passions, both contrary to divine law ; in Action IV pleasure is conceded to be a lawful aim, but a distinction is drawn between pleasures sensual and spiritual ; and in Action V the conclusion is reached that the effects of play-acting are both vicious and degrading.

Yet there is also more to the pamphlet than this ; and in Action II Gosson's reasoning assumes a more substantial form in an attempt to invalidate Lodge's argument [4] (based on Cicero) that comedy was ' an imitation of life, a mirror of manners, and an image of truth '. In the first place he shrewdly, and not unreasonably, challenges the authenticity of the much-quoted definition, and defies Lodge to find it in Cicero's writings. The truth was that the statement, long associated with Cicero's name, had hitherto been accepted on the authority of Donatus (4th Century A.D.) alone. It was not to be found in Cicero's more familiar works, but in his less-known *De re publica*,[5] as later scholarship has shown. Then, too, not content with questioning

---

[1] Hazlitt, *op. cit.* p. 145. [2] *ibid.* pp. 201–3. [3] *ibid.* pp. 159–218.
[4] See p. 113 *supra*.
[5] iv. 13, quoted in *Excerpta de Comoedia* (Wessner ed. of Donatus, i. 22).

the authoritative character of the definition—one of the main planks in the defence of the stage—Gosson endeavours in an interesting passage to reveal its unreality and lack of truth in the light of plays being produced at the time. In the first place he refuses to regard plays as in any true sense ' an imitation of life '. Thus tragedies, he points out, dealt mainly with acts of cruelty and murder, and treated of gods and kings and other exalted personages. Comedies, again, were concerned with love affairs, often of a degrading kind ; while their characters were mostly knaves and courtesans, amorous youths and foolish old men. Apart from this, the effect of tragedy was to cause men to weep unmanly tears, thus weakening their martial fibre ; whereas comedy, again, merely tickled the senses and gave rise to foolish and immoderate laughter. And as for the plots which treated of the adventures of love-sick knights, their fights with monstrous foes in foreign lands, and their return home in such plight as to be recognizable only with the help of a ring or some other trifle in their equipment—all this, declared Gosson, was sheer absurdity, with no sort of relation to actual life. The rest of the definition he treats in summary fashion. He denies that plays could be regarded as ' mirrors of manners ', for what they represented was mostly the corruption of manners, and he calls to witness a recent play, *The Three Ladies of London*. Still less reasonably could they be accepted as ' images of truth ', seeing that they were made up of feigning and fancy, as was illustrated by the play, *Cupid and Psyche*, also of recent date.

Such then is the main substance of this pamphlet, the most effective of Gosson's efforts ; and despite obvious limitations of subject-matter, it reveals a new Gosson, one not incapable of either scholarship or serious thought. In addition, it has the further interest of throwing light on the probable date of Sidney's *Apology* ; and of this something might here be said in passing. The usual assumption is that whereas Sidney in that work was replying to prejudices against poetry common at the time, he had also in mind Gosson's *School of Abuse* (1579), a work dedicated to Sidney himself, and one which, by its flashy style and daring invective, had attracted the attention of contemporary readers. However this may be, and evidence is not entirely wanting,[1] what seems more probable is that he was definitely influenced by this later work of Gosson, and particularly by certain details in the discussion of Action II. Thus the *School of Abuse* had consisted mainly of general and conventional reflexions, with the attack largely directed against the abuses of play-houses ; and

[1] See Shuckburgh's edition of the *Apology*, pp. xxxiii–xxxv.

of these matters there is little trace in the *Apology*. On the other hand *Plays confuted* had treated of plays themselves in more original, direct and specific fashion. It had expressly mentioned among current defects not only the wild improbabilities of plots, the degrading love-themes of comedies, but also the debilitating effects of tragedy and the foolish vacant laughter evoked by comedy ; and all these matters were specifically treated by Sidney. It can scarcely be doubted therefore that Sidney at the date of writing his *Apology* was already acquainted with Gosson's later venture and that therein he was replying to Gosson's weighty charges. And as *Plays confuted* was entered at Stationers' Hall in April 1582, the most likely date of the *Apology* would seem to be 1582–3, just before Sidney's re-entry into social and political activities.

Of the remaining Puritan censures at this date the most portentous was the *Anatomy of Abuses* (1583) by Philip Stubbes, an Anglican bigot, though the slightly later *Overthrow of Stage Plays* (1599) by John Rainolds, President of Corpus Christi College, Oxford, also calls for mention. The former was a savage invective in dialogue form directed against contemporary vice in general ; and Nashe later on had its author in mind when he denounced those who ' anatomized abuses and stubbed up sins by the roots, . . . that almost the things remain not whereof they admit the lawful use '.[1] For stage-plays, however, Stubbes reserved some of his sharpest darts. In his Preface, it is true, he commended plays of an edifying kind, in view of their lively appeal to both eye and ear ; but in the treatise itself he fails to discriminate. Carried away by excess of zeal, he condemns religious plays for their mixture of scurrility and theology, while secular themes rouse in him a state of blind fury. In his argument he brings to bear the weight of earlier authorities, appeals to the Bible, the early Fathers, as well as decrees of Synods and Councils ; and in his wholesale denunciation of plays and playhouses he leaves nothing unsaid, though he adds little to the diatribes of earlier pamphleteers. Interest of another kind, however, is attached to *The Overthrow of Stage Plays*, for it marks the extension of the anti-dramatic spirit to University circles, and represents the culmination of a heated controversy at Oxford which had lasted for ten years and had led to the production of some twenty or more pamphlets. In form it was a pedantic treatise devoid of any attempt to grapple with the real problem. But replete with quotations drawn from ancient classics, it rested its argument solely on such authorities, whether

[1] Smith, *op. cit.* i. p. 324.

derived from literary sources or from pronouncements on Roman civil law. Primarily intended as an attack on William Gager, a well-known Latin dramatist of the time, it drew from Gager a learned and dignified reply [1] in which academic plays, as distinct from popular plays, were skilfully defended. These then were the main lines of the attack on the drama at this date ; though opposition did not cease even after Shakespeare had written. Thomas Heywood, for instance, in his *Apology for Actors* (1612) found it necessary to defend the dramatic art against the venom of satirists and others ; *A Refutation of the Apology* by I. G. followed in 1615 ; and finally came Prynne's astounding *Histriomastix* (1632) which gathered up into its eleven hundred pages all that earlier fanaticism had urged against the theatre.[2]

Meanwhile the gradual evolution of the popular drama (1530–90) had proceeded, not altogether without critical comment ; and thus was inaugurated a new and most important phase of dramatic criticism. Chaotic in form, in substance and aim alike, and with no clear distinction between interlude, history, comedy, and tragedy, the native drama had at length emerged, slowly discarding something of its earlier formlessness by the adoption of acts and scenes, improving also on the threadbare simplicity of moralities and interludes ; and in this way a vague conception of the dramatic art was generated, as well as a sense of the need for conscious planning. For the results of this new attitude we must look to the dramatists themselves, to their Prologues and Dedications, in which were occasionally voiced their ideas on the dramatic art. Up to about 1590 such comments were scanty enough ; but after that date they became more frequent, being reinforced by significant comments in the actual plays and by remarks from other quarters. At no date, it is true, was any sort of systematic treatment forthcoming ; dramatic criticism at this date retained its sporadic and tentative character to the end. Yet an advance was made on the occasional comments of writers of academic plays. From now on more intimate relations were established with the contemporary stage. What was considered were no remote or abstract problems, but practical questions and difficulties that had confronted actual playwrights, or else there was the business of correcting manifest errors and abuses in the plays themselves. And despite the fragmentary character of the commentary thus produced, the

---

[1] See F. S. Boas in the *Fortnightly Review*, Aug. 1907.
[2] For a full account of the whole movement, see *Cambridge History of English Literature*, vi. 372–409.

net results are of value. They point to the gradual dispelling
of the earlier confusion where the drama was concerned, to the
emergence of larger and clearer ideas on dramatic technique,
and in general to a growth of insight, taste, and judgment in
dramatic affairs.

In order to appreciate the relevance of these earlier critical
remarks, however, some idea of the conditions of the contemporary drama (1558-80) must first be recalled.   And, apart from
the zealous following of Plautus, Terence, and Seneca, which
was general, and the didactic tendencies of most of the plays,
there were certain glaring abuses which were characteristic of
the period.   Of outstanding importance, for instance, was the
overwhelming vogue of comedy, often degenerating into farce,
the elements of which were thrust into every sort of play, generally
with lamentable results.   This was seen even when attempts
were made to treat of serious themes, such as R. B.'s *Apius and
Virginia* (*c.* 1563), Richard Edwardes's *Damon and Pithias* (1566)
and Thomas Preston's *Cambyses* (1569-70), all of which were
described by their authors as ' tragical comedies ', and in which
buffoonery destroyed all interest in the main stories. Then,
again, a large section of the popular plays prior to 1587 consisted
of pseudo-chivalrous tales, in which heroes and heroines underwent surprising and sensational adventures. Most of this considerable output has unfortunately perished ; but two surviving
specimens—*Common Conditions* (1568) and *Sir Clyomon and
Sir Clamydes* (*c.* 1579)—are ample witnesses of the main characteristics of such plays. Both are stories of wanderings in strange
lands where dwelt crafty enchanters, flying serpents, and other
monsters, and where whole pirate-crews were dispatched by
valiant knights single-handed ; and in these plays it is not
surprising to find that the characterization is both colourless and
unconvincing.

In the light of these conditions the critical remarks of contemporaries are seen to be both sensible and timely, touching
as they do on certain elementary but important points of dramatic
technique.   The earliest of such pronouncements came from
Richard Edwardes in his Prologue to *Damon and Pithias*; there
he asserts his right to mingle tragedy and comedy, on the ground
that ' matter mixed with mirth and care ' was best calculated
to supply the instruction and delight demanded by Horace, thus
modifying the conventional demand for instruction alone.   Yet
more illuminating are his other requirements, namely, that in
comedy life-like characters were essential, and that such characters should be revealed by the nature of their discourse.   ' In

comedies ', he states, ' the greatest skill is this, rightly to touch all things to the quick, and eke to frame each person so that by his common talk you may his nature rightly know.' The means he suggests savours of Horace's types ; roisterers, for instance, are not to preach, old men are to be sober, and young men rash. But as an aid to realism in character-drawing his advice was not without its value at this date.

Then, too, comments on other aspects of comedy came from other quarters ; and not least significant was the increasing importance now attached to its pleasure-giving function as distinct from its didactic effects. Thus Nicholas Udall in the Prologue to his *Ralph Roister Doister* (1553), while recognizing that the comedies of Plautus and Terence had contained much ' virtuous lore ', nevertheless describes the essence of his comedy (or interlude, as he calls it) as ' mirth mixed with virtue in decent comeliness ', the mirth that prolonged life and refreshed the spirits. Not that this claim was peculiar to Udall alone. Ulpian Fulwell in the Prologue to *Like will to Like* (1568) also claimed to provide a mixture of ' mirth and gravity ', explaining that ' mirth for sadness (i.e. seriousness) is a sauce most sweet ' ; and even Gosson had conceded that ' comedies nourish delight and delight should never be taken from life '.[1] But where Udall advances on the views of his contemporaries is in advocating for comedy a more refined sort of humour. He recommends a form of comedy free from scurrility and abuse, thus making the first protest against the horse-play and buffoonery of his day. Nor was the remark made by Gascoigne on yet another aspect of contemporary comedy without its significance. In the Prologue to his ' tragical comedy ', *The Glass of Government* (1575), he gives further evidence of his independent way of thinking by discouraging all slavish imitation of Roman comedy. None of Terence's phrases, he states, were employed in his work ; for times had changed since the great days of Rome, and Roman plays were not always pleasing to a later Christian age. Here, then, was a timely concession to the popular demand for comedy based on the earlier interlude ; and it was further notable as being based on historical grounds.

It was from George Whetstone (c. 1554–87), however, that the most adequate criticism of dramatic affairs came before 1590 ; and in his remarks the influence of Edwardes and others is apparent. In his Dedication to *Promos and Cassandra* [2] (1578) he sets out to explain, first, why little value was attached to the drama of his day ; and he begins by condemning the taste

[1] *Plays Confuted*, Action IV.   [2] Smith, *op. cit.* i. pp. 58–60.

of contemporary dramatists generally, foreign as well as English. Thus the Italians, he maintains, were too lascivious, a fault common to French and Spanish dramatists alike. The Germans, on the other hand, he regarded as too moralistic, often treating of matters fit only for sermons ; while Englishmen, again, were conspicuously lacking in judgment. And on this English defect he enlarges in some detail ; at the same time claiming for his own play sound moral influence and a happy mingling of serious and comic matter conducing to the necessary instruction and delight. One of the most glaring faults of English drama he held to be its choice of wildly improbable themes. Thus, ' your Englishman ', he states, ' first grounds his work on impossibilities ; then in three hours he runs through the world, marries, gets children, makes children men, men to conquer kingdoms, murder monsters, and bringeth gods from heaven and fetcheth devils from hell '. And here he is but echoing the views of Vives, Ascham, Gosson (and, later on, Sidney) regarding that ' romantic ' material which, hitherto treated in irrational and licentious fashion, Shakespeare alone was to present in artistic and convincing form.

Hardly less serious, however, was the unseemly and inartistic mingling of comic and tragic material ; for of a judicious mixture, it should be noted, he warmly approves. Thus fools, he complains, were thrust into plays, rubbing shoulders with kings, to whom, incongruously enough, they would proffer advice on state affairs. In short, everything was sacrificed to raising a laugh, and laughter, moreover, of the most vacant and crudest kind. Then, too, the character-drawing of his contemporaries, he points out, was unnatural and unconvincing ; for all dramatic characters, he maintains, in order to be effective, should speak and act in accordance with their respective natures. As it was, however, no distinction was made in matters of style, one mode of utterance being assigned to all characters alike ; whereas ' affected speech ', he points out, ' doth misbecome a clown ', while ' a crow ', he adds, ' will ill counterfeit a nightingale's sweet verse '. For the rest, he insists on the need for discrimination in action, so that all characters should behave in normal and natural fashion. This, however, he suggests, would be attained by an observance of the *decorum* of the ancients, according to which fixed and distinctive conduct should be associated with various human types, old men, young men, and the rest. Human nature, however, was not to be comprised in fixed types of this kind ; but of the value of his remarks in general there can be no doubt. It was the first substantial pronouncement on dramatic technique ; and in condemning gross improbabilities inartistically handled, the crude and ill-timed humour and unconvincing characterization of many of his contemporaries, he called attention to some of the basic principles of the dramatic art.

Such then were the slender results of dramatic criticism prior to 1590. Medieval ignorance of the real nature of the drama had been partly dispelled by Humanists who had introduced men anew to that literary form. Occasional remarks on technique had come from academic sources ; the right of the drama to exist had been fiercely challenged ; and amidst the gradual development of popular plays, attempts had been made to correct obvious excesses and to bring about a more rational form of drama. And this had been seen notably in the protests raised against incredible and fantastic themes far removed from factual truth. Moreover, breaches of fitness in style, characterization and action had been condemned ; increased stress had been laid on the element of delight in comedy, as opposed to its moral teaching ; while, concerning tragedy, little or nothing of significance had as yet been said.

It was with the rapid development of the drama after 1590, however, that dramatic criticism entered on a yet more notable phase, in which popular plays were the main concern, and a growing consciousness of dramatic values becomes perceptible ; so that this closing decade of the century marks a transition from an uncritical to a more or less critical phase where the drama was concerned. For this change of attitude many causes were responsible. By now, for one thing, the drama had become generally recognized as something more than 'the toy of an hour'; and meanwhile Lyly, Marlowe, and Kyd had written and were followed by a new race of playwrights, gifted and daring. Besides, a new official status had been won for plays and actors alike ; and altogether, in vain was the lament of the contemporary preacher that 'when the bells toll to the lecture, the trumpets sound to the stages'. Under these changed conditions some further discussion of dramatic affairs was therefore inevitable, more especially as the new vogue of satire, which became perceptible at this date, gave fresh impetus to the critical temper. Freed from the austerity of the early Reformers and the pedantry of the Humanists, men of the new age sought to improve the hitherto despised native drama and to give artistic quality to popular plays ; and as a result dramatic criticism became less vague and general, more independent and discerning. From now on, in short, dramatists and others began to have positive critical ideas and to express them more freely. At the same time such criticism as resulted still retained its earlier sporadic form, contributions being made mainly in Inductions and Prologues and incidentally in the plays themselves. In these comments many dramatists shared; and the running commentary that emerged is of considerable interest. From it may be gathered some notion of the clarification of ideas that went on. And this is revealed not only, as before, in judgments on contemporary plays and their authors, but also, and what is more important, in intermittent glimpses of that dramatic theory which determined the form of the triumphant popular drama.

Significant, in the first place, of increasing critical activities and the clarification of ideas, was the growing tendency to pass judgment on contemporary plays and their authors. And notable, to begin with, were the judicial comments on recent innovations, particularly in the field of tragedy, made by Nashe, Hall, and others. Already in 1589 Nashe was voicing his distaste for the experiments of Marlowe and his followers,[1] holding up to ridicule the grandiloquence and ' swelling bombast ' of the new school, those ' vain-glorious tragedians ' who thought themselves immortal poets if they used similes of Boreas and the like, and who made use of ' a bragging blank verse ' with its ' drumming decasyllables '. Then, too, he denounced the idea of a national drama based on Seneca, when he decried the servile imitation that had characterized many of the earlier plays. ' English Seneca read by candle-light ', he concedes,[2] ' yields many good sentences ', indeed, ' whole Hamlets and handfuls of tragical speeches '. But Seneca, he reminds his readers, was ' soon exhausted '; and then your dramatist would reveal his ' home-born mediocrity ' in mannerisms like those of Kyd, who was wont to patch up his blank verse with ' ifs and ands '. As a commentary on the tragedies of Marlowe, and even of Kyd, these remarks are obviously inadequate; they show no appreciation of the positive value of those earlier achievements, the structural and metrical improvements and the new tragic spirit. After *Tamburlaine* (1587), however, public taste insisted on a certain amount of rant and violent unmotivated action; and it was against the excess of melodrama which seemed to be threatening that Nashe's thunder was mainly directed.

The same current defects were likewise censured by Joseph Hall in his satire *Virgidemiarum* (1597–8), where, following Nashe, he derides what he regards as the excesses of the Marlowesque tradition in tragedy. Marlowe's inspiration, in the first place, he attributes to the influence of Bacchus, as that

[1] See Smith, *op. cit.* i. p. 308.   [2] *ibid.* i. p. 312.

which alone could have suggested such themes as 'the Turkish Tamberlaine'. And then he proceeds to ridicule his 'thundering threats', his hair-raising effects and 'big-sounding sentences'.[1] 'The famous Corduban', he adds, 'was never but half so high Tragedian.' After this he treats in pungent fashion the incongruous mixing of tragic and comic elements in tragedy. He describes how, in order to assuage the terror of some awful moment, the clown, self-deformed, would come leaping in among his betters to the manifest delight of the vulgar audience, in the meantime grimacing, thumping with his fists, showing jagged teeth, and laughing boisterously at his own witless folly. 'A goodly hotch-potch' and 'a goodly grace to the sober Tragic muse', are Hall's caustic comments on such situations. His conclusion is therefore that the 'tragic poesy' of his day was altogether too 'popular'[2] (i.e. degraded); and he further disapproves of the blank verse employed, in which 'unbid iambics' were said to 'flow from careless head'.

Nor were censures of this kind confined to Nashe and Hall, similar judgments being shared by many of the dramatists. Nowhere, for instance, are the crude melodramatic effects of Senecan imitations held up to fiercer ridicule than in the Induction to the anonymous play, A Warning for Fair Women[3] (1599), where a drama of the kind is analysed and it is explained

> How some damn'd tyrant to obtain a crown
> Stabs, hangs, impoisons, smothers, cutteth throats.
> And then a Chorus, too, comes howling in
> And tells us of the worrying of a cat.
> Then, too, a filthy whining ghost
> Lapt in some foul sheet or a leather pilch
> Comes screaming in, like a pig half-stick'd
> And cries Vindicta! Revenge, Revenge!

Apart from this censure of the Revenge motive there are Shakespeare's well-known references to ranting tragedians 'out-heroding Herod', to the crude ill-timed gag of comedians, whose senseless laughter 'sets on some quantity of barren spectators to laugh too':[4] and if burlesque is not actually intended in the passages of the old play recited by the actors, yet the earlier bombast and fustian is there plain enough for all to see. Equally significant, however, is Jonson's indictment of 'ill customs' of the contemporary stage,[5] in which, writing in 1616, he is obviously still influenced by Sidney. Thus he condemns what he regards

[1] Virg. I. iii. 8 ff.   [2] ibid. I. iv. I ff.
[3] See The School of Shakespeare, ed. R. Simpson, vol. ii.   [4] Hamlet, III, ii.
[5] Prol. to Every Man in his Humour, added in the Folio ed. (1616).

as absurdities resulting from breaches of the Unity of time, the ambitious attempts to represent history by means of ' three rusty swords ' and long resounding words, the use of the Chorus, again, to facilitate a change of scene, as well as sundry devices such as the interference of the gods to please the groundlings, theatrical thunder ' to make afeard the gentlewomen ', and the noise of drums to suggest a tempest.   Apart from this, not without its significance is Bobadil's vapid praise [1] of ' fine speeches ' in Kyd's *Spanish Tragedy*.   A very real hostility to melodramatic and other irrational effects is therefore obvious ; and, in general, it marks an advance in aesthetic appreciation, despite the prevailing uncertainty as to the merits of Marlowe's achievement [2] and the failure to understand as yet some of Shakespeare's methods.   Moreover, it might be added, the dislike of blank verse for dramatic purposes was not confined to Nashe and Hall. To Robert Greene, for instance, its sonorous effects were definitely distasteful, with ' each word ', as he puts it, ' filling the mouth like the faburden (i.e. faux-bourdon) of Bow Bells '.

Meanwhile plays other than tragedies were exciting comment ; and extravagances of a different kind were being ridiculed by means of parody and burlesque, those most ancient, and not the least effective, methods of passing literary judgment.   To this category belongs George Peele's *Old Wives' Tale* (1595), a farcical extravaganza in which were held up to derision the earlier plays of chivalrous romance with their myriad surprising incidents, their incoherent structures, and their incongruous mixtures of characters.[3]   The work, which consists of the story of a maiden entrapped by a magician and rescued by her two brothers, is perhaps best known as the source of the main theme of Milton's *Comus*.   Its real motive, however, is revealed clearly enough by its very title, which suggests a theme based on an old and foolish story and therefore not to be taken seriously.   The critical element emerges in the dramatic irony with which incident and character are invested.   Thus fantastic happenings and the high-flown language of magicians, Furies and others are thrown into relief by the presence of genuine and stolid rustics with their more realistic utterances ; and at the same time the literary satire which pervades the whole play is further enhanced by incidental references to Stanyhurst's unspeakable diction and to Gabriel Harvey's magniloquence in the person of

---

[1] *Every Man in his Humour*, I. v. 47 ff.
[2] cf. the ridicule of Marlowe's style in Marston's *Antonio and Mellida*, Part I, Induction.
[3] See p. 230 *supra*.

Huanebango. As the first play to deal with literary affairs the work is of interest in the critical development.

Equally unmistakable is the critical motive that lies behind Beaumont and Fletcher's *Knight of the Burning Pestle*, a mock-heroic drama first published in 1613, but probably composed some six or seven years earlier. In it the dramatic conditions of the time are treated with a delicious irony implicit in the title of the play itself ; and in the course of the action ridicule is poured on the crude taste of City playgoers, also on the type of play designed to cater for that taste. The dramatic standards of City audiences, to begin with, are effectively displayed in the ludicrous interruptions and inept remarks of an unimaginative City grocer and his wife—a device which provides the most genuine comic element in the play. By this means the bourgeois demand for far-fetched stories, forced situations and grotesque martial exploits, all redounding to the credit of London citizens, is clearly revealed and ridiculed. Then, too, significant references are made to recent plays which had subscribed to those demands. Among them were Thomas Heywood's *The Four Prentices of London* (acted c. 1600), his *If you know not me* (1606) and *The Travailes of Three English Brothers* (1607) by several authors ; all of which had dealt with the amazing adventures of City worthies. Nor was it only extravagances of plot that were censured ; for Ralph's affected use of the jargon of chivalrous romance, as well as the rant and bombast reminiscent of Kyd, are also faithfully dealt with. The play, in short, is a burlesque of a whole series of contemporary plays distinguished for their unreality and manifest absurdity ; and that the authors were inspired in their critical attitude by Cervantes's *Don Quixote*, one section of which had been translated by Thomas Shelton in 1605, would seem to be at least not wholly improbable.

Such then were the main judicial comments on plays after 1590. They were concerned mostly with censuring extravagances in contemporary tragedy and plays of a ' romantic ' kind. But certain estimates of various dramatists occasionally submitted also call for brief notice, for they witness to the growth of appreciation of a more positive kind. That the greatness of Marlowe's achievement, in spite of much detraction, was not altogether unrecognized is shown for instance by the tribute of Peele, in which he was described as ' the Muses' darling ' on account of his verse, and one

> Fit to write passions for the souls below
> If any wretched souls in passion speak.[1]

[1] *Honour of the Garter* (1593).

Then, too, there was the more sustained attempt at critical appreciation in *The Return from Parnassus*, Part I (1602–3), the third part of a trilogy, written by a University scholar and performed as a Christmas or a New Year's entertainment at St. John's College, Cambridge. There Marlowe is said to have been ' happy in his buskin Muse ', with ' wit lent from Heaven but vices sent from Hell '.[1] Marston, on the other hand, is censured for his ' ruffianly ' style ; while Ben Jonson is described as a laborious writer, ' a mere Empiric, one that gets what he hath by observation '. Most interesting, however, is the tribute paid to Shakespeare at this early date. His poems, *Venus and Adonis* and *Lucrece*, for instance, are commended as verse that ' contains heart-robbing life ' ; though advice is also given that he should choose themes of a more serious kind and thus eschew .' love's foolish languishment '. Concerning his plays, however, the praise is unqualified and is represented as the judgment of the famous actor, Will Kemp. ' Few of the University ', it is stated,[2] ' pen plays well ; they smell too much of that writer Ovid . . . and talk too much of Proserpina and Jupiter. Why, here's our fellow Shakespeare puts them all down, ay, and Ben Jonson too.' It was a notable pronouncement at the time of utterance, rendered yet more significant as the judgment of a University writer submitted to a University audience ; for it not only acknowledged the limitations of academic dramas, but it also proclaimed the supremacy of the popular playwright in the whole field of English drama. Apart from this, critical comments on dramatists are rare, though not without their interest are Webster's remarks [3] in his Preface to *The White Devil* (1612) on ' the full and heightened style ' of Chapman, ' the laboured and understanding works ' of Jonson, the worthy compositions of Beaumont and Fletcher, and ' the right happy and copious industry ' of Shakespeare, Dekker, and Heywood. Such general and one-word judgments, however, are not very illuminating. They merely suggest that appreciation of the popular drama, though genuine, was inarticulate and undiscriminating as yet.

Interesting as were these various judgments in throwing light on the slow and uncertain growth of dramatic taste, yet more valuable is that other aspect of the critical activities bound up with the dramatists themselves, from which may be gathered some general idea of those theories upon which were based the new developments of the closing decade of the century. That no systematic body of theory is anywhere elaborated, that

[1] Act I, Sc. ii.   [2] Act IV. Sc. v.
[3] See J. E. Spingarn, *Critical Essays of the 17th Century*, i. 66.

reflections on art are often coloured by dramatic considerations, and that dramatic expression must not invariably be pressed into serious doctrine ; all this is of course true. At the same time much relevant material is to be found in Prologues and the like, in incidental ironies and satirical remarks, and even in passages where the reflective poet rather than the dramatist is speaking ; and in accepting such material as of critical value we are on tolerably safe ground. To these occasional remarks Lyly, Shakespeare, and Jonson were the main contributors, though many of the other dramatists have also something to say ; and from them it becomes evident that a substantial body of dramatic theory was in the meantime forming, unformulated as yet, but instinctively applied, by the dramatists themselves. Of classical doctrine there is but little trace ; though its influence is perhaps seen in the general reaction against the formlessness of the earlier native drama. For the rest, however, the new dramatic art owed little or nothing to artistic recipes or prescriptions, whether classical or Italian. The truth was that Elizabethan dramatists were empiricists first and last, with experiment and practice engaging all attention ; and their art was no haphazard growth but an independent creation, developed along definite lines dictated by the native genius and traditions, by popular taste and stage conditions of the time. Irrespective of orthodox doctrine, they shaped their practice, and also their unwritten theory, in accordance with what they deemed to be psychologically necessary for rendering their stories attractive to popular audiences on the Elizabethan stage ; and here, if anywhere, lies the key to the understanding of Elizabethan dramatic art. A similar departure from classical precedent, it might be noted, had meanwhile developed independently in Spain ; and Lope de Vega (1562–1635), later on in his *El Nuevo Arte de hacer Comedias* (1609), was to defend his methods on the ground that ' he who wrote according to the rules would die without fame '. Those methods he described as ' a new art invented by those who sought popular applause ' ; and in view of the deference paid to native tradition and popular taste, the description is one that, with some difference, holds true of Elizabethan dramatic art.

Among the first signs which heralded the ' new art ' in England were the tentative efforts made to arrive at clearer conceptions of the main dramatic forms then current, though in confused and amorphous form, namely, comedy, tragedy, and history.[1] And of outstanding importance, in the first place, are Lyly's

---

[1] cf. the three-fold division of Shakespeare's plays in the First Folio (1623).

pronouncements on comedy; for they not only point to a conscious attempt at establishing a new comedy, they also embody principles which were to animate later dramatic developments. Not without their interest are the particular innovations he proposes in connexion with comedy, which, largely based as it hitherto was on Roman comedy, had so far outstripped tragedy in the dramatic development. From this tradition, however, Lyly deliberately breaks away, proposing a dramatic form of a vastly different kind, and emphasizing the need, already urged by earlier writers, for a refinement of comedy. The aim of comedy, he maintains,[1] should be ' to move inward delight, . . . to breed soft smiling, not loud laughing '. Of yet greater significance, however, are the principles involved in the changes proposed ; and first, there was his bold challenge of the orthodox dramatic ' kinds '. With those ancient ' kinds ' he is obviously familiar. He is also aware of the shapeless character of earlier native plays, with their indiscriminate mingling of the elements of comedy, tragedy, history, and the pastoral. The orthodox tradition however he deliberately defies ; and the native mingling of elements he claims to have been justified on account of the mixed audiences of his day. ' What heretofore ', he states,[2] ' hath been served on several dishes . . . is now minced on a charger for a Gallimaufrey.' And in refusing to classify his plays as ' comedies,. or tragedies or mere tales ', he denies that the boundaries of the dramatic species had been permanently fixed, thereby suggesting the principle of free development. At the same time further principles were involved in the position thus adopted. Not without its interest, for example, is the reason given for the changes proposed, namely, the character and taste of contemporary audiences. That the nature of the audience was a factor to be taken into account in dramatic creation was an argument now advanced for the first time in England,[3] and one which derived added force in connexion with the popular stage. Yet another important principle is advocated when the function of comedy is defined as that of giving pleasure and amusement.[4] Hitherto the moral or didactic aim had been generally accepted ; but this hedonistic conception was to grow apace and to colour much of the later work. Nor, again, must Lyly's description of his plays as ' mere pastime or plays of the imagination '[5] be overlooked. It suggested that factual truth

---

[1] Prol. to *Sapho and Phao* (acted 1582 ?) ; Prol. to *Endimion* (acted 1579).
[2] Prol. to *Midas* (1592).   [3] cf. Daniel's similar claim, p. 199 *supra*.
[4] Prol. to *The Woman in the Moon* (1597).
[5] Prol. to *Endimion* (acted 1579).

was not the only thing to be looked for on the stage; while it also gave sanction to those fanciful or ' romantic ' themes, which, ineffectively handled, had been the subject of much earlier censure. Most important of all, however, was his revelation of one of the secrets of high comedy when he remarked on the part played by brilliant dialogue and flashes of conceit and fancy in comedy. ' It is wit that allureth,' he writes,[1] ' when every word shall have his weight, when nothing shall proceed but it shall either savour of a sharp conceit or a secret conclusion.' And here he would seem to be foreshadowing that later conception of ' wit ', as distinguished from the normal Elizabethan use of that term, in advocating the use of those ingenious turns productive of ' thoughtful laughter ' which were to be seen later in the plays of Congreve, Sheridan, and others. Such then was Lyly's contribution to critical theory; and though it consists merely of scattered hints it is of outstanding value. In maintaining that dramatic forms other than classical were possible, that those forms should be determined in part by the taste of the general, that the function of the drama was simply to afford a refined pleasure, that fanciful themes were fit material for dramatic treatment, and that ' wit ' in its modern sense was an essential ingredient of comedy at its best, he was suggesting principles of fundamental importance which were to be characteristic of Shakespearean and later dramatic art.

Concerning the theory of tragedy less of a definite nature was forthcoming; and this was largely due to prevailing conditions. Before the late eighties genuine tragedy had appealed to limited academic circles only; Senecan imitations on the popular stage had achieved no very striking success; the term ' tragic ', loosely employed to describe the nondescript ' tragical comedies ', was without any definite significance; and in general, no clear conception of tragedy existed among dramatists, no feeling for tragedy among ordinary playgoers. It was left for Marlowe, and above all for Shakespeare, to create a new taste for plays in which tragic themes were developed to tragic issues. But while no coherent theory of tragedy was thus expounded, worth noting are those occasional remarks which betray an awakening interest in this new type of play. From Marlowe, Kyd, and others came, for instance, a claim for the recognition of tragedy. Thus apart from Marlowe's call to his contemporaries to abandon ' such conceits as clownage keeps in pay ',[2] Kyd in one place describes comedy as fit only for ' common wits ' and commends tragedy

[1] Quoted by G. P. Baker in *Cambridge History of Eng. Lit.* v. 128.
[2] Prol. to *Tamburlaine* (1590).

as ' fitting kings ' and containing ' matter not common things '.[1]
And still more significant in the valuable Induction to *A Warning
for Fair Women* is Tragedy's complaint to Comedy and History
that they had kept the stage too long, whereas Tragedy herself
was ' scorned of the multitude '. That more serious views on
tragedy were emerging at this date is shown by the adaptation
of old plays which no longer appealed to playgoers. Already in
1591 *Gismonde of Salerne* (1568) was presented in a revised form
as *Tancred and Gismunda*, which Webbe in his Preface to the
new version described as ' clothed in a fashion more answerable
to these times, wherein fashions are so often altered'. But the
revision was concerned mainly with formal details, the diction
being changed, blank verse substituted for rhyme, and long
speeches broken up, without any serious changes being made in
the spirit or structure of the play. Nor was much light forthcoming from the dramatists themselves, at least in the critical
sense. Marlowe, for instance, speaks of ' heroic actions ' and
' high-astounding terms ' [2] as essentially tragic elements ; while
Kyd's idea is that tragedies are acts of Death and dismal tales,
involving seas of tears and loud laments.[3] In *A Warning for
Fair Women* [4] alone is some appreciation of genuine tragedy present.
It was a domestic drama staging the recent murder of a London
merchant ; and in the course of the play some interesting remarks
are made. Tragedy, it is stated, demands passions which stir
the soul and draw tears from all eyes ; and at the end of the play
the author confesses the limitations bound up with his domestic
tragedy. Loftier themes, he suggested, were needed for tragic
effects ; since the sordid details and particular incidents of a
contemporary crime offered insufficient scope for representing
those larger issues and universal truths which true tragedy
required.

On the third of the dramatic forms under consideration at
the time, namely, the History play, no technical comments are
made, though Nashe's commendation of such plays is worthy of
note. He praises historical plays in *Pierce Pennilesse* (1592) as
fostering virtue and patriotism ; and he pays special tribute to
one particular play, possibly *I. Henry VI.* Thus he rejoices in
the immortality therein conferred on ' brave Talbot ', whose
memory was kept green by the tears of thousands of playgoers ;
and such revivals of ancient valour, he adds, were a reproach
to those Puritans who regarded all art as vanity. The prime

---

[1] *Spanish Tragedy*, IV. ii. 153 ff.   [2] Prol. to *Tamburlaine*.
[3] Induction to *Soliman and Persida* (1599).
[4] Induction to the play.

merit of such plays, however, was said to be that ' all the wily deceits gilded with holiness, all the cankers of place are there exposed. They show the evils of treason, the fall of those who mount too quickly, the miserable end of usurpers, the misery of civil strife. . . . They are (in short) sour pills of reprehension . . . rapt up in sweet words.' [1] And the passage is one that throws a vivid light on the political, non-aesthetic, character of dramatic appreciation in the last decade of the century.

But while comedy, tragedy, and history were thus the three dramatic ' kinds ' now subjected to some amount of critical comment, a word might here be added concerning the attempt to define yet another popular type of play which was neither tragedy, comedy, nor yet history. It was a dramatic form which, although not without classical or Italian precedents, had been specially designed by Beaumont and Fletcher in response to popular taste ; and in his Address to the Reader prefixed to *The Faithful Shepherdess* (1610) Fletcher attempts a definition. Tragi-comedy, he explains, ' is not so called in respect of mirth and killings, but in respect it wanteth deaths (i.e. lacks a tragic catastrophe), which is enough to make it no tragedy, yet brings some near it, which is enough to make it no comedy '. It was an attempt to justify an obvious departure from the accepted types, and it points to an increasing regard for dramatic theory as opposed to the anarchy of the earlier period.

Apart from these comments on the ' kinds ', further general principles were from time to time advanced by later dramatists explaining their methods or anticipating the objections of the ' more curious in censure ' ; and most of them are along the lines suggested by Lyly. That dramatist had already declared that for him the taste of playgoers was an important consideration ; and despite frequent expressions of scorn for the ' groundlings ' and the ' many-tongued opinion ', one of the principles generally accepted was the necessity of appealing to the ordinary man, apart from all rules. On this point Marston for one is explicit. In the Induction to *What You Will* (1601) he argues that

> Music and poetry were first approved
> By common sense ; and that which pleased most
> Held most allowance to pass. Not rules of art
> Were shaped to pleasure, nor pleasure to your rules.

Thus the earliest test, he maintains, was *communis sensus* or the approval of the general. The approval of the few, he adds,

[1] *Works of T. Nashe*, ed. Grosart, ii. 98.

'though deemed most judicious' was not enough to commend a play to a wider public.   It was a doctrine in keeping with earlier native traditions bound up with Interludes and the like ; and it was to some extent justified in its appeal to human nature over and above the rules.   The same position, moreover, was adopted by Ben Jonson in the Prologue to *The Silent Woman* (1609). He there recalls that 'of old the art of making plays was to content the people ',[1] though in his time, he added, there were writers who would 'taste nothing that was popular '.   He states, however, that with such writers he had nothing to do ; and that his aim (here following Martial [2]) was to please not 'the cook's taste but the guests' '.   Nor in this connexion must the significance of Webster's approval of Shakespeare's tragedies as the natural English forms be forgotten.   In his judgment the stricter tragedy of antiquity, with its rules relating to elevation of style, ' sentwith sen- tentious choruses ', and its lack of action supplied by Messengers' speeches, was unsuitable for English audiences.   Its 'divine raptures ', he maintains,[3] 'were poisoned by the breath of the ignorant crowd ' ; and here, by one who was himself a gifted playwright, was an early recognition of the value, not only of Shakespeare's forms and methods, but also of 'the new art invented by those who sought the public applause '.

Concerning yet another of Lyly's principles, that relating to the dramatic function, it would appear that whereas the didactic aim was still professed by some, by others the purpose of the 'new art' was held to be that of mere amusement.   Of the didactic purpose Jonson is the main representative, as may be gathered from his definite statement that

> The ends of all who for the scene do write
> Are, or should be, to profit and delight.[4]

Chapman, again, held that the purpose of tragedy was that of affording 'elegant and sententious excitement to virtue ';[5] while the closing words of Beaumont and Fletcher's *Philaster* (1610) also point in the same direction, when it is urged that from the play 'princes should learn . . . to rule the passions of their blood '.   On the other hand, by Shakespeare such moral teaching is seldom paraded ; while in more than one of his Epilogues [6] he

---

[1] cf. also *The Magnetic Lady*, Induction.   [2] *Epigr.* ix. 83.
[3] Preface to *The White Devil* (1612).
[4] *The Silent Woman*, 2nd Prol. (1609).
[5] Dedication to *The Revenge of Bussy D'Ambois* (1613).
[6] cf. Epilogues to *As You Like It* and *The Tempest*.

makes it plain that his ' project ' had been merely that of giving
pleasure. Moreover, Marston in one place [1] categorically states
that ' we strive not to instruct but to delight '. Dekker, again,
in his Dedication to *The Shoemaker's Holiday* (1599) urges that in
the play ' nothing is purposed but mirth ', and that ' mirth
lengtheneth long life ' ; while Fletcher in the Prologue to *The
Knight of the Burning Pestle* states (here following Lyly closely)
that his intent was ' to move inward lightness, and to breed . . .
soft smiling, not loud laughter '.

Of yet greater interest, however, are the various attempts
now made to commend the new drama with its fanciful or
' romantic ' themes, its departures from factual truth—features
that ran counter to the rational demand for truth to life, but
which nevertheless were cherished by popular audiences. At an
earlier date, as we have seen, far-fetched and sensational plots
had been vigorously condemned by Whetstone, Sidney, and others ;
and now it had been suggested by Lyly that such material
properly treated came within the province of dramatic art. The
chief argument advanced was that the drama was a form of
poetry, and as such it aimed at something more than a mere
reproduction of the facts of life. From Sidney himself it had
been learnt that the poet had the power of transmuting the real
and actual, and of attempting new creations in the guise of fiction.
For the dramatist was therefore claimed the ' high-flying liberty
of conceit ' of the poet, which enabled him to transcend Nature
with his ' romantic ' figments—a treatment denied to the historian,
for instance, whose themes were confined to the world of experience, to what had actually happened. Thus Marston, for one,
declares ' I have not laboured to tie myself to relate anything as
an historian, but to enlarge everything as a poet '.[2] A similar
claim is likewise made by Dekker who justifies the lack of historical
truth in his play by explaining that he had written as a poet,
not as a historian, and that these two did ' not live under one
law '.[3] Or again, there is Chapman who ridicules ' those poor
envious souls who cavil at truth's want in their natural fictions ' ;
whereas ' such authentical truth of either person or action ', he
explains, ' is not to be looked for in a poet, whose subject is not
truth but things like truth '.[4] It was an argument based on
Horace's dictum that *ficta voluptatis causa sint proxima veris*,[5]

[1] Prol. to *The Dutch Courtezan.*
[2] *Sophonisba* (1606), To the General Reader.
[3] *The Whore of Babylon* (1607), To the Reader.
[4] *The Revenge of Bussy D'Ambois* (1613), Dedication.
[5] *Ars Poetica*, l. 338.

17

and one which had previously been cited by Jonson in maintaining that

> Poets never credit gain'd
> By writing truths, but things, like truth, well feign'd.[1]

It was from Chapman, however, that the most direct statement came concerning the transforming power of the dramatist and his liberty of treatment, when he states that

> As the stuff
> Prepared for Arras pictures is no picture
> Till it be formed and man hath cast the beams
> Of his imaginous fancy through it.[2]

So, he continues, the dramatist represents ' ancient kings and conquerors as he conceived they looked, . . . though they were nothing so '. Thus was submitted a timely defence of yet another of the basic principles which were to give direction to the new art and to make for increased freedom in the dramatic development.

It now remains to consider the special contributions of Shakespeare and Ben Jonson to this dramatic criticism. Of Shakespeare, in the first place, it would be true to say that he nowhere deliberately unfolds the secrets of his art ; though hidden in his work is ample material for establishing a body of theory which, duly organized, would form a valuable counterpart to that contained in Aristotle's *Poetics*. Concerning his guiding principles and the details of his technique, however, but few direct indications are given. No explanation, for instance, is afforded of his doctrine of significant form, according to which a play should provide in its beginning an expectation of its end, in its development rational movement and in its end a sense of fulfilment. Nothing, again, is said of his conception of either tragedy or comedy, of the need for selection, compression and idealization of dramatic material, of the different methods of revealing character, of the value of contrast and relief, of the different dramatic effects of verse and prose, or of the hundred and one devices he employed for holding the playgoer's interest. The truth was that he learned his craft as he went along, improvising his methods in accordance with the nature of each particular story. From the classical tradition, it would seem, he took what he felt was needed, that is, a sense of form and fitness ; and he avoids, on the one hand, the earlier confusion of forms, and, on

---

[1] *The Silent Woman* (1609), 2nd Prol.
[2] *The Conspiracy of Charles, Duke of Byron*, III. i (1608).

the other, the classical formalism that in some quarters was threatening. Free from all abstract schemes he works from first principles, adopting such devices as were psychologically necessary in order to render his stories effective on the stage; and his dramatic theory, in consequence, remains unformulated, though everywhere implicit in his plays.

At the same time there are places where Shakespeare affords, firstly, glimpses of his views on contemporary literary and dramatic activities, and, secondly, some fragments of his conception of art in general. His judgments are conveyed mainly by means of burlesque and parody, his theories by means of suggestive *obiter dicta*, all of which, despite their dramatic occasions, may without over-ingenuity be reasonably associated with the dramatist himself. As for his literary judgments, in the first place, there can be no doubt of his attitude towards those stylistic affectations which had resulted from the earlier intemperate enthusiasm for language and the reckless abuse of formal rhetoric. In *Love's Labour's Lost*, for instance, scholastic pedantry and excessive Latinisms are ridiculed in the utterances of Holofernes, one who had been ' at a great feast of languages and had stolen the scraps '; [1] while the bombast and pomposity of Armado are also faithfully handled, as a style unnatural, altogether ' too picked, too spruce, too affected '.[2] Elsewhere the craze for Euphuism with its abuse of figurative language is occasionally derided, as in Falstaff's disquisition to Mistress Quickly.[3] But the most direct of pronouncements on the artificial and new-fangled utterance then current was the caustic reprimand of the Danish Queen to Polonius entangled in figures, when ' more matter with less art ' [4] was prescribed for his guidance. In similar fashion Shakespeare pours ridicule on the vogue of sonnet-writing, on the gross flattery and servility involved in the vapid imitations of ' the numbers that Petrarch flowed in '. To this matter he refers more than once; but of his satirical intention Proteus's recipe for the composing of ' wailful sonnets ' provides perhaps the clearest indication, when he advises Sir Thurio to ' tangle ' his mistress's desires by means of impassioned vows. ' Say ', he urges,

> That upon the altar of her heart
> You sacrifice your tears, your sighs, your heart.
> Write till your ink be dry, and with your tears
> Moist it again, and frame some feeling line
> That may discover such integrity.[5]

[1] *L.L.L.* v. i. 39.   [2] *ibid.* v. i. 14.   [3] *I. Hen. IV*, ii. iv. 446 ff.
[4] *Hamlet*, ii. ii. 95.   [5] *Two Gent.* iii. ii. 73 ff.

Then, too, on the contemporary drama Shakespeare passes
occasional judgment ; and this, apart from his treatment of the
most ' lamentable comedy ' staged by those ' hard-handed men '
who ' toiled their unbreathed memories ' in *A Midsummer Night's
Dream*. It is in the mouth of the garrulous Polonius, however,
that his most lively comment on the prevailing confusion of
dramatic forms is suitably placed.   There are mentioned, apart
from the three or four main ' kinds ', such mongrel forms as
' pastoral-comical, tragical-comical, historical-pastoral ' and the
like.[1] Or again, reference is made to plays with ' scenes individ-
able ' and to ' poems unlimited ', the former being strictly classical
types based on the ' law of writ ' (i.e. classical rules), the latter,
plays of a new kind, based on ' the liberty ' and therefore owing
nothing to the accepted rules.   The significance of this exposition
lies not only in its satire on the numerous sub-divisions of contemporary drama, but also in its recognition of the rules on the
one hand and of ' the higher law of inspired creative activity '
on the other.   With regard to his views on the different ' kinds '
Shakespeare makes no definite pronouncement ; though towards
one type of play—the pastoral—he betrays a critical attitude
which is of some significance.   In *As You Like It*, for instance, the
artificiality of pastoralism is derided by Touchstone's solemn
fooling ;[2] Jacques scoffs at the idea of Arcadia as ' a free
republic ' ;[3] and by means of both satire and parody the ethical
motive of pastoralism is held up to ridicule.   In *The Winter's
Tale*, however, a more sympathetic attitude is adopted ; and
something like a rational explanation is incidentally given.   The
main objection to pastoralism had been its unreality, its element
of artifice when contrasted with Nature ; and now Shakespeare
suggests that such characteristics need not necessarily detract
from its ultimate value.   In one of his profoundest sayings, in
speaking of the ' streak'd gillyvors ', he states through the
mouth of Polixenes that

> Nature is made better by no mean
> But nature makes that mean ; so over that art,
> Which you say adds to nature, is an art
> That nature makes.[4]

In other words he maintains that the distinction between Nature
and art was in itself artificial, that all art has its origin in Nature,
is in fact based on an observation of Nature's ways ; and here,

---

[1] *Hamlet*, II. ii. 424.   [2] III. ii. 13.   [3] II. i. 45.
[4] IV. iii. 89 ff. : cf. p. 165 *supra*.

in claiming the poet's right to transform the real and actual, he was not only adding to the chorus of some of his contemporaries, he was also echoing a doctrine long ago expounded by Quintilian [1] and others, and enunciating a vital precept of his own dramatic art.

Nor must his practical remarks on contemporary acting be overlooked. Like more than one of the earlier writers he condemns outright the rude interruptions of clowns at serious moments, the practice of introducing foolish ' gag ' or what passed for ' extemporal wit '. ' Let your clowns ', he demands, ' speak no more than is set down for them.' [2] And at the same time he censures their trick of starting an inane laugh in order ' to set on some quantity of barren spectators to laugh too '. On the other hand, he suggests that good ' fooling ' calls for qualities of a more positive kind, for keen intelligence, for instance, besides shrewd judgment and tact. And this is made plain by Viola's comment when listening to the patter of the Clown. ' This fellow's wise enough ', she exclaims,[3]

> To play the fool,
> And to do that well craves a kind of wit.
> He must observe their mood on whom he jests,
> The quality of persons and the time,
> And, like the haggard, check at every feather
> That comes before his eye. This is a practice
> As full of labour as a wise man's art.

Apart from this he pleads for moderation and good sense in expression and action alike, for an end of that melodramatic ' strutting and bellowing ' which degraded the contemporary stage. What he requires is clear and impassioned utterance, restrained gestures, moderation and self-control even in ' the whirlwind of passion ', and in general an exercise of tact and good taste which should give pleasure, if not to the groundlings, at any rate to the judicious, while also imparting an air of naturalness to the performance.[4]

Yet more interesting than these judicial comments on contemporary dramatic activities were Shakespeare's casual remarks treating of the nature and art of poetry, and of the drama in particular. Concerning the nature of poetry, to begin with, various statements are made in the course of the plays, the most conventional being those of the time-serving poet in *Timon of*

[1] *Inst. Or.* II. 17, 9 and 41 ff.   [2] *Hamlet*, III. ii. 44.
[3] *Twelfth Night*, III. i. 68 ff.   [4] *Hamlet*, III. ii. 1 ff.

Athens. He claims, for instance, that poetry is the fruit of unforced inspiration. ' Our poesy ', he states,[1]

> Is as a gum which oozes
> From whence 'tis nourish'd ; the fire i' the flint
> Shows not till it be struck.

Or again, in maintaining that it is universal in its reach, ' my free drift ', he explains,[2]

> Halts not particularly, but moves itself
> In a wide sea of wax.

Elsewhere, however, poetry is often referred to in terms of a less orthodox kind.   It is represented, for example, as an embodiment of what is not true, as a mere trick of versifying, a ' mincing ' affair, or a means by which ' fellows of infinite tongue . . . rhyme themselves into ladies' favour'.   Thus there are Theseus's scornful remarks on the wild unreason and unreality of poetry ; [3] ' the truest poetry ', according to Touchstone, ' is the most feigning ' ; [4] to Holofernes, again, its gift was a ' foolish extravagant spirit, full of forms, figures, shapes, objects and ideas . . . begot in the ventricle of memory ' ; [5] while to the fiery Hotspur and Henry V it was something beneath the dignity of plain men of action.[6] All such statements, however, are spoken in character and are therefore no certain evidences of Shakespeare's own views on the subject.   The most elaborate and reasoned of them all is Theseus's discourse ; and here, if anywhere, will perhaps be found a clue to the dramatist's real idea of the nature of poetry.

The main contention of Theseus is that the creations of the poet are none other than empty illusions, mad fancies, and ' airy nothings ', the outcome of ' tricks of strong imagination (i.e. fancy) '.   And in support of his position he recalls what Plato was thought to have said concerning the madness or ' shaping fantasies ' of ' the lunatic, the lover and the poet '.   Yet the madness discussed by Plato was not confined to the pathological kind.[7]   It included also a form of exaltation which led to a kindling of latent powers that enabled ' the prophetess, the lover and the poet ' to attain to a vision of a higher truth and beauty.[8]   As yet, however, the Renascence theory of the ' imagination ' inaugurated by Pico della Mirandola [9] was still generally accepted ;

[1] I. i. 21–3.   [2] I. i. 46–7.   [3] *M.N.D.* v. i. 1 ff.
[4] *A.Y.L.I.* III. iii. 21.   [5] *L.L.L.* IV. ii. 67 ff.
[6] *I. Hen. IV*, III. i. 133 : *Hen. V*, v. ii. 136 ff.
[7] See Willis, p. 109 *supra.*
[8] cf. *Phaedrus*, 245 a, 265 a.   [9] See p. 25 *supra.*

and that conception of 'imagination' as a mental aberration which led to indulgence in wild fancies was here adopted by Theseus. At the same time it is important to note Hippolyta's suggestive rejoinder when she maintains that 'the story of the night'

> More witnesseth than fancy's images
> And grows to something of great constancy.[1]

And here would seem to be Shakespeare's own comment on the current theory, the implication being that to him poetry was something more than mere idle figments, the poetic imagination something other than capricious fancy. Greater explicitness was prevented by the occasion and by lack of terminology ; but he seems here to be hinting at Sidney's ' high-flying liberty of conceit' of the poet as a means of arriving at substantial truth.

Concerning the art of poetry and of the drama in particular he has also some comments worthy of note. Of his conception of art in general as a methodizing of Nature's processes and a means of rendering natural efforts more effective, something has already been said. To him it was obviously something more than a matter of rules ; and in one place he laments that contemporary art had been ' tongue-tied by authority ' ; [2] while elsewhere, like Agathon and Simylus of old,[3] he recognizes the part played by happy chance in artistic endeavour, when the Princess in *Love's Labour's Lost* in commenting on Costard's unconscious humour remarks ' that sport best pleases that doth least know how '.[4] On the dramatic art he has rather more to say ; and not without its interest, in the first place, is his familiar comment on the function of the drama. That function is said to be ' to hold, as 'twere, the mirror up to nature ; to show virtue her own feature, scorn her own image, and the very age and body of the time his form and pressure '.[5] And here he claims for the drama, not so much moral teaching as a reflexion of life and human nature ; though it is curious to note that, by ' some freak of tradition ' in thus defining its value, he makes use of that simile of the mirror which Plato had previously employed to illustrate, not the value but the worthlessness of poetry, as being capable of producing only unsubstantial images.[6] On matters of technique he makes more than one important pronouncement, as when, for example, in the Prologue to *Troilus and Cressida* he explains one of his

---

[1] *M.N.D.* v. i. 25–6.   [2] *Sonnet*, LXVI.
[3] See Atkins, *Lit. Crit. in Antiquity*, i. 21–2, 179–80 : ii. 277.
[4] *L.L.L.* v. ii. 516.   [5] *Hamlet*, III. ii. 25 ff.
[6] cf. *Republic*, 596 d.

fundamental principles of dramatic construction, namely, the need for selecting the significant incidents of a story,

> Beginning in the middle ; starting thence away
> To what may be digested in a play.[1]

Or, again, there is Cassius's remark that ' men at some time are masters of their fates ',[2] where Shakespeare seems to let fall a hint of his conception of tragedy—the tragedy of character as distinct from the tragedy of error of the ancients.

Still more far-reaching is his insistence on the need for imaginative co-operation on the part of the audience—a requirement rendered necessary by the limitations of the contemporary stage in presenting stories not confined to one place and one day. Already in *A Midsummer Night's Dream* Theseus, in commenting on plays, had remarked that ' the best in this kind are but shadows, and the worst are no worse if imagination amend them ' ; [3] and subsequently in *Henry V* came the direct appeal to ' piece out our imperfections with your thoughts ',[4] an appeal that was reiterated in the later Choruses of that play.   His argument was that stage representations without the exercise of the imagination were merely ' mockeries ' ; but with the imagination at work they became alive, symbolical of the real and actual.   By such an appeal Shakespeare felt that he could generate a more vivid apprehension of things, and at the same time dispense with the Unities, since he claimed the power

> To overthrow law and in one self-born hour
> To plant and o'erwhelm custom.[5]

Other dramatists, it might be noted, were also conscious of the deficiencies of the Elizabethan stage.   But their solution was mainly the employment of a Chorus.   Thus Dekker in one place writes

> Our Muse entreats
> Your thoughts to help poor Art, and allow
> That I may serve as Chorus to her scenes.[6]

And he is followed by Thomas Heywood who notes that ' he is forced by Chorus to discourse what should have been in action '.[7] By Shakespeare, however, the problem was solved psychologically, by the suggestion of a basic principle governing all great art ;

---

[1] ll. 28–9.   [2] *Julius Caesar*, I. ii. 138.   [3] v. i. 214.
[4] I. Chor. 23 : cf. III. Chor. 25, IV. Chor. 53, v. Chor. 4.
[5] *W. Tale*, IV. Chor. 8.   [6] *Old Fortunatus* (1599), Prol.
[7] *Fair Maid of the West* (1621 ?), v. Chor.

and in asserting the need for a happy collaboration between artist and hearer (or reader) he brought to light again the profound doctrine enunciated by Theophrastus and other writers of classical antiquity.[1]

Such then were Shakespeare's sporadic remarks relating to poetry and the drama, though a word or two may here be fitly added with regard to hints given on aesthetic matters of a more general kind. To him, as to most of his contemporaries, the term ' critic ' was apparently unfamiliar in its modern and wider sense, ' carper ', ' faultfinder ', and ' cynic '[2] being the meanings attached to it in his play. As regards literary standards, he would accept only the judgment of the judicious few, ' the censure of which one ', he explains, ' must . . . o'er-weigh a whole theatre of others '.[3] Elsewhere he remarks on the difficulties of self-criticism. The artist's judgment of his own work, he suggests, is attained only by perceiving its effects on others, since

> No man is the lord of anything
> Till he communicates his parts to others.[4]

Then, too, he notes that aesthetic effects are relative, and that beauty, for instance, requires its appropriate setting. ' Nothing is good, I see,' says Portia, ' without respect ' ;[5] and later,

> How many things by season season'd are
> To their right praise and true perfection.

Or again, there are his comments on the sister art of music, and notably on its effects. In general, an appreciation of that art is for him a test of a noble nature, a doctrine illustrated by Lorenzo's speech on music ;[6] by Caesar's passing remark on the character of Cassius,[7] as well as by the different but significant reactions of Caliban and Trinculo to the strains of Ariel's songs. Here Shakespeare was embodying the Renascence doctrine of music as an aid to ' the inner harmony of the soul ', a doctrine ultimately derived from Plato's *Timaeus* in which was preserved the Pythagorean theory of music as the purgation ($\varkappa\acute{\alpha}\vartheta\alpha\varrho\sigma\iota\varsigma$) of the soul. This is made clear by Shakespeare's reference to ' the muddy vesture of decay ',[8] the barrier which prevented a hearing of the grander music of the cosmos. By music, however, men's

---

[1] See Atkins, *Lit. Crit. in Antiquity*, i. 158 ; ii. 317.
[2] cf. *L.L.L.* IV. iii. 170 : *Tr. and Cr.* v. ii. 128.
[3] *Hamlet*, III. ii. 31.   [4] *Tr. and Cr.* III. iii. 115.
[5] *M. of V.* IV. i. 99 ff.   [6] *ibid.* v. i. 83 ff.
[7] *J.C.* I. ii. 203.   [8] *M. of V.* v. i. 63.

souls were held to be brought into accord with the ' quiring ' of the heavenly bodies, and thus made to be at one with the eternal verities.

In turning now to Ben Jonson for his dramatic criticism, it becomes obvious at once that his contribution is more studied, more direct, than the casual but profoundly suggestive remarks of Shakespeare.   Apart from earlier theorists, he is in fact the first to give criticism an important place in his creative work, and to expound, as a conscious artist, his main ideas and principles. Unlike Shakespeare, he uses the term ' critic ' in its modern sense. He also has definite views on the critical function, namely, that the ' trying faculty ', being based on knowledge, consisted neither in ' affection ' (emotion) nor in ' self-tickling ' ; [1] while he also ridicules the fashionable censor who ' sits like an Aristarchus or stark ass, taking men's lines with a tobacco face '.[2]   With him, moreover, the critical habit was ever present, in his comedies, his *Epigrams, Conversations,* and the like ; and while in dramatic matters that habit is abundantly illustrated by Prologues, Pre- faces, and Dialogues between the acts, or again, by such characters as Asper, Crites, and Horace, all mouthpieces of the author, it is also significant that he was the first to indulge in scholarly comment on his own plays, the first also to publish a definitive edition in the Folio of 1616.   Up to that date his interests were primarily of a dramatic kind ; and during that period there was a frequent output of critical observations as he expounded and applied his dramatic theories.

The animating motive of his criticism throughout may be said to have been his conviction that poetry in general, and comedy and tragedy in particular, those ' excelling parts of poesy ' as Sidney had called them, were altogether in a bad way.   And, inspired by Sidney, he therefore recalls the lofty nature of true poetry, points out what seemed to him defects in contemporary drama, and submits new dramatic theories with a view to reform in practice.   Least characteristic, perhaps, though reminiscent of Sidney's influence, are his earlier remarks on poetry, written in an enthusiastic vein which later on he abandoned.   Thus already in *Every Man in his Humour* [3] (1598) he laments the condition of Poesy ' patched up in remnants and old worn rags ' ; and recalling her ancient dignity, ' attired in the majesty of art ' ; and imbued with ' sweet philosophy ', he describes her as ' blessed,

---

[1] *Catiline*, To the Reader.
[2] *Every Man out of His Humour*, Induction.
[3] Act v. : a passage omitted from the Folio (1616) version for dramatic reasons.

eternal and most true divine '. Then, too, in *The Poetaster* (1601) the same rhapsodic note is sounded. There ' sweet poesy ' is described as the ' most abstract and perfect of all earthly faculties ' ;[1] and men are urged to distinguish between those ' jaded wits that run a broken pace for common hire ',[2]

> And the high rapture of a happy muse
> Borne on the wings of her immortal thought,
> That kicks at earth with a disdainful heel
> And beats at heaven gates with her bright hoofs.

And, once again, in the Dedicatory Epistle to *Volpone* (1606) he returns to the same theme, but now in more sober vein. He mentions, for instance, as current defects, improprieties of phrase, racked metaphors, and lack of sense ; and he laments that the poet was no longer the moral educator of mankind. The principal end of poetry, he maintains, was ' to inform men in the best reason of living ', to instruct the young, to inspire men to virtue, to interpret Nature and teach things human and divine ; and he states his intention of ' raising the despised head of poesy again ', and of restoring her to her ' primitive habit, feature and majesty '.

Meanwhile his chief interest lay in ' stage-poetry ', that is, in the drama ; and he explains, to begin with, what he found defective in the plays of his time, apart from abundant ' ribaldry, blasphemy and licence ' ; though not all dramatists, he adds, ' were embarked in this bold adventure for hell '.[3] Of the Playwrights' Quarrel (1599–1602) but little need here be said. In arrogant fashion Jonson had censured Marston, Dekker, and others for certain literary and personal faults, to which Dekker had retorted by labelling Jonson as ' a mere sponge, nothing but humours and observation ', while Marston had charged him with ' filching by translation '. The battle was vigorously sustained by Jonson in *Cynthia's Revels* and *The Poetaster* (1601) ; but the whole affair was little more than an unedifying display of personalities, devoid of critical value. Of greater significance are his remarks on earlier methods and standards, as when, for instance, he ridicules the bombast of Kyd's *Spanish Tragedy* in the light of Bobadil's ill-judged praise of its ' well-penned ' lines.[4] Later on he adds that the pre-eminence formerly assigned to *Jeronimo* and *Andronicus* was a foolish judgment, then long out of date ; and at the same time he condemns those later ' romantic ' plays in which Nature was flouted, and which dealt with such themes as ' the sword and buckler age of Smithfield ', or with

[1] v. *ad. init.*
[2] I. i. *ad fin.*
[3] *Volpone*, Address.
[4] *Every Man in his Humour*, I. v. 45 ff.

' servant-monsters, . . . tales, tempests and such like drolleries ' [1]
—a palpable reference to Shakespeare's later romances.

His main indictment, however, is formulated in the Prologue
to *Every Man in his Humour*, an addition made to the revised
version of that play (1612 or earlier), and therefore representative
of his mature judgment. Here, once again, Sidney's influence
becomes perceptible, Jonson's list of ' ill customs ' being little
more than a patchwork of sentences drawn from the *Apology* and
relating to comedy, tragedy, and history. Thus he notes the
general neglect of the Unity of time in presenting ' a child, now
swaddled, to proceed man, and then shoot up past three-score
years '. He also ridicules the flagrant absurdities of historical
plays with their ' rusty swords ' and sesquipedalian words ; or
again, the use of the Chorus ' to waft you o'er the seas ', as a
device rendered necessary by failure to observe the Unity of
place. And among other stage artifices of which he disapproves
were ' the creaking thrones ' let down when gods interfered, ' the
nimble squib . . . to make afeared the gentlewomen ', the
trundling of cannon balls to simulate thunder, or again, the roll
of drums to suggest a tempest—all melodramatic devices called
into being by the nature of extravagant plots. What he objects
to in contemporary plays was, in short, their apparently unreasoned art, their blind following of outworn traditional practices.
The drama, he contended, was crude, unreal, fantastic ; it had
lost touch with life ; and moreover, he added, it no longer served
any moral purpose.

Not content, however, with indicating ' popular errors ', he
attempts, both by precept and example, to inculcate sounder
dramatic methods ; and his main theorizing, in the first place,
relates to comedy—a fact not without its significance, for the
greatest importance was attached by many to that dramatic
form. Thus Castiglione in his *Courtier* had held that the comic
writer above all expressed the true image of human life ; while
Scaliger likewise maintained that of poetry in general comedy
was the first and true form (*paene omnium et primum et verum*)
since its matter was wholly invented by the poet.[2] For the basic
ideas of his conception of comedy Jonson draws once again on
Sidney, who had defined it as treating of ' common errors of our
life . . . in ridiculous and scornful fashion ', so as to open men's
eyes to the nature of those errors and to laugh them out of court.
This general Renascence idea is now adopted by Jonson, though
not without some differences ; and thus he gives to his theory

---

[1] *Bartholomew Fair* (1614), Induction.
[2] *Poetice*, i. 2.

something of an independent colouring, together with certain caveats designed to correct the elastic notions of the comic art which then prevailed.

His first care, in view of the extravagant fancies of comic plots since Lyly's day, is to insist on the need for greater realism, so as to bring comedy into closer touch with life, and to make it once again a true *imitatio vitae* or ' image of the times '. Sidney had pointed out that ' we delight in things that have a conveniency (i.e. conformity) to ourselves or to the general nature ' ; and now Jonson's demand is for ' deeds and language such as men do use ', as well as for characters of a more realistic kind.[1] Realism, it is true, was no new element in English comedy. It had been abundantly present in plays like *Gammer Gurton's Needle*, and a movement in that direction had already become visible in the plays of Dekker, Middleton, and others. But Jonson was the first to emphasize its value as an element in comedy ; and his criticism marks a reaction against the ' romanticism ' of Shakespeare and others.

At the same time he explains that the business of comedy was ' to sport with human follies, not with crimes ',[2] a description in keeping with Sidney's ' common errors ', and with his prohibition of laughter ' at sinful things '. To this general statement, however, Jonson gives a new turn by identifying ' human follies ' with ' humours ', a fashionable term which, he allows, was ' racked and tortured ' in his day, being loosely used for any whim or affectation, but one to which he now proposes to give a more precise meaning. With the help of medieval physiology he explains that physical and mental qualities were determined by the mixture of certain fluids or humours in the body, and that there were four cardinal humours, choler, melancholy, phlegm, and blood, corresponding to the four primeval elements. Moreover, in each normal personality, he adds, there was a natural balance of humours which determined the ' complexion ' or temperament of the individual ; whereas an abnormal mixture disturbed the balance, led to excess of some one quality and resulted in those ' follies ' or foibles with which comedy should deal. As he himself states

> When some one peculiar quality
> Doth so possess a man, that it doth draw
> All his affects, his spirits, and his powers,
> In their confluctions, all to run one way,
> This may be truly said to be a Humour.[3]

[1] *Every Man in his Humour*, Prologue.   [2] *ibid.*
[3] *Every Man Out of his Humour*, Induction.

Mere passing caprice, however, would not suffice, any more than trifling affectations of dress, or external tricks of mere clowning, and he adds

> That a rook, in wearing a pyed feather,
> The cable hat-band, or the three-piled ruff,
> A yard of shoe-tye, or the Switzer's knot
> On his French garters, should affect a humour,
> O, 'tis more than most ridiculous.[1]

This, in brief, is Jonson's prescription for his comedy of humours. His characters, illustrative of 'human follies' were something other than English copies of Roman types. They were rather the outcome of his desire for realism and verisimilitude. Yet in practice they shared in the defects of those Roman types ; and in their rigidity, their one-sidedness, and their element of caricature, they lacked something of the necessary truth to life.

Then, too, concerning the function of comedy in general he has also something to say ; and here again he follows Sidney in regarding comedy as an instrument of ethical reform, a means whereby 'the time's deformity' might be 'anatomized in every nerve and sinew '.[2]   To him, in short, the comic poet is primarily a social monitor, condemning by means of satire and ridicule ; though elsewhere he defines the function of comedy as that of ' imitating justice and instructing to life ', of inculcating ' purity of language ' and of stirring up ' gentle affections (i.e. emotions) '.[3] What is striking in such statements is the stress laid on satirical and didactic intention, and the minimizing of laughter as a legitimate end.   Sidney had conceived of laughter as intimately bound up with comedy ; though he had been at pains to distinguish between farcical laughter and laughter productive of inward delight.   With most contemporaries also the amusement of playgoers had sufficed.   With Jonson, however, the provoking of laughter is merely incidental, a means to an end, and is apparently limited to laughter of a satirical kind.[4]   And here, once again, Jonson seems to be reacting against the practices of his day, this time in favour of a didactic art.

Such, then, is Jonson's theory of comedy ; and not without its significance is the claim he makes that in it he had evolved something new, something different from ancient comedy.   He points out, for instance, that the unhappy ending of *Volpone* was not in accordance with ' the strict rigour of Comic law ',[5]

---

[1] *Every Man Out of his Humour*, Induction.   [2] *ibid.*
[3] *Volpone*, Ded. Epistle, *ad fin.*   [4] See p. 330 *infra.*
[5] *Volpone*, Ded. Epistle, *ad fin.*

though he also notes that ancient comedies had not always ended joyfully. Here however, he asserts, his breach of the law had been intentional and had been dictated by his doctrine that the function of comedy was ' to imitate justice and instruct to life '. Then, too, in connexion with *Every Man Out of his Humour* [1] he confesses to a violation of the recognized laws of comedy, in that he had failed to provide for Terence's division of acts and scenes, the true number of actors, the use of a Chorus, or an observance of the Unity of time. All these, however, he describes as ' too nice requirements ' ; and tracing briefly the history of comedy from early classical times, he explains how it had developed from ' a simple and continued song ' to the master-pieces of Aristophanes, though later innovations came also from Menander and Plautus, whose changes had been made ' according to the disposition of those times in which they lived '. This then is Jonson's defence of the non-classical nature of his comedy. ' I see not ', he writes, ' but we should enjoy the same licence . . . as they did ; and not be tied to those strict and regular forms which the niceness of a few . . . would thrust upon us.'

In view of this serious attempt to legislate for a new English comedy it is somewhat surprising to find that Jonson has but little at this date to say regarding tragedy, that dramatic form on which Italian critics (following Aristotle) had written at length, and which to-day would seem to have been the greatest of Elizabethan triumphs. What he does say, however, is highly significant, for here again, as in comedy, he deliberately breaks away from classical canons. This is seen, for instance, when in commenting on his tragedy *Sejanus* [2] (1605) he freely allows that, judged by ancient standards, it was clearly irregular, since it neither observed the Unity of time nor did it make use of a proper Chorus. At the same time he notes that no modern dramatist had so far complied successfully with those require-ments ; and what was more, such requirements, he maintains, were unnecessary and almost impossible in plays intended for a contemporary audience. In his opinion it was not possible ' to observe the old state and splendour of dramatic poems with preservation of any popular delight '. And here he joins forces with most of his fellow-dramatists in recognizing that the nature of contemporary audiences was a factor to be taken into account in dramatic creation. It was a matter which he proposed to treat more fully in his projected *Observations on Horace's Ars Poetica*, a work which took the form of a dialogue between

[1] Induction.   [2] To the Readers.

Criticus (i.e. Donne) and himself, was actually written by 1619, but was unfortunately destroyed by fire some four years later.[1]

Meanwhile his conception of tragedy may to some extent be gathered from his claim to have embodied in *Sejanus* [2] what he regarded as the essential qualities of that dramatic form, namely, 'truth of argument (i.e. verisimilitude), dignity of persons, gravity and height of elocution (i.e. a lofty style) and fullness and frequency of sentence (i.e. sententious precepts) '. From this it is clear that what he has in mind is the Senecan, as distinguished from the Aristotelian, conception of tragedy, a conception previously illustrated by Sidney in his comment on *Gorboduc*, and represented also in Jonson's own practice. And this is borne out by the methods employed in *Catiline*, for instance, where he makes use of the Senecan Prologue (Sylla's ghost) and Choruses between the Acts. Nowhere is there any trace of Aristotelian doctrine, of such matters as tràgic error or tragic pity. His tragic plots are reminiscent rather of the medieval motive, the sudden fall from prosperity to adversity ; and in his occasional remarks on *protasis, epitasis, catastasis*, and *catastrophe*, he is following Scaliger [3] (not Aristotle) who had described these divisions as *partes legitimae sine quibus nequit Fabula constare*. For the rest his idea of tragedy was largely dictated by the same considerations as had given rise to his idea of comedy, namely, a demand for realism and moral teaching. Thus his tragic plots are little more than ancient conspiracies depicted with fidelity ; and of special significance is his remark that the historical details and learned quotations therein are due not to mere pedantry but to a desire to ' show his integrity in the story ',[4] in other words, its truth to life. And as for moral teaching, the main motive in each instance is the overthrow of wickedness with a view to ' imitating justice and instructing to life '. The truth was that, like most of his contemporaries in practice, and like Webster later in direct statement, he claimed new liberty for English tragedy in deference to contemporary conditions. And in his conception of tragedy the classical element is reduced to a minimum, as was shown by his prodigal use of time and place, or again, by the abundance and variety of his incidents and characters.

From this it will be seen that Jonson as a dramatic critic is but superficially a follower of classical tradition. His plays contain much classical learning but little classical technique ; and in his theorizing during his main activities as a dramatist,

---

[1] See *Underwoods*, lxi.
[2] To the Readers.
[3] *Poetice*, I. ix.
[4] *Sejanus*, To the Readers.

that is, up to 1616, he stands nearer to his ' romantic ' contemporaries than is sometimes supposed, by reason of his bold and original efforts to devise a new English drama. Even during this period, however, signs of his approval of classical artistic principles are not wholly wanting. Thus commenting in one place on the custom of playgoers to commend writers as they did ' fencers or wrestlers, who come in robustiously and are received for the braver fellows ', he points out the primary need for a conscious art. ' There is a great difference ', he states,[1] ' between those that utter all they can, however unfitly, and those that use election and a mean. For it is only the disease of the unskilful to think rude things greater than polished or scattered more numerous (i.e. rhythmical) than composed.' Here he is voicing the principle of selection and moderation as opposed to mere copiousness, a commonplace reminiscent of both Quintilian and Scaliger.[2] And the same demand for an ordered art is enunciated elsewhere when he holds that a good play is like ' a skein of silk which if you take by the right end you may wind off at pleasure '.[3] Of Jonson's inborn classical tendencies there can be little doubt ; though his reputation as a classical critic rests largely on his posthumous *Discoveries* (1641), in which he would seem to have made a closer study of classical and Aristotelian principles, endorsing and preserving his findings in that most interesting and valuable work. And of the significance of that collection something will be said later.

[1] *Alchemist* (1612), Preface : cf. *Discoveries*, § 63.
[2] *Inst. Or.* II. xii. 2–3 : *Poetice*, v. 3.
[3] *Magnetic Lady* (1635), Induction : cf. *Discoveries*, § 120.

CHAPTER IX

LATER THEORIZING: BACON, CHAPMAN, BOLTON, JONSON,
REYNOLDS, AND ALEXANDER

IN the meantime the increased liveliness in the critical sphere
which had begun in the last decade of the 16th Century was
continued, though on different lines, in the opening decades of
the century that followed, with the result of further developments
in literary theorizing. The period was one of intellectual ferment
in which new influences were brought to bear from many quarters,
and a new critical atmosphere was generated in which scholarship, hitherto overshadowed by religious and political controversies, now played a considerable part. Religious questions,
it is true, still occupied men's minds. ' I come from England ',
wrote Grotius in 1613, ' where . . . theologians are . . . the
reigning authorities.' But despite this fact, not a little concern
was shown with literary matters, and the discussions that followed
were mainly from new angles and were fortified by learning
gathered from many sources. Thus along with the silent revolu-
tion in poetry that was taking place at the time there became
visible a belated revival of Humanistic enthusiasm for learning
which made of the early 17th Century a sort of aftermath of the
15th-Century Italian Renascence, and one of the most learned
periods in English history. It was a development due in part
to the multiplication of grammar schools; partly also to the
collecting of manuscripts and the founding of libraries, interests
inspired by the Society of Antiquaries founded by Matthew
Parker in 1572; though further encouragement was derived
from the literary pretensions and scholarly tastes of the reigning
monarch, James I. At the same time the ancient classics were
now regarded, not merely as models of style, but as sources of
wisdom; a keener study of patristic writings was fostered by
the Catholic reaction; renewed interest was aroused in early
Renascence authorities such as Pico and Vives; and while the
freedom of the scientific intellect from the bondage of authority
was being claimed by Bacon, not without its effect was the
influence of foreign scholars, such as Casaubon, Heinsius, and
others, who were in direct touch with English men of letters.
Altogether at this date learning may be said to have begun to
organize itself in England. A generation of scholars appeared,
devoted to classical, patristic, historical, and even Anglo-Saxon

studies, and including among their numbers Sir Henry Savile and Sir Robert Cotton, Camden and Spelman, Richard Carew, Selden, Burton, and a host of others. It is against this scholarly and antiquarian background that the new direction now given to literary discussion is best appreciated. And in connexion with the development of the critical movement it is not irrelevant to recall the abortive attempt of Edmund Bolton to form an alliance of scholars on the decline of the Society of Antiquaries in 1616. An ambitious scheme for a royal Academy of letters was drawn up by Bolton some nineteen years before the establishment of the French Academy by Richelieu (1635). It was approved by James I; but the royal sanction being withheld until after the King's death in 1625, the project was finally dismissed by Charles I. Meanwhile Bolton had compiled a list of prospective members which included Ben Jonson, Chapman, Drayton, Sir William Alexander, and Sir John Beaumont; and these, together with Bacon and Bolton himself, were among the main contributors to literary criticism at this date. Their animating purpose in general differed from that of their predecessors in that they no longer concerned themselves primarily with earlier practical needs, with such matters as the defence of poetry and the stage, or with the art of poetry and dramatic theory. Their aim was rather to inculcate a more erudite approach to certain aspects of literature—the nature of poetry, the methods of translating, of writing history, and the like—and also tentatively to act as arbiters of taste by means of judgments passed on contemporary writers. To the former of these purposes most attention was devoted; and attempts were made to revive the teaching of antiquity as well as certain doctrines of 15th-Century Italian scholars. In the works that resulted there was consequently much that was interesting, much also that was abstruse and pedantic; and while immediate problems were but occasionally considered, for the most part the courtly charm and urbanity of such writers as Sidney, Harington, and Daniel were now exchanged for the more sober, less picturesque, vein of early Humanist scholars.

Illustrative in the first place of the new departures in critical activities of the early 17th Century is the contribution to literary theory made by Francis Bacon in his *Advancement of Learning* (1605) and elsewhere. To literary discussion, it is true, he devoted no one particular work; but in his survey of learning he has not a little to say of literary interest, and his critical views reveal not only a depth and variety of learning but also a rational trend and originality of thought, as well as a new sense of the value of historical and psychological considerations. Of interest, to begin with, is his conception of poetry, a term which, he explains, involved two separate and distinct ideas. It was said to stand, first, for an art of expression in words ; and, secondly, for the thought conveyed by means of that art. With poetry as an art, however, he does not attempt to deal, remarking merely that it was ' in measure of words for the most part restrained ',[1] that is, subject to the restraint of rules of its own. It is to the thought conveyed, the subject-matter of poetry, that his treatment is confined. To him poetry is ' a part of learning ' ; and so on the perennial question whether subject-matter or form was the essential element in poetry Bacon thus takes up a definite position.

Concerning the nature of poetry, or what he regards as its essential element, he is however explicit ; and he describes it forthwith as ' extremely licensed ', and as having to do with that part of man's understanding known as the ' imagination '.[2] Here Bacon, like Sidney and others before him, is adopting a term of medieval physiology, the fanciful nature of which had been expounded by Pico della Mirandola [3] and later by the Spaniard, Juan Huarte, whose *Examen de Ingenios* (1575) had been translated by Richard Carew in 1594 ; and he is therefore at some pains to explain his notion of that human faculty. In one place, for instance, he points out that reason is the ultimate judge of what ' sense sendeth over to imagination ' ; moreover, that in the persuasion wrought by eloquence ' imagination paints and disguises the true appearance of things ' in commending matters to the reason ; [4] while elsewhere he states yet more categorically that ' the imagination being not tied to the laws of matter may at pleasure join that which nature hath severed and sever that which nature hath joined, and so make unlawful matches and divorces of things '.[5] Hence poetry, as a product of the ' imagination ', he adds, is ' nothing else but feigned history ', in other words, narrative of a purely fanciful kind, corresponding to nothing in life itself. Yet this distortion of fact involved in the poetic process he holds to be capable of defence. Its use, he explains, was ' to give some shadow of satisfaction to the mind of man in those points wherein the nature of things doth deny it, . . . by reason whereof there is (presented) . . . a more ample greatness, a more exact goodness, and a more absolute

---

[1] *Advancement of Learning*, II. iv. I.   [2] *ibid.*
[3] See p. 25 *supra*.   [4] *Adv. of L.*, II. xii. I.
[5] *ibid.* II. iv. I.

variety, than can be found in the nature of things'.[1] Thus poetry with its chartered freedom, he maintains, represents deeds 'greater and more heroical', events rarer and more surprising, and actions that work out more in accordance with poetic justice than can be found in ordinary life, in this way satisfying man's longings for a more perfect world. In other words, the poetic process, despite its element of distortion, conduces to 'magnanimity, morality and delectation'; and in general, it has an uplifting effect 'by submitting the shows of things to the desires of the mind, whereas reason doth buckle and bow the mind unto the nature of things'.[2] At the same time it is important to note that Bacon nowhere claims for this 'feigned history' any correspondence with the truth of things. For him it is merely a form of wishful thinking, a means of palliating man's dissatisfaction with life as it actually is : and this is confirmed by his disdainful reference elsewhere to 'the enchanted palaces of the poets who build them at little cost'. It is therefore incorrect to say that 'Bacon and Aristotle do not differ in their conception of poetry'.[3] With regard to Sidney such a statement would be more or less true ; but for Bacon poetry is nothing more than 'a pleasure or play of imagination (i.e. fancy)',[4] something not to be taken too seriously. His imperfect appreciation thus recalls the earlier patronizing attitude of the Humanists ; and his excuse for the brevity of his exposition of poetry, when he turns with reverence to treat of that weightier subject, philosophy, is that 'it is not good to stay too long in the theatre'.

Yet he has also something more to say about poetry ; and of interest is the rational classification of the 'kinds'[5] which he proposes as something new, and as the most appropriate division —a matter on which he enlarges in *De Augmentis* (1623),[6] the Latin version of his *Advancement of Learning*. That classification he bases on his conception of poetry as 'feigned history'; and since poetry is said to resemble history in dealing with deeds of the past, his arrangement is determined by the different treatments accorded to such deeds. First, there is narrative (i.e. epic) poetry, with heroic actions and love as its main themes ; secondly, representative (i.e. dramatic) poetry consisting of a vivid representation of past deeds in action; and thirdly, allusive or parabolical

---

[1] *ibid.* II. iv. 2 : cf. Sir John Davies, *Nosce Teipsum* (1599).
[2] *Adv. of L.* II. iv. 2.
[3] J. E. Spingarn, *Critical Essays of the 17th Century*, I. xi.
[4] *Adv. of L.* II. xii. 1.   [5] *ibid.* II. xiii.
[6] Bacon, *Works*, ed. Ellis and Spedding, pp. 517–20.

(i.e. allegorical) poetry, in which certain deeds are presented as symbolical of ideas or doctrines. From his classification, it will be noted, he excludes such forms as satires, elegies, epigrams and odes ; and this he does on the ground that they are concerned, not with actions, but with the inner life of man, and are therefore related to philosophy or rhetoric.[1]

Then, too, concerning those ' kinds ' he has also some remarks to make.[2] Thus epic poetry, he states, treats of the dignity of man, which history for the most part denied ; while it was also said to conduce most to that ' magnanimity, morality, and delectation ' which he attributed to poetry in general. For the drama, again, which brought all the world on to the stage (*quae theatrum habet pro mundo*) considerable value was claimed, provided it was not abused. The modern stage, he held, was too often regarded as mere light amusement (*pro re ludicra*), except when it consisted of biting satire ; whereas among the ancients its aim had been that of instruction and its function a sort of ' plectrum ' of the mind (*animorum plectrum quoddam*). And to this he added one of his most illuminating psychological comments. ' It is most true ', he states, ' that the minds of men are more susceptible to emotional effects (*affectibus et impressionibus*) when gathered together in a crowd than when they are solitary ' ;[3] and this early recognition of the psychology of the crowd throws a flood of light on dramatic effects. It is to allegorical poetry, however, that he devotes most attention, as treating of things both human and divine, while appealing to reason and ' imagination ' alike. Such poetry, he explains, besides conveying valuable teaching was useful also in imparting secrets of religion or politics obscurely, when it was so desired. It was a treatment, he maintained, that had the authority of Biblical parables as well as of ancient fables, as was seen, for instance, in the riddle of the Sphinx, the fables of Aesop, or the apophthegms of ancient sages. But while he allows that a deeper meaning (*sensus mysticus*) might be read into many stories relating to the ancient gods, he is nevertheless sceptical of the allegorical theory of poetry in general. In many of the ancient stories, he contends, ' the fable was first and the exposition afterwards devised, rather than that the moral was first and thereupon the fable framed '.[4] Chrisippus (3rd Century B.C.), he notes, had obviously read into earlier poetry Stoic doctrines which could not have been present in the minds of the old poets concerned ; while Homer's stories had certainly ' no such inward-

---

[1] *de Augmentis*, II. xiii.   [2] *ibid.*
[3] *ibid.*   [4] *Adv. of L.* II. iv. 4.

ness in his own meaning '.[1] The question, however, was one on which he preserved an open mind. Allegory, he allows, was more ancient than argument ; it was also rightly applied to the interpretation of the Scriptures which, ' written for all ages, have in them infinite springs and streams of doctrine '.[2] But that it formed part of the essence of poetry, of this he is extremely doubtful ; and here was his rational judgment pronounced on the theory of poetry widely held at the time.

Nor are his further occasional comments on poetry without their interest, despite his imperfect appreciation of its true nature. Thus he recognizes, for instance, its affinity with music,[3] or again, its greater facility, compared with philosophy, in expressing emotions and passions ; while in regard to style, it was held to be not much inferior to oratory itself,[4] as earlier Humanists were wont to concede. On contemporary questions, too, he has something to say. He conceives, for example, that poetry could be written in prose form as well as in verse ; [5] and in general he decries a slavish following of the ancients. For one thing he recommends a development along the lines of native genius. ' Though men in learned tongues ', he states,[6] ' do tie themselves to the ancient measures, yet in modern languages it seemeth to me as free to make new measures of verses as of dances.' ' In these things ', he cogently added, ' the sense is better judge than the art ' ; and he quotes Martial's dictum that at feasts the guests rather than the cooks have to be considered.[7] Elsewhere he recalls that *antiquitas saeculi* is but *juventus mundi* ; [8] and condemning ' the servile expressing antiquity ', he states further that such imitation of the ancients tended to hinder development. In short, what he has to say about the teaching of antiquity, and of Aristotle in particular,[9] is not without its bearing on the literary art. On the other hand, he also denounces an excessive desire for novelty which ' cannot be content to add but it must deface '.[10] His advice is therefore to combine both convention and change, to discover what is good in ancient doctrine and methods, and then ' to make progression '.

Yet poetry after all was not Bacon's main interest. To him, as to the earlier Humanists, logic and rhetoric were ' the gravest of sciences, being the arts of arts, the one for judgment, the

---

[1] cf. Rabelais, *Pantagruel*, Prol. on the allegorical interpretation of Homer by Plutarch and others.
[2] *Adv. of L.* II. xxv. 17.   [3] *ibid.* II. iv. 2.   [4] *ibid.* II. iv. 5.
[5] *ibid.* II. iv. 1.   [6] *ibid.* II. xvi. 5.   [7] See p. 244 *supra*.
[8] *Adv. of L.* I. v. 1.   [9] *ibid.* I. iv. 12.   [10] *ibid.* I. v. 1.

other for ornament ' ; [1] and he has some interesting things to say on ' eloquence ' or style in general. To begin with, of the vicious results of an excessive preoccupation with style for its own sake—' delicate learning ', as he calls it—he has no doubts ; and he illustrates his views by a historical survey of the 16th-Century stylistic studies, their causes and effects.[2] Thus the initial cause he ascribes to the zeal of early Reformers, who in attempts to confute the doctrines of Rome had gone for their arguments to ancient authors ' which had long time slept in libraries '. Admirers, perforce, of those ancient styles, so different from those of medieval Schoolmen, they had devoted themselves anew to linguistic and rhetorical studies ; and the movement, so Bacon explains, was one which ' grew speedily to excess, for men began to hunt more after words than matter '. Hence the persistent striving for choice phrases, periodic effects and rhyming endings, together with an abundant use of tropes and figures ; and all to the neglect of sound thought and subject-matter. By Ascham and others, he recalls, the teaching of Cicero and Hermogenes had been freely expounded. The flowing styles of Demosthenes and Cicero, moreover, were regarded as the highest models ; and (in De Augmentis) [3] a noteworthy reference is also made to the more concise and pointed style of the younger Seneca and Tacitus, a style, added Bacon, which, ' not so long ago ' had begun to be acceptable to modern ears, though decried by some as being clever and not genuine, besides being affected and lacking in grace. Such then is Bacon's historical survey of rhetorical activities during the 16th Century. And it is not without its significance in the critical development ; though in attributing the main cause of such activities to early Reformers he overlooks other important factors, such as Quintilian's influence, or again, the natural desire of scholarly courtiers to acquire a heightened beauty of style.

At the same time he is not unmindful of the value of ' eloquence ', whether it be for illuminating ' the obscurity of philosophy ' or for exercising persuasion in public life. And he therefore commends to his readers the study of rhetoric or the art of eloquence as conducive to the formation of an effective style. He recalls, to begin with, that Plato had been unfair in regarding rhetoric as ' a voluptuary art ' and in ' resembling it to cookery that did mar wholesome meats ' ; [4] though this attitude, he recognizes, had been justly occasioned by hostility

[1] Adv. of L. II. Ded. § 12.   [2] ibid. I. iv. 2–4.
[3] Works, ed. Ellis and Spedding, i. 452.
[4] Adv. of L. II. xviii. 3 : cf. Plato, Gorgias, 462 C.

to the false rhetoric of the Sophists. He then proceeds to give reasons for the cultivation of rhetoric as a means of adding emotional value to expression. Rhetoric, he explains, is to the ' imagination ' what logic is to the understanding, its function being ' to apply reason to imagination for the better moving of the will ' ;[1] and he recalls in passing the ancient distinction, ascribed to Zeno, of logic as the closed fist and rhetoric as the open palm.[2] Moreover, if human emotions, he adds, were merely obedient to reason, then ' naked proofs ' or sheer argument would suffice to convince readers ; but in view of the subtle character of the emotions some further appeal was necessary. In other words, ' reason would become captive . . . if eloquence of persuasions . . . did not win the imagination '.[3] So that rhetoric was something more than a means of perverting facts or producing false impressions by means of fine language. It was, in short, a genuine art which, unlike logic, called for discrimination in its appeal to auditors or readers. Further into the details of rhetorical study, however, he does not go, his object being merely to recall certain basic principles, or, as he himself puts it, ' to stir the earth a little about the roots of the science '.[4] Yet two caveats of his are perhaps worthy of note as emphasizing the need for clear and natural expression. There is, for instance, his warning against obscurity in style resulting from a loose use of words (Idols of the market-place) characteristic of the ' vulgar sort '.[5] He recalls with approval the familiar commonplace attributed to Aristotle, *loquendum ut vulgus sentiendum ut sapientes*;[6] but he also reminds his readers that ordinary speech is often vague in its use of language, and that clarification of terms was therefore needed, especially in controversial writings. Or, again, there is his denunciation of a laboured or pedantic style. Thus ' speech that is uttered with labour or difficulty, . . . that savoureth of the affectation of art, . . . or is framed after the imitation of some pattern of excellence, all this ', he states, ' though never so excellent, hath somewhat servile ' ;[7] and he advocates accordingly utterance of a natural and un-affected kind.

These remarks on poetry and rhetoric may be said to represent Bacon's main contribution to literary theory. At the same time scattered throughout his works are further comments on literary matters which, though brief and varied in kind, are nevertheless worth noting, since they point to a widening of

[1] *ibid.* II. xviii. 2. [2] *ibid.* II. xviii. 5 : cf. Quin. *Inst. Or.* : II. 20. 7.
[3] *ibid.* [4] *ibid.* II. xviii. 2.
[5] *Adv. of L.* II. xiv. 11. [6] See p. 86 *supra*. [7] *Adv. of L.* I. Ded. § 2.

critical interests at this date. It is not only that he reveals something of the old Humanistic spirit in his attitude to literature generally. For him books enshrine the immortal thoughts of men, rendering those thoughts ' capable of perpetual renovation ', by generating ideas in the minds of others and giving rise to infinite actions and thoughts in succeeding ages ; so that letters, he states, are like ships which ' pass through the vast seas of time and make ages so distant to participate of the wisdom, . . . the one of the other '.[1] But apart from this glowing eulogy he has also some practical remarks to make on books themselves, and on ancient texts in particular, as presented to contemporary readers. Thus he notes how textual critics had rashly presumed that that which they understood not was ' false set down ', and how that as a result of their emendations ' the most corrected texts ' were ' commonly the least correct ' ; while, again, editors of such texts, he adds, were wont to ' blanch (i.e. avoid) the obscure places and discourse upon the plain '.[2] More relevant to our present purpose is his recommendation that brief appreciations of literary works should be prepared for the guidance of readers,[3] thus heralding the most fruitful kind of criticism that was to develop in later years. Of definite critical value, too, is the hint casually thrown out that ' the times often give great light to the true interpretation (of texts) ',[4]—a basic principle of historical criticism, which Colet alone had previously grasped and had applied in his interpretation of Biblical literature. Equally interesting, however, and certainly more surprising, is his denunciation of the system of patronage as it affected literature.[5] ' The modern dedication of books . . . as to patrons ', he writes, ' is not to be commended ; for that books . . . ought to have no patrons but truth and reason.' And here, by a century and more, he was forestalling the famous Letter of Dr. Johnson (1755), that ' far-famed blast of doom, proclaiming . . . that patronage should be no more ', as Carlyle described it.

Nor is this all ; for of interest, too, are sundry remarks of his relating to various literary forms and to aesthetic matters generally. Thus, for instance, like many of his contemporaries, he is gravely concerned about the defective state of historical writings. Ancient history, with some notable exceptions, he held, consisted mainly of fables and fragments ; whereas English history, too, had hitherto been inadequately treated.[6] The true function of the historian, he maintained, was ' to represent the events themselves, together with the counsels, and to leave . . .

[1] *Adv. of L.* I. viii. 6. [2] *ibid.* II. xix. 1. [3] *ibid.*
[4] *ibid.* [5] *ibid.* I. iii. 9. [6] *ibid.* II. ii. 7.

the conclusions thereupon to . . . every man's judgment ' ; [1]
and, in addition, he recommends the writing of a history of letters
as a means of throwing light on the intellectual life of the past.[2]
Elsewhere he denounces more than once what he calls ' the
canker of epitomes ', those ' corruptions and moths of history
which hindered the development of knowledge ; [3] and, on the
other hand, he is the first to recognize and comment on the essay
form. ' The word " essay " ', he explains,[4] ' is late, but the
thing is ancient ; for Seneca's *Epistles to Lucilius* . . . are but
essays, that is dispersed meditations.' Then, too, he has here
and there some highly suggestive remarks on art in general ;
as when, for instance he states, as if in anticipation of later
' romantic ' ideals, that ' there is no excellent beauty that hath
not some strangeness in the proportion '.[5] Or again, there is
his further comment that in the sister arts of music and painting
the artist attains excellence, not by rule, but by ' a kind of
felicity ' [6] which enables him to achieve ' those nameless graces
which no methods teach '. Moreover, not without its significance
is the fact that in his theorizing he adopts for the most part
psychological methods. Thus the emotional value of discord
in music he describes as that of heightening the pleasure of the
harmony that follows ; while the effects of an occasional avoidance of the normal close or cadence in music are said to resemble
those of the rhetorical figure, *praeter expectationem*, since, as he
explains, ' there is a pleasure even in being deceived '.[7]

Such then is Bacon's contribution to literary and artistic
ideas ; and despite its casual nature and its limited scope, it is
of interest in the critical development. His conception of poetry
may be inadequate, his treatment of rhetoric merely general ;
while his interest in contemporary literature is limited, possibly
by imperfect literary sympathies, more certainly by his preoccupation with scientific matters and by his strange distrust of
English and other modern languages, which, he maintained,
would ' play the bankrupt with books '.[8] At the same time his
theorizing on literature is of a germinal nature, everywhere
characterized by an independence of thought, which, without
relying on traditional classical doctrine, evolved new theories
built up in logical and systematic fashion. His methods, moreover, are throughout of a psychological kind ; he works from first
principles and is for ever tracing the affinities of art with human

---

[1] *ibid*. II. ii. 12.   [2] *ibid*. II. i. 2.   [3] *ibid*. I. v. 4 ; II. ii. 4.
[4] *Essays* (1612 ed.). Dedication.   [5] *ibid*. XLIII.   [6] *ibid*.
[7] *Sylva Sylvarum*, cent. ii. 113.
[8] *Letter to Toby Matthews* (1623).

nature. Apart from this, many of his casual utterances are highly
suggestive and of first-rate importance ; as, for instance, his
refutation of the allegorical theory of poetry, his advice concerning ' imitation of the ancients ', or again, his explanation
of the principle of ' the psychology of the crowd ' in connexion
with the drama. And, further, in his concern with such matters
as historical writings and the ' mystical ' interpretation of poetry
he anticipates the themes of later writers thus giving new
direction and a wider scope to literary inquiries. Bacon's
writings, it has been said, have always the fascination of deep
waters ; and his scattered critical remarks are not wholly wanting
in that quality.

Further evidence of changes in critical interests at this date
was supplied by signs of a more serious treatment given to the
craft of translation, a problem that was to receive increasing
attention in the course of the century. In the Tudor and
Elizabethan periods there had been no lack of free translations,
often of a racy, and even a startling, kind ; for it was instinctively
felt that too literal a rendering would impair the sense of the
original as well as the style of the new version. As yet, however,
no serious attempt had been made to discuss the real problem.
Whereas in France Dolet's treatise *La Manière de bien traduire
d'une langue en aultre* (1540) had already appeared, in England
occasional comments on the process were all that were forthcoming. Such remarks were mostly of a linguistic kind. Thus
statements had been made that English was fully capable of
expressing the ideas of antiquity ; that it had more in common
than Latin with the idioms of Greek and Hebrew ; and that a
selection of the language used by Englishmen was the fitting
medium of translation. As for the process itself, it was beginning
to be realized that as an art it presented greater difficulties than
original composition ; that each language had its own peculiar
idiom ; that word for word translation had in general to be
sacrificed to preserve the sense of the original ; and that a plain
style, free from ornateness and obscurity, was needed to appeal
to the understanding of the unlearned.[1]

It was in the work of the translators of the Bible, however,
that this earlier phase culminated, with a hint or two of their
animating principles supplied in the Address to the Reader prefixed to *The Authorized Version of the Bible* (1611).[2] A body of
some fifty-four scholars, they entered upon their task with a full
sense of the care and labour involved. Decrying the haste in

---

[1] For fuller details, see E. J. Sweeting, *Early Tudor Criticism*, pp. 23–57.
[2] See Pollard, *Records of the English Bible*, p. 369.

which the *Septuagint* was said to have been prepared, and with
Tyndale's and Coverdale's versions ever before them, they
' feared no reproof for slowness, nor coveted praise for expedi-
tion ' ; but with scrupulous care concerning both subject-matter
and style, free also from self-conscious artistry and vain pedantry,
they endeavoured to produce a correct and acceptable version
by means of untiring revision and by ' ever bringing back to the
anvil what they had hammered '. Implicit criticism is thus
present on every page ; and whereas those nameless graces which
give to their translation its enduring vitality were doubtless
inspired by a kind of felicity and the genius of the age, in one
respect at least the translators seem to have revealed a secret of
their art. Avoiding all ' niceness in words, . . . the next step
to trifling ', as well as a slavish dependence on the letter which
would have obscured the real meaning, they refused ' to tie
themselves to an uniformity of phrasing or to an identity of
words, . . . for ', as they explained, ' there be some words that
be not of the same sense everywhere '. That is to say, where
variety was not misleading they claimed the right to use different
terms to express a given Greek or Hebrew word ; and this free
use of synonyms contributed greatly to the euphony, the flexi-
bility of rhythm and the power of expressing subtle shades of
meaning which are among the distinguishing features of the art
underlying the English Bible.

It was from George Chapman (1559–1634), however, that
this business of translation received yet fuller treatment, when in
the introductory remarks prefixed to the two earlier drafts of
his translation of the *Iliad* (1598), as well as in the later Prefaces
to the *Complete Works of Homer* (1616), he not only expounded
his idea of the process, but also entered on a spirited defence of
Homer, revealing at the same time something of his conception
of poetry. At the outset he makes it clear that his chief aim in
translating had been, first, ' to observe Homer's sentences,
figures and forms of speech, his true sense and height ' ; and then
' to adorn them with figures and forms of oration fitted to the
original in the same tongue to which they are translated '.[1] In
other words, it was necessary to understand Homer's true meaning and to appreciate his qualities ; and then to resort to devices
of expression calculated to reproduce in English some measure
of Homeric effects. His conception of translation has thus to
do not only with subject-matter but also with literary qualities ;
and this implied translation of a free, as opposed to a literal,
kind. For this he claimed the authority of Horace ; and word

[1] Smith, *op. cit.* ii. p. 296.

for word translation he described as nothing more than ' pedantical and absurd affectation ',[1] a process that caused the loss of the free graces of natural speech. Hence, he explains, his liberties in the matter of diction, his ' far-fetched and beyond-sea manner of writing ', which, while avoiding ' ink-pot terms ', embodied new words, ' significant and not ill-sounding '. This procedure he defends as a means of enriching the native language, noting besides, that all other languages had developed along those lines, whereas Chaucer, by whom he would ' authorize true English, had more new words . . . than any man needs to devise now '.[2] Then, too, he commends the use of periphrasis for expressing Homer's sense with greater effect ; and he recalls in support the example of L. Valla, who in his Latin translation of the *Iliad* (1447) had freely resorted to that device.[3] And as for verse-forms, he defends his use of both the fourteener line and the heroic couplet. Homeric verse by reason of its length, he suggests, requires a spacious line in translation ; while elsewhere he holds that ' unless it be in couplets ' Homer shall never be fitly translated in octaves, canzonets and such light measures.[4]

Apart from these remarks on translation the Prefaces of Chapman are notable also for an enthusiastic defence of Homer, in the course of which a savage attack is made on the elder Scaliger, who in his *Poetice*,[5] after a lengthy and detailed comparison of Homer with Virgil, had magisterially declared in favour of the Roman poet and had even asserted that Homer's epics were inferior to Musaeus's *Hero and Leander*. In this apologia of Chapman's is heard an echo of that 15th-Century controversy [6] which, having degenerated into the Virgil-worship of the century following, found in Scaliger its most dogmatic exponent ; and Chapman for his part makes it plain that he himself writes not as a detractor of Virgil but as a vindicator of Homer. Thus Homer, he contends to begin with, was a great original genius, while Virgil wrote in ' a courtly, laborious and imitatory spirit ',[7] freely borrowing from Homer his similes, ideas and characters. Then, too, Homer was said to excel in quality, ' imitating none nor ever worthily imitated of any ', as Velleius Paterculus,[8] he noted, had long ago pointed out ; so that whereas Virgil's work was ' gilt and embroidered silver ', that of Homer was described as ' plain massive gold '. It was true, added Chapman, that

---

[1] Spingarn, *Crit. Essays of the* 17th *Cent.* i. p. 72.
[2] Smith, *op. cit.* ii. p. 305.   [3] Spingarn, *op. cit.* i. p. 70.
[4] Smith, *op. cit.* ii. p. 307.   [5] v. iii.
[6] See p. 32 *supra.*
[7] Smith, *op. cit.* ii. p. 298.   [8] *Historia romana*, i. 5.

Homer's real majesty could not be grasped if read ' capriciously in dismembered fractions '. For a just appreciation ' the whole drift, weight and height ' of his work had first to be estimated. Moreover, he was said to be ' a bottomless fountain ' of learning and wisdom ; all arts (according to Plutarch) [1] were ' to be deduced, confirmed or illustrated from him '. And finally Chapman recalls some of the praises accorded to him from Plato onwards ; [2] how Silius Italicus [3] had represented Scipio as longing in Elysium for him to sing the praises of Rome to wondering nations, how the elder Pliny [4] had described him as ' having given to antiquity her living fire ', while Politian [5] at a later date had maintained that ' in Homer's sun all other ancient poets lost their light ', and that Apollo had confessed Homer to be his equal. As for the censure of the ' soul-blind Scaliger ',[6] Chapman dismisses its author with the biting jibe that his ' diminuation of Homer ' was the only original part of his treatise, and that nowhere in his ' all-countries-exploded filcheries ' was his ' drossy spirit ' more clearly revealed.

But while these remarks on translation and the defence of Homer thus constitute the main substance of Chapman's criticism, not without its interest is the conception of poetry incidentally revealed,[7] a conception which, influenced apparently by the French scholar, Spondanus, translator of Homer's works (1583), is ultimately based on post-classical and patristic teaching. Hence poetry is said to perform best the main duty of man which is ' to sing the glories of God ' ; and since its creation is not merely the outcome of labour and art, its real nature is none other than that of ' a divine infusion '. As such it is held to be something different from ' the bold rhymes of every impudent braggart ' or ' the idle weaving of cobwebs '. It is, in short, of wisdom all compact, and therefore superior to all other branches of know- ledge. Thus poetic fiction, according to Chapman, is no mere licence but a symbolic revelation of the profoundest truth and wisdom ; and of this his interpretation of *Achilles Shield* (1598) as ' a divine rapture ',[8] in which the whole world is depicted, is a good illustration. Moreover, he endorses the esoteric idea of poetry, according to which obscurity of utterance was necessary to conceal truth from the irreverent. Thus poetry, he explains, is ' the flower of the sun and disdains to open to the eye of a candle ; so kings hide their treasure and counsels from the

---

[1] *De vita et poesi Homeri*, ii. i.
[3] *Punica*, Bk. 13.
[5] *Nutricia*.
[7] Spingarn, *op. cit.* i. pp. 67 ff.

[2] Spingarn, *op. cit.* i. pp. 74–6.
[4] *Natural History*, vii. 29.
[6] Smith. *op. cit.* ii. p. 301.
[8] Smith, *op. cit.* ii. p. 297.

vulgar (*ne euilescant*) '. And the interest of this theorizing is two-fold. It points not only to the survival of non-Aristotelian doctrine, but also to that search for abstruse meanings (*sensus mysticus*) in poetry which was characteristic of theorists at this particular date.

Meanwhile a further extension of critical activities becomes perceptible in Edmund Bolton's *Hypercritica* (1618), a work of considerable learning though lacking in literary graces, which represented an attempt to improve the methods of writing history, a field of literature which, he asserted, ' hath as many praises as any Muse among the Nine '. Its immediate occasion would seem to have been the complaint of Sir Henry Savile that ' our historians . . . have defiled the history of England with most fusty fooleries ',[1] and his wish that the handling of history might equal the majesty of the argument. At the same time there were other and more general causes which also fostered interest in this branch of literature. First, there was a widespread consciousness of the defects of Tudor and Elizabethan Chronicles, with their encyclopaedic contents and their strange mixture of fact and legend— ' vast vulgar tomes ', as Bolton described them, ' tumultuary and centonical writings', resembling ' some huge disproportionable temple '.[2] Then, too, during the 16th Century many formal treatises on the subject had appeared in Italy, one of which, Patrizzi's *Della Historia* (1560), had been translated by Thomas Blundeville as *The True Order and Method of writing and reading Histories* (1574) ; and such works had led to a profounder sense of the purpose and methods of writing history. Or again, there was the controversy raging at the time over the authenticity of Geoffrey of Monmouth's *Historia Regum Brittanniae*, with its romantic stories of Brutus and Arthur. Bolton notes that it had been attacked by Giraldus Cambrensis, Whethamstede, Vives, and others, whereas medieval chroniclers, supported by Leland, Dr. Keyes (Caius) and many Welsh antiquarians had accepted the work as genuine.[3] And recalling further that Geoffrey himself had implied that his Welsh source was nothing more than mere satire or rhapsody pieced together from bardic ballads, he therefore questions the historical value of such work.

In defence of the value of historical writings generally Bolton, in the first place, quotes the testimony of various authorities, including those of Bede and William of Malmesbury. Cicero, too, it was stated, had described it as ' the light of truth and mistress

[1] Spingarn, *op. cit.* i. p. 96.   [2] *ibid.* pp. 97–8.
[3] *ibid.* i. p. 87.

of life ' ; [1] Sir Thomas North had asserted that ' histories are fit for every place, serve for all times, teach the living, revive the dead, so excelling all other books as it is better to see learning in noble men's lives than to read it in philosophers' writing " ; [2] and, again, there was Casaubon's notable reminder that history was ' nothing else but a kind of philosophy using examples '.[3] Then turning to his main theme Bolton refers to particular defects of earlier historians. For one thing, he explains, an adequate sense of the workings of Providence in human affairs had for the most part been wanting, pagan historians having ignored that influence entirely ; whereas Christian writers on the other hand had generally neglected the natural causes of events.[4] Equally flagrant, however, were the prejudices and bias with which history had often been written. Disinterestedness, indeed, he describes as an absolute necessity and the glory of the historian ; [5] and Bede's generous praises of Aidan,[6] in spite of differences of opinion, are recalled as an inspiring example. Such integrity, it was allowed, was often difficult and inconvenient ; but the establishing of the immortal memory of great men was a sacred business. ' There goes a great deal of conscience to the compiling of a history,' [7] wrote Sir Thomas Browne ; and historians, asserted Bolton, should thus refrain from pandering to current prejudices or indulging their own predilections. Moreover, too much reliance, he added, had been placed on wild etymologies.[8] ' The licence of deriving nations from supposed gods and puissant worthies ' was said to be universal. Yet the practice had been condemned by St. Augustine ; and Geoffrey's derivation of the name ' Britain ' from ' Brutus ' was seriously to be questioned.

What, on the other hand, was required from the historian was, first, a strict adherence to facts and a discarding of the fabulous, while early traditions were to be accepted sceptically.[9] Truth was, in short, the essential element, all other qualities being merely subsidiary ; and Bolton recalls how for want of that quality Lucian had condemned Herodotus and others to his hell,[10] and had elsewhere commended plain speaking in advising the historian to call ' a spade a spade ' (τὰ σῦκα σῦκα).[11] At the same time a collection of facts alone was not sufficient. An explana-

---

[1] *De orat.* ii. 9, 36. [2] Preface to his trans. of *Plutarch's Lives.*
[3] Spingarn, *op. cit.* i. p. 98. [4] *ibid.* i. p. 84.
[5] *ibid.* i. pp. 91 ff. [6] *Eccles. History*, iii. 17.
[7] *Religio Medici*, ed. Morison, p. 90.
[8] Spingarn, *op. cit.* i. pp. 89 ff. [9] *ibid.* i. pp. 85, 95.
[10] *True History*, ii. 32. [11] *Teaching of Rhetoric*, § 9.

19

tion of causes was also required ; and Thomas Lodge, it might be noted, in his translation of the *Works of Josephus* (1602) had already emphasized the need for judgment in determining the significance of historical events. Such causes, Bolton allows, are intricate enough ; but he who ' relates events without their premisses and circumstances deserves not the name of historian '.[1] In fact, the main duty of a historian, he adds, is in handling ' the counsels and causes of affairs ' ; and here was said to be the difficulty of historical writing, ' its mystery and also its felicity '.[2] Nor, as his third requirement, does Bolton omit to insist on a fitting style for the historian.[3] Fine expression alone, he states, was no substitute for truth ; for without truth art and style are said to be mere impostures. On the other hand, a good style added lustre to a work and gave delight to the reader, so that both truth and eloquence were needed. And here Bolton is reiterating one of the great doctrines of the early Renascence, namely, the intimate relations existing between wisdom and eloquence.[4] On the matter of style, however, he has little to say except that history should be clothed in the garment of English idiom. As a sort of guide he submits, not without diffidence, a ' tumultuary catalogue ' of ' books of warrantable English ', with comments on their styles.[5] But this, he confesses, was ' rather *parergon* ', or subsidiary to his main purpose, which was that of inculcating truth and judgment in the treatment of history, qualities which were to be displayed in Bacon's *History of Henry VII* (1622).

While, however, such matters as the methods of translation and of writing history were thus engaging critical attention at this date, serious questions relating to poetry were also being discussed by others than Bacon and Chapman. Of minor interest, though worthy of note, are the remarks of Henry Peacham and Sir John Beaumont (1583–1627), elder brother of Francis Beaumont, the dramatist. The former in his *Compleat Gentleman* (1622) had devoted one section (Chapter X) to some consideration of the subject, whereas the latter had addressed to James I certain verses *Concerning the True Form of English Poetry*, which are worthy of note. Peacham's contribution, in the first place, is merely a compilation made up almost wholly of commonplaces relating to poetry drawn from Puttenham's *Arte*, together with judgments on poets, both ancient and modern, based largely on Scaliger's *Poetice*, and the treatment is designed, as the title indicates, to provide a short and easy path to literary

[1] Spingarn, *op. cit.* i. p. 84. [2] *ibid.* i. p. 100.
[3] *ibid.* i. p. 83. [4] See p. 18 *supra.* [5] See pp. 291–2 *infra.*

culture for leisured readers. Thus Strabo's definition of poetry as ' the first philosophy '[1] is quoted, as is also Lucretius's description of it as none other than natural and moral philosophy sweetened with verse, just as honey is placed in the cup to make wormwood pleasing.[2] Or, again, poetry is said to enshrine mysteries, high and divine, to have been employed by St. Paul and many Christian Fathers ; and while its effects were said to be elevating and an inspiration to courage, it was claimed to have had powerful patrons in every age, though but lightly esteemed in latter days. Of rather more interest is the survey of poets that follows, embodying Scaliger's judgments on the ancients, together with some estimates of English poets ; and of these some account will be given later.

A more original treatment of the subject is supplied in the heroic couplets of Beaumont,[3] where the writer enlarges on his conception of the poetic art. He notes, to begin with, that rhyme, which by then had established itself as ' the relish of the Muse ' in all European languages, was a form of verse well adapted for English poets, its repeated chimes being likened to ' the closing sounds of some delightful bell '. Its use, however, was said to call for both skill and discretion. Capable of producing many and varied effects, it was nevertheless described as most expressive in its simplest form ; and here apparently Beaumont was advocating the use of the heroic couplet, as opposed to those ' fettered staves ' or complicated stanzas, which involved such ' vain care and needless repetition '. Then, too, such rhyming verse was said to be capable of those same qualities which had given distinction to the works of ancient Greeks and Romans. For this, however, was needed the observance of certain classical principles ; the choice, for instance, of a noble and uplifting theme to fire the imagination, the use, besides, of ' pure phrase, fit epithets, sober metaphors ', and similes ' not vexed by learning ', as well as fresh and striking figures and a simple unaffected diction, free from archaisms on the one hand and from ' those Latin shreds by which the pedant climbs ', on the other. It was altogether an orthodox and a sensible attempt, at a time of some confusion, to expound a form of English verse in which something of the classical form and spirit might be successfully enshrined.

Of greater interest in the critical development were Jonson's casual remarks on poetic theory preserved mainly in his *Conversations with Drummond* (1619). Concerning the Preface to his translation of Horace's *Ars Poetica* and the *Discourse of Poetry*

---

[1] *Geography*, i. 2, 3.   [2] *De Nat. Rerum*, i. 926 ff.
[3] Quoted by W. J. Courthope, *History of English Poetry*, iii. 197–8.

written in reply to both Campion and Daniel, little or nothing is
known, and of his *Discoveries* something will be said later ; so
that for his views on matters of current interest, views not without their influence on his contemporaries, we must turn primarily
to the hints supplied in the recorded *Conversations*. Characteristic, to begin with, of his attitude to the poetic art in general
is the importance he attaches to the subject-matter or thought
of poetry. Thus ' verses ', he claimed, ' stood by sense without
either colours or accent ' ; [1] though this, according to Drummond,
' at other times he denied '. That he shared Bacon's views on
this particular question is however suggested by his further
claim to have written all his verses ' first in prose ', adding that
' so his master, Camden, had learned him '. But of the nature
of this subject-matter he has little to say, beyond stating that
in practice he avoided the theme of love, and that ' the god of love
into his rhymes could ne'er be got by any art '.[2]

At the same time his comments are concerned mostly with the
formal aspects of poetry, with matters of verse and various
poetic forms. And highly significant, in the first place, especially
in view of later developments, is the supremacy he assigns to the
heroic couplet among all verse-forms ; for in spite of his *Fit of
Rhyme against Rhyme* he was conscious, as his works show, of the
value of rhyme in general. Moreover, ' couplets ' be held to be
' the bravest sort of verses, especially when they are broken like
hexameters ' ; [3] whereas, on the other hand, ' cross-rhymes and
stanzas ', he maintained, ' were all forced ', and even Spenser's
stanzas, he added, ' pleased him not '. Equally interesting,
however, are his remarks on certain poetic forms, though their
scope is somewhat limited. Almost all of his poems were of an
occasional kind, consisting of epigrams, epitaphs, elegies, odes
and the like ; and it is on the epigram, strangely enough, that
he makes his main pronouncements. Concerning the epic or
heroic poem, one of the main themes discussed by earlier Italian
critics, as well as by English theorists in the later half of the
17th Century, he has but little to say. He had apparently
designed an epic of his own, to be called *Heroologia*, which was
to sing the praises of English notabilities in couplet form. But
it embodied a conception far removed from the orthodox epic
theory ; and for the rest he is content to commend ' King
Arthur's fiction ' as the most fitting of epic themes [4]—a subject
subsequently considered by Milton and accepted with unhappy
results by Sir Richard Blackmore. Nor are his remarks on the

---

[1] Spingarn, *op. cit.* i. p. 214.   [2] *Forest*, i.
[3] Spingarn, *op. cit.* i. p. 210.   [4] *ibid.* i. p. 213.

sonnet any more extensive or illuminating ; for the sonnet-vogue having declined by 1619, he expresses his dislike of it as a poetic form. Thus he is said to have ' cursed Petrarch for redacting verses to sonnets ',[1] which in his opinion had all the defects of the Procrustean bed. And from this it would appear that his condemnation was based not so much on the sentimental love-themes associated with that form of verse, nor again, on the intricacy of its rhyming pattern, but rather on its rigid and restricted form which prevented the free treatment of a given theme. It was, in fact, a misleading pronouncement, probably not without its influence on later writers, yet devoid of the keener insight and judgment displayed earlier by Daniel in his treatment of the sonnet-form.[2]

In his remarks on the epigram, however, Jonson is more helpful and constructive ; for here he endeavours to restore to a form of verse much cultivated at the time something of its ancient range and quality. Earlier experiments had been made by Wyatt and John Heywood ; later on came the *Epigrams* (c. 1590) of Sir John Davies, who was followed by Harington and a host of others. And meanwhile the growing taste for satire and recondite wit had restricted the epigram to little more than mere ' laughter and a jest ', a short satiric poem concluding with a witty and pregnant close, denouncing current follies and extravagances. Throughout its development in England the accepted model had been Martial, who had described the epigram as satirical in intention, brief and pungent in form, and a *genre* admitting of a certain lasciviousness of treatment, since *jocosa carmina*, he held, were ineffective without prurience.[3] Such a description represented a decline from the wider and nobler conception of the *Greek Anthology*, that collection of epigrams, re-edited by a monk, Planudes (1301), and first brought to light by Salmasius (1606) in the Palatine Library at Heidelberg. In that collection were embodied thoughts on life in general, including graceful epitaphs and elegies, delicate literary appreciations, satires, eulogies and light love-poems, all touched into life with a magical simplicity of expression ; and Jonson now attempts to revive the older tradition, of which Martial in practice, it is true, had been by no means unconscious. Thus his collection of *Epigrams* (1616), while including some of the satirical kind, contains also dignified epistles, touching epitaphs, thoughts on life and death, and themes chosen from the whole range of human interests. And he does more than this ; for by his occasional

---

[1] *ibid.* i. p. 211.   [2] See p. 203 *supra.*
[3] Martial, *Epigrams*, vii. 12, 25 ; i. 35.

comments he makes plain the reform he advocates. In one place, for instance, he concedes that to some readers his epigrams may seem new ; whereas, he protests, ' it is the old way and the true '.[1] Moreover he refuses to limit them to satirical poems of a ' sharp and toothed ' kind, ' hurling ink and wit as madmen stones ' ; [2] or again, here breaking definitely with the Martial tradition, he defends his epigrams against the charge of lacking ' salt ', ' the tongue of epigrams ', a charge brought by those to whom ' salt ' or wit meant merely obscenity.[3] Elsewhere he has something to say on the technique of this verse-form ; for he condemns ' bare narrations ', like those of Harington, where no striking reflexion brought the poem to a close.[4] He also decries the practice of others, the concluding lines of whose epigrams bore no relation to the thought previously expressed.[5] In one place Jonson calls his *Epigrams* ' the ripest of his studies ' ; [6] and compared with those of his contemporaries they represent a reaction against the prevailing licentious treatment ; though the results of his teaching are probably best seen in Herrick whose later epigrams bear a marked resemblance to those of the Greeks. Apart from this his critical comments are a further attempt to introduce order and decency into a popular poetic form of his day ; and this he does by advocating a return to ancient methods and standards.

Of lesser importance, perhaps, is the work of Henry Reynolds who theorizes on poetry in his *Mythomystes* (1632), a treatise which, despite obvious limitations, is still of considerable interest, especially interest of a historical kind. It has been described as ' perverse ', ' a tropical forest of strange fancies ' ; and from a modern standpoint there is much in the work to justify such a description. Moreover, the treatise is seriously lacking in literary grace ; it is strewn with unwieldy parentheses which make heavy going amidst the vast erudition with which the argument is supported. Yet, read with sympathetic understanding of its historical background and with the contemporary reaction to Elizabethan poetic conventions in mind, it has definite value. It throws a vivid light on current speculations regarding poetry, as well as on the conditions which led to the activities of Donne, Vaughan, and others, and to the later speculations of the Cambridge Platonists in philosophy.

At the outset Reynolds makes it plain that what he intends to submit are his views on the ' essence ', or the true nature, of

---

[1] *Epigrams*, xviii.
[2] *ibid*. ii.
[3] *ibid*. xlix.
[4] Spingarn, *op. cit.* i. p. 211.
[5] *ibid*. i. p. 214.
[6] Dedication to *Epigrams*.

poetry. Earlier writers, he maintains, had dealt merely with its ' accidents ' or accessories ; with metrical matters, for instance, or again, with tropes and figures, the flowers of rhetoric, those aids to expression which suggested themselves naturally to your true poet, but which, employed artificially, came but ' lame to the business '.[1] These things, he allows, had been freely discussed by earlier ' curious wits ' ; but none had gone really to the heart of the matter. And highly significant in its bearing on contemporary thought is the wish he expresses that Sidney had handed on ' an encomiastic poem ' in place of his *Apology*. He therefore makes bold to open up the question anew and thus to vindicate poetry from the light esteem in which it was still commonly held. The results of that estimate, he asserted, were plain enough in the poetry being then produced ; though, indeed, he has little to say for the activities of Western Europe generally. Thus, with few exceptions, he dismisses as trifling the earlier vernacular poets of Spain and France, Italy and England. They were said to have been concerned merely with style and expression, the ' bark and clothing ' of poetry, and, like Ixion of old, to have embraced clouds and begotten monsters. As for contemporary English poems, they were nothing more than ' slight flashes of ungrounded fancies, ingenious nothings and mere embroideries upon cobwebs ' ; [2] or else they were pedlar's wares hawked about for the amusement of fools and children. What had led to this state of things, he maintained, was not so much the degraded taste of readers as the mistaken ideas of poets themselves, with their unedifying fables, their mercenary flatteries of greatness and their neglect of that wisdom which poetry should normally contain. And these conditions he attempts to rectify by expounding a loftier conception of what poetry really was.

In the first place, like Bacon and Jonson before him, he holds that the essence of poetry consists in its subject-matter ; and for the true subject-matter of poetry he refers to the ' never-enough honoured ancients ', whose constant aim had been a disinterested search for the highest truth. This search he finds commended in Platonic theory,[3] for which he draws freely on Pico della Mirandola's treatise on Plato's teaching.[4] According to that theory, the poet, inspired by heavenly love, sought through the medium of earthly beauty to arrive at the beauty of things divine ; and by the contemplation of that ideal beauty his rational being was raised aloft above earthly things to sing in ecstasy of his vision of divine truth. An important feature of

---

[1] Spingarn, *op. cit.* i. p. 143.　　[2] *ibid.* i. p. 154.
[3] *ibid.* i. pp. 150–3.　　[4] *Omnia Opera*, i. (Basle, 1572).

the poetic process was held to be the detachment from all earthly vanities ; and Pico had noted that Homer and Tiresias of old were said to have become blind by much gazing on the heavenly vision. Moreover, such poets were in the beginning ' the founts of knowledge and nurses of wisdom '. From the teaching of Orpheus and Zoroaster, as Pico had explained, was drawn the wisdom of Pythagoras and other philosophers ; whence Plato's description of the earliest poets as ' interpreters of the gods ', and their poems as ' the gifts and graces of heaven '. This search for the highest truth, apart from all earthly distractions, was therefore for Reynolds the real essence of poetry ; and of such elements he could find no trace in contemporary poetry.

Further light on the nature of poetry, however, was said to be forthcoming from the ancients in virtue of their particular method of conveying the profound truths thus acquired. From the first both poets and philosophers were credited with writing in cryptic fashion, thus concealing their knowledge from the vulgar ; and Reynolds, in accordance with the meticulous scholarship of his day, is at pains to establish the importance of this fact.[1] Thus he recalls, for instance, the hieroglyphics of Egyptian priests, the enigmas and riddles of the Greeks, and the esoteric methods commended by both Plato and Aristotle. Elsewhere Plato is cited as evidence that Orpheus within the folds of fables had hidden the mysteries of his doctrines ; Politian's statement in *Ambra* is also recalled, affirming that Homer's poems, though the fountain-heads of all learning, were yet to ordinary readers nothing more than ' two fictitious impossible tales ' ; while Pythagoras's well-known precept, again, ' give not readily thy right hand to every one ', is interpreted as an injunction to refrain from communicating to unworthy minds instruction intended for ' sublime wits '. Nor, so it was stated, was the process confined to profane writers only ; for esoteric methods were commanded by the angel in the Apocryphal *Book of Esdras*. Moreover, the same device was attributed to Moses in writing the Pentateuch, in which, according to Pico, the Mosaic law was duly published, but not its hidden meaning, those abstruse mysteries communicated by God on the Mount. Such then was the widespread practice of antiquity ; and from it, adds Reynolds, there developed the art of mystical writing in numbers known as *Scientia Cabalae*, the origin of which Pico[2] had traced back to Orpheus. It was an art based on the mysterious properties of numbers, on harmonious numerical arrange-

[1] Spingarn, *op. cit.* i. pp. 155–62.
[2] *Apologia*, fol. 83.

ments which were said to make of the universe a cosmos ; [1] and this doctrine, recognized by Hebrew, Greek, and Arabic authorities alike, had since been seriously treated by many of the Christian Fathers. It was therefore on the strength of this united testimony of antiquity that Reynolds argues the need for the use of the esoteric method in poetry, for a discreet treatment of poetic truths by means of allegory and the like.

But while the highest truths allegorically treated thus constituted for Reynolds the real essence of poetry, he has yet a further comment to make, in the light of ancient practice, on the character of those truths which it was the proper function of poetry to reveal. He recognizes, to begin with, that moral doctrine had frequently been treated by recent poets in allegorical fashion, whereas ' the mysteries and hidden properties of God's handmaid, Nature ', had hitherto received from them no sort of attention. [2] These latter truths, however, he asserts, led men more surely to a knowledge of the inscrutable being of God than did moral teaching derived from pagan philosophies ; and such truths were therefore in his opinion the most fitting matter for poetry. For a knowledge of these matters he refers his readers to the ancients, to those ' who lived nearest to the time of the gods ' ; though he is also aware that many scholars of his day, his friend Chapman among them, held that moral meanings alone were to be read into those ancient writings. That moral doctrine had indeed formed part of ancient teaching, this he readily concedes, in view of the works of Zoroaster, Orpheus and the like ; or again, there were the old fables of gods and heroes in which vices and virtues had been abundantly illustrated. Yet, he asserts with confidence, far more of such fables had related to the workings of Nature than to matters of morality, seeing that many stories of the gods, with ' their riots, rapes, and murders ' were obviously no fit instruction for the race of men. For the actual truths revealed concerning the hidden workings of Nature he refers to Pico's exposition of *Magia naturalis* or natural wisdom, [3] which was defined as ' the exact and absolute knowledge of all natural things '. And then he points to the light thrown by Orpheus and others on such subjects as ' the generation of the elements, fire and water, the courses of the stars, the qualities of metals or the secrets of vegetable life '—themes, he very properly allows, ' too infinite to pursue '. It was true, he adds, that such fables in some quarters were regarded as ' a legacy

---

[1] cf. Sir Thomas Browne's disquisition on the quincunx in *The Garden of Cyrus*, ch. ii.

[2] Spingarn, *op. cit.* i. pp. 162 ff.   [3] *Apologia*, fol. 112.

of mere old wives' tales ' ; and he alludes with scorn to the inconsistency of a contemporary, by no means ' unlearned ',[1] who had extracted wisdom from many of the fables and had then denied that such allegorical meanings had originally been present in the minds of the writers. Moreover, he laments the lack of contemporary interest in the arcana of Nature, apart, that is, from their utilitarian value in bringing to the relief of man's estate such things as ' diving-boats . . . to take crabs under water with ', or again, ' water-bellows . . . to blow the fire withal '.[2] Yet, in spite of all this, he repeats that disinterested speculation on the secrets of ' our great God of Nature ' was the need of contemporary poets, as being most conducive to spiritual growth ; and if there were obvious difficulties it was worth remembering that ' the ripest fruits of knowledge grow ever highest '.

These, then were Reynolds' views on the essence of poetry ; and they represent a plea for its recognition as an esoteric art, a means of conveying to the initiated hidden truths concerning the mysteries of Nature—in short, what he advocates seems at first sight to be little more than a modified version of the allegorical theory of medieval times. Ostensibly based on the authority of the ancients, its real source was the multifarious but uncritical learning of the early Italian Renascence represented by Pico primarily, but by Politian as well, together with the later Alexandrian, Farra, and others. Of the teaching of Aristotle's *Poetics* or of the 16th-Century Italians there is no trace. The main inspiration throughout is drawn from 15th-Century Platonism, which failed to distinguish between the original doctrines of Plato and those of the later Neo-Platonists, while it also embodied a heterogeneous mass of fanciful thought derived from Zoroaster, Pythagoras, and even ' Moses ', and handed down through Alexandrian and medieval Jewish schools. Hence the place given to cabalistic mysteries, *magia naturalis* and the rest ; or again, the value attached to the teaching of the remote Zoroaster and the doctrines of the mythical Orpheus, whose accredited poems are all forgeries of the Hellenistic period. For the interpretation of Nature, which was to constitute the main theme of poetry, Reynolds thus depended on the principle of authority, and looked solely to the *a priori* theories attributed to legendary writers. It was a line of approach which Bacon had already discredited by his scientific teaching of experience

---

[1] i.e. Bacon, see p. 266 *supra*.
[2] cf. Bacon's *New Atlantis* (1627), ed. Gough. pp. 35 ff., for schemes of invention.

as the only source of knowledge and of induction as the only fruitful method ; and in the treatise therefore there is but little that is of intrinsic and lasting value.

On the other hand the historical value of *Mythomystes* is definite and by no means inconsiderable. For one thing it throws light on the ideas of poetry current in the early 17th Century ; on the significant absence of Aristotelian doctrine, for instance, or again, on the equally significant use made of Neo-Platonic theory ; and at the same time it also points to the persisting influence of 15th-Century Italian thought at this date. More than this, however, and despite its disordered erudition, its vague occultism, it voices an actual tendency in the poetic activities of the time, unremarked upon elsewhere, namely, a striving for a range of feeling in poetry unknown to the Elizabethans generally, and seen more particularly in the later efforts to arrive at a spiritual interpretation of the Universe. Incidentally this explains why Pico figures as the chief influence and guide ; for to him, possessed with a sense of the unity of all knowledge, every object in the natural world was a symbol of some higher truth in the world of spirit. But the full significance of Reynolds' treatise emerges only in the light of contemporary developments, and against the background of the mystical poetry cultivated at this date. This is most clearly seen in Vaughan's efforts to break up, as he himself puts it, ' some seals which none had touched before ' and to reveal some of the deeper truths bound up with Nature. This he did, it is true, not by following methods suggested by Reynolds, but by means of intuition, imagination, and a subtle analysis of personal moods and emotions ; as when, for example, he affords glimpses of the ' shadows of eternity ' in ' gilded cloud or flower ', or reads ' sublime truths ' into ' the mystical deep streams ' of the waterfall. Yet Reynolds seems to have foreshadowed this development in his attempt to commend to poets the task of unravelling ' the mysteries and hidden properties of God's handmaid, Nature '. His effort was obviously of an ill-directed and wrong-headed kind ; but he was the first in English critical history to advocate the cultivation of themes which were to extend the poetic vision and ultimately to lead to Wordsworth's Nature-poetry, with its belief in the spiritual apprehension of truth beyond the understanding.

There yet remains for consideration one other addition to the theorizing on poetry during the early years of the 17th Century, namely, the *Anacrisis* (1634 ?) of Sir William Alexander (*c.* 1567–1640), a Scottish *littérateur* who, having followed James I into England, became subsequently Secretary of State for

Scotland (1621) and Earl of Stirling (1633), and whose contributions to poetry won for him some reputation at the time, though now he is perhaps best remembered as author of the tragedy, *Darius* (1604), certain lines of which are said to have inspired the sublime utterance on 'cloud-capped towers', in Shakespeare's *Tempest*. The *Anacrisis* was dedicated by Alexander to his friend and compatriot, Drummond of Hawthornden, and, written as it was, in a period of retirement, it consists of stray thoughts on critical standards and also on poetry which are of some interest. Unlike many of his contemporaries, he does not share their prejudices against modern writers, whom, he protests, he finds 'in no way inferior' to the ancients, though they had written in the vernacular 'to grace their own country'. At the same time he contends that poems were often praised for the wrong things, for mere skill in diction, for instance, whereas vitality and thought might be wholly lacking. For his part he regarded language as but 'the apparel of poetry', which might give beauty but not strength; and he proceeds to explain his own methods of forming poetic judgments. Thus by an analysis of the general structure of a poem and by neglecting for the time being that 'external gorgeousness consisting in the choice or placing of words', he seeks for qualities which seemed to him more essential.[1] Not that skill in expression was without its importance; for it might add grace to truth and to the thought conveyed. More importance, however, he maintained, should be attached, as in surveying a garden, to fitness and effectiveness in the arrangement of the parts, and to a pleasing variety in the effects attained; while, apart from this, what gave him greatest delight was a weighty sentiment embodying wisdom, a 'witty conceit' which exhilarated the spirits, and an emotional uplift 'whereby the mind might be inflamed for great things'. His tests were thus of considerable merit; they were based on no rigid rules, but on qualities of a structural and aesthetic character.

Another defect to which he refers in the critical judgments of the time was the tendency to ascribe to some favoured poet all the artistic virtues; whereas, Alexander maintains, 'every author has his own genius, directing him by a secret inspiration to that wherein he may most excel, and excelling in some things but not in all'.[2] Elsewhere he remarks that 'men's works, like themselves, are not all of one quality, nor ever alike'; and in view of these facts he suggests that greater discretion should be exercised in forming judgments. In each of the old Roman

---

[1] Spingarn, *op. cit.* i. p. 182.   [2] *ibid.*

poets he had discerned, not all, but distinctive and characteristic, qualities, while Tasso, again, did not always maintain the high level of his *Jerusalem Delivered*. And this leads him to question Scaliger's estimate of Virgil in attributing to that poet a faultless art, while at the same time vilifying Lucan who was said ' to bark rather than to sing '. Yet blemishes, he held, were to be found in Virgil, as for instance, his lack of judgment in representing Turnus in a cowardly light, thus detracting from the valour of his epic hero Aeneas. This, he suggests, was an error more serious than any to be found in Lucan. And it was with astonishment that he viewed this glaring example of biassed judgment, especially as coming from one ' deservedly renowned and admirably learned ' ; though at the same time he defends his action in criticizing so great an authority by recalling ' Scaliger's example in censuring all his betters '.

He then turns to deal briefly with the current theory that poetry was necessarily based on ' feigned history ' or fiction, thus limiting ' the boundless liberty of the poet '.[1] It was true, he noted, that the fables of ancient poets apparently supported such a doctrine ; yet to the ancients those narratives had been something more than mere fanciful creations, being held to embody profound truths concerning gods and heroes. And his contention therefore was that, in general, truth, not fiction, was the ultimate basis of poetry. At the same time he allows that some modifications were necessary in treating the several ' kinds '. The epic, for instance, ' should consist altogether of a fiction ', so as to enable the poet in his flight above the course of Nature to create his picture of the perfect hero. On the other hand tragedy, more serious, called for a treatment of ' true history ', as being more likely to produce emotional effects. And as for satires and epigrams, they required a mixture of both truth and fiction, in which actual persons might be dealt with under assumed names, or modern times censured by allusions to antiquity. Here our author is obviously commenting on Bacon's theory of poetry, while his conception of tragedy would seem to have been influenced by his own and Jonson's practice. But what is perhaps most significant is the continued absence at this date of any reference to Aristotelian teaching, which had dealt at length with the problems here discussed.

With this, Alexander brings his remarks to a close, though he cannot refrain from a passing shot against those of ' a pretended theological austerity ' who condemned all reading of fiction on the ground that it fostered ' a contagious dissoluteness '

[1] *ibid.* i. p. 185.

that poisoned the minds of readers.[1] On the contrary, he
maintained, such works were really a source of both profit and
delight ; and while he finds much to admire in such a work as
the *Aethiopica* of Heliodorus, Sidney's *Arcadia* he regards as
' the most excellent work that . . . hath been written in our
language ', since, as in an epic poem, it afforded types of perfection for both the sexes '. In his youth, he states, he had
attempted unsuccessfully an imitation of Sidney's work ; but
then, as he added, *non cuivis homini contingit adire Corinthum*.
Apart from this he has nothing but praise for the pastoral
romances in prose which had become a feature of modern
literature. He refers in this connexion to the works of Sannazaro,
Montemayor and D'Urfé, as a new departure ; and here was
an early recognition of the possibilities of ' the epic in prose ',
that is, of the modern novel.

Such then was the main substance of the theorizing that
went on during the early 17th Century ; and amidst much
confusion of thought it becomes clear that fresh interests were
engaging the attention of critical minds. As before, groping
attempts were being made to expound the nature of poetry,
though new and independent doctrines were now to some extent
forthcoming. At the same time pronouncements were being
made on the proper method of translating and on the principles
which should underlie the writing of history. A wider conception
of the epigram was also advocated, which led to the production
of much occasional verse in place of the earlier sonnet ; and while
the merits of the heroic couplet were now for the first time being
emphasized, there were also signs that men were beginning to
reflect on the principles of taste and standards of judgment.
The main influences were still those of patristic writers and
Italian Humanists of the 15th Century ; though there was also
evidence of some amount of independent and rational thinking.
It is true that comment on the new ' metaphysical ' trend in the
poetry of the day is entirely absent ; yet signs are not wanting,
though imperfectly expressed, of the need felt for a more profound meaning to be read into the poetry.

[1] Spingarn, *op. cit.* i. p. 186.

CHAPTER X

LATER CRITICAL JUDGMENTS : BOLTON, PEACHAM, CAREW, DRAYTON, SUCKLING, JONSON

MEANWHILE in the opening decades of the 17th Century there had become visible a notable advance in literary appreciation and judgment which now assumed various forms, and which, despite much that was trite and conventional, occasionally betrayed a keen insight into literary qualities and values. To this judicial criticism most of the writers already mentioned contributed ; though to their number must be added the names of Thomas Carew, Drayton, Suckling, and others. Some, for example Bolton and Peacham, were content to continue along earlier lines with second-hand lists of writers accompanied by short critical remarks. Of greater importance, however, was the criticism in verse-form associated with Jonson, Carew, Drayton, and Suckling. Theirs was a new development embodying memorial verses, epistles, mock-heroic poems, and the like ; and to this section belongs at least two of the most striking appreciations. In addition there were the casual utterances of Jonson and others, free, outspoken, and challenging, which likewise witnessed to the growing tendency to pass judgment on contemporary literature. In short, critical judgment at this date was becoming articulate, even though old prejudices of the learned against vernacular works were still harboured in some quarters. Conventional efforts were still made to expound the qualities of ancient classics ; but increasing efforts, some of outstanding value, were also made to pronounce judgment on the native literature. Thus Speght in his edition of Chaucer's works (1602), in insisting on the regularity of the poet's verse, ascribes apparent defects to the ' negligence and rape ' of Adam Scrivener ; and altogether a new liveliness in literary appreciation becomes apparent at this date.

Least interesting, though not without their value, are the critical remarks of Bolton and Peacham. The aim of Bolton, in the first place, was confessedly limited in *Hypercritica* to discussing the styles of those ' books of warrantable English ', the reading of which was likely to improve the expression of intending historians ; and he begins by recognizing, on the one hand, the inherent disabilities of the English tongue owing to its lack of ' certainty ' in matters of grammar and orthography, and, on the other, the existence of a standard English which he describes as ' nearest to the phrase of Court ' and the speech of educated Londoners. He then passes briefly in review those works of earlier English writers which he regards as most helpful, and tentatively submits his ' private true opinion ' in a ' tumultuary catalogue '.[1] Thus he has a word of praise for the clearness and propriety of the English of Sir Thomas More ; whereas Sidney's ornateness in *Arcadia* he notes, but hesitates to recommend it for practical purposes. On the other hand, Raleigh's style he duly commends ; Hooker is said to have provided a rare and ' choice parcel of our vulgar language ' ; while to Bacon is attributed ' the freshest and most savoury form and aptest utterances ' in English. Nor does he look to prose-writings alone for his ' garden-plots ', his models of style. He glances rapidly over earlier poets, though his judgment, he protests, ' is nothing at all in poems and poesy '. The earliest poets, and Spenser as well, he dismisses forthwith on account of their archaic diction ; but he has rather more to say for the ' brave language ' of Chapman's *Homer*, and for the style of Daniel, ' fitter for prose than verse ' ; while Gascoigne, he coldly allows, ' may be endured '. His remarks on other poets, ranging from Wyatt to Donne, are mostly of a conventional kind ; though for Jonson a high, and what is more, a personal, tribute is reserved. ' I never tasted English ', he writes, ' more to my liking, nor more smart, and put to the height of use in poetry than in that vital, judicious, and most practicable language of Benjamin Jonson's poems ' ; but, for the rest, the chief merit of his survey must be said to lie in its laudable attempt to establish a worthy standard of English prose in the light of earlier masters.

Rather more extensive, but also more conventional, is Peacham's survey of poetry in his *Compleat Gentleman*, compiled with the aim of guiding his readers through the garden of the Muses, and of acquainting them with estimates of both Latin and English poets which it behoved every cultured Englishman to know. For his judgments he draws on Scaliger and Puttenham ; though occasionally he is indebted to patristic and other sources, as for instance, in his noteworthy passing reference to the *Psalms*.[2] Here he quotes St. Hilary's happy description of those sacred poems as a bunch of keys opening doors which give entrance to ' prayer, rejoicing, repentance and thanksgiving ' ; though their further appreciation is based merely on rhetorical considerations, on their effective use of similes, allegories and such figures as *epiphonema*, *prosopopoeia*, and the like.

[1] Spingarn, *op. cit.* i. p. 107.   [2] *ibid.* i. p. 117.

It is, however, with Latin and English poets that he is mainly concerned ; and he proceeds forthwith to deal at some length with Virgil, who alone is said, in accordance with Scaliger's teaching, to conform with that critic's requirements for the true poet.[1] Those requirements he enumerates as follows : first, Prudence, that is, a fitting treatment of both action and diction in relation to place, time, and manner ; secondly, Efficacy (i.e. ἐνέργεια), the vivid and animated presentment of things ; thirdly, Variety of incidents, descriptions, and the like ; fourthly, Sweetness, those graces and beauty that give delight ; and these points he illustrates by passages from the *Aeneid*. With the remaining Latin poets he deals in more summary fashion. Thus Ovid is praised for the sweetness and smoothness of his style ; and as for his alleged wantonness, ' with the weeds ' are said to be found ' delicate flowers in those walks of Venus '. Next, Horace is described as the most artistic of lyric poets, and, on Scaliger's authority, ' more accurate and sententious ' than even Pindar. His *Satires* moreover are said to be lively, less bitter than those of Juvenal ; while his *Ars Poetica* is described as ' his worst piece ', for, so it is explained, ' while he teacheth the art, he goeth unartificially (i.e. inartistically) to work, even in the very beginning '. On the other hand, Juvenal is praised as the best of the Roman satirists ; whereas Persius is censured for his harsh and obscure style. Martial, again, is commended for his witty epigrams, on account of which, so it is urged, his wantonness should be ' winked at '. Moreover, Lucan's style is described as spirited but inflated in places ; whereas that of Statius is ranked nearest to the Virgilian manner, some of his lines being said to be superior to those of Homer. And as for the dramatists, Plautus, it was stated, was to be admired for his skill in comedy, Terence on account of his pure and elegant style ; while Seneca, though indebted to the Greeks for his tragic plots, was held to surpass Euripides in *cultu et nitore*, and to be distinguished by a majesty of style all his own. In these estimates there is obviously much that is debatable and misleading. Their interest, however, lies in the fact that here more clearly than elsewhere in English is reflected the dogmatic teaching of that ' Prince of all learning and Judge of judgments, the divine Julius Caesar Scaliger ', with its Roman bias, its Virgil-worship, and its failure to realize the qualities of the great Greeks.

To this account of Latin poetry Peacham adds a series of judgments on English poets,[2] beginning with some consideration

[1] *ibid*. i. pp. 120 ff : cf. Scaliger, *Poetice*, iii. cap. 25 ff.
[2] *ibid*. i. pp. 129 ff.

of the works of English Latinists, and including the 12th-Century Joseph of Exeter, the ' rough-hewn, slovenly and rude ' Buchanan, and Sir Thomas More, ' a man of most rich and pleasant invention '. Of greater interest perhaps is the brief survey of vernacular poets, based mainly on Puttenham ; and most notable is the praise accorded to Chaucer, though not always for the right things. Thus his archaic style, it is conceded, may be displeasing ; yet under a bitter and rough rind ' there is said to be ' a delicate kernel of conceit and rich invention ', while he is also given credit as ' a sound divine who saw in those times without his spectacles '. In addition it is claimed that his artistic handling of his characters and his use of similes and *exempla* all add to the beauty of his work, just as ' threads of gold in the rich Arras '. And if in general his poems are represented as mere translations, yet the *Canterbury Tales* at least are recognized as original creations reflecting contemporary life ; and altogether Peacham's advice to his gentle readers is ' to account Chaucer among the best of the English books in your library '. Apart from this, he has little to add concerning either medieval or more recent poetry. The ' moral ' Gower is briefly dismissed as a ' poor and plain ' poet, lacking in originality, and obscure by reason of his affectation of French words and phrases. To Lydgate, described as a translator who wrote in tolerable verse, is ascribed that ' bitter satire *Peirs Plowman* ' ; whereas Skelton's claim to the title of poet-laureate comes in for mere derision. Nor is much information supplied concerning later Tudor and Elizabethan poetry, beyond a brief catalogue ranging from Wyatt to Daniel ; though the Elizabethan era, it is true, is recognized as a golden age, the like of which ' could hardly be hoped for in any succeeding age '. The truth was, as Bacon pointed out in another connexion, ' water will not ascend higher than the level of the first spring-head ' ; and Peacham has nothing to add to Puttenham's judgments. His account is of an impersonal kind ; and its chief value is that it reflects views which persisted well into the 17th Century.

So far but little, if any, advance on earlier Elizabethan procedure had become perceptible in literary judgments at this date. In the meantime, however, fresh impulse was being given to literary appreciation by the adoption of verse-form for critical purposes ; though, as before, sporadic remarks on current tendencies and fashions continued to come from the poets themselves. Chapman, for instance, had already declared against the adoption of hexameters in English verse. ' Sweet Poesy ', he stated,

Will not be clad in her supremacy
With those strange garments (Rome's hexameters),
As she is English ; but in 'right prefers
Our native robes (put on with skilful hands—
English heroics) to those antic garlands.[1]

Then, somewhat later, the comments of George Herbert and Habington are worthy of note. Thus Herbert, for instance, protests strongly against the endless harpings on tawdry love-themes, as well as against the artificialities of the pastoral and allegorical conventions of the Spenserian school. And in his demand for loftier and more substantial themes he exclaims :

Who says that fictions only and false hair
Become a verse ? Is there in truth no beauty ?[2]

And again,

Is it no verse, except enchanted groves
And sudden arbours shadow coarse-spun lines ?
Must purling streams refresh a lover's loves ?
Must all be veiled, while he that reads, divines,
Catching the sense at two removes ?[3]

Habington's comment is of a different kind, and is directed against the licentious cynicism with which the love-theme was being handled by Suckling and others. In his *Castara*[4] (1634) he states that ' when woman . . . is the supreme object of wit, we soon degenerate into effeminacy ' ; nevertheless he laments the loss of the chivalrous attitude to woman and pleads for something like a return to the Petrarchan tradition in poetry.

Of yet greater significance, however, were the judgments that resulted from the use of memorial verses, epistles, and mock-heroic poems for critical purposes. And of these most important, in the first place, were the memorial verses enshrining graceful tributes to men of letters and others, which as a result of the more generous conception of the epigram advocated by Jonson, became now a characteristic feature of the literary output of the period. The most imposing of such contributions was the miscellany known as *Jonsonus Virbius* (1638) ; and to this collection some thirty ' friends of the Muses ' had contributed. As a rule, such verses were more notable for generous enthusiasms than for penetrating judgments ; as Doctor Johnson later on explained, ' in lapidary inscriptions a man is not upon oath '. And *Jonsonus Virbius* is no exception to the rule ; for it consists

---

[1] *Shadow of Night* (*Hymnus in Cynthiam*) (1594), ll. 86–91.
[2] *Jordan*, ll. 1–2.   [3] *ibid.*, ll. 6–10.   [4] *Address to the Reader.*

of unbounded praise of Jonson's achievement mostly in general terms. At the same time it has also historical value in that it reveals some of the specific qualities for which Jonson was then admired, and his literary standing among his contemporaries. Thus his learning, his ' wit ' and his judgment are invariably commended. Sir John Beaumont describes him as ' the great refiner of our poesy ' ; Cleveland as ' he who first reformed our stage by justest laws '. Reference is also made to the nature of his satire which ' whipped the vices yet spared the man ' ; to his style, frowned on only by pedants, in which ' in few words a man may utter much ' ; though the chief praise is reserved for his dramatic works. Thus all agree on the didactic and elevating effects of ' the ethic lectures of his comedies ' ; whereas his tragedies are said to reveal ' all the disorders of a tottering state '. One writer adds that the works of Shakespeare and Beaumont were to be read, those of Jonson to be studied, the former being works of chance, the latter works of judgment ; but, in the opinion of all, Jonson ' in writing his works had built his monument '. Such complimentary verses were therefore capable of something more than unchecked exuberance or vapid praise. At their best they opened up new possibilities for the expression of literary judgment ; and of this development Jonson in particular, and Thomas Carew as well, provide excellent examples, verses in which illuminating judgments are gracefully couched in dignified and memorable phrase beyond the reach of mere pedestrian prose.

Among the memorial verses written by Jonson of interest, in the first place, are his tributes paid to Beaumont, Donne, and others. More substantial, however, are his lines addressed to Sir Henry Savile [1] whom he praises for his insight into events and their causes, and for his impartial handling of history, a treatment characteristic of one who ' dared not write things false nor hide things true ' ; and the tribute, it might be added, was one of special significance at this date. Moreover, this tribute is of further interest as embodying the method adopted by Jonson in the famous remarks on Shakespeare and Bacon in his *Discoveries*, where he adapts passages from ancient classical authors to express his ideas. Here, almost word for word, a passage from Cicero's *De oratore* [2] is utilized ; and Savile is credited with a technical knowledge of ' the graces of history ', and with knowing where brevity or splendour, where sweetness or weight, were required for the appropriate effects.

[1] *Epigr.* xcv.
[2] ii. 62–3 : quoted by Courthope, *History of English Poetry*, iii. 181.

It is in the verses *To the Memory of my beloved Master, William Shakespeare*, however, lines inserted in the First Folio of Shakespeare's works (1623), that we find Jonson's finest effort at versecriticism of this sort ; for there, into a eulogy of the usual formal kind he has worked a judicial estimate in the main both generous and just. The generosity was called for by the occasion, but the justice was a revelation of critical insight ; and both are surprising when all things are considered. From the outset, as if conscious of the greatness of his theme, Jonson states his intention of avoiding the empty raptures of ignorant but well-meaning minds as well as the faint but damning praise of pens of the baser sort. And then with fine judgment he indicates what he regards as Shakespeare's position in the world of letters and the outstanding merits of his work. For him, to begin with, is claimed a place above all English poets and dramatists ; above Chaucer and Spenser, above Lyly, ' sporting Kyd ', and even Marlowe with his ' mighty line '. Possessed though he was of ' small Latin and less Greek ', his sole compeers were said to be the great tragedians of antiquity. He alone challenged comparison with the artistic triumphs of ' insolent (i.e. rare) [1] Greece and haughty Rome ' ; and to him besides was due the homage of all Europe. Hence, argued Jonson, the universality and permanence of his appeal. ' He was not of an age but for all time '—a pregnant phrase, in which Jonson was unconsciously applying the ' Longinian ' test of all great literature. A further merit was indicated in the part played by Nature in all his creations, which were described as the fruit of native genius and thus endowed with the freshness and originality of those times when ' the Muses were in their prime '. In this respect he was said to have outmoded the comedies of the ancients ; and Nature, added Jonson, was ' proud of his designs '. Concerning the artistic merits of Shakespeare's style, however, Jonson is less happy and convincing ; for, while conceding that art as well as Nature had gone to fashion his work, he attributes to Shakespeare his own deliberate processes of writing and commends in particular his ' well turned and true filed lines ', describing them as a faithful reflexion of the dramatist's character. Elsewhere Jonson modifies this particular statement when freed from the pious obligations of memorial verses ; [2] but, for the rest, his remarks must be described as of positive and lasting value. In claiming for Shakespeare an unchallenged supremacy in English poetry, a right to be alone classed with the greatest of the ancients, an originality born of native genius, and above all a universality and perman-

[1] See p. 163 fn. *supra.*   [2] See pp. 306–7 *infra.*

ence of appeal, he had given utterance to more than one profound truth concerning Shakespeare's achievement, was in fact laying the foundations of future Shakespearean criticism. That his findings have become the commonplaces of to-day in no wise detracts from their actual value ; for they were dictated, not by arbitrary rules, but by his own aesthetic reactions to the works in question. They are besides all the more commendable as the pronouncements of a normally captious critic on a fellow-dramatist who had catered, and catered successfully, for the despised popular stage, and one whose genius moreover was alien to his own. These Folio verses are, in short, one of the outstanding pieces of contemporary judicial criticism ; and more than one of their memorable phrases have become part and parcel of our critical tradition.

No less striking, however, is the later *Elegy upon the death of the Dean of St. Paul's, Dr. John Donne* by Thomas Carew (1595–1639 ?) in which yet another master-mind of the period is acutely and justly appreciated, and not in ' unkneaded dough-baked prose ', but in the more lofty and suggestive form of verse. After a passing tribute to Donne's flaming pulpit eloquence that had melted all hearts and taught what ' fancy could not reach ', Carew turns to deal with his poetic achievement, and shrewdly explains something of those qualities which arrested attention at the time and led to a transformation of poetry for a generation or more. His main theme is Donne's audacious break-away from Elizabethan conventions and from that ' servile imitation ' which had characterized much of the earlier poetry. ' The Muses' garden with pedantic weeds o'erspread ', he asserts, had been purged by Donne and ' fresh invention planted ' ; and, not content with generalities, he has something further to say on the specific changes wrought by the poet's innovations. Thus earlier artificialities, he states, had been dispensed with ; the ' mimic fury ' of poets simulating the passion of Anacreon or Pindar, the ' licentious thefts ', the juggling with ' two-edged words ' or compounds, and the everlasting play with ancient gods and goddesses. In their place, he maintains, Donne had opened up ' a mine of rich and pregnant fancy ', had moreover clothed his thought in ' masculine expression ', which, added Carew, would have been approved by ' old Orpheus or all the ancient brood our superstitious fools admire '. Earlier English poets there had been, more tuneful perhaps ; but to none had Donne yielded precedence, save in the matter of time. Nay, more, his achievement was in reality all the greater in that, coming later, he had moulded anew ' our stubborn English ',

making it a fit medium for his ' giant fancy ' which had proved
' too stout for their soft melting phrases '. And, besides, whereas
poets before him had ' culled the prime buds of invention ',
leaving ' bare lands ' and ' rifled fields ', yet Donne had cultivated
new themes of his own devising and had gathered in a richer
harvest than had been reaped before. The secrets of such poetry,
adds Carew, would be too subtle for those who followed ; the
hackneyed themes of classical myth would later be recalled to
' swell the windy page '. Yet in his judgment the triumph of
Donne was assured ; and he hails him as ' a king that ruled as
he thought fit the universal monarchy of wit '. It was altogether
·an illuminating judgment on a contemporary which recognized
and commended a new depth and range of feeling as well as the
strange harmonies resulting from the use of a colloquial idiom
and a more masculine style. Donne's fame as a poet was
destined to undergo strange vicissitudes ; but it was not left for
the 20th Century alone to realize his originality and his positive
merits.

While these memorial verses of Jonson and Carew were thus
the most serious of the contributions to criticism in verse during
this period, less substantial, though yet of interest, were the
further additions to verse-criticism made by Epistles and mock-
heroic poems which also throw light on the literary taste of the
time. Of these, Drayton's *Epistle to Henry Reynolds* (1627),
in the first place, is a poem in heroic couplets written in the
familiar Horatian style, in which the writer conveys to his friend,
the author of *Mythomystes*, his views on English poets in general,
though in a fashion that marks an advance on the ' tumultuary
catalogues ' of earlier critics. To the earliest poets little more
than conventional tributes are paid ; to Chaucer, for instance,
as ' the first . . . that ever brake into the Muses' treasure ' and
the first to speak in ' weighty numbers ', enriching English with
his rhymes and giving to the language new powers of expression ;
whereas ' honest Gower ', it was stated, had ' only sipped at
Aganippe's brim '.[1] Hardly less superficial, however, are his
comments on the early Tudors and Elizabethans. Thus Wyatt
and Surrey are commended for ' many dainty passages of wit '
in their contributions to *Tottel's Miscellany* ; but the works of
Gascoigne and Churchyard, ' great meterers ' in their day, are
said to be already out of date. ' Grave moral Spenser ', again, is
warmly approved for his learning and brave fancies ; while
Sidney, described as master of both prose and verse, comes in
for special praise as having checked the baneful Euphuistic craze,

[1] Spingarn, *op. cit.* i. pp. 135–6.

that endless ' playing with words and idle similes ', that ' talking of stones, stars, plants ', and the like.

It is with his more immediate contemporaries, however, that Drayton's remarks become more personal in kind ; and not without their significance, to begin with, are his comments on certain of the dramatists.   On Marlowe, for instance, enthusiastic praise is showered on account of his primitive force, his ' raptures all air and fire ' ; and with him are associated a ' fine madness ' and ' those brave sublunary things that the first poets had '.[1] Shakespeare, on the other hand, is referred to in a somewhat lower key, though he is credited with success in comedy and with passion unsurpassed in the field of tragedy.   It is ' learned Jonson ', however, who commands most admiration.   He is confidently hailed as ' lord of the theatre ' ; and in both tragedy and comedy his correctness and skill are said to be such as to challenge the supremacy of Seneca and Plautus.   Of the remarks on other contemporary writers those on Nashe, Daniel, and Chapman are the most interesting.   Thus Nashe is praised for his keen satiric touch, his unique power of ' scorching and blasting ' with words.   Concerning Daniel the current criticism that he was ' too much historian in verse ' is quoted, but without further comment ; whereas Drayton's own estimate is that while his verses were smooth ' his manner better fitted prose '.   On the other hand to Chapman the highest praise is accorded for his translations which had successfully transplanted Homer and other Greek poets into the English tongue.   And, finally, with brief references to his select circle of literary friends, which included Sir William Alexander, Drummond of Hawthornden, the two Beaumonts and William Browne, Drayton brings his *Epistle* to a close, noting that his comments had been confined to published works alone, and deprecating the private circulation of works in manuscript form as ' though the world unworthy were to know their rich composures ' [2]—a remark not without its significance in view of the omission of Donne from his survey. From the various judgments submitted by Drayton it is obvious that no great claim can be made for his *Epistle* as a contribution to judicial criticism.   That it reflects current opinion in graceful fashion and at the same time embodies some happy phrases characteristic of criticism in verse, these are perhaps the chief merits of the work and they constitute a claim for notice in the critical development.

Interest of another kind is attached to the verse-criticism bound up with those mock-heroic or burlesque poems, the work

[1] Spingarn, *op. cit.* i. p. 137.   [2] *ibid.* i. p. 139.

of Drayton, Suckling, and others, which represent new and picturesque vehicles for passing literary judgments. The first of these, Drayton's *Nymphidia* (1627), is a playful skit on the old romances, apparently designed to laugh out of court the fairy way of writing. Its story tells of the struggle between Oberon and the knight Pigwiggin for the love of Queen Mab, in which Oberon, maddened with jealousy, attacks all and sundry, takes a wasp for Pigwiggin, a glow-worm for the devil, and finally plunges into a lake which cools his ardour. Meanwhile Queen Mab has been hidden by the fairy, Nymphidia, in a hazel-nut, which renders her invisible to the prying Puck, and thus happily averts a dreadful tragedy. It is all a delightful fantasy, with humorous reminiscences of Chaucer's *Sir Thopas* (including his stanza), of Ariosto's *Orlando Furioso*, and Shakespeare's *Midsummer Night's Dream* ; and if the burlesque treatment suggests a critical pronouncement, the criticism is nevertheless devoid of the animus of earlier attacks on romances and the like. In lighter vein Drayton would seem to be tilting against themes fantastic and incredible, but he does so in a manner free from strong feeling. With his Lilliputian elves there creeps into the poem something of the beauty and charm of the fairy world ; and his critical effort is therefore the less convincing, inasmuch as, like Cervantes, he obviously loved the things he laughed at.

Different in character, both in form and intention, were those contributions of Suckling and others, in which was adopted for critical purposes a new and striking device that was destined to attain considerable popularity. Those works were *A Sessions of the Poets* (1637) by Sir John Suckling, *The Great Assizes holden in Parnassus* (1645) ascribed to the poet Wither, and *A Socratic Session* (1651) by one Samuel Sheppard ; and the device they embodied was one that had been suggested by Trajano Boccalini's *Ragguagli di Parnasso* (1612).[1] That remarkable Italian work, the influence of which persisted well into the 18th Century, was first translated into English as *Advertisements from Parnassus* (1657) by Henry Cary, Earl of Monmouth, though it was well known in England long before that date. Indeed its fame was of a European character, as was seen from the numerous translations and imitations which appeared from time to time. Its popularity was due to the ingenious and piquant form adopted for discussing political, literary, and intellectual affairs. In the imaginary realm of Parnassus, Apollo, attended by the Muses

---

[1] For a discussion of this work and its influence on English literature, see Spingarn, *op. cit.* i. pp. xxiii–xxv : and for a more detailed treatment the article by Richard Thomas in *Aberystwyth Studies*, vol. iii. pp. 73–102.

and eminent men of all the ages, was represented as holding his court in which judgments were pronounced on questions submitted by the ' gazetteer ', who was Boccalini himself. Thus, in connexion with literary affairs, Justus Lipsius was reproved for his attack on Tacitus on account of his impiety; Castelvetro was arraigned for rejecting Tasso's famous epic because it had not observed Aristotelian rules, whereupon Aristotle, in attendance at court, protested that he had prescribed no rules ; or again, pronouncements were made on the claims of those who sought immortal fame by admission to Parnassus. The work is of a mock-heroic kind, satirical, bizarre, and ironical, but with a vein of seriousness running throughout ; and as an attractive medium for conveying literary judgments it caught the imaginations of contemporary writers.

Of the English works which made use of this device that of Suckling is little more than a lively lampoon on the coterie of poets, scholars, and courtiers who frequented the cultured gatherings of Lucius Cary, Lord Falkland, in his Oxfordshire home at Great Tew. Its immediate occasion would seem to have been the vacancy in the Poet-Laureateship caused by the death of Ben Jonson in 1637, a post filled in the year following by Sir William Davenant through the influence of the Queen ; and Suckling in characteristically mischievous fashion represents all members of that coterie as candidates for election. Apollo presides at the ceremony ; the various applications are considered ; and the laurel is ultimately awarded to a prosperous alderman, on the ground that ' the best sign of good store of wit's to have good store of coin '.[1] In Wither's *Great Assizes* the machinery is more elaborate ; for there Apollo as judge is assisted by Assessors who include Renascence scholars as well as the poets Shakespeare, Massinger, Drayton, and Jonson ; and judgment is then sought on the beginnings of English journalism, on the conduct of such periodicals as the *Mercurius Aulicus*, *Mercurius Britannicus*, and the rest. Then, too, in the *Socratic Session* the scene once again is the Court of Parnassus, to which the ancients are summoned by Apollo for judgment ; and Scaliger is now indicted for his treatment of Homer.

Of actual literary judgments in these works there is not much to say. From Suckling's *Sessions* [2] we get a glimpse of Lord Falkland's circle, with the ' ever-memorable ' John Hales, Waller, Chillingworth, and others ; but of serious criticism there is little or nothing. Jonson, it is true, is pilloried for his arrogance in claiming to have written ' works ', not plays, and to have

[1] Spingarn, *op. cit.* i. p. 193.   [2] *ibid.* i. pp. 190–3.

purged the stage ; Thomas Carew, curiously enough, is denounced for his ' hard-bound Muse ', his laboured writing ; Suckling himself is represented as having ' loved not the Muses so well as his sport ' ; while Montague, author of *The Shepherd's Paradise* (1629) is derided for his obscurity. The work, in fact, is little more than a piece of light ridicule directed by a cynical poet against the intellectuals of his day, and against the method of assigning honours in the literary field. Hardly more notable are the comments in *The Great Assizes* on the earliest efforts of English journalists ; though there are reflected the suspicion with which they were viewed, and their alleged tendencies to pervert the truth, to inculcate false doctrine and to seduce readers from more profitable pastures. And as for *A Socratic Session*, its chief interest lies in the fact that it embodies yet another attack on Scaliger for his depreciation of Homer, for which he is now consigned to the lower regions. It will therefore be seen that these works are of little positive value in the critical development. At the same time they are not without their significance ; for they represent a search for an attractive medium for critical purposes before the possibilities of the essay had become apparent.

Such then were the main attempts at judicial criticism in verse during this period, and for judgments and appreciations of a more substantial character we must turn to the criticism in prose, and in particular to the scattered remarks of Jonson in his *Conversations with Drummond* and his *Discoveries*. Here the comments, in spite of occasional prejudices, exaggerations, and contradictions, in spite, too, of their casual and often unreasoned form, will nevertheless be found to be for the most part suggestive and illuminating, thus marking the greatest advance in criticism of a judicial kind. Of significance, in the first place, is the fact that he has something to say, not only on the defects of contemporary criticism generally, but also on the true function of the critic himself. Thus nothing in his day, he states, was ' more preposterous than the running judgments upon poets and poetry ',[1] by which praise was being given to writings with which a man would scorn ' to light his tobacco ', and for the treatment of which Martial's device [2] of ' a sponge dipped in ink ' would amply suffice. Hence the debased taste that in general prevailed. The trivial works of John Taylor, the Water poet, (1580–1653), for instance, were preferred to those of Spenser ; or again, the crowd commended writers ' as they did fencers and wrestlers, thinking rude things greater than polished and

---

[1] *Discoveries*, § 63.   [2] *Epigr.* iv, 10, 4.

scattered more numerous (i.e. rhythmical) than composed '.[1] Moreover, such estimates were not confined to the sordid multitude, for ' the neater sort of . . . gallants . . . differed only in clothes, not in judgment or understanding '. Nor were those meticulous critics, the grammarians, any more helpful with their emendations of what had been written ; wherefore such critics were described as ' a kind of tinkers that make more faults than they mend '.[2] The truth was, as Heinsius [3] had put it, that ' the office of a true critic or censor was not to throw by (*ejicere*) a letter or damn an innocent syllable, . . . but to judge sincerely of an author and his matter '. And to this Jonson adds the more debatable statement that ' to judge of poets is only the faculty of poets, and not of all poets but the best '.[4] It was a doctrine that had come down apparently from the *Rhetorica ad Herennium*, was widely accepted in the 17th Century, but was subsequently denounced in the century following.

A further sign of the development of the critical faculty is seen in Jonson's general comments on current literary conditions and tendencies which he analyses with ancient authorities and standards ever in mind. Like Sidney and others before him, he laments, for instance, the low esteem in which poets were held, the name ' poet ', he explains, being still little more than ' a contemptible nickname '.[5] This, however, he accounts for, not on the earlier ground that poets had dealt with flimsy fancies and untruths, but rather as being due to the prevalence of scurrilous satire, which, since Nashe, Hall, and others had written, had become ' the diet of the times '. ' The writer must lie ', he states, ' and the gentle reader rests happy to hear the worthiest works misinterpreted, the clearest actions obscured, and the innocentest life traduced ' ; and this he describes as ' the disease of the age '.

It is in his diagnosis of the specific defects in contemporary literature, however, that Jonson's critical acumen and his acquaintance with ancient authorities and standards yet more plainly appear. He holds, to begin with, that some poets wrote only for show, and were therefore concerned merely with the ' colours ' and superficial aspects of their work, to the neglect of subject-matter and thought.[6] Others, again, aimed deliberately at ' a rough and broken style ', as a result of which their

---

[1] cf. Quin., *Inst. Or.* II. xii. 1–3.   [2] *Disc.* § 130.
[3] *Ad Horatium de Plauto et Terentio judicium, ad fin.*
[4] *Disc.* § 130 (cf. Pliny, *Letters*, I. Ep. x. De pictore, sculptore . . .
judicare nisi artifex non potest). See also Spingarn, *op. cit.* i. pp. 229–30.
[5] *ibid.* § 42.   [6] *ibid.* § 65 n. 3.

poems were wont ' to run like brewers' carts upon the stones, hobbling ' ; [1] and of these he has rather more to say. Such poets, he adds, regarded ' that style more strong and manly that struck the ear with a kind of unevenness ; and here he is evidently recalling the younger Seneca's censure of poets who *virilem putant et fortem quae aurem inaequalitate percutiat*,[2] as well as Martial's attack on the crude ill-formed verses of his day *quae per salebras* (i.e. ruts) *altaque saxa cadunt.*[3] Versifying of this kind, so Jonson explained, was nothing more than an affectation to attract attention ; though its danger lay in the fact that it had set a fashion. And here he was doubtless referring to the principle laid down by Hall in the postscript to his *Virgidemiarum*, and accepted by later satirists, namely, that satire was naturally ' both hard of conceit and harsh of style ' and thus ' unpleasing both to the unskilful and over-musical ear '. At the same time Jonson also calls attention to a contemporary defect of the opposite kind, to verse that was tuneful enough but otherwise colourless and vapid. Such verse, he states, ' runs and slides and only makes a sound ',[4] (here recalling Seneca's *blanditur et molliter labitur*) ; [5] and the work of these ' women's poets ' he contemptuously describes as being ' as smooth, as soft, as cream ' and utterly shallow in thought.

Nor are these all the current abuses that evoke his censure. There were the writers, for example, who dealt with themes which were the result of wide but indiscriminate reading, and who wrote without any sense of fitness or consistency in their efforts to turn to account their latest find. Such writers, Jonson explains, ' bring all to the stake raw and undigested ' ; [6] they merely ' confess what book they have read last '. And among these ready writers he includes, strangely enough, ' all the essayists, even their master, Montaigne '—a judgment also pronounced by Sir John Daw in *The Silent Woman*,[7] when he described Plutarch and Seneca as ' mere essayists, a few loose sentences, that's all '. Then, too, there were other writers, men of some repute, who on occasion indulged in spurious references and quotations ; [8] and besides them, cunning plagiarists who denied that they owed anything to the works of others, thus endeavouring to ' cool the scent of their fox-like thefts ', which often consisted of ' whole pages usurped from one author '.[9] Most blatant of all, however, were those who prided themselves

[1] *ibid.* §§ 65 n. 4, 137.   [2] *Ep. ad Lucilium*, cxiv.
[3] *Epigr.* xi. 90.   [4] *Disc.* § 65 n. 5.
[5] *Ep. ad. Lucilium*, cxiv.   [6] *Disc.* § 65 n. 6.
[7] II. ii.   [8] *Disc.* § 65 n. 7.   [9] *ibid.* n. 8.

on their own unaided geniuses, and who, ignorant of all art, derided the idea that care and effort were necessary in writing. These men, Jonson asserts, were wont ' to utter all they can think with a kind of violence and indisposition (i.e. disorder) ; . . . and the more wilful and stubborn they are . . . the more learned they are esteemed of the multitude, . . . who think those things the stronger that have no art '.[1] At the same time he recognizes that some good things might occasionally be uttered by men of this sort, though their rare felicities did not make up for the lack of more essential qualities. ' Their jests and their sentences (i.e. epigrams),' added Jonson,[2] ' which they only and ambitiously seek for, stick out and are more eminent because all is sordid and vile about them, as lights are more discerned in a thick darkness than a faint shadow.' And here Jonson once again, in accordance with his common practice, is applying to his own generation the judgment of an ancient classical authority, this time Quintilian,[3] on the methods characteristic of 1st-Century writers. Finally he has a word to say concerning the heat and violence generated by theological controversy in his day, and its futility for the most part. He likens such disputants to swaggerers in a tavern who, snatching at candle-sticks or pots as weapons, often fight blindly and vainly beat the air. In such controversies, he notes, ' most times the truth is lost . . . or left untouched ' ; and he adds laconically, ' such fencers in religion I like not '.[4]

Yet more arresting are Jonson's judgments pronounced on individual writers, in which he gives free expression to his reactions to their works, thus throwing further light on his critical standards and methods. Most notable, in the first place, are his remarks on Shakespeare, and more especially on his style. He had noted that the praise often accorded to his contemporary rested on the claim that he had ' never blotted out (a) line '.[5] To this Jonson's reply had been, ' would he had blotted a thousand '. In order, however, to clear himself of any charge of malice or captiousness he repeats his tribute paid elsewhere to Shakespeare's personality and writings, and now states that he had ' loved the man and honoured his memory on this side idolatry ', adding that ' he was indeed honest (i.e. honourable) and of an open and free nature, had an excellent phantasy, brave notions and gentle expressions '. Nevertheless, an outstanding defect in his work, so Jonson maintained, was his unchecked facility which sometimes resulted in careless and ridiculous passages ; though the instance quoted

---

[1] *Disc.* § 65 n. 9.   [2] *ibid.* n. 10.   [3] *Inst. Or.* II. xi. 1–3.
[4] *Disc.* § 81.   [5] *ibid.* § 64.

from *Julius Caesar* [1] by Jonson to illustrate his point is somewhat puzzling. The Folio version of 1623 reads differently and intelligibly enough ; and it remains doubtful whether Jonson, relying on memory, has quoted the passage incorrectly, or whether he is referring to an earlier draft which Shakespeare subsequently revised. That occasional obscurities exist in Shakespeare's texts, owing to the rapidity of his working, this much may be conceded ; but, in any case, the neglect of the ' file ' involved in Shakespeare's methods ran counter to Jonson's conception of the art of expression. He therefore condemns Shakespeare's unlaboured style and supports his position by a reference to the judgment passed by Augustus on Haterius, a verbose and impassioned orator of Rome, to the effect that *Haterius noster sufflaminandus est* (a brake must be applied to our friend Haterius). The judgment had been recorded by the elder Seneca,[2] along with other comments of his own ; and Seneca's whole passage is here literally adopted by Jonson to serve as his criticism of Shakespeare. Not only is Shakespeare's ' facility ' condemned and restraint recommended, but included also are the generous phrases with which Seneca had concluded his remarks. So that of Shakespeare, even more truly than of Haterius, it is asserted that ' he redeemed his vices with his virtues. There was ever more in him to be praised than to be pardoned.' [3]

This, then is Jonson's main comment on Shakespeare's art ; and it is significant that in it he confines his attention solely to Shakespeare's style or mode of expression, to his rich fancy, his noble ideas and graceful phrasing on the one hand, and to what he regards as his regrettable fluency on the other. In this way he modifies the tribute paid to Shakespeare elsewhere under different conditions, when he had credited him with his own deliberate methods of writing and with lines well and truly ' filed '. What, however, is further notable is that neither here nor elsewhere does he comment at any length on the technique of Shakespeare's dramatic art. It is true that he derides such things as the absurdities involved in historical plays by breaches of the Unities or the loose use of the Chorus ; he also ridicules Shakespeare's ' romances ' in his references to ' tales and tempests ' already mentioned ; [4] and again in his *Conversations with Drummond* he notes as a palpable absurdity Shakespeare's representa-

---

[1] III. i. 47. J.'s version is ' Caesar never did wrong but with just cause ' : cf. also his parody of the passage in *The Staple of News*, Induction.
[2] *Controversiae*, iv. Pref. 7.
[3] *ibid.* Pref. 11 : cf. *redimebat tamen vitia virtutibus* &c.
[4] See p. 256 *supra*.

tion in *The Winter's Tale* [1] of ' a shipwreck in Bohemia, where there is no sea near by some 100 miles '. But beyond these departures from factual truth and truth to life he has little· or nothing to say on Shakespeare's dramatic qualities and methods. There is of course his further blunt and uncompromising statement in the *Conversations* that ' Shakespeare wanted art ' ; [2] but into that statement too much may easily be read. It can scarcely have been, as is often supposed, an indictment of Shakespeare for the non-observance of rules expounded by Italian critics, for in both tragedy and comedy Jonson himself was an innovator and no strict follower of either classical tradition or ' neo-classical ' laws. What therefore he had primarily in mind would seem to have been Shakespeare's alleged defects in the art of expression. With the subsequent development of ' neo-classical ' theory, however, Jonson's statement took on a new and wider meaning ; and the charge that ' Shakespeare wanted art ' became the theme of much of the later Shakespearean criticism, until the realization of the truth, by Lessing, Coleridge, and others, that Shakespeare, besides being a great natural genius, was also a profound and accomplished artist.

A similar preoccupation with the art of expression is also found in Jonson's appreciation of ' the learned and able, though unfortunate ' Francis Bacon, who, by his eloquence, is said ' to have performed that in our tongue which may be compared or preferred either to insolent Greece or haughty Rome '.[3] And here, once again, Jonson is adapting for his own purposes the judgment of the elder Seneca,[4] this time on the eloquence of Cassius Severus, a Roman advocate who had denounced the trivial declamatory oratory of his age. To Bacon is therefore ascribed just those qualities of style in which Shakespeare had been described as wanting, qualities which to Jonson were basic and essential. Thus his language is said to be ' nobly censorious (i.e. severe). No man ever spake more neatly, more pressly (i.e. concisely), more weightily, or suffered less emptiness . . . in what he uttered.' Moreover his style is described as a faithful reflexion of his character ; he is said to have controlled the emotions of all his hearers ; and altogether he is represented as ' the mark and ἀκμή of our language ', in an age of noisy and confused utterance. Nor is it irrelevant to note Jonson's personal tribute added to this literary estimate, for it represents those

---

[1] III. iii. : see Spingarn, *op. cit.* i. p. 213.
[2] Spingarn, *op. cit.* i. p. 211.
[3] *Disc.* § 72 : cf. Seneca, *Controversiae*, i. Pref. 6.
[4] *ibid.* § 71 : cf. Seneca, *Controversiae*, iii. Pref.

qualities of Jonson as a prose-writer which gave weight to his criticism.

My conceit of his person [he writes] was never increased toward him by his place or honours. But I have and do reverence him for the greatness that was only proper to himself, in that he seemed to me ever by his work one of the greatest men and most worthy of admiration that had been in many ages. In his adversity I ever prayed that God would give him strength ; for greatness he could not want.

It was a criticism of the man and his work that is of lasting validity ; and together with the eulogy of Shakespeare, it represents one of the earliest literary portraits in English.

For Jonson's further remarks on contemporary *littérateurs* we are indebted mainly to the reported *Conversations* which, despite imperfections due to the occasion and manner of delivery, are nevertheless of value as throwing light on his literary tastes and opinions. His reaction against the Spenserian tradition, for instance, is revealed by his remarks on Spenser, whose stanza-forms he dislikes, as well as his subject-matter ; [1] though the latter statement he modifies in his *Discoveries*,[2] where he allows that the poet might well be read for his matter, but with the discretion with which ' Virgil read Ennius '. Then, too, he notes as a defect of *The Faerie Queene* that the significance of its design and allegory does not emerge clearly enough from the poem itself ; and that a prefatory letter addressed to Raleigh was found necessary for that purpose [3]—a weighty objection by no means unfounded. Perhaps his most famous comment on Spenser, however, was that ' in affecting the ancients he writ no language ' ; [4] and it is worth noting that in connexion with this judgment there has been some amount of misunderstanding, owing to the statement being read apart from its context. It has generally been taken to imply a sweeping censure on Spenser's use of archaic diction on artistic grounds, just as Sidney had previously condemned such usage in the alleged absence of classical precedent. Yet read in its proper setting Jonson's comment has clearly a different meaning. He was considering at the time what writers were likely to be helpful to youthful readers in forming an effective style, and he advises the neglect at first of those whose styles presented difficulties or involved departures from normal usage. In this connexion he notes that Spenser's artificial diction corresponded to nothing in actual life ; and therefore was unsuitable for the purpose he had in mind. No further condemnation was here

---

[1] Spingarn, *op. cit.* i. p. 210.
[2] § 116.
[3] Spingarn, *op. cit.* i. p. 211.
[4] *Disc.* § 116.

involved ; and elsewhere,[1] like 'E. K.', he shows himself to be fully alive to the subtle aesthetic effects which were obtained by a judicious use of archaic and dialect forms.

Of considerable interest, too, are Jonson's remarks on Donne, whose genius, vitally different from his own, comes in for admiration, though the poet's methods and qualities are not always understood. Thus Jonson is evidently puzzled by some of Donne's experiments in verse-form and style ; and he gives forcible expression to his perplexity in the familiar comment that ' Donne for not keeping of accent deserved hanging '.[2] That Donne's verse in places is rugged and harsh owing to the wrenching of accent is nowadays a commonplace. And it may well have been that in condemning these metrical liberties Jonson had in mind those poets who deliberately cultivated a ' rough and broken ' style for purposes of satire, or else as a mere affectation. But more than this was involved in Donne's irregularities. Partly no doubt a revolt against the smooth and conventional harmonies of Spenserian verse, they were also an attempt at producing novel and startling effects giving expression to his intricate thoughts, moods, and passions, and attained by an abandonment of metrical patterns and a resort to the rhythm of colloquial speech. These effects were, however, obtained not without some loss of simplicity and lucidity, as was seen, for instance, by Jonson's misinterpretation of Donne's *Anniversary*. That poem he describes as full of profanity and blasphemy, with qualities attributed to an unknown, qualities, so Jonson maintained, which could be justly associated with the Virgin Mary alone.[3] Nor is he satisfied with the poet's explanation that woman in the ideal had been the theme ; for he persists in thinking that ' Donne, for not being understood, would perish '.[4] Nevertheless, in spite of all difficulties, some measure of Donne's greatness had successfully appealed to Jonson ; for from him comes also the unmistakable pronouncement that ' Donne was the first poet of the world in some things '.[5] And this estimate, it might be added, was not confined to Jonson only. Carew's tribute has already been mentioned, and Drummond, too, bore testimony to his remarkable achievement. ' Donne, among the Anacreontic lyrics ', he writes, ' is second to none and far from all second ' ;[6] or again, ' he might easily be the best epigrammatist we have found in English '. And such enthusiastic appreciations are of interest at this date, for they go far to explain Donne's influence on 17th-Century poetry.

[1] *Disc.* § 119 b : see also p. 150 *infra*.
[2] Spingarn, *op. cit.* i. p. 211.   [3] *ibid.* i. p. 211.
[4] *ibid.* i. p. 213.   [5] *ibid.* i. p. 212.   [6] *ibid.* i. p. 216.

Of lesser value, though still of interest, are Jonson's further literary impressions recorded in the *Conversations*. And in the first place, of significance, in relation to his theorizing, is the marked preference he displays among the writers of antiquity for those of the Silver Age at Rome, for Quintilian, the younger Pliny, Petronius, Tacitus, and Martial, while also attributing the best Latin, not to Cicero, but to Petronius, the younger Pliny and Tacitus.[1] It is with contemporary literature, however, that his comments are mainly concerned ; and not a few of his judgments have survived the test of time, though others again are short-sighted or unduly censorious. Thus, in his opinion, the position of Sidney, Hooker, Selden, and others was already assured ; among the translators Chapman is commended despite his use of the long fourteener line ; Beaumont and Fletcher's tragi-comedy, *The Faithful Shepherdess*, with its lyrical element is very properly praised ; and at the same time he also points out the merits of single poems such as Wotton's *Character of a Happy Life* and Southwell's *Burning Babe*. On the other hand he makes short work of Stow and his *Chronicles* with their ' monstrous observations ', adding, rather unkindly and unnecessarily, that ' he was of his craft a tailor '. He is also less than fair to Daniel whom he describes as ' no poet ', and points out that his *Civil Wars* contained not a single battle. The contemporary fame of Du Bartas he more justly decries, describing him as a mere ' verser ' because he wrote not fiction, and condemning also Sylvester's translation of his work as faulty. These then are among the uncoordinated notes found among Drummond's papers at his death ; and their subsequent history is perhaps worthy of note. More than one later writer deplored their publication as detracting from Jonson's character and fame ; and Drummond was even accused of something like treachery in that he ' had set down in malice, abridged without judgment and published without shame ', judgments lightly expressed in private conversation. Nowadays the heat thus generated seems to have been wholly uncalled for ; since the record was not intended for publication. It is true that remarks detached from their context are easily misinterpreted, and that table-talk at its brightest may assume pungent and exaggerated form. But when all allowance is made the *Conversations* will be found to provide material of definite value which throws an interesting side-light on Jonson's literary impressions and on the critical discussions which now became a feature of social gatherings at the Mermaid and elsewhere.

[1] Spingarn, *op. cit.* i. p. 213.

CHAPTER XI

THE LAST PHASE : JONSON AND MILTON

THERE yet remains for consideration one further phase of the critical development in England, a phase which may be said to have brought Renascence influence to a close. Hitherto the course of that development, since Ascham had written, had been mainly determined by problems that had arisen in connexion with the native literature. The nature and art of poetry in general had been discussed, as well as some of the principles underlying the new drama ; sporadic judgments had also been pronounced on literary works ; and all this had been done largely by the light of Nature or reason, but also with the help of occasional but indiscriminate references to classical, post-classical, patristic, and Humanistic sources. As yet, however, apart from casual references, the teaching of classical antiquity on literature had not been directly presented, either by means of translation or treatise ; while the exposition of Aristotelian theory by 16th-Century Italian theorists had, with few exceptions, failed to influence English thought. And now, with the increased scholarship of the early 17th Century, not only were the esoteric doctrines of Pico and others recalled, but something like the enthusiasm of early Italian Humanists was recaptured, and deliberate attempts were made, for the first time in English, to expound classical doctrine with direct reference to the original authorities. This, then, was the contribution of Jonson and Milton to literary theory at this latest stage.

For the causes which led to this belated addition to earlier theorizing we must look, in the first place, to the classical bias which characterized the genius of each of the contributors. Both were widely read in classical literature ; Jonson, more particularly, in the works of the Silver Age at Rome, Milton in those of both Greece and Rome alike. And both discerned qualities in that ancient literature which responded to their innate conceptions of literary values, qualities which they found treated in the critical literature of classical antiquity. At the same time further inspiration was also derived from works which had recently appeared, thus witnessing to the growth of a classical movement. Not without its significance, for instance, was the revival of interest in the works of Vives revealed by the publication of the Latin text of his *De tradendis disciplinis* in 1612 by Henry Jackson,

an Oxford scholar ; and definite signs of an acquaintance with
his *De corruptis artibus* were also apparent in a work by George
Hakewill written in 1630. Yet more important, however, was
the development at this time of a school of classical scholarship
in Holland which influenced the growth of criticism throughout
all Europe. Already at Leyden the younger (Joseph Justus)
Scaliger (1540–1609) had prepared the way for a more intelligent
study of classical literature by the fresh light he had shed on
ancient chronology and history in his famous *Thesaurus Temporum*
(1606). In this task he had been preceded by Justus Lipsius
(1547–1606), and was followed by Daniel Heinsius (1580–1655),
whose treatise *De tragoediae constitutione* (1611), since described
as ' the quintessence of Aristotle's *Poetics* ', became one of the
most influential works of the early 17th Century. Such then were
the conditions under which Jonson and Milton wrote at this later
date. The aim of each was to recover the wisdom of the ancient
classics ; ' to be ', in Milton's words, ' an interpreter of the best
and sagest things . . . in the mother dialect '. And this was
achieved by Jonson in his *Discoveries*, and by Milton in various
Prefaces and utterances of an occasional kind.

In the *Discoveries* of Jonson, to begin with, we have what is
undoubtedly one of the most suggestive and valuable of all the
contemporary critical writings. Owing to its unique character,
however, it presents difficulties of interpretation, and its real
significance has therefore been commonly misunderstood until
quite recent times. To it was accorded by later generations some
amount of recognition and praise. Dryden, for one, found in it
' as many and profitable rules . . . as any wherewith the French
can furnish us ' ;[1] Joseph Warton, later on, admired it sufficiently
to add certain of its sections to his reprint of Sidney's *Apology*
(1757) ; Gifford,[2] again, commended ' the elegance, judgment and
learning ' displayed on every page ; while from Swinburne[3]
came an unbounded eulogy of ' the wonderful little book ' on
account of its keen insight, its profound wisdom and effective
style. All, however, were agreed in regarding the work as an
original composition, a collection of Jonson's own thoughts ' as
they had flowed out of his daily readings '. And it was left for
the scholarship of yesterday[4] to reveal its real character, that of
a series of striking passages gathered from ancient and later

---

[1] *Essays of Dryden*, ed. Ker, i. 83.
[2] *Works of Ben Jonson*, Pref. p. 51.
[3] *Essay on Ben Jonson* (1889), pp. 127–81.
[4] cf. Schelling (1892), Castelain (1907), Spingarn (1907), Simpson, and
others.

writers, and translated, sometimes literally, sometimes more freely, with modifications adapted to the needs of the time. As a result a new approach to the work was rendered possible, an approach which revealed its true nature without detracting in any great measure from its actual value.

First published as a posthumous work (probably by Sir Kenelm Digby) in the Folio edition (1640–1) of Jonson's writings, it was obviously one of those commonplace books kept by contemporary writers as repositories of arresting thoughts on which to draw in the course of their creative activities. Apparently it was not intended for publication ; and indeed, the actual date of writing is also uncertain, though it is not without reason assigned to the latter part of Jonson's life, and more particularly to the years 1620–35. Some of the passages, however, appear in modified form in works of his belonging to an earlier period (1605–15) ; and it is thus possible that a collection previously made was destroyed in the fire of 1623, and that Jonson after that date renewed with increased zest his exploration of ancient theory. At any rate it is important to note that the dramatic theory expounded at the end of the work has but little bearing on his earlier dramatic creations. But while the work is thus a notebook made up of material garnered from various sources, the result is something more than a mere compilation as a comparison with Milton's uninspiring *Commonplace Book* [1] would plainly show. The truth is that Jonson has given to the work an air of originality by diffusing throughout something of his own personality and tastes. And this is seen in the character of the passages selected, as well as in his treatment of his borrowed material. Thus his choice of matter, in the first place, is of no haphazard kind. His extracts in general consist of thoughts which found a ready response in his own nature ; and his selection of critical passages more especially is therefore of significance as representing views on literature which commended themselves to his own particular genius. Then, too, he transformed what he borrowed by presenting it in a fashion suitable for his own literary purposes. And this he does by means of a free translation, abridging, expanding or adapting as he saw fit, while employing for that purpose his own vigorous prose, with its clear, compact, picturesque, and masculine qualities. Such treatment it is that has doubtless commended the work to later generations ; but over and above this is the insight thus afforded into Jonson's views on fundamental literary matters. His material, it is true, was originally borrowed ; but in selecting and thus endorsing that

[1] Camden Soc.

material he has not only recalled some of the wisest teaching of antiquity, but has also incidentally revealed what he regarded as some of the guiding principles of the literary art.

It is therefore with the bearing of the *Discoveries* on Jonson's critical ideas that we are here primarily concerned ; and in view of his indebtedness to the ancients, it is important to note at the outset the spirit in which he makes his extensive borrowings. Thus early in the work he makes it clear that he is no servile follower of the ancients *qua* ancients, that he does not ' take all upon trust from them ', that, in short, his attitude throughout is of a judicial kind. ' It is true ', he concedes,[1] (here quoting Vives [2]) that ' they opened the gates and made the way that went before us ; but as guides not commanders '. And their pronouncements, he adds, should therefore be examined in the light of reason and submitted to the test of truth alone. Nor, he protests, does he challenge the ancients in any captious or presumptuous spirit. His desire is merely to have his reasons ' examined with theirs ', and so to arrive at what was true.

Nothing is more ridiculous [he continues later [3] (here summarizing passages in Bacon) [4]] than to make an author a dictator, as the schools have done Aristotle. . . . For to many things a man should owe but a temporary belief and a suspension of his own judgment, not an absolute resignation of himself or a perpetual captivity. Let Aristotle and others have their dues ; but if we can make farther discoveries of truth and fitness than they, why are we envied ?

But this rational and judicial temper does not altogether explain his critical attitude towards the teaching of the ancients. He has also reasons of a more positive kind, inasmuch as he shares with most of the Elizabethans a well-founded confidence in the possibilities of the national genius where art was concerned. And here, once again, he culls from Vives certain pronouncements in support of his position. Thus ' Truth ', he states,[5] ' lies open to all ; it is no man's several '. Or again, ' no art ', he adds, ' is at one stroke discovered and perfected '. And, finally, he expresses more fully his belief in the progress of art when he states his confidence in the unfailing fecundity of Nature. ' I cannot think Nature is so spent and decayed ', he writes,[6] ' that she can bring forth nothing worth her former years. She is always the same, like herself ; and when she collects her strength she is abler still. Men are decayed, and studies ; she is not.'

[1] *Disc.* §§ 21–2.
[2] Watson, *op. cit.* pp. 9–10.
[3] *Disc.* § 123.
[4] *Adv. of L.*, ed. Wright, i. pp. 34 ff.
[5] *Disc.* §§ 21–2 : cf. Watson, *op. cit.* pp. 9–10.
[6] *ibid.* § 20 : cf. Watson, *op. cit.* p. 8.

This independent attitude towards the teaching of antiquity is therefore an essential feature of Jonson's theorizing ; and in this matter he by no means stood alone. Bacon for one had declared against a blind adherence to ancient doctrine ; Elizabethan literature as a whole was a silent protest against the superstition of classical authority ; and indeed the actual questioning of authority was more general at this date than is sometimes realized. In Italy, for instance, Aristotle's authority had already been challenged by Cinthio (1504–73) in connexion with the *romanzi* ; Castelvetro [1] (1505–71) besides freeing the epic from Aristotelian restrictions had declined to allow Aristotle to prescribe unconditionally for the drama ; Patrizzi (1529–97) had already decried his claims as a philosopher ; while Bruno (1549–1600), a visitor to England in 1585, had vigorously condemned ' those who judged poetry by the rules of Aristotle '.[2] Symptomatic of the same trend, and therefore not without its significance, was also the appearance of Robert Ashley's *Interchangeable Course of Things* (1594), a translation from the French, which among other things had urged that ' we ought by our invention to augment the doctrines of the ancients '.[3] Or again, there was George Hakewill's *Apology or Declaration of the Power and Providence of God in the Government of the World* (2nd ed. 1630), in which it was denied that modern ages had decayed ; while more than once was quoted the passage from Vives denouncing the saying of Bernard of Chartres, that, compared with the ancients, the moderns ' were as dwarfs on the shoulders of giants '.[4] It is therefore clear that the stage was already set for the later conflict between the ancients and the moderns in which, among others, Perrault in France, Swift and Wotton in England, all played their parts. And in this more independent and rational attitude towards antiquity Ben Jonson also definitely shared.

Nevertheless, in spite of his critical approach to ancient theorizing, and his intention ' as an explorer ' to ' call former time into question ', of his deep-seated reverence for the ancients there can be no doubt, as was shown by his wide reading and his constant reference to their guidance in literary matters. Indeed, it is not too much to say that by this discreet treatment the value of his findings was actually enhanced ; for what he thus submits is so much sifted teaching, doctrines commended, not by mere

---

[1] See Charlton, *Castelvetro's Theory of Poetry, passim*.

[2] For further details, see Spingarn, *Lit. Crit. in the Renaissance*, pp. 112–24, 162–7.

[3] See Watson, *op. cit.* p. cvi. fn.

[4] Watson, *op. cit.* p. cvi. fn. : see p. 45 *supra*.

authority, but by his genius, his good sense and experience as well. What he looks for in his researches is further light on matters which he regards as of the first importance. They were those same subjects which had already engaged the attention of earlier critics ; and his collection of passages, though unsystematic in kind, is therefore concerned with three main topics, namely, the art of expression in words (§§ 1–126), poetry (§§ 127–30), and certain aspects of the drama(§§ 131–7). On each of these subjects he has much of interest to say, doctrines gathered from all sorts of sources and embodying things new and old, some of universal and lasting value.

In accordance with ancient and Humanistic traditions he devotes considerable attention, in the first place, to the art of expression in words, to the principles underlying a sound and effective style. It has already been stated that the idea of wedding eloquence and wisdom had been fundamental in Humanistic thought. Vives, for example, had emphasized the need for a lighter touch in connexion with all branches of learning ; and Jonson reiterates his teaching, and also his phrasing, in demanding that prose writing should be not only clear but elegant as well. ' A man should so deliver himself ', he writes,[1] ' as to redeem arts (i.e. studies) from their rough and braky seats, where they lay hid and overgrown with thorns, to a pure, open and flowery light, where they may take the eye and be taken by the hand.' Apart from this he is conscious of the glaring defects of many of his contemporaries. Thus he complains of the craze for studied artifice, and states that in his day ' nothing is good that is natural '.[2] Moreover, ' that which is writhed and tortured ', he adds, ' is counted the more exquisite. Cloth of bodkin or tissue must be embroidered ; as if no face were fair that were not powdered or painted, no beauty to be had but in wresting and writhing our own tongue.' Then, too, there were also those ' who ran away from Nature ' in their deliberate cultivation of an inflated and grandiose style, thereby imitating ' the Tamerlanes and Tamerchams ' with their loud appeals to ' the ignorant gapers '.[3] Such writers, he contended, with their ' furious vociferation ' knew no other way of being impressive ; whereas your true ' artificer ' (i.e. artist) followed different methods, even though in so doing he was dubbed ' barren, lean, and a poor writer '. Or again, elsewhere he refers to those who, like Homer's Thersites, spoke without judgment or measure ;[4] and against such garrulous and long-winded speakers (and writers) he recalls

---

[1] *Disc.* § 19 : cf. Watson, *op. cit.* pp. 6–7.   [2] *ibid.* § 62.
[3] *ibid.* § 65 n. 10.   [4] *ibid.* § 46.

many wise sayings collected by Aulus Gellius,[1] relating to such *futiles et importuni locutores.*

It is to correct such abuses and to formulate sound ideas that Jonson collects in his reading such passages as bear on ' eloquence ' and the secrets of good writing. His main authorities for this purpose are Quintilian and Vives, though he draws occasionally on other sources ; and his findings, freed from the pedantries of earlier Rhetorics, are for the most part of an eminently practical kind. Concerning ' eloquence ' in general he has some suggestive remarks to make. He recalls, for instance, the ancient commonplace, *oratio imago animi,* pointing out that style is an expression of personality, and that ' language most shows a man ' since ' it springs out of the most retired and inmost parts ' [2] of his being. Or again, he notes the intimate relation existing between words and sense. The sense, he explains, is as ' the life and soul of language, without which all words are dead ' ; [3] and careless speech, he adds, detracts from the worth of subject-matter.[4] Moreover, for the cultivation of a good style he recommends the reading of the best authors, a study of the best speakers and constant exercise in actual writing ; [5] all in accordance with ancient teaching. On the other hand, highly significant is his omission of any reference in this connexion to the process of imitating great writers. And here he would seem to have been influenced by Quintilian, who had pointed out the dangers of a mechanical copying, as a result of which defective features might easily be imitated, while the subtler and more vital effects of the original would defy imitation ; and in any case the copy would of necessity be inferior to its model.[6] On this point Jonson himself has one remark to make. As if by way of commenting on the earlier Ciceronians he recalls the saying of the elder Seneca, that ' one though he be excellent . . . is not to be imitated alone. For never no imitator ever grew up to his author ; likeness is always on this side truth.' [7]

In his more detailed notes on style he calls attention, in the first place, to the need for a choice of suitable diction, recalling in that connexion the familiar saying of Julius Caesar, *delectus verborum origo est eloquentia.*[8] His first requirement is for a due observance of *decorum* or fitness, for writing according to the

---

[1] *Noctes Atticae,* i. 15.
[2] *Disc.* § 121 : cf. Vives, *De rat. dic.,* ii. (*Opera,* i. 103).
[3] *ibid.* § 119.   [4] *ibid.* § 124.   [5] *ibid.* § 115.
[6] See Atkins, *Lit. Crit. in Antiquity,* ii. 278 ff.
[7] *Disc.* § 71 : cf. *Controversiae,* i. Pref. 6.
[8] Cic., *Brutus,* lxxvii. 253.

capacity of the reader. Words in common use, he urges, should
normally be employed ; since ' words are the people's '.[1] Yet
discrimination should also be exercised in the actual choice. The
words chosen should be in keeping with the person speaking, the
subject treated, as well as the occasion of utterance, different
vocabularies being needed for the pulpit, the law-court, the camp,
and the ordinary affairs of life. Furthermore, in making the
choice, custom or usage should be the guide ; in other words,
' that speech which is the consent of the learned '.[2] New-minted
words and archaic forms should be sparingly employed ; for ' the
chief virtue of style ', he explains, ' is perspicuity ', and no
interpreter should be needed. At the same time he concedes that
' words borrowed of antiquity do lend a kind of majesty to style
and are not without their delight sometimes ' ; for, so he asserts,
they bring with them not only the authority of age but an element
of freshness as well. What he therefore recommends is, in
Quintilian's phrase, ' the eldest of the present and the newest of
the past ' ; [3] for archaic forms, he adds, were once in common
usage. To this approval of archaic forms reference has already
been made ; [4] though works strongly coloured with archaisms are
described as unsuitable models for young readers. Virgil, it is
pointed out, had used them sparingly ; whereas Lucretius's
style with its many archaisms was ' scabrous and rough ' ; as
were also the styles of Jonson's own contemporaries who made
an undue use of Chaucerisms which were ' better expunged and
banished '. Hence for young writers Jonson advises the reading
of Livy before Sallust and Sidney before Donne ; while Gower
and Chaucer were to be kept for a later date. For the rest he
recommends the use of certain words the function of which was
to add ' ornament and beauty ' to style, just as flowers are
gathered to ' strew houses or make garlands '.[5] But such words,
he adds, should be naturally and unostentatiously introduced.
They should ' grow to our style, as in a meadow where, though
the mere grass . . . delights, yet the variety of flowers doth
heighten and beautify '.
  A choice of suitable diction in itself, however, did not necessarily ensure good writing ; and Jonson enlarges further on those
principles which seemed to him to lie at the root of effective
expression in words, drawing as before mainly on the teaching of
Quintilian and Vives. His first requirement is one that had been
reiterated by all ancient authorities from Plato onwards. It was

[1] *Disc.* § 119 : cf. Vives, *De rat. dic.*, i. (*Opera*, i. 85 ff.).
[2] *ibid.* § 119 b : cf. Quin. *Inst. Or.* i. vi. 3.
[3] *Inst. Or.* i. vi. 41.   [4] See p. 310 *supra*.   [5] *Disc.* § 119 b.

an insistence on the basic need for clear thinking, and for having something definite to say—a commonplace, perhaps, but one which was (and is) often disregarded, and to the neglect of which Bacon had referred in his remarks on ' fantastic learning '. Concerning this fundamental need, however, Jonson is peremptory. ' In style ', he writes,[1] it is necessary ' to consider what ought to be written, and after, what manner. The writer must first think and excogitate his matter.' Or again, elsewhere he states that the successful writer is one ' who apprehends the consequence of things in their truth and utters his apprehensions as truly ' ; [2] and in support he recalls Cicero's pronouncement that clear impressions were needed for sound expression, and that *dicere recte nemo potest, nisi qui prudenter intelligit.*

At the same time he recognizes that matter and manner are vitally related and that thought must be properly arranged before it can be persuasively and attractively expressed. And here again Jonson is recalling an essential principle that had been maintained by all classical authorities. Thus he states that for a man to write well ' he must take care in placing and ranking both matter and words, that the composition be comely '.[3] Yet ' comeliness ' alone would not suffice. A natural development of the thought with easy transitions was also needed ; and with Quintilian's help a practical method of attaining those qualities is therefore indicated. While ' election and a mean ' (i.e. discrimination and restraint), so he states, are everywhere needed, it was further recommended that the writer should constantly ' look back to what was intended at first ',[4] so as to ' make all an even and proportioned body '. And to this practice of turning back he attaches considerable importance, for he enlarges on the matter more than once in his work. Thus elsewhere he explains the effects of such continuous reference to what was already written. ' It helps ', he asserts, ' the consequence (i.e. the sequence of thought) and makes the juncture better ; [5] it quickens the heat of imagination, that often cools in the time of setting down ; and gives it new strength, as if it grew lustier by the going back. As we see in the contention of leaping, they jump farthest that fetch their race largest.' It was advice well calculated to produce the classical qualities of order, proportion, and clarity, those qualities, in short, in which earlier prose had been frequently lacking. And this essential need for an orderly

---

[1] *Disc.* § 115 : cf. Quin., *Inst. Or.* x. iii. 4.
[2] *ibid.* § 124.
[3] *Disc.* § 115 : cf. Quin., *Inst. Or.* x. iii. 5.
[4] *ibid.* § 65, n. 10.   [5] *ibid.* § 115 : cf. Quin. *Inst. Or.* x. iii. 6.

development of thought with easy transitions he stresses elsewhere. Thus, ' order ', he explains,[1] ' helps much to perspicuity, as confusion hurts ' ; or again, ' our style should be like a skein of silk, to be . . . found by the right thread, not ravelled or perplexed '.

Apart from these basic requirements of appropriate diction and sound thought effectively arranged Jonson has something more to say on style, including notes of a more or less technical character, and what is perhaps yet more valuable, general advice of an eminently practical kind. To begin with, he recognizes the need for the heightening of style produced by the use of figurative expressions ; though it is noteworthy that he makes no attempt to deal with figures as a whole. Nevertheless he allows that ' some writings need sunshine ' ; and departures from the ordinary way of writing he justifies mainly on the score of pleasure and variety, ' as travellers turn out of the highway, drawn by the commodity of a footpath or the delicacy and freshness of the field '.[2] His treatment of figures, however, is limited to ' translations ' (i.e. metaphors), hyperboles, and the like. The use of metaphors, he explains, is on occasion necessary ; not only because they add an element of beauty and elegance, but also because they often supply the most effective and fitting expression.[3] Yet care was to be exercised in their employment ; for far-fetched metaphors led to obscurity, pretentious metaphors to a loss of grace, while unsuitable metaphors were merely ridiculous, as when a divine used expressions of the tavern or a rustic the language of the sea. And as a further instance of the misuse of metaphors he quotes (following Quintilian [4]) the ugly conceit of an old epic poet of Rome, namely, [*Juppiter*] *cana nive conspuit Alpes* (J. with white snow the Alps bespewed). Then, too, the mixing of metaphors, he adds, should be avoided ; a metaphor drawn from ' sea and billows ' should not end in ' flame and ashes '.[5] Nor again, should a metaphor be too long sustained ; lest the effect be confused and savour of affectation. Concerning hyperboles he has less to say. He notes, for instance, that their use varies in different languages, that there are hyperboles ' which become one language that will by no means admit another '. Moreover, he explains, however daring they may be, they must always be plausible and acceptable ; ' they may be above faith but never

---

[1] *ibid.* § 120 : cf. Vives, *De rat. dic.* i. (*Opera*, i. 98 ff).
[2] *ibid.* : cf. Vives, *De rat. dic.* i. (*Opera*, i. 102).
[3] *ibid.* § 119 : cf. Vives, *De rat. dic.* i. (*Opera*, i. 85 ff).
[4] *Inst. Or.* VIII. vi. 7.
[5] *Disc.* § 120 : cf. Vives, *De rat. dic.* i. (*Opera*, i. 101).

above reason '. And from the elder Seneca [1] he draws striking examples of their use and misuse.

Equally conventional are his remarks on the different styles, as when, for instance, he recalls the traditional kinds—high, middle, and low—and the defects usually associated with each.[2] Thus the ' high ' style, he states, easily degenerates into an inflated, bombastic style, the ' low ' style into an abject and colourless style. And in his further descriptions he makes use (following Cicero) of analogies drawn from human physiology, as when he refers, for instance, to the ' fleshy ' style as excessively periphrastic and rotund, or again, to the ' bloodless ' style as arid and colourless. His main interest, however, is concentrated on the brief and forcible style ; though periods are beautiful, he concedes, when they are not too long. And on the various kinds of this more forcible style he enlarges in some detail. Thus a ' strict and succinct ' style he describes as that from which nothing can be taken without loss ; the ' brief ' style as that which expresses much in little : the ' concise ' style as that which leaves something to the imagination ; and the ' abrupt ' style as being broken and irregular. His ultimate advice, however, is ' to write what we can the nearest way, so we keep our gait and not leap ' ; for excessive brevity, he explains, may be difficult to understand, while undue length is not easy to remember. He would prefer in general ' a plain downright wisdom to a foolish and affected eloquence ' ; ' our style ', he adds, ' should be neither dry nor empty, nor winding and wanton with far-fetched descriptions '.

Finally, of greater interest is the practical advice he gives on the methods of cultivating an effective style, mainly gathered from Quintilian. In the first place he recognizes that to be content with the meticulous precepts of the grammarians is not enough ; for ' their extreme anxieties and foolish cavils ', he urges,[3] can hamper expression and ' break a wit in pieces '. At the same time the need for consideration is said to be ever present. The first ideas and words that come to mind were not to be adopted forthwith ; [4] for the very ease with which they presented themselves should render them suspect, and besides, ' all that we invent doth please us in their conception '. Hence the unceasing need for care and judgment ; even though it involved at first slow and laborious methods. Yet such, it is stated, was the practice of the best writers in their beginnings. ' They did nothing rashly ;

---

[1] *Suasoriae*, i. 11–12.
[2] *Disc.* §§ 120–1 : cf. Vives, *De rat. dic.* i. (*Opera*, i. 95 ff., 103 ff.).
[3] *ibid.* § 118 : cf. Quin., *Inst. Or.* viii. Pref. 18.
[4] *ibid.* § 115 : cf. Quin., *Inst. Or.* x. iii. 7–10.

they aimed first at writing well, and then custom made it easy and a habit.'[1] And, so Jonson adds, 'ready writing makes not good writing ; but good writing brings on ready writing '. Here then was a clear enunciation of classical principle, enjoining, not so many rules, but the exercise of judgment, restraint, and ordered expression, so as to write well knowingly. At the same time it is obvious that it is no rigid procedure that he thus advocates. For on occasion, he allows, less laboured methods were possible ; it was permissible ' to spread our sails, so the favour of the gale deceive us not '. In youthful writings, moreover, undue exuberances were to be condoned, provided that they were subsequently pruned ; while elsewhere he insists that, despite the inspiration derived from the reading of the best authors, each writer should be free to develop his style in accordance with his own genius.[2] Nor wholly irrelevant is his further advice on matters less fundamental ; as for instance when he points out the value of illuminating quotations aptly introduced, or again, when he shrewdly suggests that greater care should be bestowed on the beginning and end of a composition than on the middle, and on the end more than on the beginning.[3]

Such then is the substance of Jonson's notes on style in general ; though his supplementary remarks on epistolary style are also worth noting. His main ideas he draws from the *Epistolica Institutio* of Justus Lipsius, but what he borrows he transforms by his own lively treatment ; and the teaching represents a marked advance on the rigid system of the medieval *ars dictaminis*. For the most part the guiding principles are in keeping with those already formulated, namely, the need for clear ideas, orderly arrangement, a sense of fitness, and the rest. But for letter-writing in particular the special qualities required are said to be brevity, perspicuity, liveliness, and discretion ; and on each of these requirements Jonson has something of interest to say. Significant, in the first place, is the importance attached to brevity of expression ;[4] for as a result of the use made of empty complimentary phrases, round-about expressions, parentheses and the like, sentences that went ' a-begging for some meaning and laboured to be delivered of the great burden of nothing ', were all too frequent in ordinary correspondence. Only the most significant words should therefore be used ; and moreover, it is urged, that ' letters should not be treatises, except to learned men, and even among them there is a kind of thrift and saving of words '.

---

[1] *ibid.* § 115 : cf. Quin., *Inst. Or.* x. iii. 9–10.
[2] *ibid.*   [3] *ibid.* § 119 b.
[4] *ibid.* § 126 : cf. Lipsius, *Ep. Inst.* cap. vii.

Nor was the brevity obtained by terse and broken sentences always successful. And here Jonson recalls Quintilian's statement that ' there is a briefness of the parts that makes the whole long ' ; so that ' oftentimes a short journey is made long by unnecessary baits '.[1] This, in his opinion, had been a defect of some earlier Humanists ; and ' perhaps Seneca ', he adds, ' may be impeached of it ; I accuse him not '.

In connexion with the second of these requirements, perspicuity,[2] he emphasizes once again the need for a natural sequence of thought, so that ' every clause may give the Q, one to another, and be bespoken ere it come '. Then, too, ease and simplicity of expression are said to be especially necessary. Letters, he points out, should not be ' penned like English statutes ', or cumbered with the obscure terminology of learned men. That is why scholars, he explains, often speak ' fumblingly ' and why ' talkative and shallow men do often content their hearers (or readers) '. Nor, again, was the general treatment to be too precise and formal. ' A diligent kind of negligence ', he states, should be cultivated, ' as ladies do in their attire ' ; and besides, too frequent a resort to expressions ' perfumed ' and fashionable was also to be avoided. On the further matters of liveliness and discretion he has less to say. He is content to state, for instance, that freshness and animation may be obtained by a proper use of conceits, allusions, wise commonplaces, and the rest. And as for discretion, this, he asserts, is attained by an ever-present sense of what is fitting. It is a quality, he adds, that is the fruit of ripe judgment. But it is acquired from no knowledge of art, being a gift of Nature and of God himself.

So far attention has been given to Jonson's notes on style ; and his observations on poetry have next to be considered, as affording some idea of what he regarded as most valuable in ancient poetic theory. Of the essential value of poetry he has no doubt. It is, for instance, described as ' the most prevailing (i.e. effective) eloquence ' ; [3] though elsewhere he recalls that estimate of Cicero's which placed eloquence first in the scale of values, with poetry a good second. Thus, ' the poet ', he writes,[4] ' is the nearest borderer upon the orator and expresseth all his virtues, though he be tied more to numbers ; is his equal in ornament and above him in his strength '. Then, too, (following Plutarch [5]) he points out that poetry was closely related to the sister art, painting, ' poetry being a speaking picture and

---

[1] *Inst. Or.* IV. ii. 41.   [2] *Disc.* § 126 : cf. Lipsius, *Ep. Inst.* cap. viii–x.
[3] *ibid.* § 127.   [4] *ibid.* § 130 : cf. Cic., *De orat.* i. 16.
[5] *ibid.* § 109 : cf. Plutarch, *De aud. poetis*, 17 f.

picture a mute poesy '. Both, he explained, were arts of imitation, ' inventing and feigning, with pleasure and profit as their common object ' ; yet of the two, he added, ' the pen is more noble than the pencil, for that can speak to the understanding, the other but to the sense '. At the same time he notes that latterly poetry had been discredited, not as before, for lack of truth, but because of its want of seriousness, and more especially because of the abuses and calumnies of contemporary satirical writers. From such abuses, however, he claims that his own satirical writings had been free, in virtue of their impersonal character. In those works, he asserts, ' I name no persons, but deride follies ' ; and for support of such treatment he refers to judgments pronounced by Jerome and Erasmus.[1]

Elsewhere in his collection he submits in a more or less system-atic form certain doctrines concerning the nature of poetry gathered from classical and post-classical authorities. First come some remarks of a general kind,[2] for which he claims the authority of Aristotle. Thus the poet is described as ' above all a maker or feigner ' ($\varkappa \alpha \tau$ ' $\dot{\varepsilon} \xi o \chi \dot{\eta} \nu \ \dot{o} \ \pi o \iota \eta \tau \dot{\eta} \varsigma$). His art is said to be ' an art of imitation or feigning, expressing the life of man in fit measures, numbers, and harmony '. Moreover, he is called a poet, not because he writes ' in measures only ', but because ' he feigneth and formeth a fable and writes things like the truth ' ; for ' the fable and fiction ', it is added, ' is the form and soul of any poetical work '. Here, it is true, something of Aristotelian doctrine is recalled ; his definition of poetry, for instance, as an art of imitation, an art concerned, not with mere versifying, but with depicting the life of man in fictional form, which was said to constitute the essential element of poetry. At the same time it is clear that his conception of ' imitation ' is non-Aristotelian ; for it is represented as a process of mere ' feigning ' or fancy, with elements based on actual life, thus treating of ' things like the truth ', yet productive of fiction only, and without any correspondence to truths of a higher kind. With Aristotle, however, the term involved something more than a fanciful transcript of life which had the virtue of veri-similitude ; it stood rather for an imaginative and a creative process in which were revealed the permanent and universal characteristics of human life and thought. Jonson's position, in short, was not so very different from that of Bacon, to whom poetry was nothing more than a product of the ' imagination ', resulting in narratives of a purely fanciful kind.

[1] *Ep. ad Martinum Dorpinum* (XL). (*Opera*, ix. pp. 4 ff.)
[2] *Disc.* § 128.

For the further discussion of poetry he adopts the Hellenistic three-fold category of *poema, poesis, and poeta*, a scholastic distinction that had been utilized, not only by Graeco-Roman critics of old,[1] but by many of the 16th-Century Italian theorists [2] as well.   Concerning *poema* he has little to say, beyond mentioning its various forms of epic, dramatic, lyric, elegiac, and epigrammatic ; [3] while his treatment here of *poesis*, or the poetic art, is also of a limited kind, being concerned solely with justifying its description as ' queen of arts '.[4]   Thus, of divine origin, to begin with, it is said to have been first received by the Hebrews, then treasured by the Greeks and by them transmitted to the Latins and all civilized peoples.   For it moreover was claimed a beneficent influence.   There was Aristotle's testimony that it conduced to ' the good life ' ; while Cicero's familiar statement [5] regarding the manifold benefits it conferred on mankind under all sorts of conditions is quoted at length.   Then, too, it is recalled that it had been described as ' a dulcet and gentle philosophy ', that with ' a ravishing delight and incredible sweetness ' led men on to noble deeds.   It is on *poeta*, or the requirements of the poet alone, that he enlarges at some length and thereby submits his views on poetry in general.

With this object in view he brings together various pronouncements of ancient authorities on what went to the making of a poet.   And these requirements he sums up as native genius, constant practice, help derived from earlier master-poets, wide reading, and a knowledge of art.[6]   In the first place he insists on the need for a specially gifted nature, over and above that measure of understanding required for other intellectual pursuits ;   and this he supports by well-known utterances of Plato, Aristotle, and Seneca.   One thus endowed, and duly inspired, was said to be capable of the highest flights in the realms of thought, as was indeed implied in ancient allusions to Pegasus, Helicon, and Parnassus.   And this requirement was why your true poet was rarely found.   ' Every beggarly corporation ', Jonson asserts, ' affords the state a major (i.e. mayor) or two bailiffs yearly ;   but *solus rex aut poeta non quotannis nascitur* '. Jonson was here adapting a picturesque phrase of Petronius ; [7] and he plays with the idea more than once elsewhere in his works.[8]

---

[1] See Atkins, *Lit. Crit. in Antiquity*, i. 170–1, ii. *passim*.
[2] See Spingarn, *Lit. Crit. in the Renaissance*, 27, n.   [3] *Disc.* § 129.
[4] *ibid.* § 130.   [5] *Pro Archia*, 12–30.   [6] *Disc.* § 130.
[7] *Fragmenta Poetica*, ed. Nisard, p. 101.
[8] cf. *Every Man in his Humour*, v. v. 37 :   *New Inn*, Epilogue : *Epigrams*, 79.

In the second place frequent exercise was said to be necessary, even for one well endowed with poetic gifts ; and, in addition, all such attempts were to be submitted to ' forge and file ', since the quality of the ancients could only be slowly won. Virgil, for instance, was said to have ' brought forth his verses like a bear, and, after, formed them with licking ' ; [1] while Euripides, so it was stated, had reproved the tragic poet, Alcestis, for hasty writing. ' I have met many of these rattles ', added Jonson, ' that made a noise and buzzed ' ; whereas ' things wrote with labour deserve to be so read and will last their age '.

Yet industry and meticulous care alone were not enough. Imitation of the best poets was also recommended ; and the particular sense in which Jonson uses that term is worthy of note. On the authority of Horace [2] he dismisses the idea of servile copying, of borrowing indiscriminately what was good and what was ' raw and undigested '. He represents it rather as a process like that of the bee gathering honey from the choicest flowers ; or, in terms reminiscent of the Pléiade teaching, as a process of converting the substance of a poet's work into nourishment for another's use. And here, it might be added, Jonson has rightly interpreted the ' imitation ' first prescribed by Isocrates and inculcated later by Cicero, Horace, Quintilian, and other Graeco-Roman critics.[3] By them it was propounded as a process, not of mere copying, but of ' re-creation ', a means, that is, of attaining originality by creating something new out of the old. And Jonson further recalls the successful working of the process in antiquity, as seen in Virgil's imitation of Homer, Horace's imitation of Archilochus, and the rest.

Concerning the fourth requirement—wide reading—Jonson has little to say beyond emphasizing the need for that mental equipment afforded by ample and careful study. And, adapting a well-known passage of Persius's *Satires*,[4] he bluntly asserts that no man ' can leap forth suddenly a poet by dreaming he hath been in Parnassus, or having washed his lips (as they say) in Helicon '. It is to the fifth and last requirement—the need for a knowledge of artistic principle—that Jonson attaches perhaps the greatest importance. Such knowledge alone, he asserts, ' can lead the poet to perfection ' ; and, referring to Cicero as his authority, he aptly quotes in addition the neat saying of Simylus, a didactic poet of the Hellenistic period, fragments of whose works

[1] Donatus, *De P. Virgilii . . . Vita*, ix (33).
[2] cf. *Ars Poetica*, ll. 131 ff.
[3] See Atkins, *Lit. Crit. in Antiquity*, i. 128 ; ii. 29, 100, 280 &c.
[4] *Prologus*, ll. 1 ff.

had been collected by Stobaeus [1] (*c.* A.D. 500). The lines thus quoted were as follows :

> Nature of Art bereft will not suffice
> For any work whate'er in all the world ;
> Nor Art again, devoid of Nature's aid.[2]

But further suggestions would also seem to have been drawn from the same source when Jonson goes on to point out in this same connexion the value of the aid afforded by the judicious critic. He who is content to learn only from himself, so Jonson explains, has but ' a fool to his master ' ; and the poet should therefore accept guidance from the wisest teachers, ' among whom Horace and (he that taught him) Aristotle, deserved to be the first in estimation '.

To this advice of a general kind Jonson, however, adds some interesting remarks, first, on the nature of those artistic principles, and, secondly, on the source whence guidance might most effectually be sought. Thus, ' I am not of that opinion,' he writes,[3] ' to conclude a poet's liberty within the narrow limits of laws which either the grammarians or the philosophers prescribe. For before they found out those laws there were many excellent poets that fulfilled them, amongst whom none more perfect than Sophocles.' Here, by means of a close translation, he is embodying the views of Heinsius ; [4] and, continuing that scholar's argument, he recalls further examples of the freedom from petty rules characteristic of the great Greeks. ' Which of the Greeklings ', he asks, ' durst ever give precepts to Demosthenes ? Or to Pericles whom the age named heavenly, because he seemed to thunder and lighten with his language ? Or to Alcibiades, who had rather Nature for his guide than Art for his master ? '

But while petty and restricting rules were thus to be discounted, there were at the same time certain principles of art to be observed : and in stating that those principles were to be found in Aristotle's *Poetics*, Jonson pays a reasoned and striking tribute to that authority as the supreme guide in literary matters, and as one who embodied in his theories the teachings of genius and experience alike.

Whatsoever Nature : . . . dictated to the most happy [5] [he writes (still following Heinsius [6])] or long exercise to the most laborious,

---

[1] *Florilegium*, ed. Meineke, ii. 352.
[2] See Sandys, *History of Classical Scholarship*, i. 56 ; and Atkins, *Lit. Crit. in Antiquity*, i. 179–80.
[3] *Disc.* § 130. [4] *De tragoediae constitutione*, cap. I.
[5] *Disc.* § 130. [6] *De trag. const.*, cap. I.

that the wisdom . . . of Aristotle hath brought into an art because he understood the causes of things. And what other men did by chance or custom he doth by reason ; and not only found out the way not to err, but the short way we should take not to err.

These, then, are Jonson's reasons for accepting Aristotle as guide ; and this tribute is by no means inconsistent with his refusal elsewhere to accept that authority as dictator. In a further notable passage he even emphasizes his respect for Aristotle as a critic, when he describes him as ' the first accurate critic and truest judge ; [1] nay, the greatest philosopher the world ever had. . . . He taught us two offices, . . . how we ought to judge rightly of others, and what we ought to imitate specially in ourselves.' Allusions to Aristotle had occasionally been made by earlier critics ; but this was the first discerning appreciation from one who was himself a keen and exacting critic.

Such then, in the main, are Jonson's notes relating to poetic theory ; and he concludes his collection with some additional remarks on dramatic poetry [2] chiefly, commenting, first, on the function of comedy, and secondly, on the correct method of constructing a plot. The former of these subjects had been suggested to him by a note in Heinsius's edition of Horace [3] (1612), commenting on Horace's expressed preference for Terence as compared with Plautus ; [4] the latter, by his own realization of the importance of the fable or plot in poetry generally—an element which he had previously defined as ' the form and soul of poetry '. And throughout his treatment of those matters he follows Heinsius closely, in places resorting to a literal translation of his teaching.

To comedy, in the first place, Jonson had already assigned special importance, in accordance with views current in antiquity. Of all poets, he had maintained, [5] the comic poet came nearest to the orator, not only by reason of his elegant language, but also on account of his power of ' expressing to the life ' so many and varied emotions, in which skill he was said to surpass both painter and sculptor. This statement he now supplements by certain remarks of Heinsius relating to the function of comedy —views which probably coincided with his own. Thus, noting to begin with, that in the matter of structure ' the parts of a comedy are the same with a tragedy ',[6] Jonson states, as his main

---

[1] *Disc.* § 130.   [2] *ibid.* §§ 131 ff.
[3] pp. 78 ff. : republished (1635) as a dissertation, *Ad Horatii de Plauto et Terentio judicium.*
[4] cf. Hor., *Epis.* ii. i. 58–9, 170 : *A.P.* 270 ff.
[5] *Disc.* § 130 : cf. Quin., *Inst. Or.* x. i. 65, 71.   [6] *ibid.* § 131.

point, that the function of comedy no less than that of tragedy was ' to delight and teach ', adding that comic poets had been called διδάσκαλοι or teachers by the Greeks.   In support of this view, however, he proceeds to deprecate, and even condemn, the element of laughter in comedy, a position that had been maintained by more than one earlier Humanist.   He asserts, for instance, that ' the moving of laughter is not always the end of comedy ' ;   that, indeed, it was nothing more than a ' fowling ' (i.e. a snare) to entrap and befool popular audiences.   And as his authority for such a statement he quotes Aristotle as having described laughter as ' a fault in comedy, a kind of turpitude that depraves some part of a man's nature without a disease '. But such a statement is nowhere to be found in Aristotle.   The passage as quoted is none other than a serious misinterpretation on the part of Heinsius ;   for what Aristotle actually wrote was as follows :   ' the laughable is merely a species of the ugly or bad ; it consists in some defect or ugliness which is neither painful nor harmful '.[1]

On this mishandling of Aristotle's text, however, Heinsius had based his theory, for which he contrived to find further support in antiquity ;   and Jonson here adopts his theorizing as a whole.   Thus he condemns outright the laughter caused in comedy by ' a wry face ', or again, ' by a rude clown dressed in a lady's habit and using her action '.[2]   He notes also the distrust of laughter evinced by ancient philosophers ;   how Plato, for instance, had condemned Homer for sacrilege in representing the laughter of the gods ;   how, too, Aristotle had declared that ' to seem ridiculous is a part of dishonesty and foolish '.[3]   Moreover, he maintains that the defects of the Old Attic Comedy were largely the outcome of the desire to cause scornful laughter. ' Insolent (i.e. *inusitata*) and obscene speeches ', it is stated, as well as jests on good men and attacks on individuals, all alike were designed for that particular purpose ;   so that ' scurrility came forth in place of wit '.   Of such comic poets Aristophanes was described as the chief ;   and examples of these abuses were indicated in his derisive and scandalous treatment of Socrates, or again, in his absurd investigations into the activities of a flea.[4] He is said, in short, to have expressed ' all the moods and figures of what is ridiculous ' ;   and as ' vinegar is not accounted good until the wine be corrupted, so (it is added) jests that are true and natural seldom raise laughter with . . . the multitude '. The truth was that this theory denying a place to laughter in

[1] Aristotle, *Poetics*, 1449 a.   [2] *Disc.* § 131.   [3] *Ethics*, iv. 9.
[4] Aristophanes, *Clouds*, 217 ff., 144 ff.

comedy was based neither on sound authority nor yet on actual experience ; though owing to the prestige of both Heinsius and Jonson, its later influence proved to be considerable in France and England alike.[1]

In his concluding notes on the fable or plot Jonson is on safer ground in reproducing, with the help of Heinsius [2] again, certain details of Aristotle's teaching on that subject. He assumes throughout that, generally speaking, the same principles of construction apply to tragedy, comedy, and the epic ; though he also recognizes that, from the very nature of things, the epic can run to greater lengths than either of the dramatic forms. He begins, however, by defining the main features of a plot. It is described as ' an imitation of one entire and perfect action ', the parts of which ' are so joined . . . together as nothing in the structure can be changed or taken away without impairing the whole ', while in the parts themselves there must be ' a proportional magnitude '. In this way he emphasizes, first, the need for unity of action ; the story must supply all necessary details ; it must also omit all that is irrelevant. Then, too, that unity should be of an organic kind, with ' a beginning, a midst and an end '. In other words, there should be a definite development in the incidents employed. The action should embody an intelligible beginning, a satisfactory end, and a middle which, besides being the outcome of what had gone before, led on naturally to the conclusion. Moreover, besides this necessary cohesion of the parts, the parts and the whole as well should be of ' a proportional magnitude ' ; that is, ' neither too vast nor too minute '. ' If the action be too great ', he adds, ' we can never comprehend the whole together ' ; if again ' it be too little . . . it affords no view to stay ' in the memory.

To these, the main Aristotelian principles underlying the formation of plots, Jonson adds some further remarks.[3] And, first, he deals with the appropriate length of the action, stating that no action would be of merit without ' its fit bounds '. Those limits, he states, are of no arbitrary kind ; they are determined by the nature of the story itself, by the incidents required to mark the change (in tragedy) ' from good fortune into the worse, or (in comedy) the change from worse into the better '. Apart from this he suggests that the action should ' not exceed the compass of one day ', and that some scope should be left for subsidiary episodes. He therefore accepts the so-called Unity of time, though of the Unity of place he makes no mention.

---

[1] See Spingarn, *Crit. Essays of the 17th Cent.*, i. 231–2.
[2] *De trag. const.*, cap. IV.   [3] *Disc.* §§ 134–5.

Then, too, he stresses at some length the caveat uttered by Aristotle relating to the faulty conception of the Unity of action held in his time. Thus that Unity, Jonson states, does not consist in the unity of the hero ; ' since by one and the same person many things may be severally done which cannot fitly be referred or joined to the same end '. The necessary unity, for instance, could not be found in stories of Theseus and the like, which in relating the manifold exploits of their respective heroes, contained ' many parts that had no coherence nor kindred with other, so far were they from being one action, one fable '. On the other hand the greatest of ancient poets, both epic and dramatic, had duly observed the necessary Unity of action. Homer in his *Odyssey*, for example, had not included all the adventures of Ulysses, but only such as ' tended to one and the same end ' ; similarly, Virgil in his *Aeneid* had ' pretermitted many things ', while relating merely ' how Aeneas came into Italy ' ; and Sophocles, in his *Ajax* again, had attained the necessary unity by confining his treatment to the madness of his hero. Here, then, apart from Sidney's effort, was the first serious attempt to represent in English certain important details of Aristotelian dramatic theory.[1] It is true that Jonson's teaching is here derived at second hand from Heinsius, and is thus coloured in many places by that scholar's faulty readings. Moreover, neither here nor elsewhere does Jonson show any true understanding of the Aristotelian term ' imitation ', the deeper meaning of which Sidney alone would seem to have grasped. Nevertheless this attempt to grapple with Greek critical theory is not without its significance ; for it points to a widening of critical interests and to the continuing influence of the Renascence at this date.

It is then these remarks on style, on poetry, and dramatic theory, together with the judgments on Shakespeare, Bacon, and other contemporary writers and writings mentioned above, that constitute the main critical *loci* in Jonson's *Discoveries*. And altogether they represent a deliberate attempt to recover from the ancients some of their basic literary theories and standards of judgment. The task was accomplished with Jonson's characteristic good sense and critical acumen, though not without limitations. Thus the use made of Latin authorities is more general, and also more fruitful, than that made of the Greeks. For Greek theory, as we have seen, he depended apparently on second-hand authorities, whose mistakes he unwittingly adopted, while the knowledge he reveals of Aristotle's more recondite

[1] cf. *Poetics*, 1450 b, 24 ff. ; 1451 a, 15 ff.

theories is of a markedly tenuous kind. At the same time such classical teaching as he embodies consists of not a little that is fundamental ; he has throughout an eye to practical and immediate problems ; and what he borrows he transforms by means of his racy, massive and flexible prose. Nor is it wholly irrelevant to add that these critical notes are far from exhausting the interest of this ' little golden book '. For the collection is otherwise full of good things ; autobiographical remarks, for instance, advice on life and conduct, besides shrewd sayings felicitously expressed and relating to moral, political and educational affairs. Thus ' memory of all powers of the mind ', Jonson asserts,[1] ' is most delicate and frail ' ; and adds that in his youth he ' could have repeated all that he ever made '. Or again, there are such sayings as : ' A cripple in the way out-travels . . . a post out of the way ' ; ' Expectation of the vulgar is more drawn . . . with newness than with goodness ' ; ' Greatness of name in the father ofttimes . . . o'erwhelms the son ' ; ' Affliction teacheth a wicked person sometime to pray, prosperity never ' ; ' Nothing is a courtesy unless it be meant us ' ; ' Too much pickedness is not manly ' ; ' Flattery is a fine picklock of tender ears.'[2] These are shrewd and pregnant ideas culled at random from the wisdom of the ancients ; and they doubtless account in part for Swinburne's extravagant comment that ' a single leaf of the *Discoveries* is worth all his lyrics, tragedies, elegies, and epigrams together '.

Bearing in mind the varied nature of Jonson's critical activities —the dramatic criticism, the literary theorizing and judgments of his earlier years, together with the later classical studies of the *Discoveries*—what can now be said of his critical achievement as a whole ? As a literary theorist, in the first place, he has been loosely described as ' a champion of the rules ', an early advocate of those constricting doctrines bound up with the later neo-classical system. Yet nothing in reality could be farther from the truth. Actuated throughout by a profound respect for the ancients, at no stage did he recommend a slavish following, to be attained by means of fixed and mechanical rules. In this matter he would probably have agreed with Bacon that ' to make judgment wholly by their rules is the humour of a scholar (pedant) '.[3] What he strove for, in view of current extravagances, was a return to the ordered harmony, the spirit, of the ancients, to those permanent and fundamental principles that had inspired their art ; and in this sense alone can he be regarded as a classicist.

[1] *Disc.* § 56.   [2] *ibid.* §§ 28, 49, 50, 26, 54, 102, 84.
[3] Essay, *On Studies.*

Apart from this he is an Elizabethan, to whom, as to most of his contemporaries, Nature or reason was the ultimate guide, and who recognized that departures from ancient methods were both natural and inevitable. This he makes clear in his theory and practice alike ; as when, for instance, he refers to the ' too nice ' requirements of ancient dramatic technique, defends his comedy against the charge of infringing ' the strict rigour of Comic law ', or justifies his methods in tragedy on the ground that classical technique would have made no sort of appeal to contemporary playgoers. Yet this liberal classicism did not hinder him from drawing freely on earlier teaching, notably from Horace and Quintilian among the ancients, from Vives and Heinsius among later scholars ; and while Sidney must be reckoned as his earliest guide, towards the end he strove to understand and expound something of Aristotle's doctrines. What he extracted from them all, however, is not so much abstract theories or definite systems as practical advice on formal aspects of both poetry and prose. On the nature of poetry, for instance, he does not dwell ; to him, as to most of his contemporaries, it was nothing more than mere ' feigning or fancy '. On the other hand, he enlarges at some length on the actual process of poetic creation, calling attention to the need for constant effort, for the use of ' forge and file ', as well as to the freedom permitted to poetic genius and the inspiration to be derived from earlier masterpieces. In addition he treats of the more formal side of poetry ; and though he has little or nothing to say on the epic, his remarks on the epigram, the sonnet and the heroic couplet are of definite interest in literary history. Most valuable of all, however, are his injunctions regarding prose style ; for they embody principles of enduring value and are the findings of one who was himself a master of English prose.

But the liberal classicism of his theorizing also goes to explain the nature of his achievement as a judicial critic ; for his judgments are largely the result of applying classical principles to literature in the concrete. Hence his censures of all breaches of classical discipline with its demands for fitness, good sense and orderly craftsmanship. And this is seen, not only in his remarks on the ' ill customs ' and extravagances of the contemporary stage, or in his condemnation of the luxuriant Spenserian tradition and Shakespeare's unchecked facility, but also in his attacks on all affected styles, the tortured, the profuse, the rough, the obscure, and the like. At the same time he is bound by neither classical traditions nor standards. For in both Shakespeare and Donne he discerns qualities of an original kind, for which there was no classical precedent ; and the insight, the judgment, and the happy phrasing he there displays are qualities associated with a great and generous critic. Before him there had been ' snarling pedants and courtly eulogists ' ; but apart from Sidney, with his reaction to *Chevy Chace*, Jonson is the first to introduce effectively the personal touch into critical appreciation. That his judgments were not without their limitations is of course true. Many are arrogant, prejudiced, and even contradictory ; some are concerned mainly with stylistic effects, as opposed to effects of a more general aesthetic kind ; and some, again, read later apart from their context, gave rise to misunderstandings, as for instance, the somewhat blunt pronouncements that Shakespeare ' wanted art ', or that Spenser had ' writ no language '. Then, too, his criticism may be said at times to be lacking in subtlety and in a realization of the finer effects of the great literature of his day. Yet it embodied the judgments of one who, richly endowed with the critical temper, brought to the task an understanding robust, practical, and keen. In him appeared, in short, the first great English critic, one who gave to criticism a definite place in literary activities, and who did much in diffusing a critical atmosphere and in conveying his love of letters to his own and later generations. It may be true to say with Dryden that there are few serious thoughts that are new in him. But at least he endeavoured to acquaint his fellow-countrymen with the best that had been thought and said on literature in antiquity ; he remained to the end a critic and inquirer, *tamquam explorator* ; and he was also the first to place Shakespeare on the lofty pedestal upon which he has since towered.

It yet remains to mention the contribution of Milton to this last phase of Renascence criticism in England ; for he, like Jonson, was also instrumental thus late in the day in calling attention to the best that had been thought and said on literature in antiquity. His contribution, it is true, was of a casual nature, consisting of remarks on literature and literary theory scattered here and there in pamphlets or set forth more formally in brief *Prefaces* to his greater works. Nevertheless, such doctrines as he submits are of considerable interest. Now, practically for the first time, certain elements of Aristotelian theory are clearly and accurately set forth ; while the views expressed concerning poets and poetry are the views of a great poet drawing obviously on his own experiences. Then, too, the spirit which animates his theorizing is reminiscent in part of the early Humanists, with deference paid to classical antiquity in the main, regardless of that crystallizing of ancient theory into what is known as the neo-classical system—a process that was taking place in France at the time. Of the development of neo-classical doctrine in England many of his contemporaries, beginning with Davenant, were already giving signs ; and meanwhile, in addition, a new aesthetic was being formulated by Hobbes. Such developments, however, left Milton wholly unaffected ; in his theorizing, as in his creative work, his was the last voice of the Renascence in England.

Nothing, to begin with, is more eloquent of the spirit with which he was animated than the glowing enthusiasm which characterized his praise of literature in general, the constant theme of Humanists from John of Salisbury onwards. In his *Areopagitica* (1644), for instance, that unspoken speech written, so he claimed, ' after the true Attic style ', he reveals his conception of the mysterious powers of great literature, namely, its inexhaustible vitality and its additional faculty of communicating the living spirit therein enshrined to all ages and readers. Thus, ' books ', he writes,[1] ' are not absolutely dead things, but do contain a potency of life in them . . . as active as that soul was whose progeny they are '. Moreover, he adds, ' as good almost to kill a man as kill a good book ', . . . for ' a good book is the precious life-blood of a master spirit, embalmed and treasured up on purpose to a life beyond life '. These are memorable and familiar words, embodying one of the profoundest truths concerning literature. And Milton's metaphor here suffers nothing in comparison with that employed by Plato's Socrates who had attributed to poetry the stored-up energy and radiating influence of the magnet.[2] Nor does he limit his eulogy to ' good ' books only ; for books of a less worthy kind, if read with discretion, are said to have their uses. Thus Selden, he recalls, had shown by his learned writings that ' all opinions, yea, errors, known, read, and collated, are of service . . . towards the . . . attainment of what is truest ' ;[3] and, as he adds further, ' a wise man will make a better use of an idle pamphlet than a fool will do of sacred Scripture '.[4] Moreover, there is his highly significant comment elsewhere on the art of reading, when he states that he

> who reads
> Incessantly, and to his reading brings not
> A spirit and judgment equal or superior,
> . . . .
> Uncertain and unsettl'd still remains.[5]

[1] *Areopagitica*, ed. Cotterill, p. 5.
[2] Plato, *Ion*, 533.
[3] *Areopagitica*, ed. Cotterill, p. 14.
[4] *ibid.* p. 19.
[5] *Paradise Regained*, iv. 322 ff.

Here Milton is insisting on the need for active judgment on the part of the reader and for his imaginative co-operation with the writer. The same principle had been advocated by more than one Greek critic in connexion with oratory ; [1] and it had been reiterated by Shakespeare in his appeal to his audience in *Henry V*.

In the field of literature, however, Milton's main interests were manifestly bound up with poetry ; and his scattered remarks on literary theory are therefore above all concerned with poets and the poetic art, in the course of which he supplies information of a unique autobiographical value. Unlike Jonson and the earlier Humanists, he pays but little attention to the study of rhetoric or prose style. To him prose was an inferior form of expression, a manner of writing in which he had but the use of his ' left hand ' ; and in *The Reason of Church Government* he speaks contemptuously of his prose activities (1640–60), which had condemned him to ' club quotations with men whose learning and belief lay in marginal stuffings '.[2] At the same time he regards the study of rhetoric as a useful preliminary to the cultivation of the art of expression in general ; and in his *Treatise of Education* [3] (1644) he indicates its place in a scheme of literary training. He maintains that it should follow the study of logic, designed to cultivate accurate thinking, and then, with its teaching of the graces of expression, it should in turn lead on to the study of poetics. As for its guiding principles, those he asserts were to be gathered from the works of Plato, Aristotle, Phalereus,[4] Cicero, ' Longinus ' ; and here is revealed not only Milton's acquaintance with the main course of the critical development in antiquity, but also his advance on the earlier Humanistic position where literary theory was concerned. The study of poetry is no longer regarded as ancillary to rhetorical studies ; the authorities in rhetoric are held to be, not Trapezuntius, Melanchthon, and the rest, but the ancient classical writers from Plato onwards ; and not without its significance is the fact that here for the first time mention is made of the work of ' Longinus '.

It is in his remarks on poetry in *The Reason of Church Government*, however, that Milton may be said to have broken new ground, more especially in his conception of its nature and function. For to him poetry is something more than an ingenious

---

[1] See Atkins, *Lit. Crit. in Antiquity*, i. 158 ; ii. 206.
[2] Spingarn, *op. cit.* i. pp. 194, 200.   [3] *ibid.* i. p. 206.
[4] Probably a mistaken reference to Demetrius Phalereus (3rd Cent. B.C.), to whom was ascribed the work of Demetrius (1st Cent. A.D.) : see Atkins, *Lit. Crit. in Antiquity*, ii. 197–9.

game of verse-writing, the work of ' vulgar amorists ' or ' libi-
dinous and ignorant poetasters ', with their vicious precepts
enclosed in sweet pills. With the hackneyed teaching of
antiquity in mind he therefore denounces as inadequate not only
the vague references to inspiration derived from the Muses or
from ' the vapours of wine ', but also the arid moral and philo-
sophic teaching suggested by Horace and Plutarch ; and at the
same time he expounds in terms more definite and idealistic
what he conceives to be the true nature and function of poetry.
That inspiration, in the first place, was needed for every poetic
venture, of this he is firmly convinced. But such inspiration,
he adds, was ' the gift of God rarely bestowed, but yet to some
. . . in every nation '.[1]   It was, moreover, a gift to be obtained
' not by the invocation of Dame Memory and her siren daughters,
but by devout prayer to that eternal Spirit who can enrich with
all utterance and knowledge, and sends out His seraphim with
the hallowed fire of His altar to touch and purify the lips of whom
He pleases '.[2]   To Milton, therefore, the poetic function was of
a prophetic kind, to instruct, to move, to ennoble. In other
words its task was ' to inbreed the seeds . . . of virtue, to allay
the perturbations of the mind and set the affections in right
tune ' ; to tell of changes of fortune and of man's deepest
thoughts ; to celebrate the glories of Almighty God and to do
all this in delightsome fashion, for ' those of soft and delicious
temper who will not so much as look upon Truth herself, unless
they see her elegantly dressed '.[3]

This, then, being Milton's conception of the high and sacred
calling of the poet, his long period of self-dedication and his
' inward promptings . . . to leave something so written to after-
times as they should not willingly let it die ',[4] both alike become
intelligible. And as Wordsworth, another dedicated spirit, was
later on to give some account of the growth of a poet's mind,
so Milton incidentally records something of that training which
he had found helpful in his own poetic development. In the first
place, the wide reading prescribed for young orators in antiquity
he now recommends for the nourishment of the poet's mind.
And he recalls how his adventures among all kinds of classical
writers had enabled him to judge and admire all human excellences and had given him ' a ear that could measure a just
cadence '.[5]   But moral as well as intellectual qualities had also
to be cultivated ; and with this object in view he endorses the
Stoic doctrine of the poet (and orator) as *vir bonus*, declaring that

---

[1] Spingarn, *op. cit.* i. p. 197.   [2] *ibid.* i. p. 199.
[3] *ibid.* i. p. 197.   [4] *ibid.* i. p. 195.   [5] *ibid.* i. p. 204.

' he who would not be frustrate of his hope to write well . . .
in laudable things ought himself to be a true poem '.[1]   In this
opinion, he states, he had been confirmed by his reading, not only
of the sublime loves of Petrarch and Dante, but also of the
knightly chivalry of those old romances, which, he significantly
adds, ' to many others had been the fuel of wantonness and loose
living '.   And finally he recommends an acquaintance with
actual life, the acquiring of ' insight into all seemly and generous
arts and affairs '.

Apart from these general remarks, however, Milton has also
something of value to say on the ' sublime art ' of poetry, which,
to begin with, he distinguishes from the art of rhetoric as being
' more simple, sensuous and passionate ' ; [2] in other words, more
free from verbal and other tricks, more varied in its aesthetic
appeal, and more impressive in its emotional effects.   In addition,
the poetic art, he explains, is concerned with something more
than mere prosody.   It is said to treat of poetic creation in general,
of the laws relating to the epic, the drama, and the lyric, besides
the essential need for the observance of *decorum* or fitness throughout.   And all this, he added, was to be gathered from recognized
authorities, such as Aristotle, Horace, Castelvetro, and Tasso.
At the same time a comment of his on verse-form is not without
its interest ; for in introducing *Paradise Lost* (1667) to his readers
he defends his choice of unrhymed verse, possibly in reply to a
controversy raging at the time.   In adopting blank verse for his
great epic Milton had doubtless been guided by a sound poetic
instinct ; for hitherto, as Daniel had remarked of Campion, ' his
commendable rhymes . . . had given . . . the best notice of his
worth '.   And in contending that rhyme was ' no necessary
adjunct . . . of poem or good verse, in longer works especially ',[3]
he was undoubtedly on sound ground.   To this, however, he adds
the conventional and less convincing argument that rhyme was
' the invention of a barbarous age ' devised ' to set off wretched
matter and lame metre ' ; and that although it had been adopted
latterly by some famous poets it had seriously hindered a free
and natural expression, and had consequently been discarded by
certain Italian and Spanish poets, as well as by the best writers
of tragedy in English.   Moreover, rhyme, he declared, was
' trivial and of no true musical delight ', since it consisted mainly
of ' the jingling sound of like endings, a fault avoided by the
learned ancients both in poetry and . . . oratory '.   On the
other hand the true beauty of verse, he maintained, lay in ' apt
numbers, fit quantity of syllables and the sense variously drawn

[1] *ibid.* i. p. 202.   [2] *ibid.* i. p. 206.   [3] *ibid.* i. pp. 206–7.

out from one verse into another '. And in thus claiming for verse suitable metrical, accentual and rhythmical effects, together with the freedom of movement that resulted from the use of run-on lines, he was clearly revealing some of the secrets of his own wonderful blank verse. In his description of rhyme, it must be confessed, he is less than just ; his strictures are obviously of the nature of special pleading. What he had in mind, however, was to justify his instinctive use of blank verse in an epic ; and this he does in illuminating fashion by demanding a more varied music, a less fettered movement, than was afforded by the use of the heroic couplet.

Of autobiographical interest are also his remarks on the various poetic ' kinds ', revealing thereby his groping efforts towards arriving at clear conceptions of their several forms. Writing in 1641 his ideas are evidently in a more or less fluid form. In his *Reason of Church Government* he is considering conceptions drawn from various quarters ; and although it is significant that he looks primarily to the Greeks among the ancients for guidance, yet along with Aristotle's doctrine he has also in mind patristic teachings as well as those of Tasso and others. Of the epic, to begin with, he can conceive of several legitimate forms.[1] First, there was the ' diffuse ' epic with Homer and Virgil as models, and secondly, the ' brief ' form, after the fashion of the *Book of Job* ; or again, there was the epic in which the rules of Aristotle were strictly followed, while yet another and more original form was possible, a form dictated by Nature and artistic judgment alone. Into further details he does not enter, except to imply (here following Tasso's teaching in his *Discorsi* (1587)) that the epic hero should be taken from Christian history ; though elsewhere [2] he states his intention of selecting his hero from the ancient history of Britain, which, he noted, had previously been mal-treated by ' the unskilful handling of monks and mechanics '.[3] Then, too, his conception of the drama is of the same undetermined character ; and since his interest is confined to the more serious forms, he considers neither comedy nor the successful innovations of the Elizabethan popular stage. His main concern is with tragedy ; and here, as with the epic, Greek traditions being uppermost in his mind, he therefore recommends as models, not Seneca, but Sophocles and Euripides. At the same time he calls attention to other possibilities, to the pastoral drama of *The Song of Solomon*, with its two *personae* and a double Chorus,[4] or again, to the ' high and stately tragedy ' of the *Book of the*

---

[1] Spingarn, *op. cit.* i. p. 196.   [2] *ibid.* i. p. 195.
[3] See p. 276 *supra.*   [4] *ibid.* i. p. 196.

Revelation, with ' its solemn acts and scenes and its seven-fold chorus of Hallelujahs '. And similarly with the lyric. The Greeks, Pindar and Callimachus, are here suggested as reliable guides ; though there were also those ' incomparable ' Hebrew songs scattered throughout the pages of the Old Testament. These comments are perhaps mainly of historical interest. But they illustrate effectively the ' spacious circuits ' of a great poet's musings, and the deference paid to Greek and Biblical traditions, at a time when literary theory elsewhere was crystallizing into the rigidity of the neo-classical system.

Nor should his further comments on tragedy in his Preface to *Samson Agonistes* (1671) be overlooked ; for there he supplements by some scholarly remarks those casual, and sometimes misleading, expositions of Aristotelian doctrine previously made by Jonson and others. To begin with, at a time when the epic, or ' heroic poem ' as it was called, was engaging the attention of most critics, of Davenant in England and Chapelain in France, for instance, Milton now (following Aristotle) describes tragedy as ' the gravest, the moralest and the most profitable of all other poems '.[1] In support of that statement he resorts to the customary appeal to authorities of the past. He notes, for instance, the use made of tragic poets by Cicero, Plutarch, and St. Paul ; or again the tragedies produced by the younger Seneca and Augustus Caesar, as well as the *Christus Patiens* (12th Century ?) of uncertain authorship, which, however, he attributes to Gregory Nazianzen, a famous bishop of the 4th Century. In this way he commends tragedy to Puritan readers, and counteracts the prejudices with which it was viewed on account of earlier levities and abuses.

Most notable of all, however, is his exposition of ancient Greek tragedy, in the course of which he calls attention to Aristotle's conception of the function of tragedy, and to other features of the Greek tragic drama. Thus either from a first-hand acquaintance with Aristotle's text,[2] or from his reading elsewhere, of Minturno [3] and others, he propounds Aristotle's theory of the effects of tragedy, and gives for the first time in English a clear and correct idea of the ' catharsis ' or purgation, which later on was to be subjected to various interpretations. ' The effect of tragedy ', so he explains, ' was by raising pity and fear or terror, to purge the mind of those and such-like passions ; that is, to temper and reduce them to just measure with a kind of delight stirred up by reading or seeing those passions well imitated.' [4]

---

[1] Spingarn, *op. cit.* i. p. 207.
[2] *Poetics,* 1449 b, 27–8.
[3] *L'Arte Poetica,* p. 77 (Venice, 1564).
[4] Spingarn, *op. cit.* i. p. 207.

23

In this way he makes it plain that a medicinal, not a moral, effect is involved. Unhealthy conditions of the soul are remedied by a sort of homoeopathic treatment ; and the process, he further explains, is analogous to that of medicine on the body, inasmuch as ' just measure ' or emotional balance is restored by the working-off of morbid feelings. For the rest he notes the importance of the Chorus in Greek tragedy, the absence of acts and scenes, the element of ' uniformity ' or consistency in character-drawing, plots that might be ' intricate ' (complex) or ' explicit ' (simple), the general observance of verisimilitude and *decorum*, as well as the limitation of the action to one day. And with this belated reference to Greek dramatic standards, Renascence influence on English criticism may be said to have practically ceased. To these matters Cheke and Ascham had previously called attention ; and Milton enlarges on the teaching of those earlier Humanists, though French influences and native developments were in the meantime presenting new problems to critical minds.

CHAPTER XII

CONCLUSION

THE main details in the development of English Renascence criticism have now been recalled ; and it remains to discuss the outstanding features of the achievement and its significance in critical history. In the first place, as has been seen, the critical output obviously embodies something more than a treatment of what have been doubtfully described as the two real problems of specific interest, the advocacy, that is, of the ' two lost causes ', classical verse and classical drama. To these matters undue attention has been devoted in the past, though they were after all of but secondary interest to contemporaries. Then, too, it is no less clear that this phase of criticism is by no means limited to tiresome reiterations of stock theories relating to poetry, or to a series of pedantic pronouncements on the poetic art, thus reproducing (in Milton's phrase) ' divine and human learning raked out of the embers of forgotten tongues '. Such well-worn doctrines, it is true, are to be found mostly in formal treatises ; but there is also much else of value besides. Nor, again, can the net result be described as the emergence of a tentative ' classicism ', a claim which, so far from being based on actual facts, has all the appearance of arguing down from the theory to the facts ; while, in addition, Rymer's later judgment that Ben Jonson in his day ' had all the critical learning to himself, and . . . England was as free from critics as it was from wolves ', this, too, can safely be dismissed as being far from the truth. Criticism must always be largely a matter of emphasis ; and estimates such as these do not represent what was actually accomplished at this date.

On the other hand, a true judgment is likely to be formed only when the work is viewed in its proper perspective ; and, approached from this standpoint, contemporary criticism is perhaps best described as a continuous but unregulated effort to lay anew the foundations of the native literature in the light that had dawned at the Renascence. What was primarily needed at the time was work of a pioneer and fundamental character ; firstly, basic teaching in the art of expression, both in prose and verse, and secondly, the exposition of intelligible views concerning the nature and art of poetry. Such elementary instruction was now forthcoming, and it forms the main gist of contemporary criticism, though with it went also an intermittent treatment of immediate problems, the correction of glaring abuses, for instance, some valuable constructive suggestions regarding literary and dramatic methods, besides judgments and appreciations of more than passing interest. That some amount of dead matter was embodied in the critical ferment must be readily conceded ; though such doctrine was not wholly without its influence on creative work. On the other hand, many fundamental truths and principles of universal validity were also enunciated ; and they constitute the enduring part of Renascence criticism. Altogether the findings were the result of free minds bent on investigating matters both old and new, working meanwhile from first principles. No system was adopted, no authority regarded as final. The teaching of antiquity was in general subjected to the light of Nature or reason ; and where necessary, regard was paid to native instincts and traditions.

For the initial inspiration of this critical movement attention has been directed above to the influence mainly of 15th-Century Italian Humanists. Attempts, however, have at times been made to establish a claim in this connexion for Italian theorists of the 16th Century ; [1] and concerning this claim something must here be said in the light of the facts previously presented. That sporadic ideas in the works of English critics may occasionally be traceable to the writings of these later Italians, this much may be granted. Sidney, for one, undoubtedly wrote with some acquaintance with Daniello, Minturno, Scaliger, and Castelvetro ; while Harington apparently made use of Cinthio, Pigna, and others. For the rest, however, the evidence for an intimate knowledge of the main body of Italian theory is slight and unconvincing, little more than could be explained by the casual use of doctrines in the air at the time, as, for instance, the allusions to Castelvetro's theory of the three Unities. It is not only that definite references by English critics to these Italian scholars are extremely rare ; whereas the authorities freely mentioned are Cicero and Quintilian, Plato, Horace, Plutarch, the Neo-Platonists, and others rendered familiar by earlier Humanists, while it is to Aeneas Sylvius, Politian, and Pico,[2] among others, that Daniel's mind reverts when he thinks of the Revival of Learning. This argument of course is by no means conclusive, as the Elizabethans, it is well known, were not careful always to acknowledge debts of this kind ; and, moreover, greater weight would normally be attached to the authority of the ancients. At the same time it

[1] cf. Smith, *op. cit.* i. pp. lxxvii–lxxxvii, and Spingarn, *Lit. Crit. in the Renaissance*, pp. 253–310.

[2] Smith, *op. cit.* ii. p. 369.

is also worth noting that no single treatise of these important Italian critics was translated into English during this period; though versions of other foreign works bearing on literary matters were by no means uncommon, as was shown by the English translations mentioned above and attributed to T. B. Gent, Sandford, Bavande, Fenton, Blundeville, and Ashley.

What, however, is more significant is that in the subjects treated, and in its treatment generally, English theorizing differs vitally from that of the Italian critics. The main concern of the Italians had been to expound abstract theories of poetry in general and to prescribe forms for the epic, for tragedy and comedy in particular, with, as Scaliger maintained, a standard of perfection for each of the 'kinds'; all of which was ostensibly based on the teaching of Aristotle's *Poetics*. Of the English critics, however, Sidney almost alone seems to have grasped the importance of the theory of poetry thus submitted, the significance of Aristotle's *mimesis* and his vindication of poetry as a revelation of universal truth; and as for Italian theories of the epic and tragedy, it is worth noting that no serious attempt was made as yet to commend them in any detail to English readers. Apart from this, one of the most striking features of English criticism at this date is the slight acquaintance shown with Aristotle's teaching, the exposition of which had largely inspired Italian theorizing. Certain of his ideas, some falsified or badly interpreted, had indeed been occasionally set forth. Glimpses of his theories appear for instance in the writings of Willis, Puttenham, Jonson, and Milton. On the other hand, Jonson, who pays him a notable tribute, failed (here following Heinsius) to expound correctly his idea of comedy; while the references made yet earlier by Ascham and Harington had also betrayed a serious lack of understanding. So that, compared with the volume of Aristotelian doctrine available, but little use was made of his teaching by English writers. 'He was much named but little read', as Harvey, writing in 1579, complained of the study of Aristotle at Cambridge at that date.

Nor is there any ground for thinking that substantial Italian influence in the matter of theory may nevertheless have been exercised in indirect fashion, especially in view of the manifold borrowings from Italian sources that otherwise went on. That Italian critics fostered the critical spirit in England and that they suggested new forms, such as the *Apologies* and *Discourses* for critical work, this much is likely, and at this stage it represented stimulus of a valuable kind. But it is unnecessary to attribute to Italian influence all the more enlightened theory found in English critical works. Thus Castelvetro, Robortelli, and others had insisted that art was primarily designed to give pleasure, and pleasure alone ; and similar pronouncements were made by Lyly and Puttenham. Yet the conditions which in practice had called forth the ' new art ' of Shakespeare and Lope de Vega would adequately account for such pronouncements. Like the Italians in question the English writers were here exercising an independence of judgment based on natural instinct.

Then, finally, of significance, too, is the attitude displayed towards certain aspects of Italian teaching. Scaliger is perhaps the most frequently mentioned. He is deferred to, for instance, by such a writer as Peacham ; and use is made elsewhere of such matters as his three-fold classification of poets, the theological, the philosophical, and poets who imitated human life, or again, of his divisions of a play, the *protasis* and the rest. On the other hand, Alexander respectfully questions his estimates of Homer and Virgil ; Chapman derides his judgment in more scathing terms ; while basic doctrines of his, that verse for instance was the essence of poetry, or that Aristotle was a perpetual dictator, such notions were scouted by English theorists. Of the value of the theorizing of these 16th-Century Italians there can be no doubt ; and its assimilation by English theorists at this date would have changed completely the subsequent course of English criticism. In the following century their influence was abundantly felt by French critics ; but despite the undoubted value and suggestiveness of much of the Italian theorizing its effect was but vague and sporadic where English writers at this date were concerned. It would therefore seem that the case for this Italian influence in contemporary English criticism has yet to be made out. Englishmen, busied with immediate problems, were unable as yet to grasp the larger questions opened up by the Italians ; or was it that old prejudices against Italian teaching still lingered, prejudices originally inspired by the arrogance of earlier Italian scholars towards the ' barbarians ' north of the Alps ? The necessary changes in English criticism at this date, so states a modern authority,[1] ' were effected with the minimum of direct foreign influence '. And the truth would appear to be that English Renascence criticism was not something which began in the 16th Century under contemporary Italian inspiration, but was rather a continuation of medieval efforts, coloured anew by classical influences derived from 15th-Century Italian Humanists, and invigorated by a constant appeal to the laws of Nature or reason.

[1] G. Saintsbury, *op. cit.* p. 27.

But whatever may have been the decisive influences on this phase of English criticism, of greater importance is the nature of what was actually accomplished by English critics at this date. And here, compared with the sporadic efforts of previous generations, a sudden and a marked advance becomes evident, an advance in theorizing, judging, and appreciating alike. Not least important, in the first place, was the fresh light now thrown on the fundamental principles of all good writing, notably by Wilson and Jonson, in their efforts to inculcate a more intelligible and generous conception of rhetoric as the art of effective expression in words. In view of the formless character of the medieval, and much of the early Tudor, prose, in view too of the imperfect conception of rhetoric that had been handed down, such efforts at the time were badly needed, and they were instrumental, practically for the first time, in calling attention to the value of literary form and to not a few secrets of an attractive literary style. Their great achievement was in re-vitalizing doctrines which had long been petrified in the mechanical and schematic teaching of earlier and current works on rhetoric. And this they did by calling men away from the rules and routine of the school-rhetorics to the illuminating principles laid down by Quintilian and others, at the same time submitting those principles in a form acceptable to cultured and reasonable minds. Thus were recalled some of the basic principles evolved in classical antiquity from the time of Plato onwards, but since overlaid by the accumulated hair-splitting and complicated terminology of scholastic theorists.

Of the ancient principles thus revived the most notable perhaps was the fundamental and indispensable need for clear thinking, as opposed to concentration on formal artifice or tortured phrase. And this was accompanied by further demands for an orderly development of thought with easy transitions, for a diction and a manner in keeping with the theme, the occasion and the reader, as well as for a discreet use of those figurative devices in which human emotion has always found artistic expression. Apart from this the necessity for constant practice and a concealment of art was also inculcated ; style, it was pointed out, was inevitably an expression of personality ; and its highest qualities were said to be realized, not in an array of flowers, but in order, proportion, simplicity, and above all, perspicuity. As Quintilian long ago had stated, the aim in writing should be ' not merely to enable a reader to understand but to make it impossible for him not to understand '. Thus was discountenanced the ' gaudy English ', the ungirt prose, of writers of the day ; and what above all was inculcated was a sense of structure, the truth that prose was a formal craft with laws subtle and flexible, since 'meaning never runs the better for having its clothes dirty and unbuttoned'.

Nor less notable was the manner of conveying these truths. Rhetoric was no longer presented as the arbitrary pronouncements of pedantic grammarians ; neither was its ultimate authority based solely on the teaching of the ancients.   Stripped of unnecessary technicalities, of complicated divisions and sub-divisions, its principles were now submitted as being primarily in accordance with Nature or reason, and therefore psychologically necessary ; as when, for instance, figures are shown to be no mere capricious tricks but devices with an appeal to human nature, by means of which expression rose above bare statement and acquired strange and arresting effects.   Moreover, few traces remain of the medieval confusion between rhetoric and poetic ; while such pedantries as the distinction drawn between figures of poetry and figures of prose are boldly discarded.   And such rational methods were accompanied by occasional hints of a practical kind ; as when Jonson, for instance, in emphasizing the need for coherent thought with easy transitions, recommended constant reference to what had gone before, as not only ensuring due sequence of thought but also making the junctures easier and quickening the imagination.   These and other similar injunctions were doubtless the fruit of actual experience ; and they are simple truths of perennial value.   So that altogether it may be said that the rhetorical teaching of the time embodied many new and sound precepts, as well as an abundance of basic doctrines essential for the attainment of an effective prose style.   That such precepts are to-day sometimes ignored by teachers of the art of composition is but an illustration of a common human tendency, first, to dismiss fundamental truths as obvious and commonplace, and then to forget and ignore them entirely in practice.   The principles of rhetoric need to be re-interpreted in every age and re-stated in the terminology of the day.   And this is what was successfully accomplished by Renascence critics in the light of classical teaching, as tested by the laws of Nature or reason.

Expositions of the art of writing in prose, however, were not the only, nor yet the chief, concern of contemporary English criticism.   More general were the attempts made to arrive at clear ideas on the nature and art of poetry.   From medieval times, it has already been stated, there had come but a flickering light on this most elusive of subjects.   What theorizing there was was at second-hand ; theorizing which rested on the authority of post-classical and patristic writers. And now in the 16th Century, with earlier traditions by no means exhausted, the confused clash of ideas became yet more pronounced by the addition of doctrines derived mainly from classical sources. Nor was this distraction of many voices the only cause of perplexity. English Humanists, strangely enough, had thrown but little light on the subject ; poets in many quarters were alluded to as fanciful creatures ; while the Puritans, for their part, had darkened counsel by denouncing all poetry as an evil and a dangerous art. Fresh interest, however, was aroused by more courtly and cultured minds with whom a vague but inarticulate sense of its value was present ; and efforts were accordingly made, amidst the prevailing confusion, to give reasons for the faith that was in them, by attempts at vindicating poetry and at explaining something of its art. Nowadays the value of poetry admits of no question ; but for 16th-Century readers the position was different. The truth was that it was no mere academic inquiry that was then in progress ; and significant of its seriousness was the fact that quite late in the century Puttenham was still urging the value of poetry and protesting moreover that an art of English poetry was quite conceivable.

Of the views thus expressed concerning the nature of poetry, in the first place, the most prevalent was that which held that poetry was essentially allegorical and esoteric in kind, conveying moral and philosophical truths in hidden fashion. It was a view shared by Wilson, Ascham, and Lodge, Nashe, Harington, and Chapman ; and in a modified form it was later on submitted by Reynolds. This of course was none other than the medieval conception, derived from post-classical and patristic sources, but reinforced at this date by the teaching of Plutarch, whose influence generally was greater than is sometimes realized. The theory was acceptable in that it met more than one of the current objections to poetry, by associating with the poetic art a didactic function and some amount of moral teaching. Its later modification by Reynolds was due to a deepening sense of the mystery of poetry and a vague desire that poets should concern themselves not only with moral precepts but also with the mysteries and hidden properties of physical Nature. A great secret wisdom, Reynolds maintained on the authority of Pico and the Neo-Platonists, had been enshrined in such writers as Zoroaster, Orpheus, and Pythagoras ; and disinterested speculation on the hidden workings of external Nature he regarded as the highest function of this allegorical and esoteric art. To modern readers this allegorical theory is obviously of historical interest only ;

for it fails to account for those qualities that have characterized great poetry throughout the ages. And Bacon had already decried the general validity of the theory, in denying that allegory formed part of the essence of poetry. Then, too, the obscurity bound up with an esoteric art forms no essential element of poetry. Art, it has been said, exists to betray, not to keep, secrets ; and though the poet's methods may be oblique and suggestive in kind, his appeal is not confined to coteries of the initiated, nor is obscurity with him a primary aim.

More suggestive and illuminating, however, were the theories submitted by Sidney, Puttenham, and Bacon. To Sidney, for instance, poetry was an exercise of the free creative faculty, in which the poet transcended the limitations of actual life, yet succeeded by means of his fictions in giving a delightful and inspiring revelation of ideal and universal truth. Puttenham likewise regarded poetry as a product of the creative faculty ; but, according to his theory, the poet's fictions dealt, not only with extra-natural worlds, but with what was true, fabulous, or probable, representing things with the primary purpose of affording delight. To Bacon, again, the essence of poetry consisted in fanciful narratives which, like those of Sidney, corresponded to nothing in actual life, but which were designed to present, not ideal or universal truth, but merely a glorified picture of things to satisfy the unfulfilled aspirations of the human soul. In all three doctrines there are significant features. All, for instance, were agreed on ' the high-flying liberty of conceit ' of the poet, on the essential element of fictitious narratives, and on the pleasure-giving, rather than the didactic, function ; thus marking a break-away from allegorical restrictions. But there were also characteristic differences as well. Thus Sidney suggested that the figments of the poet were something more than idle fancies, a view which Shakespeare apparently also shared. Following Plato and Aristotle, Sidney emphasizes the value of poetry as a great dynamic force and a means of revealing universal truth ; and these are qualities that belong to great poetry of all the ages. Puttenham, for his part, notes that poetry might nevertheless treat of actual life, and was not confined to ' feigned history ' ; whereas Bacon contended that poetic fictions had no necessary correspondence with the truth of things, and were merely of the nature of palliatives. And in so doing he was in a sense anticipating the later conception of ' romantic ' poetry, with its element of ' escapism ', its day-dreams inspired by man's ' divine discontent ', and his restless longing for a more perfect world. Such theories as these marked a distinct advance on the medieval position, though, approached as the subject was from a purely intellectual standpoint, its real nature only partially emerged. To a rational age truth was naturally the highest thing to look for, whereas aesthetic and spiritual qualities were not easily perceptible by human reason : and, moreover, terminology was wanting. What, however, had been shown was that poetry was not all moonshine and delusion ; something of its positive value, its mysteries of sound and sense had been revealed ; while the Platonic ban had also been tentatively refuted. And, meanwhile, the discussion, it may be added, is one that is by no means exhausted at the present day.

Equally interesting, and yet more extensive, were the efforts made to treat of the art of poetry, those principles which were held to govern the processes of artistic creation generally, as well as the forms of the several particular ' kinds '. In the first place, nothing is more significant than Puttenham's attempt to introduce to his readers a just conception of art itself, when, with Aristotle apparently as his guide, he explains it as something other than a body of arbitrary rules, and as a means, based on Nature's methods, which enabled men to reproduce, transform, and even to transcend, Nature's normal effects. And from the original illustration he supplies by his reference to gardening, it is not unreasonable to infer that Shakespeare in a well-known passage may have been influenced by his exposition. At the same time there was general agreement that a woeful state of ignorance prevailed concerning the principles of the poetic art ; though equally general was the conviction that no fixed rules were possible, not even those of the ancients. On the other hand, for the task of poetic creation ' inspiration ' was deemed to be essential ; and attempts were made to rationalize the traditional conception of that term, which was vaguely represented as a sort of madness brought about by the workings of a pagan Muse. Willis, for instance, qualifies that conception by suggesting that the ' madness ' was not of a pathological kind, but was rather a state of distraction or exaltation induced by intense concentration on the part of the poet. Sidney and Milton were content to describe it as a gift from God himself ; whereas the suggestion to-day is that it is ' less an active than a passive and involuntary process '.

But while ' inspiration ', it was conceded, was a necessary feature of the poet's equipment, less agreement existed concerning the part played by ' imitation ' in connexion with the poetic art. The term itself was employed in more senses than one, some of which related to the nature, rather than the art, of poetry. Thus, apart from the Aristotelian *mimesis* or ' artistic idealiza-

tion ', which explained the relations existing between art and
Nature, there was also the use of the term to define the relations
between art and life, as when the drama was described as an
imitation or reflexion of the life of men. Yet more general,
however, was the ' imitation ' which stood for an aid to literary
creation in general, the aid afforded by the best models, that is,
the practice of the ancients ; and this has sometimes been taken
to represent the leading doctrine at the Renascence. For this
doctrine, which had been advocated in various forms by a long
list of eminent critics in antiquity from Isocrates onwards, there
is indeed much to be said ; and Ascham revived the ancient
teaching in admirable fashion, pointing out in so doing the defects
in the versions of the theory submitted by earlier Humanists.
What he advocated was no slavish copying of ancient technique,
of verbal or structural details, but rather a judicious study of
ancient artistic methods and effects, with a view to evolving on
sound lines fresh literary developments ; and such a process of
re-creation, it is worth noting, was something vitally different
from the later static conception of ' imitation ' characteristic of
neo-classical theorists, with their code of fixed rules and standards.
Yet the true significance of Ascham's teaching was apparently
not realized by later English critics ; at any rate it was never
seriously advocated, any more than the blind following of the
ancients condemned by Daniel, Jonson, and others. Isolated
attempts were made to imitate classical technique in connexion
with both verse and the drama. But true progress lay, as Daniel
pointed out, in striving for development along the lines of native
tradition. And in practice and theory alike native genius and
native traditions, together with the dictates of Nature or reason,
were to be the governing factors, as was shown by the emergence
of the ' new art ' of Shakespeare and others. In short, the
classicizing tendency of contemporary English criticism and the
influence of the theory of ' imitation ' have been considerably
over-rated in the past.

Apart from these general principles, however, other aspects
of the poetic art, elementary in character, were from time to time
discussed, notably questions relating to diction and verse. In
the matter of diction, for example, there was a widespread revolt
against all artifice such as fantastic coinages or excessive borrowings from foreign or other sources, usage or custom being prescribed as the ultimate criterion. At the same time it was also
recognized that the occasional use of strange words brought with
them an element of pleasing surprise ; while ' E. K. ', for one,
defends the use of dialect forms in poetry on aesthetic grounds.

Of yet greater interest were the efforts made to expound basic principles, and even some of the mysteries, underlying verse-forms ; for, despite Sidney's equivocal position, verse was accepted by all as an essential component of poetry, and this for various reasons. To Puttenham, for instance, it was none other than a fundamental law of Nature ; and more than one critic points to the affinity of rhythm and metre with the soul of man, which, it was asserted, had been created in special relation to the principles of harmony and rhythm. From the first, both Gascoigne and Puttenham had submitted many sensible and helpful comments on the artistic effects, the varied harmonies, of lines and stanzas. And at the same time, in consequence of prejudices harboured against rhyming verse, the adoption of classical metres was advocated by Harvey and others ; but only to find that such a procedure was repugnant to the genius of the language and therefore impracticable. Then, too, from time to time further light was thrown on matters of prosody, with special reference to contemporary activities. Thus Puttenham, dis-cussing the qualities of those artificial figure-poems condemned by Harvey and others, points out what he regards as their ingenuity, their symmetry, and their appeal to the eye. He also describes rhyming verse as the natural English form, at the same time countering current prejudices by a historical sketch of its development. From Daniel came a yet more convincing defence of rhyme, as well as an illuminating appreciation of the sonnet-form and the peculiar artistic delight afforded by its restricted dimensions ; while Hall maintained that verse of a rugged kind was required for satire. Meanwhile Campion had pointed out (in practice at least) the possibilities of unrhymed verse ; though, strangely enough, a just appreciation of blank verse, after all the great achievement of the period, was still to come. On the other hand, the heroic couplet was already being commended by Jonson ; Sir John Beaumont, moreover, had advocated its employ-ment as being free from the complications of stanza-forms, while also providing some of the qualities of classical verse ; and not least important was Jonson's attempt to revive in that much-cultivated verse-form—the epigram—something of the lost grace and dignity of the Greek tradition.

Less effective, perhaps, though still of considerable interest, were the tentative efforts to make plain the several ' kinds ' of poetry that were possible, as well as the nature of one at least of those particular ' kinds '. Thus Sidney, to begin with, cites the traditional classification, namely, epic, dramatic, lyric, and the rest ; but he is careful to note that the classification was defective, in that it was based on considerations, partly of metre, partly of subject-matter. Webbe, however, with an eye to contemporary activities, proposes as his classification, poetry comical, tragical, and historical. In the first of these divisions he would include epigrams and eclogues, in the second, complaints and sad stories, in the third, chronicles and complimentary poems ; thus omitting from his survey all mention of epic poetry. A more rational classification was suggested by Puttenham in preference to the traditional grouping ; and this, with contemporary developments also in mind, he bases on what he regards as the elementary needs of mankind, both public and private. First, there were the social needs which required the correction of vice and the praise of virtue ; and of these, the necessary reproof was provided by comedy, tragedy, and satire, while virtue was commended in heroic poetry, complimentary poems, and epitaphs. Secondly, there were the private emotional needs of man that called for expression ; and these were provided by such forms as odes and ballads, songs and sonnets, elegies and epigrams. Then, again, there was Bacon's attempt at a reasoned statement on the subject. By him the ' kinds ' were differentiated in accordance with the various treatments of their basic element, which he defined as ' feigned history ', or fanciful stories dealing with human actions. Thus epic poetry was held to treat of heroic deeds in narrative fashion ; dramatic poetry of the deeds of men represented in more vivid and realistic style ; while parabolical (or allegorical) poetry was said to present human deeds with symbolical ends in view. From his treatment, however, he excludes such forms as satire, odes, and elegies on the ground that they dealt, not with actions, but with the thoughts of men. These varied efforts at outlining the field of poetry are obviously imperfect ; but they are nevertheless not without their interest. Apart from the confusion and incompleteness displayed, they witness to independent and rational attempts at classification based, not on the ancients, but on current activities ; and these, during the greater part of the 16th Century, were mainly concerned, not with the epic and the drama, but with such minor forms as epigrams and epitaphs, complimentary poems, songs, sonnets, and the like.

Of a detailed treatment of the various ' kinds ' little at first sight appeared during this period. For the most part discussions on the nature and art of poetry in general engaged the attention ; and it is significant that at no stage was any definite treatise on the specific forms forthcoming. Nevertheless, both before and after 1590, when the drama was revived, dramatic technique was from time to time incidentally discussed, but concerning the epic, lyric, and other forms, little or nothing was said. And not least important in the criticism of the time was that body of theory relating to the drama and its several forms. From the first, efforts were made by Humanists to obtain recognition for ancient literature as such. This had become necessary owing to the confused ideas of dramatic form handed down from the Middle Ages and embodied, not only in the formless miracles and moralities, but also in those tales in verse (undramatic in form) which went by the names of tragedies and comedies. Then in the light of the traditions of Plautus, Terence, and Seneca, attempts were made in plays of an academic kind to recover some of the lost secrets of the dramatic art ; and fragments of dramatic theory were casually expounded, such as, for instance, the need in tragedy for grave themes, an imposing style and moral ' sentences ', or again, in comedy, for moral teaching conveyed by stock characters. Not that the exposition, even at this early stage, was confined to ancient classical doctrine ; for already arguments were advanced for disregarding the Unities, as well as the law which forbade the mingling of comic and tragic material. Moreover, Ascham had also directed attention from Senecan standards to the supremacy of Greek tragedy, to the precepts of Aristotle and the example of Euripides.

After Ascham's day the traditions of Plautus, Terence, and Seneca were for a time maintained ; though protests were being raised by Udall, Gascoigne, and others against a slavish imitation of Roman drama. Apart from this an observance of verisimilitude and classical *decorum* was regarded as essential. Farfetched themes, for instance, were rigorously condemned, and stock characters were recommended for comedy ; while Whetstone called attention to an important principle when he insisted that all such characters should act and speak in accordance with their respective natures. And to this tradition Sidney's dramatic theorizing to some extent belongs ; though eclectic in kind, it embodies much else besides, being drawn from various sources and infused with his own good sense and penetrating insight. In his conceptions of both tragedy and comedy, for instance, he embodies ideas medieval, classical, and Italian ; but he also emphasizes certain points of considerable technical importance. Thus he requires a free treatment of tragic material, pointing out that tragedy was not subject to the laws of history ; while he also stresses the importance of an effective opening scene, which should deal, not with the actual beginning, but with a significant incident, of the tragic story. And as for comedy, in that connexion he advocates the cultivation of plays of a more intellectual

kind, and directs attention to ordinary life as the natural storehouse of comic characters—sound counsel which is not without
its bearing on later dramatic developments.   Already by the close
of the century, however, the tradition of Plautus, Terence, and
Seneca was being seriously challenged and thus underwent a
marked decline.   Nashe, for one, attacked Seneca's melodramatic
effects with characteristic violence ;   crude Senecan imitations
were ridiculed by more than one writer ;   and new conceptions
of comedy were formulated by Jonson and others.   In tragedy,
it is true, Jonson, during his earlier years as a playwright, still
adhered to the ideals of Seneca ;   but, later on, he expounds
certain doctrines of Aristotle, and in this he was followed in yet
more scholarly fashion by Milton.   It was, however, a belated
revival of ancient classical doctrine which was without effect on
current dramatic activities.

These fragments of ancient doctrine, however, were not the
only contributions to dramatic theory during this period.   Of
far greater significance were the comments which characterized
the flowering time of the popular drama, and which suggested
that the ' new art ' of Shakespeare and others was no haphazard
growth but was firmly rooted on principles of its own.   With the
status of the drama assured by the close of the century, there
came a sense of the need for conscious and independent planning ;
and attempts were made, not only to clarify views concerning
comedy, tragedy, and the rest, but also to justify the new developments on the ground that dramatic forms other than classical
were possible and inevitable.   The main lines of the new doctrine
(with special reference to comedy) were sketched in the first
place by Lyly, who maintained that amusement rather than
instruction was the true dramatic function, that the nature of
contemporary audiences was a factor to be considered in determining the character of English plays, that fanciful themes
were fit subjects for dramatic treatment, and that wit in its
modern sense was the spice of comedy.   And these principles
were confirmed later by Marston, Dekker, Chapman, Webster,
and others, who emphasized more especially the important
principles that the business of the dramatist was to please not
' the cook's taste but the guests' ', and that factual truth was not
essential, since the drama was of the nature of poetry, not history ;
so that for the dramatist might be claimed full liberty of treatment, that ' high-flying liberty of conceit ' described by Sidney.

Nor were the incidental pronouncements of Shakespeare and
Jonson on the new dramatic art without their interest.   Thus
Shakespeare, for instance, realizing the limitations of the stage

of his day as well as the necessity of appealing successfully to contemporary audiences, demands in consequence the active and imaginative co-operation of playgoers. And here he is enunciating a principle of universal validity, a general principle advocated not only in antiquity, but also later on by Milton; and it went far towards justifying the daring flights of 'romantic' dramatists. Then, too, he suggests that the dramatic function was not to give moral teaching, but to amuse and to afford a reflexion of human life. He also hints at such matters as the importance of the opening scene, that the underlying motive of his tragedies was to suggest that character was Fate, that fiction might bring into light some of the inner recesses of human nature, while he also has a word to say on the part played by 'happy chance' in all artistic creation. More explicit, however, were the remarks of Jonson, who, while he insists on the moral purpose of comedy and its satirical treatment of human foibles, yet stands for a new form which ignored the 'too nice requirements' of ancient drama. He is less concerned with pleading the suitability of fanciful themes than with advocating the need for realism and the observance of verisimilitude. But his main doctrine, reiterated in connexion with comedy and tragedy alike, is the need for a modification of classical canons, such as the rules which required an observance of the Unity of time, the use of a chorus and the like. As has already been stated, his conception of tragedy is coloured to some extent by Senecan influence; but the outstanding fact is that, for both comedy and tragedy, he prescribes a new liberty for English dramatists, claiming as their right the freedom previously exercised by the ancients, more especially as ancient requirements, he asserted, were impossible in plays intended for contemporary English audiences. By such scattered hints the way was prepared for a reasoned justification of the new 'romantic' drama, while the suggestion was that the methods of the new dramatists were not wholly empirical in kind, but were dictated by some sound psychological principles.

Apart from all this theorizing on the secrets of good prose as well as on the nature and art of poetry, contemporary criticism, it will have been seen, made also a useful beginning with the judging and appreciating of literature. Least important were the 'tumultuary catalogues' of ancient and contemporary writers compiled by Webbe, Peacham, and others, in which second-hand judgments for the most part were submitted. And of greater significance were the efforts made to correct prevailing literary defects as viewed in the light of Nature or reason.

24

To a rational generation factual truth and moral teaching were naturally the highest things to look for in poetry. Hence the judgments passed on the far-fetched themes of medieval romances and contemporary plays ; on the artificiality of the contemporary lyric, and more especially on the hackneyed love-themes of the sonnets with their inevitable but faded Petrarchan sentiment ; while more than one protest was raised against the sensual treatment of classical myth. Moreover, there were the defects due to a lack of the sense of fitness. The pastoral and allegorical conventions, for instance, the mingling of Christian with pagan material, or again, Suckling's cynical handling of the theme of love, all alike came in for some amount of censure. And as for Jonson's arraignment of the poets of his day, he remarks on those who were wont to write in superficial and showy fashion, on others, again, who deliberately sought a rough or broken style or else affected a colourless and insipid manner ; and, besides, he has some hard words to say about shameless plagiarists and about others who dealt with undigested matter or who wrote in defiance of all art.

Then, too, judgments and appreciations of a more constructive kind were by no means lacking, thus revealing signs of a new sense of literary values, though the estimate formed of Du Bartas, for example, was strangely misleading. In the first place a key to the interpretation of earlier literature had been provided when Colet read Biblical literature in the light of its historical background, or when Cheke attributed the defects of Sallust's style to contemporary causes. It was the earliest use made of the historical method by English critics ; but some time was to elapse before its value was generally appreciated. On the other hand, definite signs of an aesthetic appreciation were not slow in appearing, and mostly in connexion with contemporary works. Of medieval poetry, it is true, but little was actually known ; and while Chaucer came in for some amount of conventional praise, it was often for the wrong things. Thus his *Canterbury Tales* and his *Troilus* were duly commended, and his verse was declared to be less irregular than was generally supposed ; but it was as a moral reformer that he was mainly admired, and it was left for a later age to see in him the genial humorist. For the rest, however, discerning judgments of contemporary works were forthcoming from Sidney, Puttenham, and others ; and they marked a distinct advance in critical activities. Classical standards, it is true, were frequently applied, as when *Chevy Chace* was said to lack the grandeur of Pindar's lyrics, or again, the *Shepherd's Calendar* to embody features not found in either Theocritus or Virgil. On the other hand evidence of sound and independent judgment was also supplied when the works of Wyatt and Surrey, Spenser's *Shepherd's Calendar* and his *Faerie Queene*, were singled out for special praise. And when Sidney calls attention to the genuine lyrical note of the *Psalms*, the narrative excellences of the Parables, and the moving effects of the old ballads and romances, he had in mind neither rules nor theories, but was initiating judgments of a new and more fruitful kind, based on his own reactions to varied aesthetic qualities. Nor was this impressionistic criticism the only development which marked an advance in the appreciation of literature at this date. In the memorial verses of Jonson and others a new instrument had been forged for the graceful expression of literary judgment; and the verse-criticism of the early 17th Century points not only to more serious critical ventures as compared with the earlier sporadic remarks, but also to a growing sense of the value of literary appreciations in and for themselves. Moreover, judgments of a more profound and penetrating kind now become available. Jonson's tribute to Shakespeare, for instance, with its claim for supremacy and universality of appeal, is of outstanding quality and permanent value; while in the treatment of Donne by Carew and Jonson there is revealed an ability to appreciate a new depth and range of feeling as well as novelty in thought and idiom alike.

With this then as a summary account of the main findings of Renascence criticism, its theorizings and judgments, it remains finally to suggest its historical significance and the place it occupies in the critical development in England. That it marked a considerable advance on the sporadic efforts of medieval times is of course obvious; and nowhere is this more clearly perceptible than in the attempts to commend poetry to 16th-Century readers. Much of the medieval theory, it is true, is still retained; but despite all limitations, the conceptions of the poetic art now submitted are worlds away from those of an earlier day, when, as in the 12th Century and later, it was seriously doubted whether poetry was an independent art at all, or whether it was anything more than versified rhetoric, a more persuasive form of logic and the rest. Moreover, critical activities now became more conscious, more widespread and diversified. The earlier Areopagus of Sidney and Spenser developed into the habit of literary discussion at the Mermaid, where Jonson and other notabilities held forth. And in occupying this wider platform criticism was beginning to assume the status of a new literary *genre*, the exponents of which attempted from time to time to define its function ; as when attacks were made on ' poet-haters ' or on ' tinkers who made more faults than they mended ', or again, when Sir William Alexander commented in general on critical methods and standards. Then, too, besides dispelling medieval mists and fostering literary judgment anew, this body of criticism was not entirely without its influence on contemporary literature. The way for the new dramatic art, for instance, would seem to have been prepared in part by Lyly and Sidney, while Shakespeare apparently was not above borrowing suggestions for his characters as well as other details from his reading of Wilson, Sidney, and Puttenham.

Of yet greater interest, however, is the relation in which this Renascence criticism stands to later phases in the critical development ; for it is none other than an integral part of modern English criticism, reproducing ancient truths and anticipating modern doctrines, besides treating of themes and betraying qualities which were to distinguish the critical activities of the generations that followed. Already the need for scanning and augmenting ancient theories had been widely recognized, positive value being claimed for modern theories. And when definite protests came from Jonson, Hakewill, and others that modern ages had not necessarily decayed, it was the preliminary skirmishing that heralded the later battles between the Ancients and the Moderns. Then, too, it was now that the earliest application of the historical method in interpreting literature occurs in the works of Colet and Ascham ; that with Daniel begins a genuine appreciation of the Middle Ages despite Humanistic prejudices ; and that through ' E. K. ', Sidney, Bacon, and others, stray glimpses are caught of ' romantic ' principles and standards ; all of which were to be subsequently developed in the works of such writers as Dryden, Warton, and Hurd. And, in addition, it was now that the merits of the heroic couplet were first expounded and commended, and that references were first made to such things as the evils of the system of patronage and the vice of plagiarism —matters which were to receive the attention of later critics.

Most significant of all, however, were the spirit and methods that gave direction to this Renascence criticism ; for they embodied features that with some modifications were to characterize English critics of the centuries following. At no time, broadly speaking, have English critics been wholly subservient to precepts found in books, to systems and rules ; and this independence, we have seen, was characteristic of Renascence criticism. From the first, literature was approached in the light of Nature or reason, with the changeless needs of human nature ever in mind ; and the results were a keen scrutiny of ancient doctrine, and the formulation of new and independent doctrines as dictated by the native genius. In the neo-classical movement that originated in France in the 17th Century, however, men were content to accept the fundamental truths about poetry as already settled by the ancients ; and formal laws and rules were established on that basis as final, fixed, and indispensable. But later English critics as a whole did not subscribe to these rigid and authoritative doctrines. Their tests in general remained those of human nature, reason, and experience. The course of English criticism up to the 19th Century was in fact one long attempt to escape from the false position thus created in France. And just as the first objection to the formal imitation of the ancients had already been made in the earlier rejection of classical metres on rational grounds, so, later on, neo-classical prescriptions for the drama and the epic were challenged by Dryden, Warton, and others, in the light of the achievements of Shakespeare, Spenser, and the old ballad-writers. In short, the animating spirit of Renascence criticism survived throughout the centuries that immediately followed. And it survived as being characteristic of the national genius ; for of the actual performance of those earlier critics little or nothing was known for some time to come.

Such then is the many-sided interest attached to Renascence criticism in England ; though, it might perhaps be added, for a full account of the critical ideas then current some further notice would be required of that unwritten theory implicit in much of the creative work of the time. The truth is that the Elizabethans, and Shakespeare more particularly, viewing literature in close relation to man, as Aristotle and others before them had done, arrived independently and by psychological processes at some of the fundamental doctrines of classical antiquity, though they are nowhere formulated ; and this is best seen in the evolution of the new dramatic art. Of Shakespeare's hints in matters of this kind something has already been said ; and to this might be added further definite principles bound up with his actual practice. Thus he recognizes, for instance, in *The Tempest* and elsewhere, the rightful place of the marvellous and fanciful in poetry, and that ' a likely impossibility is preferable to an unconvincing possibility ', points previously made by Aristotle, though sometimes ignored by later generations ; while in the coherent structure of his plays he revives Aristotle's principle of artistic logic, that of ' a probable or necessary sequence ' requiring a rigorous connexion of the incidents employed. Aristotelian, again, are such things as the demands for

unity of action, for consistent character-drawing and propriety
of expression, all of which are illustrated by Shakespeare's art.
Most striking of all, however, is his conception of tragedy, which
he shared with few, if any, of his contemporaries, the conception
that tragedy was essentially a matter of revealing some of the
mysterious ways of Destiny. ' Shakespeare ', it has been well
said,[1] 'joins hands with Aeschylus . . . in making his chief
tragic engine "the pity of it", the sense that there is infinite
excuse, but no positive justification, for the acts which bring
their heroes and heroines to misfortune.' It was in virtue of
such implicit doctrine that Lessing later on protested that
Shakespeare had approached more nearly to Greek tragedy in
essentials than had Corneille with his more formal imitation.
And in view of the conditions of classical cholarship in the
England of Shakespeare's day, when the feeling for classical art
was enthusiastic and vague rather than exact and discriminating,
it can only be inferred that Shakespeare's theory and technique
were of his own devising. Similar psychological processes inspired by genius, with twenty centuries between, had, in short,
led to the evolving of unformulated principles which, if not
identical, had much in common ; and not least interesting in the
whole range of contemporary critical thought is this unwritten
theory of Shakespeare.

For the rest, the critical material that has actually come
down has a positive and enduring value of its own, especially
in the light of what came before and after. Limitations in the
methods and findings of course there are. Nature or reason,
for instance, as the critical instrument, was not capable of
sounding or solving the profounder mysteries of the literary art ;
crude and mistaken judgments moreover sometimes occur ; and
there was also the lack of an adequate terminology, with however
the consequential avoidance of such jargon as later became
common. On the other hand, many great, simple truths were
revealed for the first time to English readers ; and something
of the formal traditions of the ancients was recaptured, with a
difference. A growing sense of the beauty of restrained and
regulated form was instilled, when the subtle laws of an effective
prose were unfolded. Poetry was vindicated for minds perplexed ; and such things as the charms, not only of the ' distant
rhyme ', but also of rhythm, that primitive harmony, ' the
technique of Creation ' were also inculcated. Meanwhile from
the first there was an unfailing belief in literary progress, and
fresh developments were conceived of, born of contemporary

[1] G. Saintsbury, *History of Criticism*, i. p. 39.

needs. It was also freely recognized that art, being an expression of the common interests of mankind, had an appeal for all men, and not merely for coteries ; and upon this assumption were based the lasting triumphs of the great Elizabethan drama. Nor were these revelations set forth in pedestrian fashion, or with that ' peevish affectation of words ' which Puttenham rather unkindly described as ' the besetting sin of scholars '. Much of the work submitted is literature itself, with the unique quality of Elizabethan prose, memorable by reason of its pregnant, picturesque and racy phrases, and graced with a simple dignity that has since been lost. Altogether an auspicious start had thus been made in the business of vitalizing critical activities in England. Fresh light had incidentally been thrown on the workings of the minds of Elizabethan men of letters, and a chapter of sorts added to the history of contemporary thought ; though it is also true to say that this Renascence period closes with a sense of mysteries yet to be revealed. In the varied pronouncements of critics differing greatly in temperament and genius alike, there are many passages that appeal with special force to modern readers. Yet nothing is perhaps more striking than that spacious vision of Daniel in *Musophilus*, when, in the days before the setting forth of the Pilgrim Fathers, he dreams of the beneficent future of English literature flowing into new worlds, ' to enrich ', as he puts it, ' unknowing nations in the yet unformed Occident with the treasures of our tongue '. It was a bold prophecy that was destined to be gloriously fulfilled. But it was also instinct with the true spirit of English Renascence criticism, with its daring initiative, its generous enthusiasms, and its unfailing confidence in the lasting and spiritual influence of all great literature.

INDEX

365